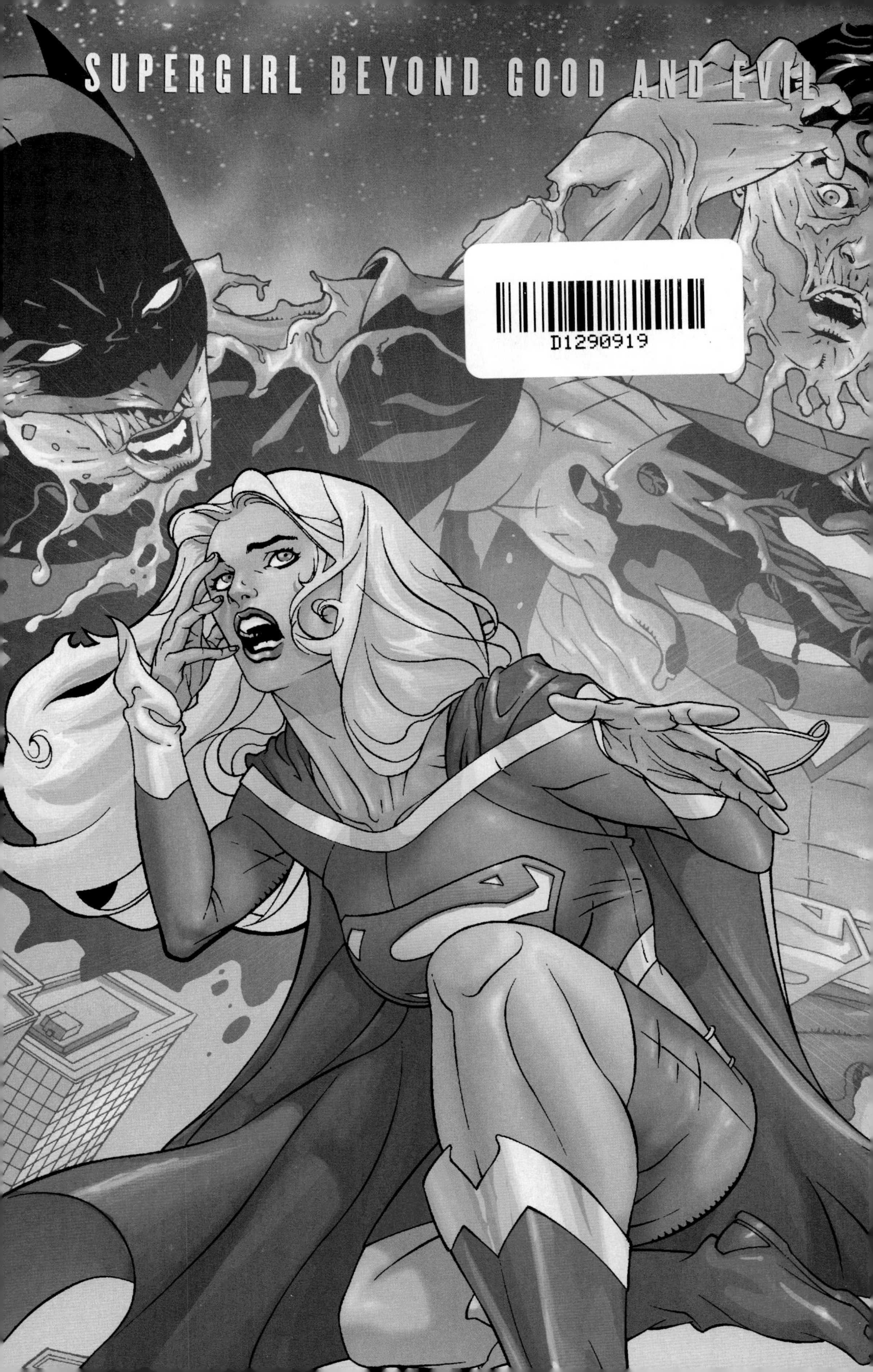
SUPERGIRL BEYOND GOOD AND EVIL

Kelley Puckett   Kurt Busiek   Fabian Nicieza   Geoff Johns Writers
Drew Johnson   Renato Guedes   Lee Ferguson   Rick Leonardi Pencillers
Ray Snyder   José Wilson Magalháes   Marc Deering   Dan Green Inkers
Brad Anderson Colorist
Rob Leigh   Jared K. Fletcher   Travis Lanham   Steve Wands Letterers

Superman created by Jerry Siegel and Joe Shuster

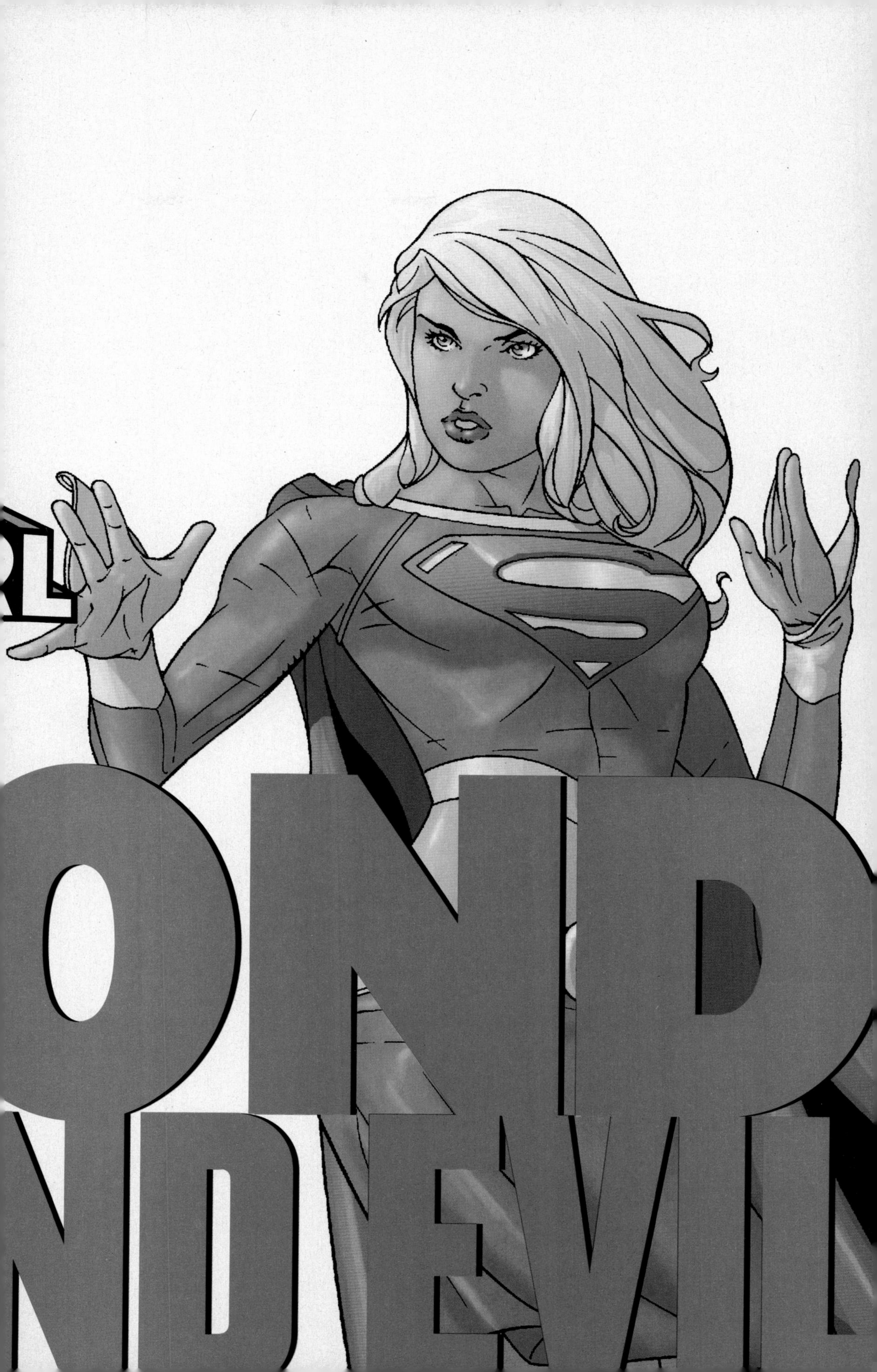
OND
NDEVIL

Dan DiDio Senior VP-Executive Editor
Matt Idelson Editor-original oeries
Nachie Castro Tom Palmer, Jr. Associate Editor-original oeries
Bob Joy Editor-collected cdition
Robbin Brosterman Senior Art Director
Paul Levitz President & Publisher
Georg Brewer VP-Design & DC Direct Creative
Richard Bruning Senior VP-Creative Director
Patrick Caldon Executive VP-Finance & Operations
Chris Caramalis VP-Finance
John Cunningham VP-Marketing
Terri Cunningham VP-Managing Editor
Alison Gill VP-Manufacturing
David Hyde VP-Publicity
Hank Kanalz VP-General Manager, WildStorm
Jim Lee Editorial Director-WildStorm
Paula Lowitt Senior VP-Business & Legal Affairs
MaryEllen McLaughlin VP-Advertising & Custom Publishing
John Nee Senior VP-Business Development
Gregory Noveck Senior VP-Creative Affairs
Sue Pohja VP-Book Trade Sales
Steve Rotterdam Senior VP-Sales & Marketing
Cheryl Rubin Senior VP-Brand Management
Jeff Trojan VP-Business Development, DC Direct
Bob Wayne VP-Sales

Cover art by Renato Guedes

SUPERGIRL: BEYOND GOOD AND EVIL
Published by DC Comics.
Cover and compilation Copyright © 2008 DC Comics.
All Rights Reserved.

DC Comics, 1700 Broadway, New York, NY 10019
A Warner Bros. Entertainment Company
Printed in Canada. First Printing.

ISBN: 978-1-4012-1850-8

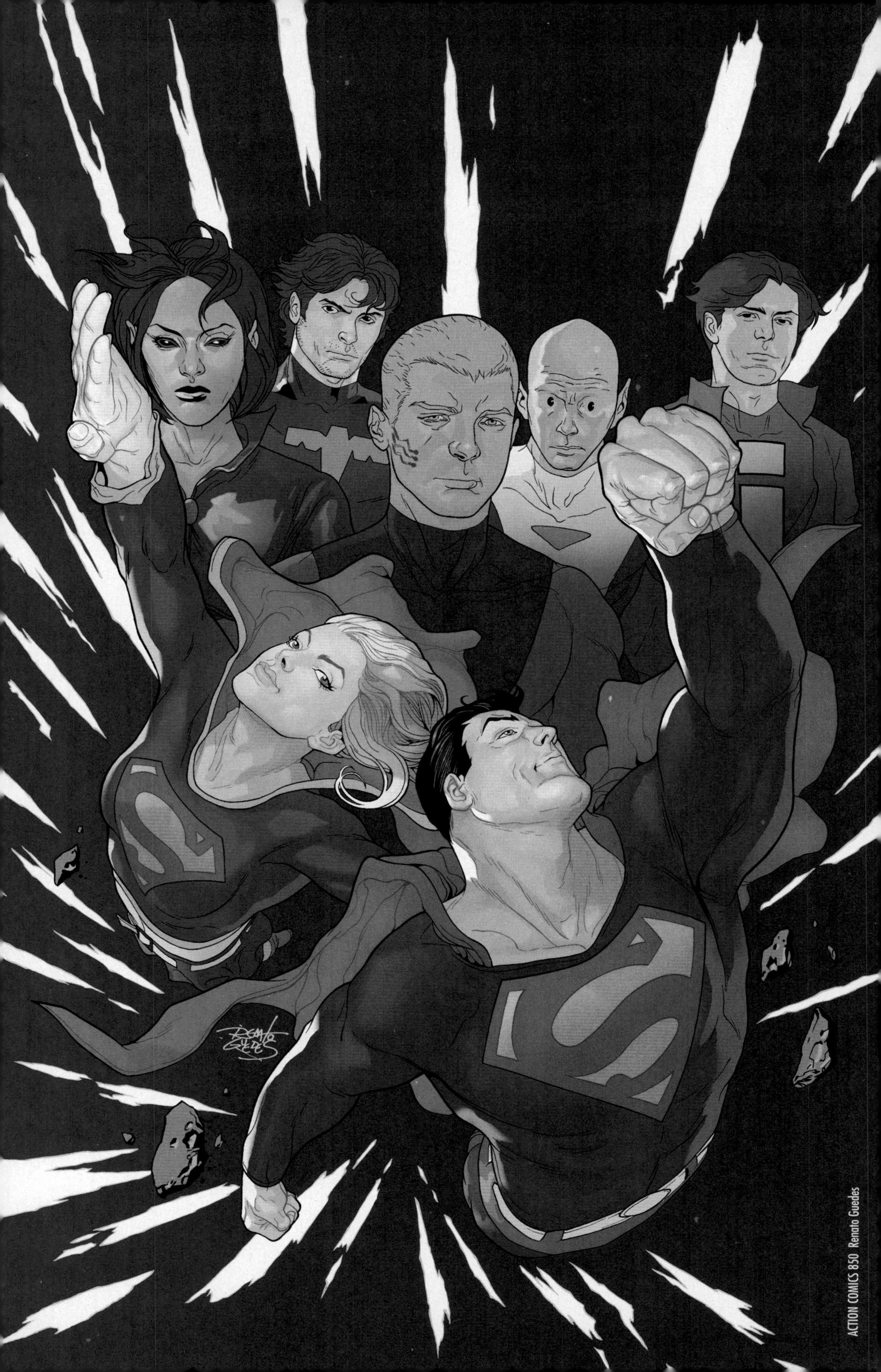

ACTION COMICS 850 Renato Guedes

SUPERMAN: FAMILY

KURT BUSIEK FABIAN NICIEZA GEOFF JOHNS WRITERS
RENATO GUEDES PENCILS & COLORS
JOSÉ WILSON MAGALHÁES INKS

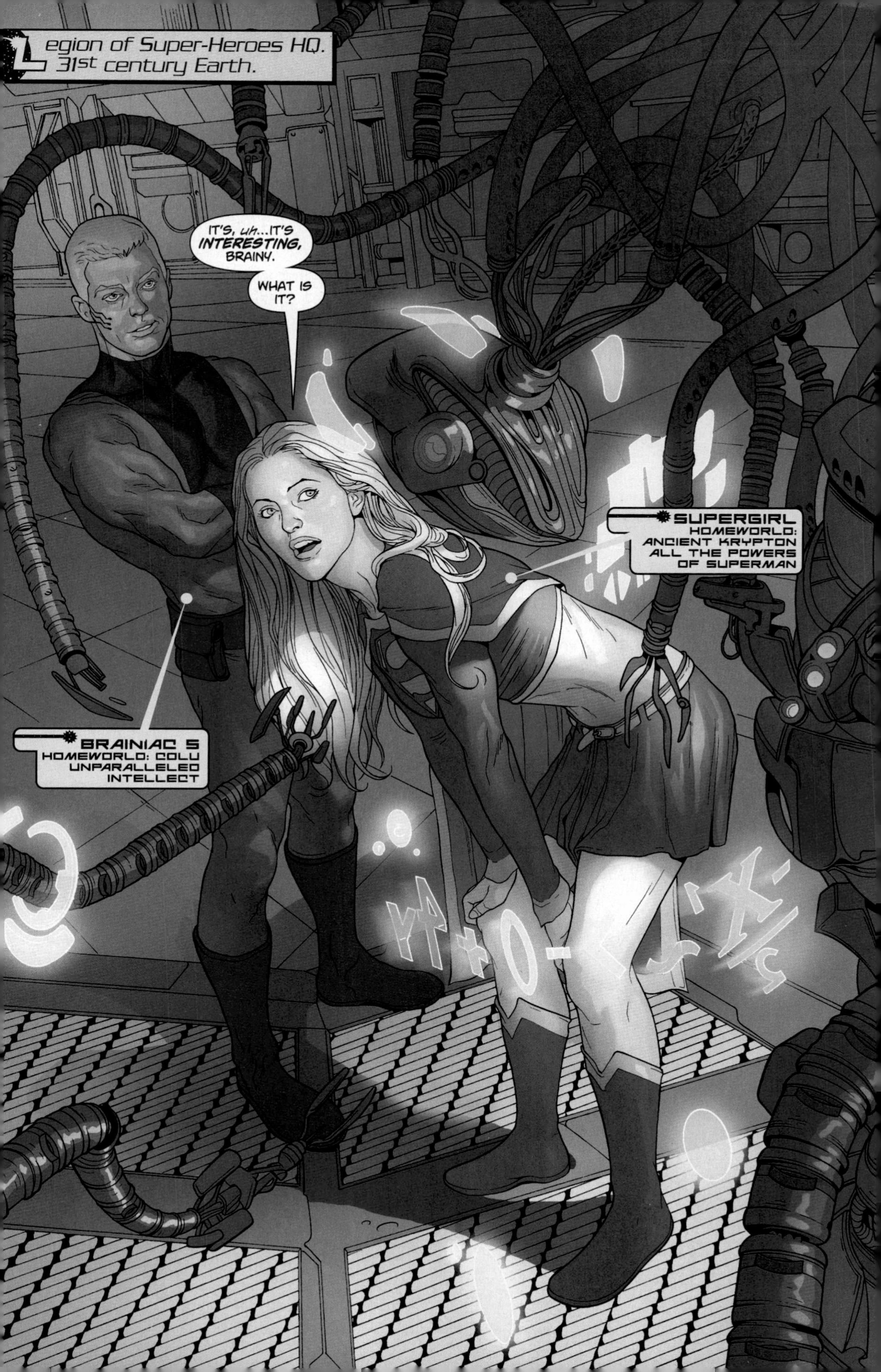
Legion of Super-Heroes HQ. 31st century Earth.
IT'S, uh...IT'S INTERESTING, BRAINY.
WHAT IS IT?
SUPERGIRL HOMEWORLD: ANCIENT KRYPTON ALL THE POWERS OF SUPERMAN
BRAINIAC 5 HOMEWORLD: COLU UNPARALLELED INTELLECT

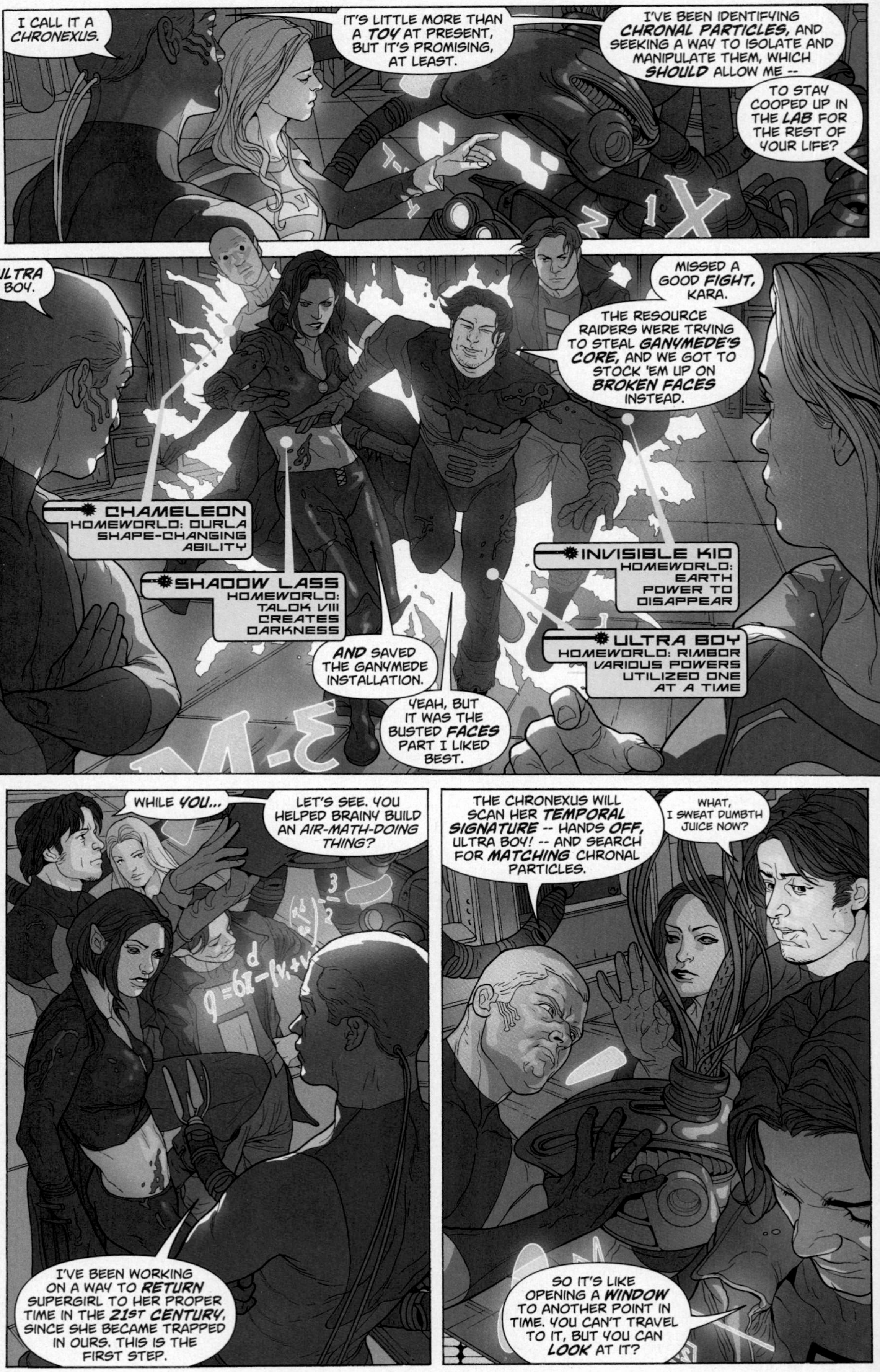
I CALL IT A CHRONEXUS.
IT'S LITTLE MORE THAN A TOY AT PRESENT, BUT IT'S PROMISING, AT LEAST.
I'VE BEEN IDENTIFYING CHRONAL PARTICLES, AND SEEKING A WAY TO ISOLATE AND MANIPULATE THEM, WHICH SHOULD ALLOW ME --
TO STAY COOPED UP IN THE LAB FOR THE REST OF YOUR LIFE?
ULTRA BOY.
MISSED A GOOD FIGHT, KARA.
THE RESOURCE RAIDERS WERE TRYING TO STEAL GANYMEDE'S CORE, AND WE GOT TO STOCK 'EM UP ON BROKEN FACES INSTEAD.
CHAMELEON
HOMEWORLD: DURLA
SHAPE-CHANGING ABILITY
SHADOW LASS
HOMEWORLD: TALOK VIII
CREATES DARKNESS
INVISIBLE KID
HOMEWORLD: EARTH
POWER TO DISAPPEAR
ULTRA BOY
HOMEWORLD: RIMBOR
VARIOUS POWERS UTILIZED ONE AT A TIME
AND SAVED THE GANYMEDE INSTALLATION.
YEAH, BUT IT WAS THE BUSTED FACES PART I LIKED BEST.
WHILE YOU...
LET'S SEE. YOU HELPED BRAINY BUILD AN AIR-MATH-DOING THING?
I'VE BEEN WORKING ON A WAY TO RETURN SUPERGIRL TO HER PROPER TIME IN THE 21ST CENTURY, SINCE SHE BECAME TRAPPED IN OURS. THIS IS THE FIRST STEP.
THE CHRONEXUS WILL SCAN HER TEMPORAL SIGNATURE -- HANDS OFF, ULTRA BOY! -- AND SEARCH FOR MATCHING CHRONAL PARTICLES.
WHAT, I SWEAT DUMBTH JUICE NOW?
SO IT'S LIKE OPENING A WINDOW TO ANOTHER POINT IN TIME. YOU CAN'T TRAVEL TO IT, BUT YOU CAN LOOK AT IT?

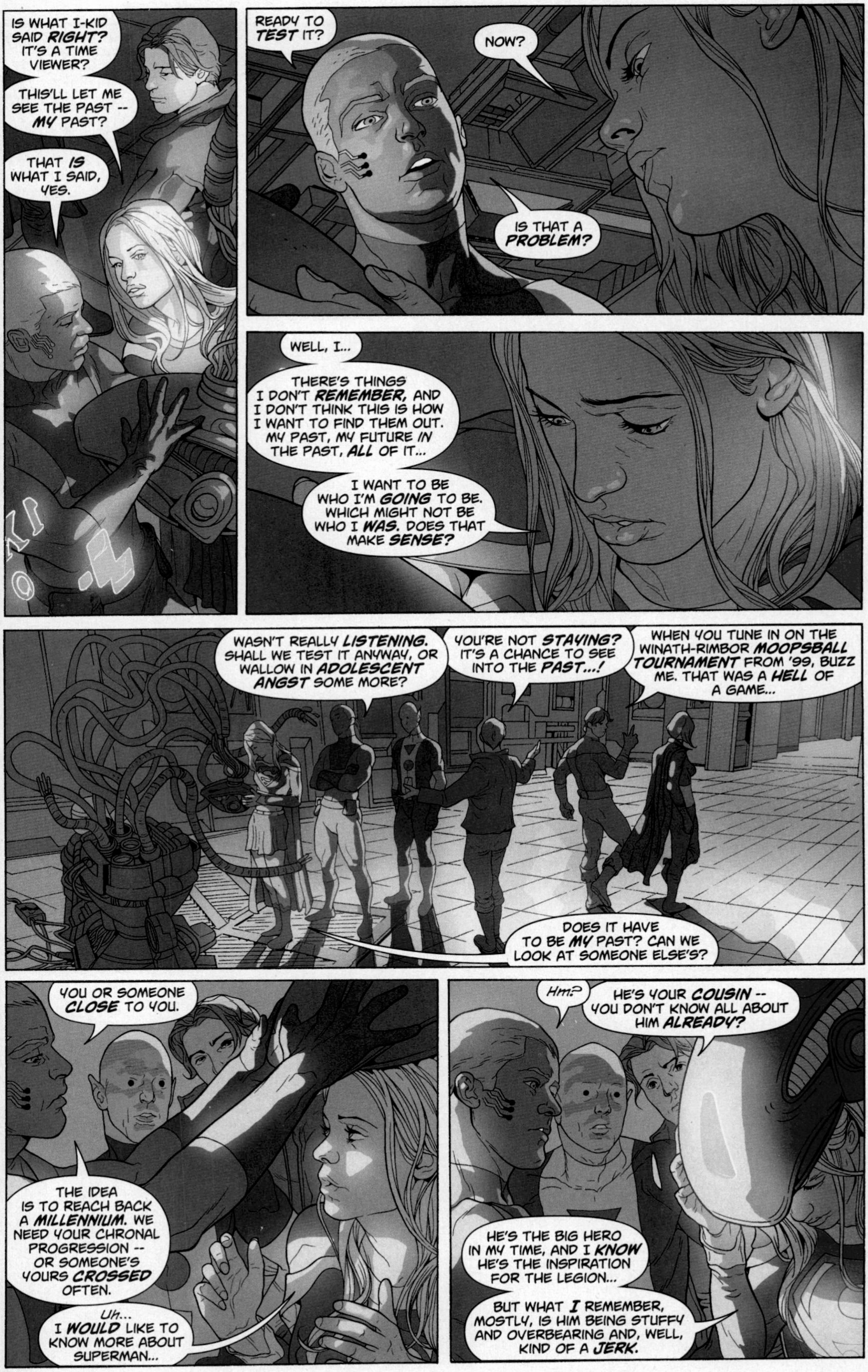

IS WHAT I-KID SAID RIGHT? IT'S A TIME VIEWER?
THIS'LL LET ME SEE THE PAST -- MY PAST?
THAT IS WHAT I SAID, YES.
READY TO TEST IT?
NOW?
IS THAT A PROBLEM?
WELL, I...
THERE'S THINGS I DON'T REMEMBER, AND I DON'T THINK THIS IS HOW I WANT TO FIND THEM OUT. MY PAST, MY FUTURE IN THE PAST, ALL OF IT...
I WANT TO BE WHO I'M GOING TO BE. WHICH MIGHT NOT BE WHO I WAS. DOES THAT MAKE SENSE?
WASN'T REALLY LISTENING. SHALL WE TEST IT ANYWAY, OR WALLOW IN ADOLESCENT ANGST SOME MORE?
YOU'RE NOT STAYING? IT'S A CHANCE TO SEE INTO THE PAST...!
WHEN YOU TUNE IN ON THE WINATH-RIMBOR MOOPSBALL TOURNAMENT FROM '99, BUZZ ME. THAT WAS A HELL OF A GAME...
DOES IT HAVE TO BE MY PAST? CAN WE LOOK AT SOMEONE ELSE'S?
YOU OR SOMEONE CLOSE TO YOU.
THE IDEA IS TO REACH BACK A MILLENNIUM. WE NEED YOUR CHRONAL PROGRESSION -- OR SOMEONE'S YOURS CROSSED OFTEN.
Uh... I WOULD LIKE TO KNOW MORE ABOUT SUPERMAN...
Hm?
HE'S YOUR COUSIN -- YOU DON'T KNOW ALL ABOUT HIM ALREADY?
HE'S THE BIG HERO IN MY TIME, AND I KNOW HE'S THE INSPIRATION FOR THE LEGION...
BUT WHAT I REMEMBER, MOSTLY, IS HIM BEING STUFFY AND OVERBEARING AND, WELL, KIND OF A JERK.

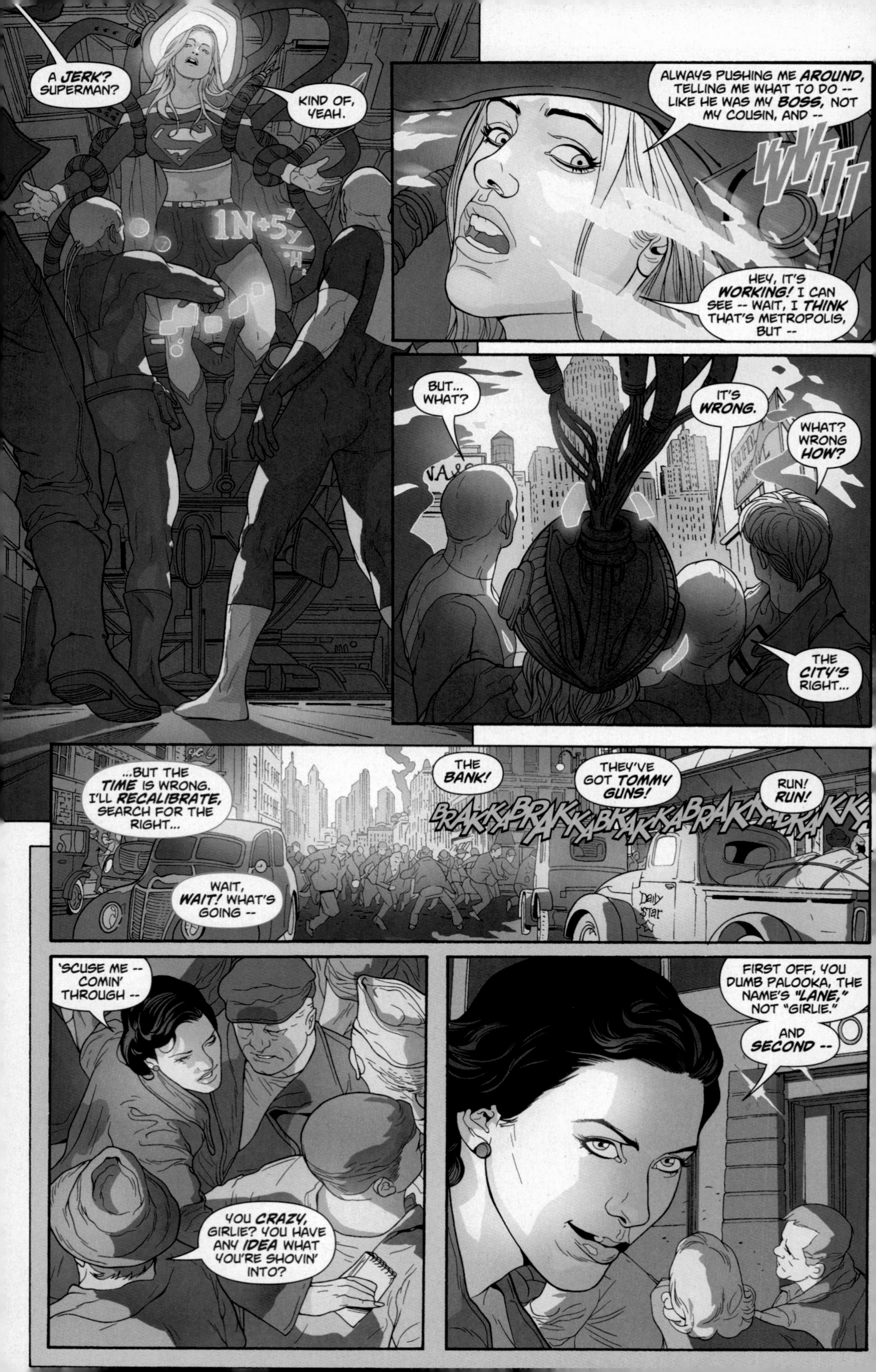
A JERK? SUPERMAN?
KIND OF, YEAH.
1N+5
ALWAYS PUSHING ME AROUND, TELLING ME WHAT TO DO -- LIKE HE WAS MY BOSS, NOT MY COUSIN, AND --
VVVTTT
HEY, IT'S WORKING! I CAN SEE -- WAIT, I THINK THAT'S METROPOLIS, BUT --
BUT... WHAT?
IT'S WRONG.
WHAT? WRONG HOW?
THE CITY'S RIGHT...
...BUT THE TIME IS WRONG. I'LL RECALIBRATE, SEARCH FOR THE RIGHT...
THE BANK!
THEY'VE GOT TOMMY GUNS!
RUN! RUN!
BRAKKABRAKKABRAKKABRAKKABRAKKABRAKKA
WAIT, WAIT! WHAT'S GOING --
Daily Star
'SCUSE ME -- COMIN' THROUGH --
YOU CRAZY, GIRLIE? YOU HAVE ANY IDEA WHAT YOU'RE SHOVIN' INTO?
FIRST OFF, YOU DUMB PALOOKA, THE NAME'S "LANE," NOT "GIRLIE."
AND SECOND --

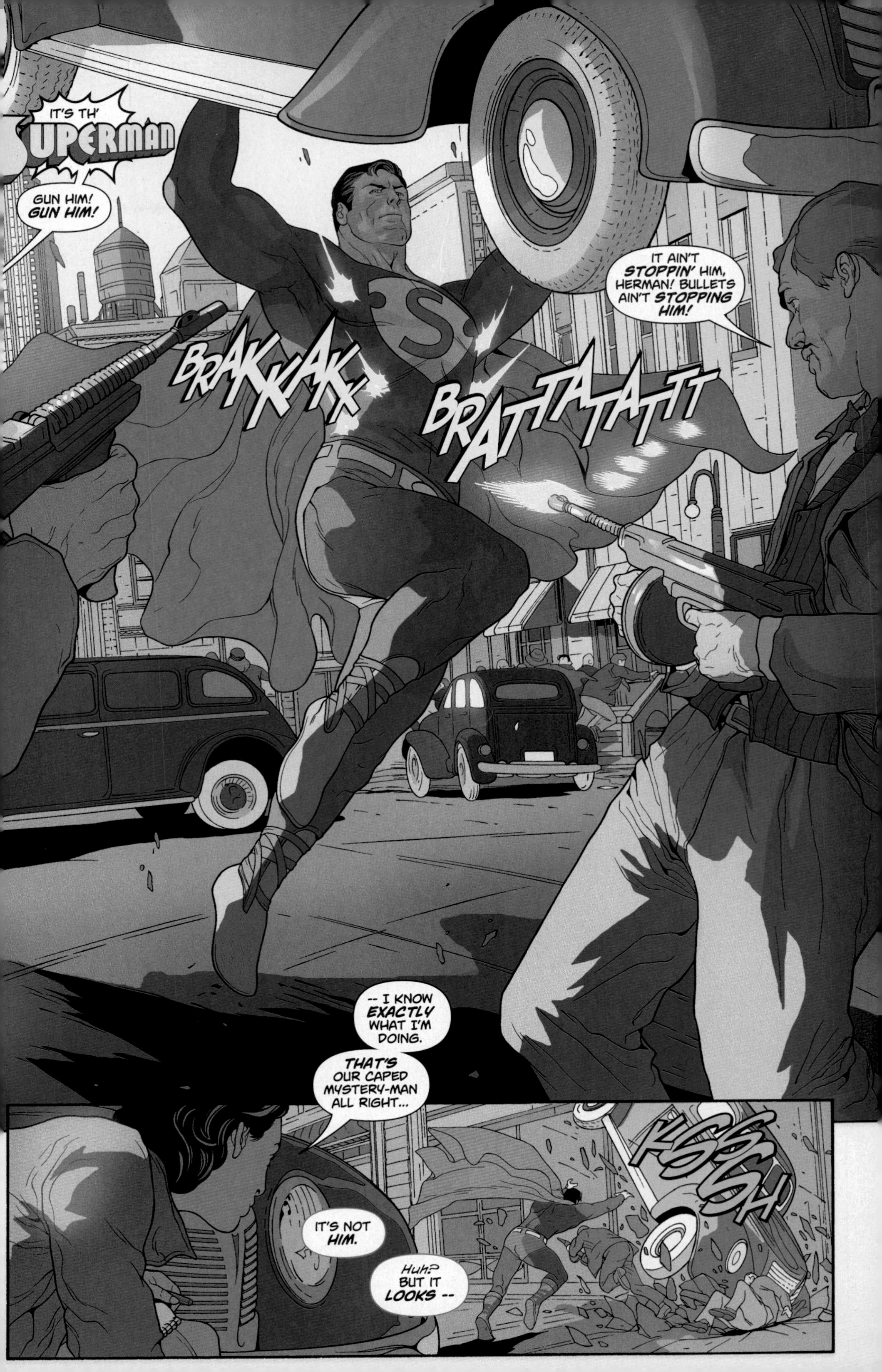
IT'S TH' SUPERMAN
GUN HIM! GUN HIM!
IT AIN'T STOPPIN' HIM, HERMAN! BULLETS AIN'T STOPPING HIM!
BRAKKAKK
BRATTTATATTT
-- I KNOW EXACTLY WHAT I'M DOING.
THAT'S OUR CAPED MYSTERY-MAN ALL RIGHT...
KSSSH
IT'S NOT HIM.
Huh? BUT IT LOOKS --

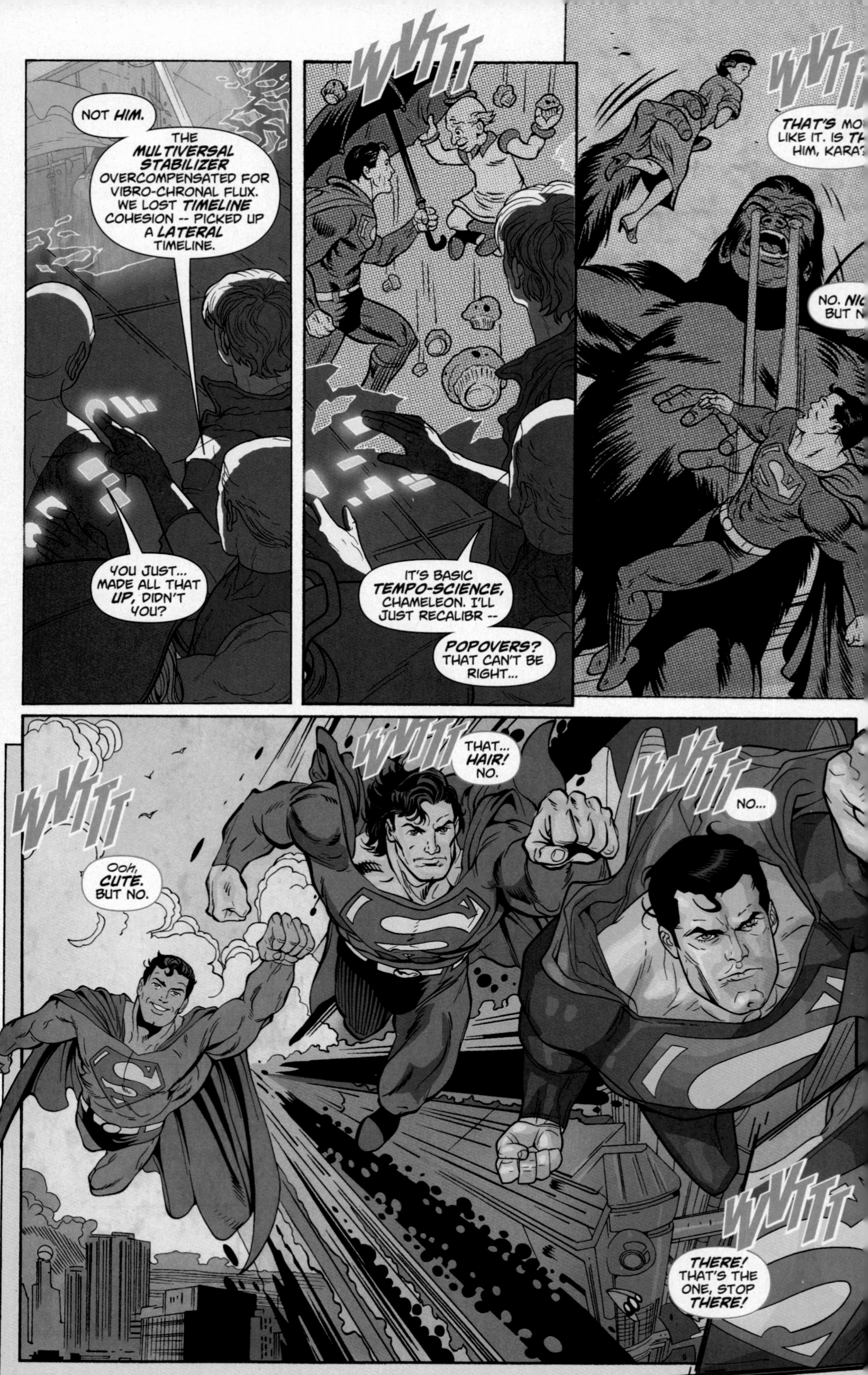

NOT HIM.
THE MULTIVERSAL STABILIZER OVERCOMPENSATED FOR VIBRO-CHRONAL FLUX. WE LOST TIMELINE COHESION -- PICKED UP A LATERAL TIMELINE.
YOU JUST... MADE ALL THAT UP, DIDN'T YOU?
WVTTT
IT'S BASIC TEMPO-SCIENCE, CHAMELEON. I'LL JUST RECALIBR --
POPOVERS? THAT CAN'T BE RIGHT...
WVT
THAT'S MO
LIKE IT. IS TH
HIM, KARA?
NO. NIC
BUT N
WVTTT
Ooh, CUTE. BUT NO.
WVTTT
THAT... HAIR! NO.
WVTTT
NO...
WVTTT
THERE! THAT'S THE ONE, STOP THERE!

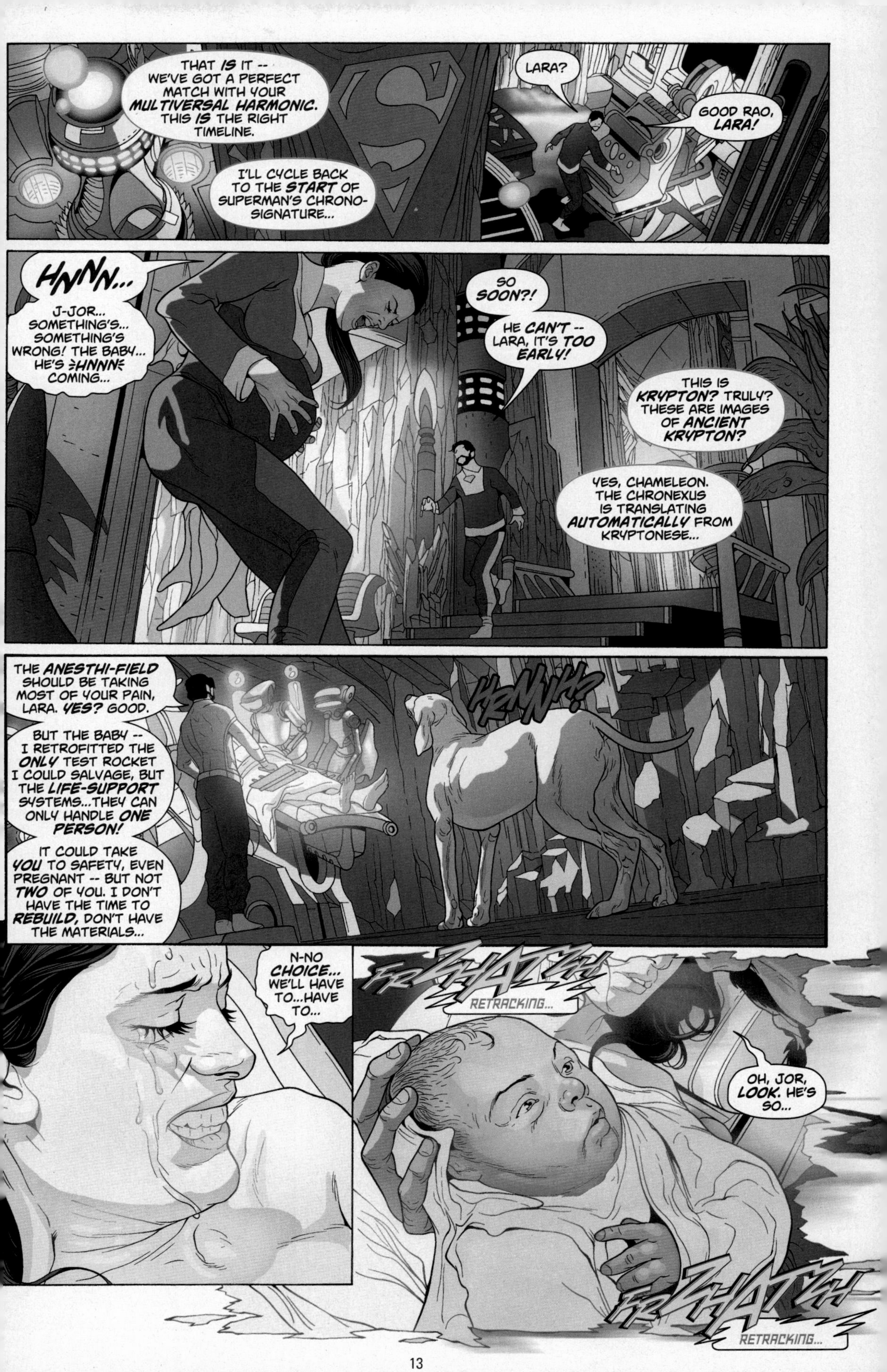

THAT IS IT -- WE'VE GOT A PERFECT MATCH WITH YOUR MULTIVERSAL HARMONIC. THIS IS THE RIGHT TIMELINE.
I'LL CYCLE BACK TO THE START OF SUPERMAN'S CHRONO-SIGNATURE...
LARA?
GOOD RAO, LARA!
HNNN...
J-JOR... SOMETHING'S... SOMETHING'S WRONG! THE BABY... HE'S HNNN COMING...
SO SOON?!
HE CAN'T -- LARA, IT'S TOO EARLY!
THIS IS KRYPTON? TRULY? THESE ARE IMAGES OF ANCIENT KRYPTON?
YES, CHAMELEON. THE CHRONEXUS IS TRANSLATING AUTOMATICALLY FROM KRYPTONESE...
THE ANESTHI-FIELD SHOULD BE TAKING MOST OF YOUR PAIN, LARA. YES? GOOD.
BUT THE BABY -- I RETROFITTED THE ONLY TEST ROCKET I COULD SALVAGE, BUT THE LIFE-SUPPORT SYSTEMS...THEY CAN ONLY HANDLE ONE PERSON!
IT COULD TAKE YOU TO SAFETY, EVEN PREGNANT -- BUT NOT TWO OF YOU. I DON'T HAVE THE TIME TO REBUILD, DON'T HAVE THE MATERIALS...
HRNNH?!
N-NO CHOICE... WE'LL HAVE TO...HAVE TO...
FRZHATCH
RETRACKING...
OH, JOR, LOOK. HE'S SO...
FRZHATCH
RETRACKING...

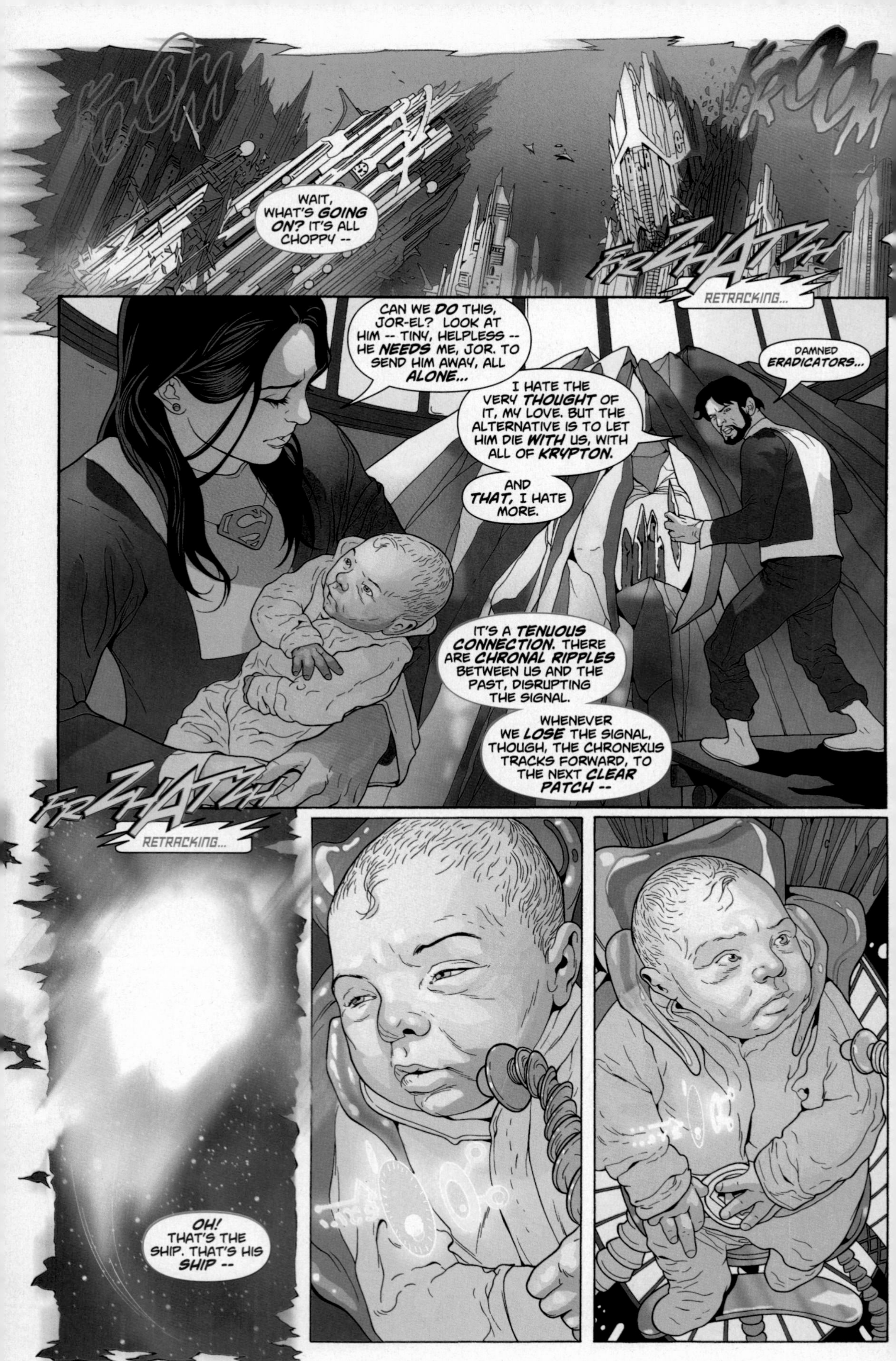
KROOM
WAIT, WHAT'S GOING ON? IT'S ALL CHOPPY --
KROOM
FRZHATH
RETRACKING...
CAN WE DO THIS, JOR-EL? LOOK AT HIM -- TINY, HELPLESS -- HE NEEDS ME, JOR. TO SEND HIM AWAY, ALL ALONE...
I HATE THE VERY THOUGHT OF IT, MY LOVE. BUT THE ALTERNATIVE IS TO LET HIM DIE WITH US, WITH ALL OF KRYPTON.
AND THAT, I HATE MORE.
DAMNED ERADICATORS...
IT'S A TENUOUS CONNECTION. THERE ARE CHRONAL RIPPLES BETWEEN US AND THE PAST, DISRUPTING THE SIGNAL.
WHENEVER WE LOSE THE SIGNAL, THOUGH, THE CHRONEXUS TRACKS FORWARD, TO THE NEXT CLEAR PATCH --
FRZHATH
RETRACKING...
OH! THAT'S THE SHIP. THAT'S HIS SHIP --

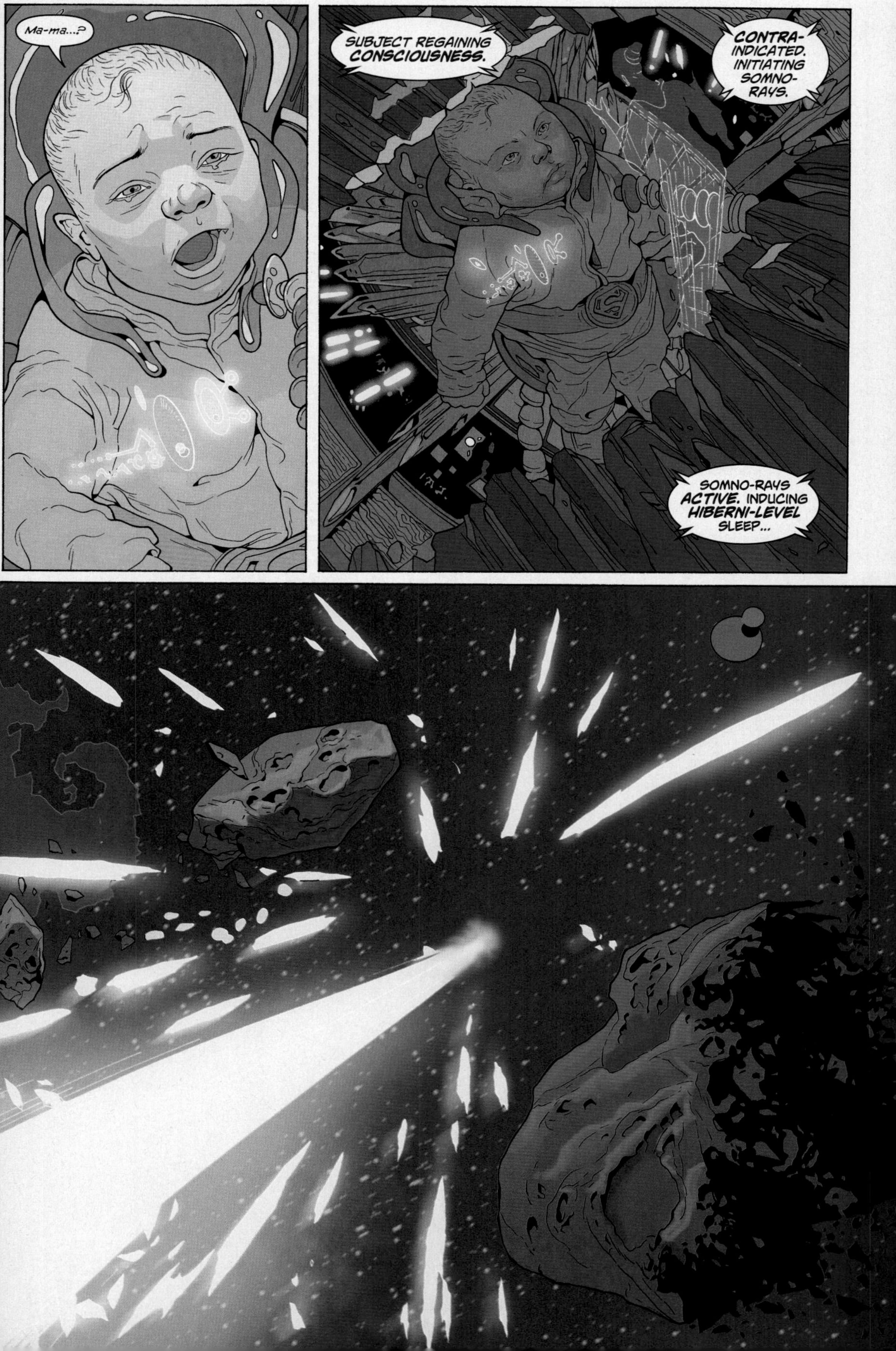
Ma-ma...?
SUBJECT REGAINING CONSCIOUSNESS.
CONTRA-INDICATED. INITIATING SOMNO-RAYS.
SOMNO-RAYS ACTIVE. INDUCING HIBERNI-LEVEL SLEEP...

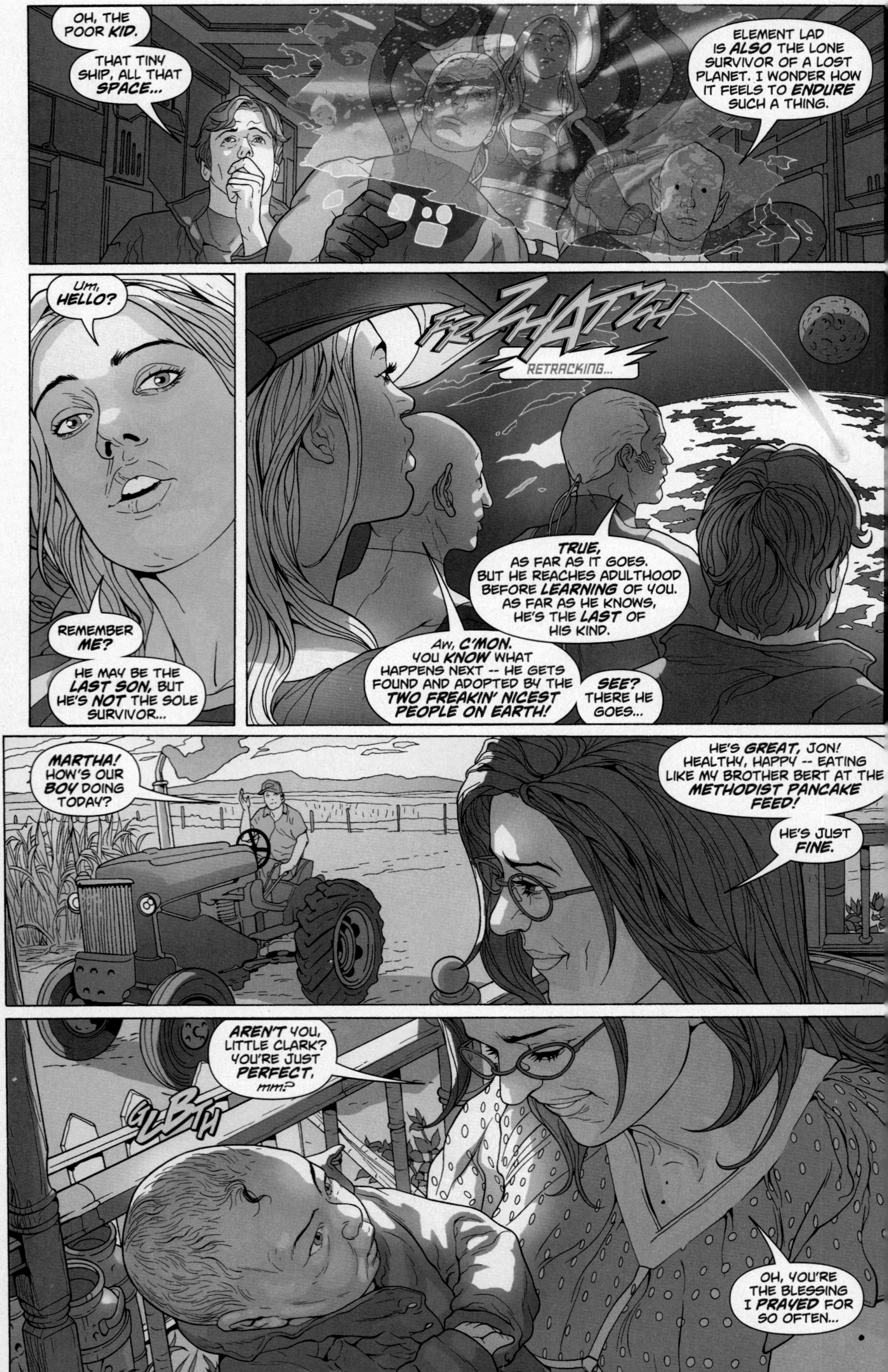
OH, THE POOR KID.
THAT TINY SHIP, ALL THAT SPACE...
ELEMENT LAD IS ALSO THE LONE SURVIVOR OF A LOST PLANET. I WONDER HOW IT FEELS TO ENDURE SUCH A THING.
Um, HELLO?
REMEMBER ME?
HE MAY BE THE LAST SON, BUT HE'S NOT THE SOLE SURVIVOR...
FRZHATZH
RETRACKING...
TRUE, AS FAR AS IT GOES. BUT HE REACHES ADULTHOOD BEFORE LEARNING OF YOU. AS FAR AS HE KNOWS, HE'S THE LAST OF HIS KIND.
Aw, C'MON. YOU KNOW WHAT HAPPENS NEXT -- HE GETS FOUND AND ADOPTED BY THE TWO FREAKIN' NICEST PEOPLE ON EARTH!
SEE? THERE HE GOES...
MARTHA! HOW'S OUR BOY DOING TODAY?
HE'S GREAT, JON! HEALTHY, HAPPY -- EATING LIKE MY BROTHER BERT AT THE METHODIST PANCAKE FEED!
HE'S JUST FINE.
AREN'T YOU, LITTLE CLARK? YOU'RE JUST PERFECT, mm?
GLBTH
OH, YOU'RE THE BLESSING I PRAYED FOR SO OFTEN...

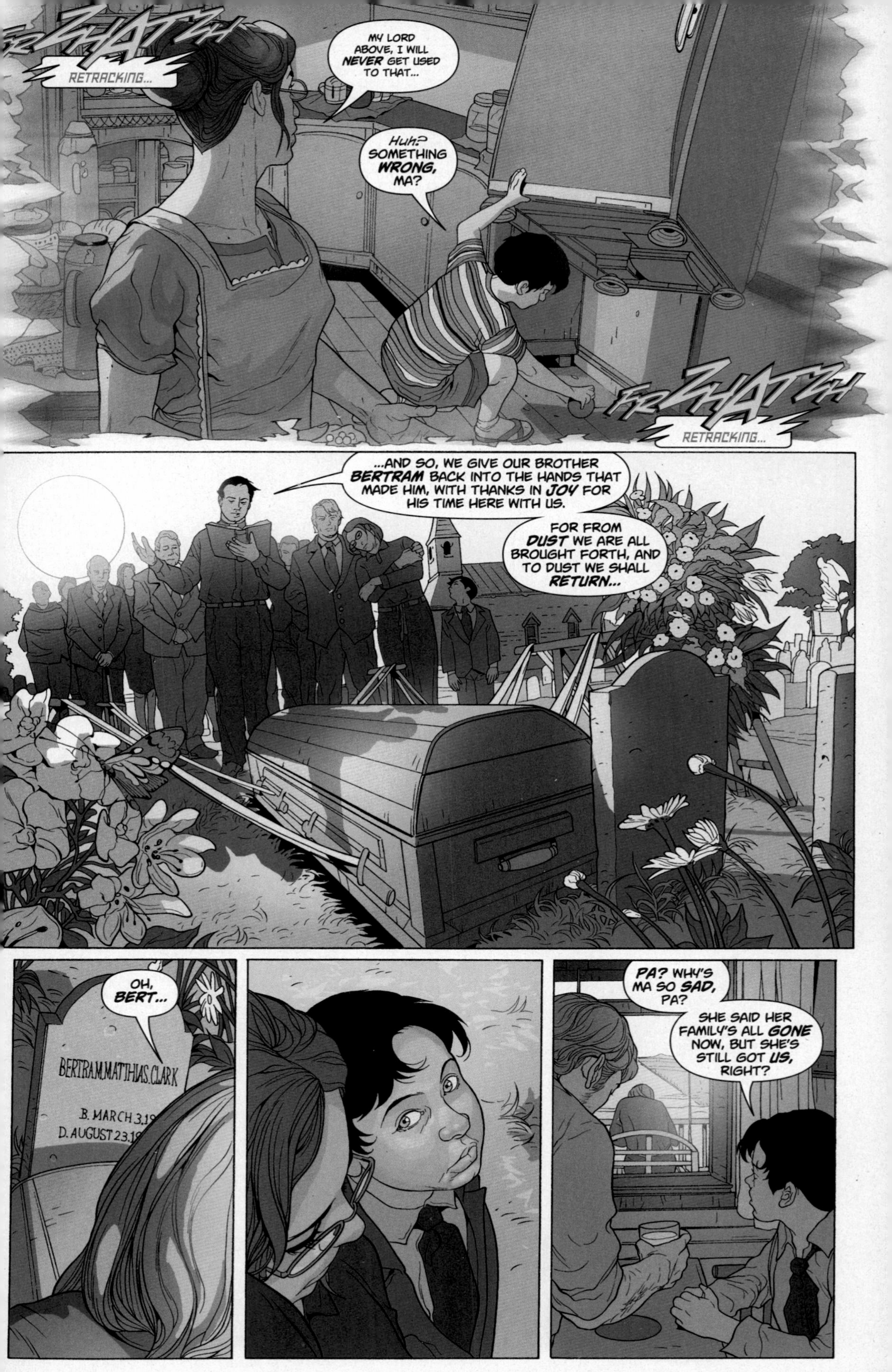
FRZHATZH
RETRACKING...
MY LORD ABOVE, I WILL NEVER GET USED TO THAT...
Huh? SOMETHING WRONG, MA?
FRZHATZH
RETRACKING...
...AND SO, WE GIVE OUR BROTHER BERTRAM BACK INTO THE HANDS THAT MADE HIM, WITH THANKS IN JOY FOR HIS TIME HERE WITH US.
FOR FROM DUST WE ARE ALL BROUGHT FORTH, AND TO DUST WE SHALL RETURN...
OH, BERT...
BERTRAM.MATTHIAS.CLARK
B. MARCH 3.19
D. AUGUST 23.19
PA? WHY'S MA SO SAD, PA?
SHE SAID HER FAMILY'S ALL GONE NOW, BUT SHE'S STILL GOT US, RIGHT?

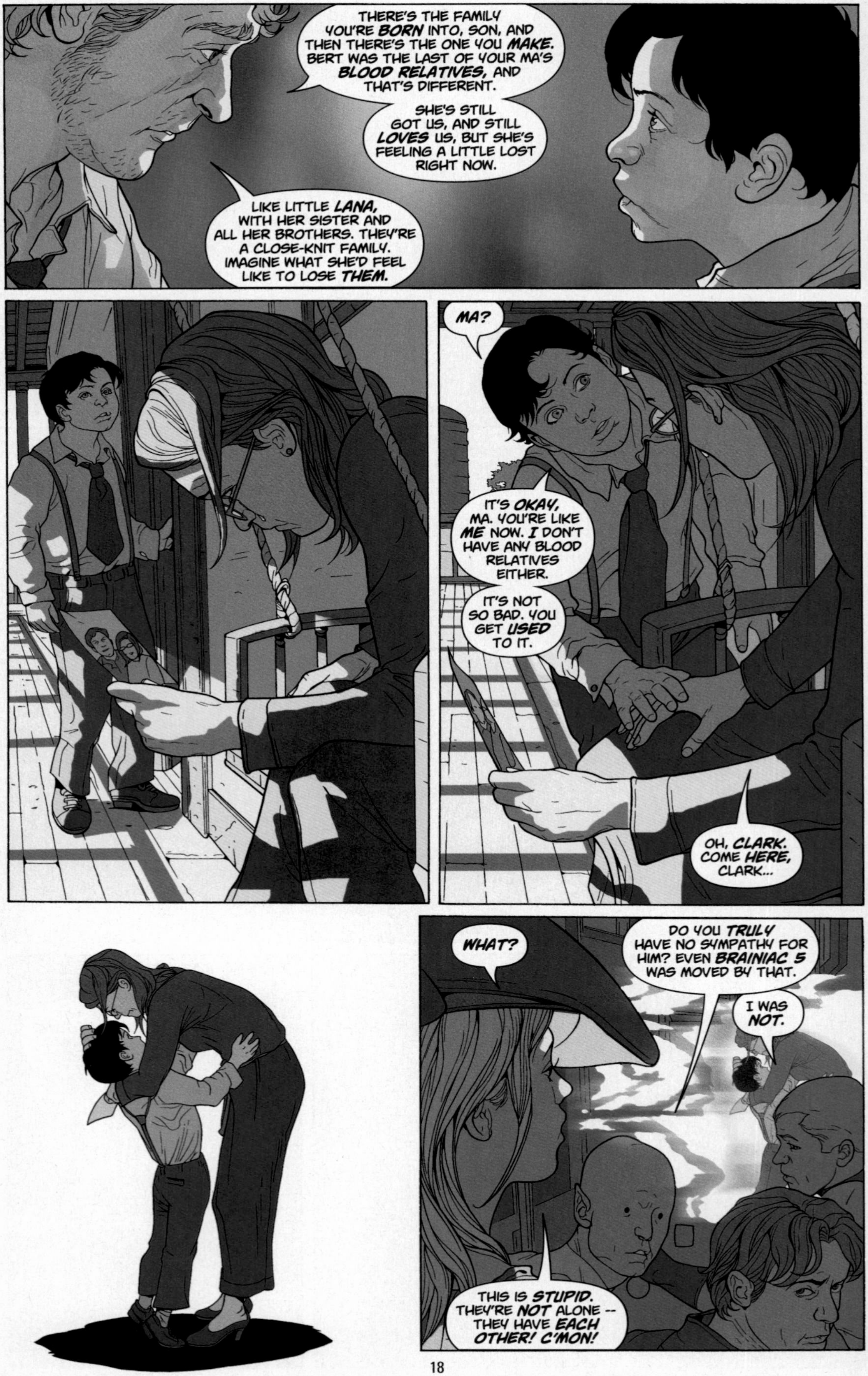
THERE'S THE FAMILY YOU'RE BORN INTO, SON, AND THEN THERE'S THE ONE YOU MAKE. BERT WAS THE LAST OF YOUR MA'S BLOOD RELATIVES, AND THAT'S DIFFERENT.
SHE'S STILL GOT US, AND STILL LOVES US, BUT SHE'S FEELING A LITTLE LOST RIGHT NOW.
LIKE LITTLE LANA, WITH HER SISTER AND ALL HER BROTHERS. THEY'RE A CLOSE-KNIT FAMILY. IMAGINE WHAT SHE'D FEEL LIKE TO LOSE THEM.
MA?
IT'S OKAY, MA. YOU'RE LIKE ME NOW. I DON'T HAVE ANY BLOOD RELATIVES EITHER.
IT'S NOT SO BAD. YOU GET USED TO IT.
OH, CLARK. COME HERE, CLARK...
WHAT?
DO YOU TRULY HAVE NO SYMPATHY FOR HIM? EVEN BRAINIAC 5 WAS MOVED BY THAT.
I WAS NOT.
THIS IS STUPID. THEY'RE NOT ALONE -- THEY HAVE EACH OTHER! C'MON!

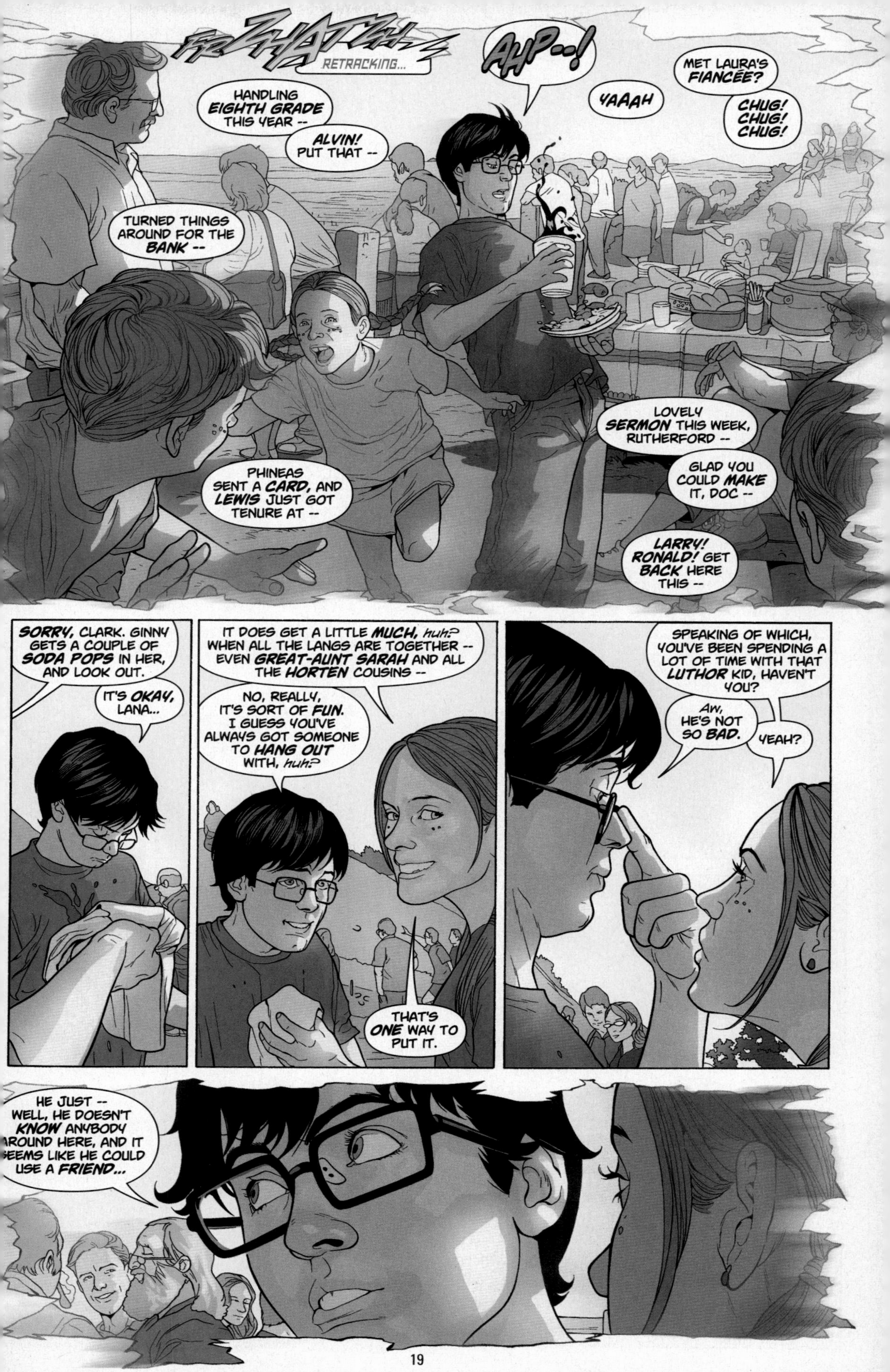

FRZHATCH
RETRACKING...
AHP--!
HANDLING EIGHTH GRADE THIS YEAR --
ALVIN! PUT THAT --
YAAAH
MET LAURA'S FIANCÉE?
CHUG! CHUG! CHUG!
TURNED THINGS AROUND FOR THE BANK --
LOVELY SERMON THIS WEEK, RUTHERFORD --
PHINEAS SENT A CARD, AND LEWIS JUST GOT TENURE AT --
GLAD YOU COULD MAKE IT, DOC --
LARRY! RONALD! GET BACK HERE THIS --
SORRY, CLARK. GINNY GETS A COUPLE OF SODA POPS IN HER, AND LOOK OUT.
IT'S OKAY, LANA...
IT DOES GET A LITTLE MUCH, huh? WHEN ALL THE LANGS ARE TOGETHER -- EVEN GREAT-AUNT SARAH AND ALL THE HORTEN COUSINS --
NO, REALLY, IT'S SORT OF FUN. I GUESS YOU'VE ALWAYS GOT SOMEONE TO HANG OUT WITH, huh?
THAT'S ONE WAY TO PUT IT.
SPEAKING OF WHICH, YOU'VE BEEN SPENDING A LOT OF TIME WITH THAT LUTHOR KID, HAVEN'T YOU?
AW, HE'S NOT SO BAD.
YEAH?
HE JUST -- WELL, HE DOESN'T KNOW ANYBODY AROUND HERE, AND IT SEEMS LIKE HE COULD USE A FRIEND...

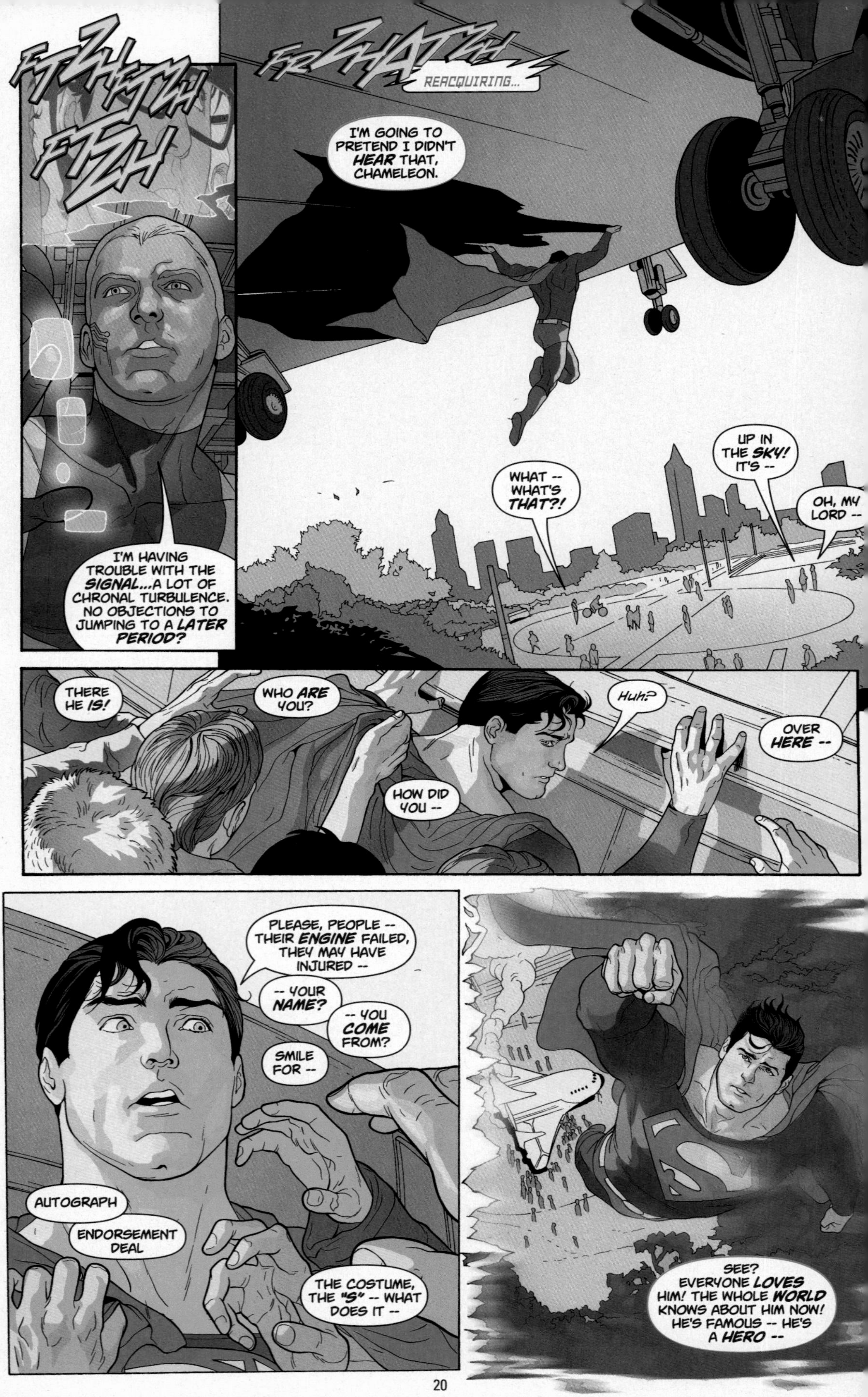
FTZHETZH
FTZH
FRZHATZH
REACQUIRING...
I'M GOING TO PRETEND I DIDN'T HEAR THAT, CHAMELEON.
I'M HAVING TROUBLE WITH THE SIGNAL...A LOT OF CHRONAL TURBULENCE. NO OBJECTIONS TO JUMPING TO A LATER PERIOD?
WHAT -- WHAT'S THAT?!
UP IN THE SKY! IT'S --
OH, MY LORD --
THERE HE IS!
WHO ARE YOU?
HOW DID YOU --
Huh?
OVER HERE --
PLEASE, PEOPLE -- THEIR ENGINE FAILED, THEY MAY HAVE INJURED --
-- YOUR NAME?
-- YOU COME FROM?
SMILE FOR --
AUTOGRAPH
ENDORSEMENT DEAL
THE COSTUME, THE "S" -- WHAT DOES IT --
SEE? EVERYONE LOVES HIM! THE WHOLE WORLD KNOWS ABOUT HIM NOW! HE'S FAMOUS -- HE'S A HERO --

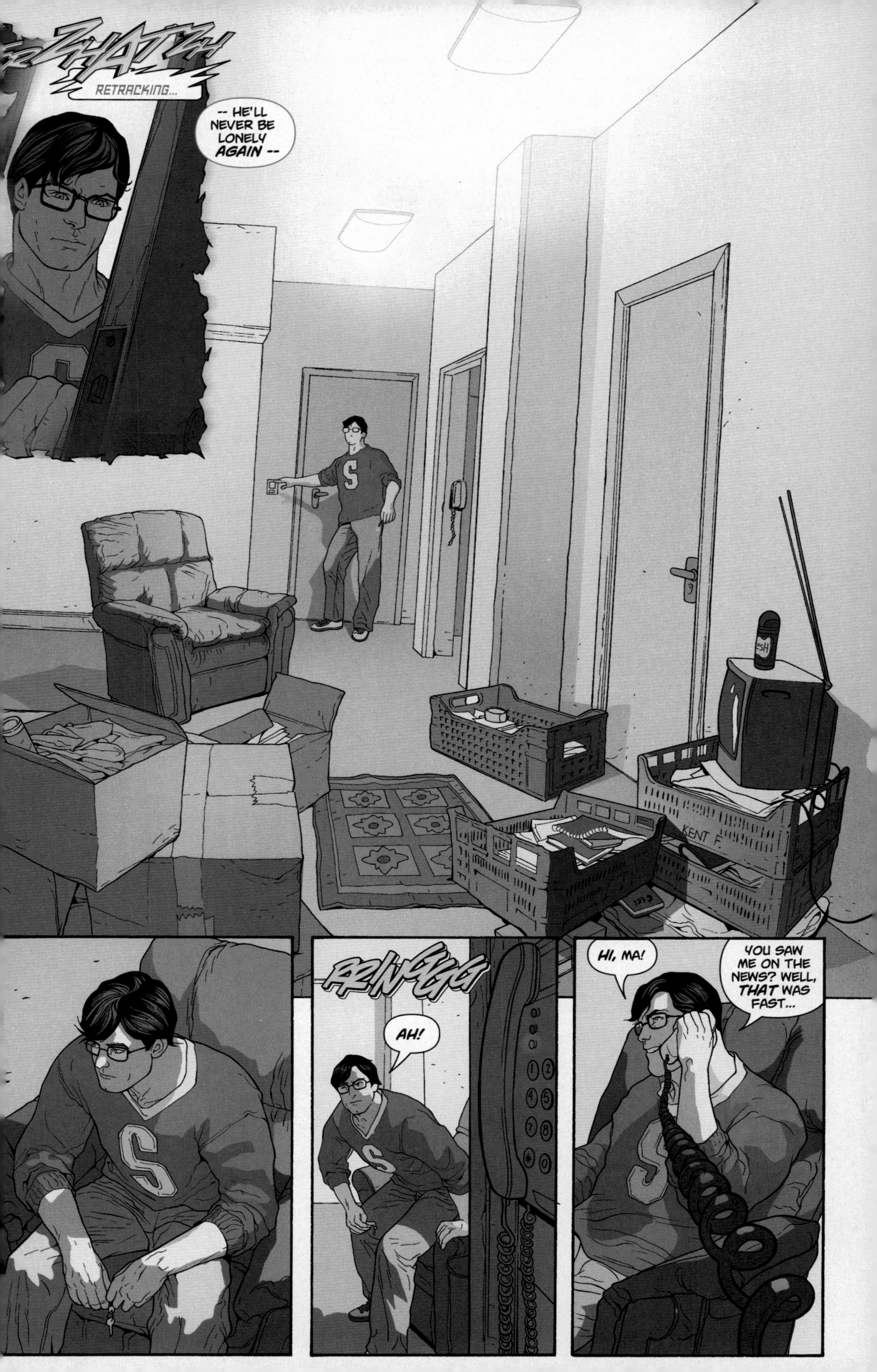
ZHATZH
RETRACKING...
-- HE'LL NEVER BE LONELY AGAIN --
KENT F.
BRINGG
AH!
HI, MA!
YOU SAW ME ON THE NEWS? WELL, THAT WAS FAST...

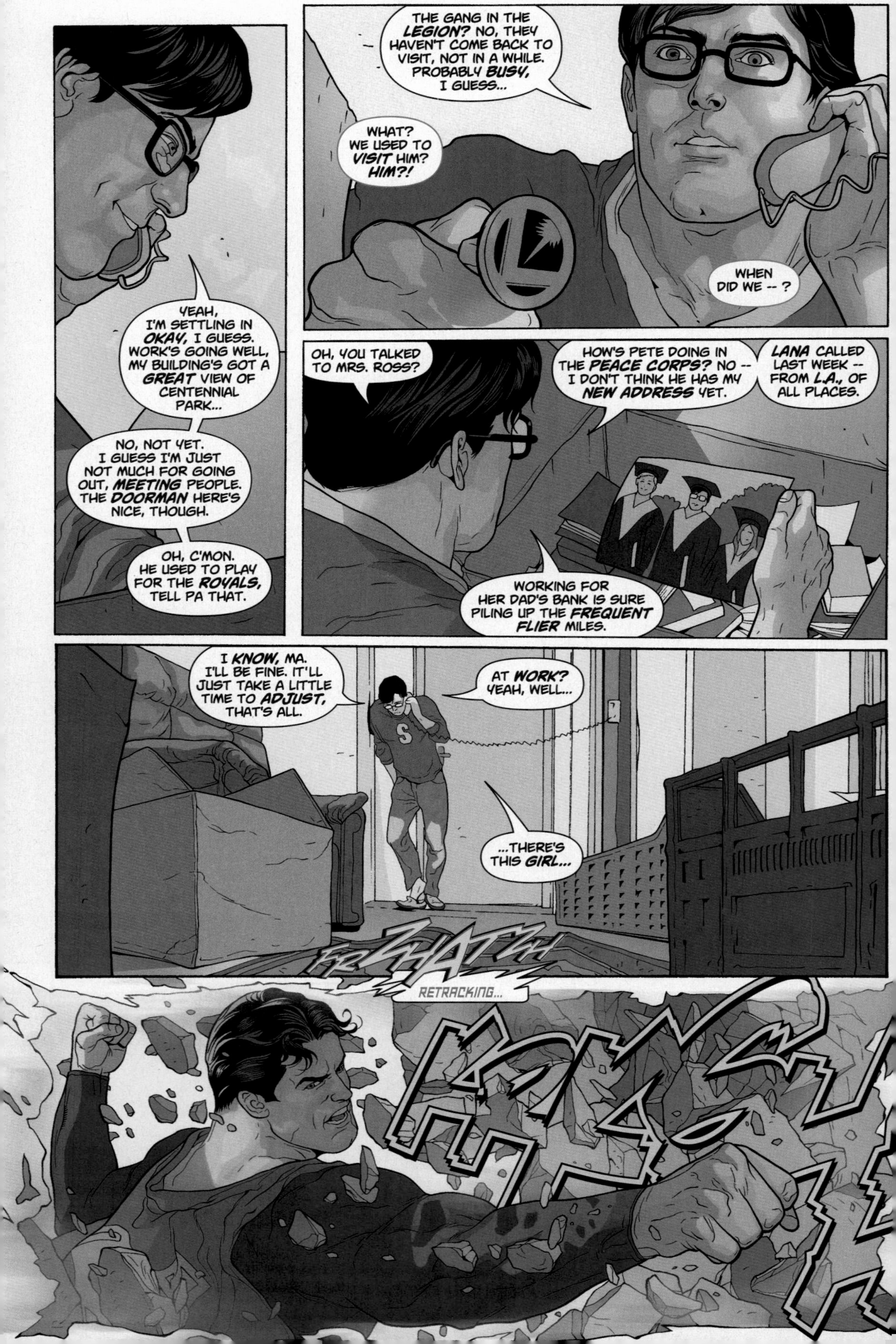

YEAH, I'M SETTLING IN OKAY, I GUESS. WORK'S GOING WELL, MY BUILDING'S GOT A GREAT VIEW OF CENTENNIAL PARK...
NO, NOT YET. I GUESS I'M JUST NOT MUCH FOR GOING OUT, MEETING PEOPLE. THE DOORMAN HERE'S NICE, THOUGH.
OH, C'MON. HE USED TO PLAY FOR THE ROYALS, TELL PA THAT.
THE GANG IN THE LEGION? NO, THEY HAVEN'T COME BACK TO VISIT, NOT IN A WHILE. PROBABLY BUSY, I GUESS...
WHAT? WE USED TO VISIT HIM? HIM?!
WHEN DID WE -- ?
OH, YOU TALKED TO MRS. ROSS?
HOW'S PETE DOING IN THE PEACE CORPS? NO -- I DON'T THINK HE HAS MY NEW ADDRESS YET.
LANA CALLED LAST WEEK -- FROM L.A., OF ALL PLACES.
WORKING FOR HER DAD'S BANK IS SURE PILING UP THE FREQUENT FLIER MILES.
I KNOW, MA. I'LL BE FINE. IT'LL JUST TAKE A LITTLE TIME TO ADJUST, THAT'S ALL.
AT WORK? YEAH, WELL...
...THERE'S THIS GIRL...
RETRACKING...

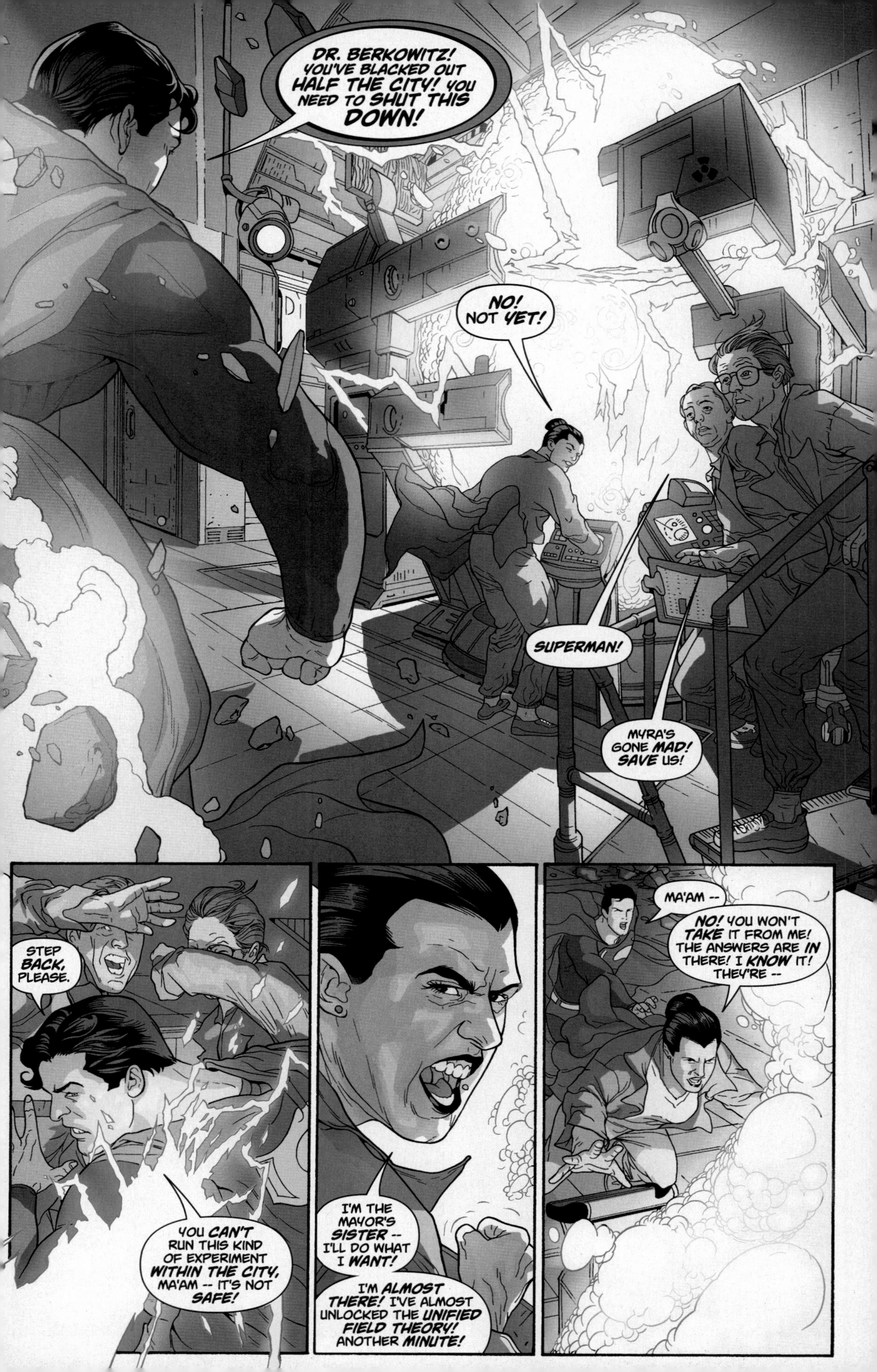
DR. BERKOWITZ! YOU'VE BLACKED OUT HALF THE CITY! YOU NEED TO SHUT THIS DOWN!
NO! NOT YET!
SUPERMAN!
MYRA'S GONE MAD! SAVE US!
STEP BACK, PLEASE.
YOU CAN'T RUN THIS KIND OF EXPERIMENT WITHIN THE CITY, MA'AM -- IT'S NOT SAFE!
I'M THE MAYOR'S SISTER -- I'LL DO WHAT I WANT!
I'M ALMOST THERE! I'VE ALMOST UNLOCKED THE UNIFIED FIELD THEORY! ANOTHER MINUTE!
MA'AM --
NO! YOU WON'T TAKE IT FROM ME! THE ANSWERS ARE IN THERE! I KNOW IT! THEY'RE --

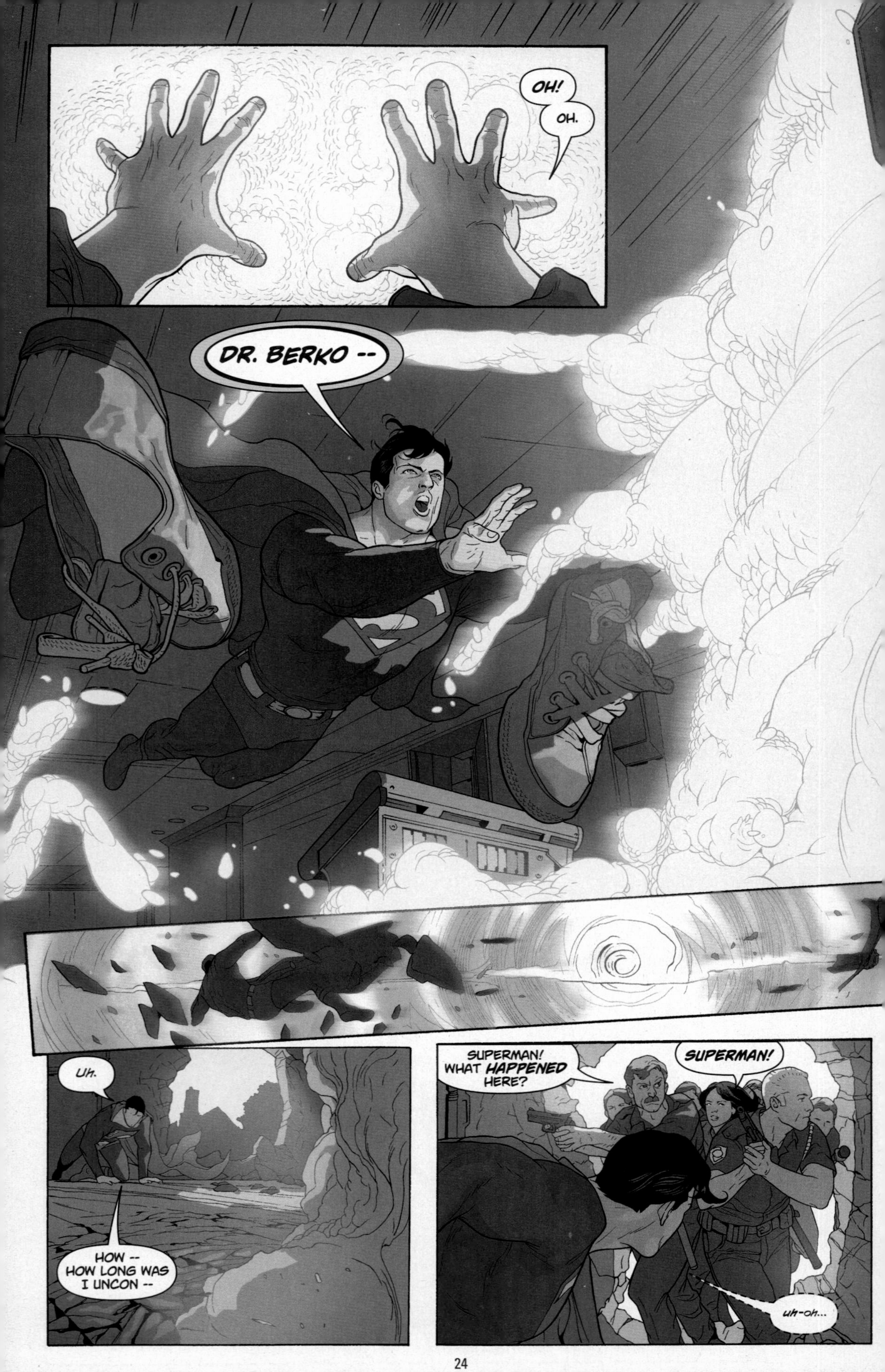
OH!
OH.
DR. BERKO --
Uh.
HOW -- HOW LONG WAS I UNCON --
SUPERMAN! WHAT HAPPENED HERE?
SUPERMAN!
uh-oh...

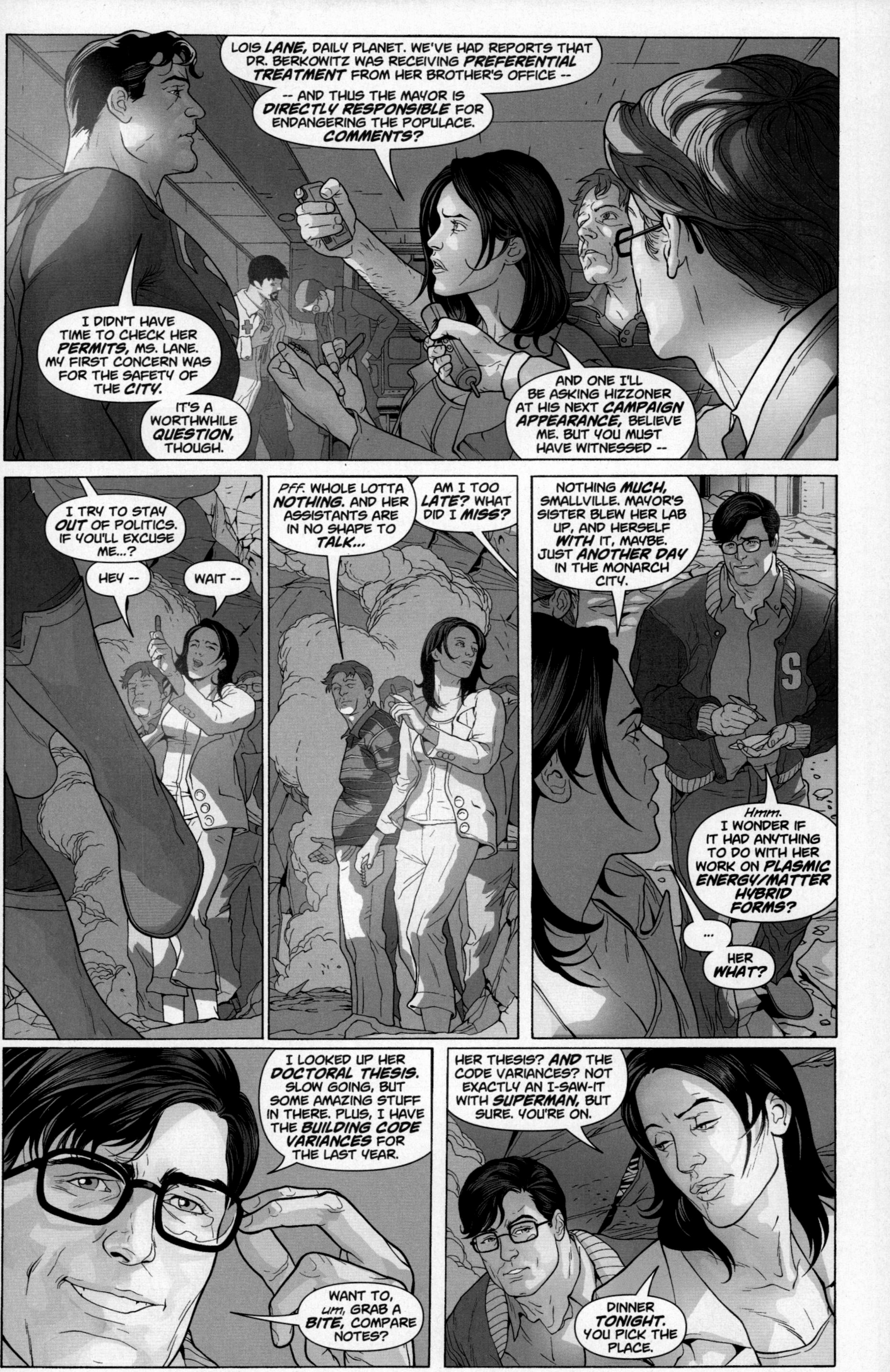
LOIS LANE, DAILY PLANET. WE'VE HAD REPORTS THAT DR. BERKOWITZ WAS RECEIVING PREFERENTIAL TREATMENT FROM HER BROTHER'S OFFICE --
-- AND THUS THE MAYOR IS DIRECTLY RESPONSIBLE FOR ENDANGERING THE POPULACE. COMMENTS?
I DIDN'T HAVE TIME TO CHECK HER PERMITS, MS. LANE. MY FIRST CONCERN WAS FOR THE SAFETY OF THE CITY.
IT'S A WORTHWHILE QUESTION, THOUGH.
AND ONE I'LL BE ASKING HIZZONER AT HIS NEXT CAMPAIGN APPEARANCE, BELIEVE ME. BUT YOU MUST HAVE WITNESSED --
I TRY TO STAY OUT OF POLITICS. IF YOU'LL EXCUSE ME...?
HEY --
WAIT --
PFF. WHOLE LOTTA NOTHING. AND HER ASSISTANTS ARE IN NO SHAPE TO TALK...
AM I TOO LATE? WHAT DID I MISS?
NOTHING MUCH, SMALLVILLE. MAYOR'S SISTER BLEW HER LAB UP, AND HERSELF WITH IT, MAYBE. JUST ANOTHER DAY IN THE MONARCH CITY.
Hmm. I WONDER IF IT HAD ANYTHING TO DO WITH HER WORK ON PLASMIC ENERGY/MATTER HYBRID FORMS?
...
HER WHAT?
I LOOKED UP HER DOCTORAL THESIS. SLOW GOING, BUT SOME AMAZING STUFF IN THERE. PLUS, I HAVE THE BUILDING CODE VARIANCES FOR THE LAST YEAR.
WANT TO, um, GRAB A BITE, COMPARE NOTES?
HER THESIS? AND THE CODE VARIANCES? NOT EXACTLY AN I-SAW-IT WITH SUPERMAN, BUT SURE. YOU'RE ON.
DINNER TONIGHT. YOU PICK THE PLACE.

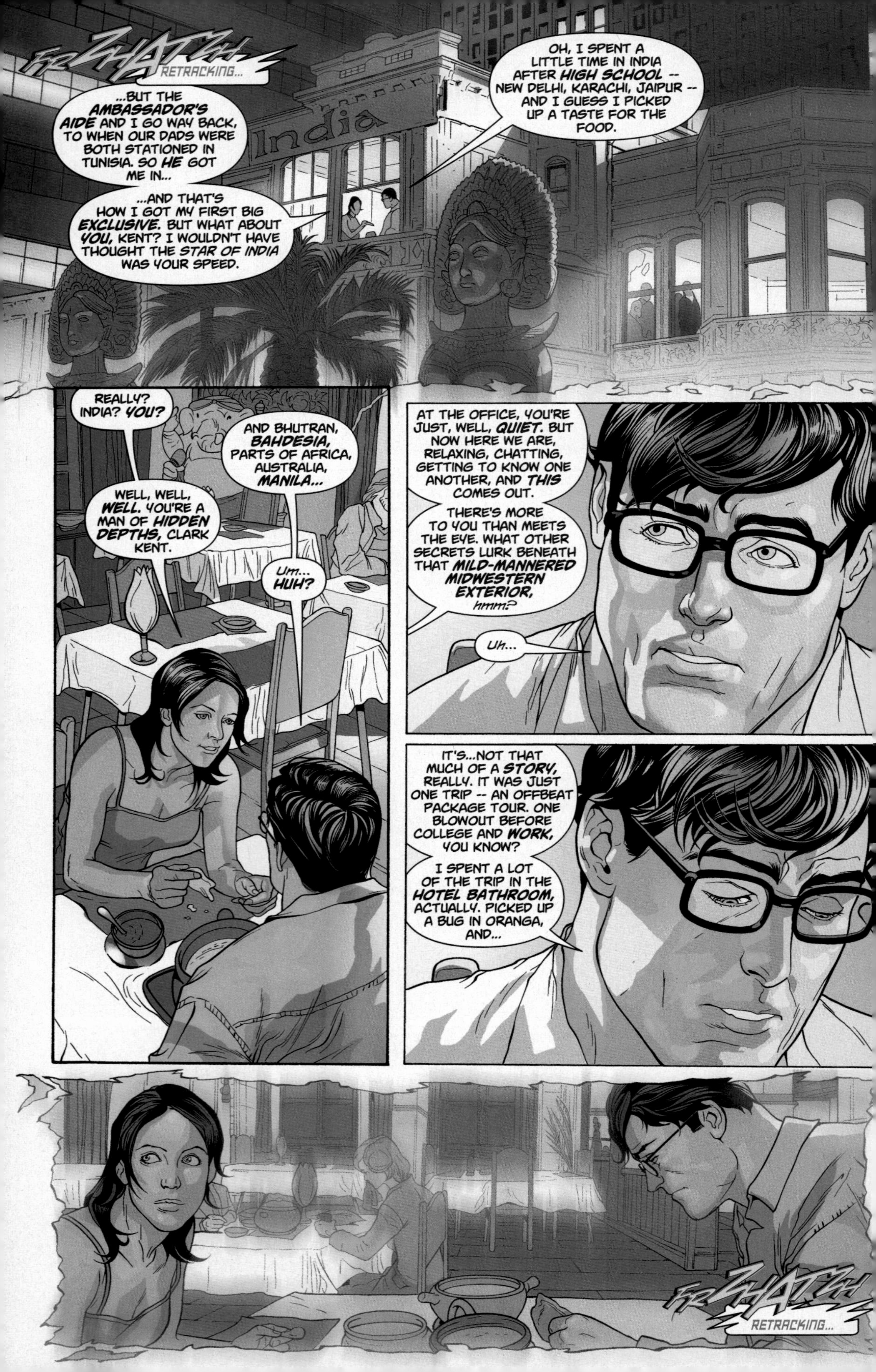
FRZHATZH
RETRACKING...
...BUT THE AMBASSADOR'S AIDE AND I GO WAY BACK, TO WHEN OUR DADS WERE BOTH STATIONED IN TUNISIA. SO HE GOT ME IN...
...AND THAT'S HOW I GOT MY FIRST BIG EXCLUSIVE. BUT WHAT ABOUT YOU, KENT? I WOULDN'T HAVE THOUGHT THE STAR OF INDIA WAS YOUR SPEED.
OH, I SPENT A LITTLE TIME IN INDIA AFTER HIGH SCHOOL -- NEW DELHI, KARACHI, JAIPUR -- AND I GUESS I PICKED UP A TASTE FOR THE FOOD.
India
REALLY? INDIA? YOU?
AND BHUTRAN, BAHDESIA, PARTS OF AFRICA, AUSTRALIA, MANILA...
WELL, WELL, WELL. YOU'RE A MAN OF HIDDEN DEPTHS, CLARK KENT.
Um... HUH?
AT THE OFFICE, YOU'RE JUST, WELL, QUIET. BUT NOW HERE WE ARE, RELAXING, CHATTING, GETTING TO KNOW ONE ANOTHER, AND THIS COMES OUT.
THERE'S MORE TO YOU THAN MEETS THE EYE. WHAT OTHER SECRETS LURK BENEATH THAT MILD-MANNERED MIDWESTERN EXTERIOR, hmm?
Uh...
IT'S...NOT THAT MUCH OF A STORY, REALLY. IT WAS JUST ONE TRIP -- AN OFFBEAT PACKAGE TOUR. ONE BLOWOUT BEFORE COLLEGE AND WORK, YOU KNOW?
I SPENT A LOT OF THE TRIP IN THE HOTEL BATHROOM, ACTUALLY. PICKED UP A BUG IN ORANGA, AND...
FRZHATZH
RETRACKING...

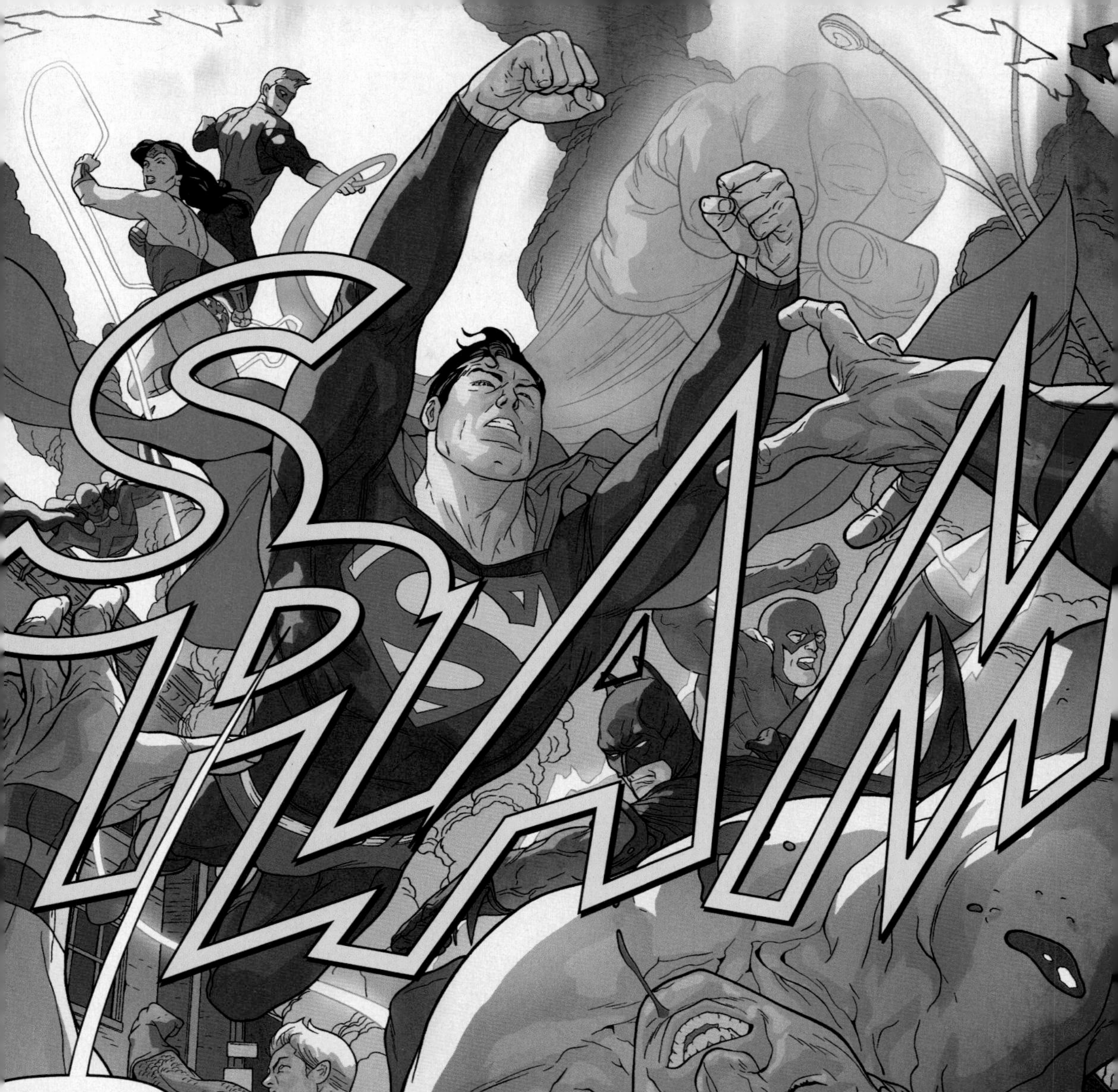
SLAM
JUSTICE
EAGUE --
--TOGETHER!

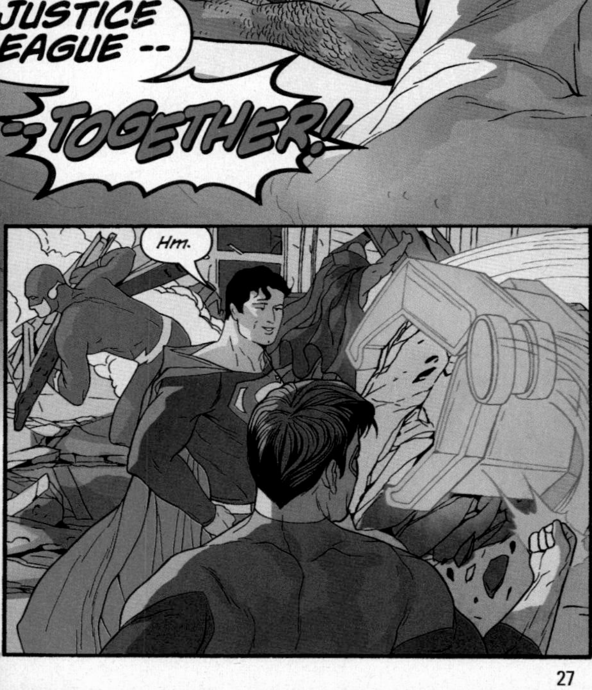
Hm.

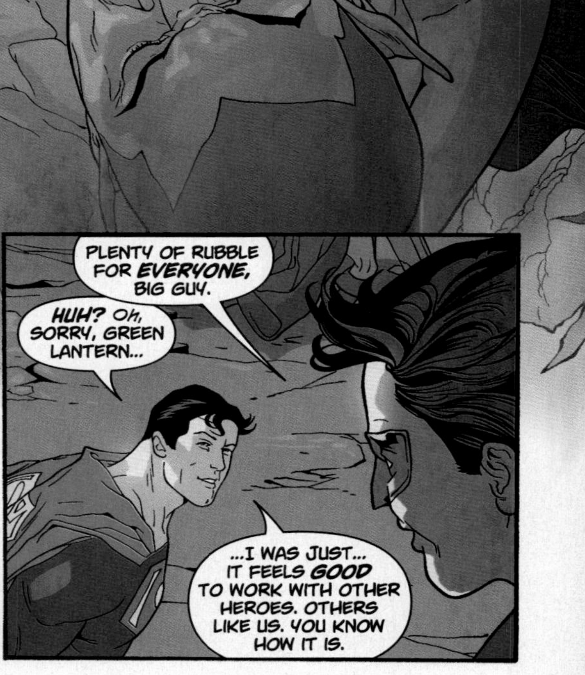
PLENTY OF RUBBLE FOR EVERYONE, BIG GUY.
HUH? Oh, SORRY, GREEN LANTERN...
...I WAS JUST... IT FEELS GOOD TO WORK WITH OTHER HEROES. OTHERS LIKE US. YOU KNOW HOW IT IS.

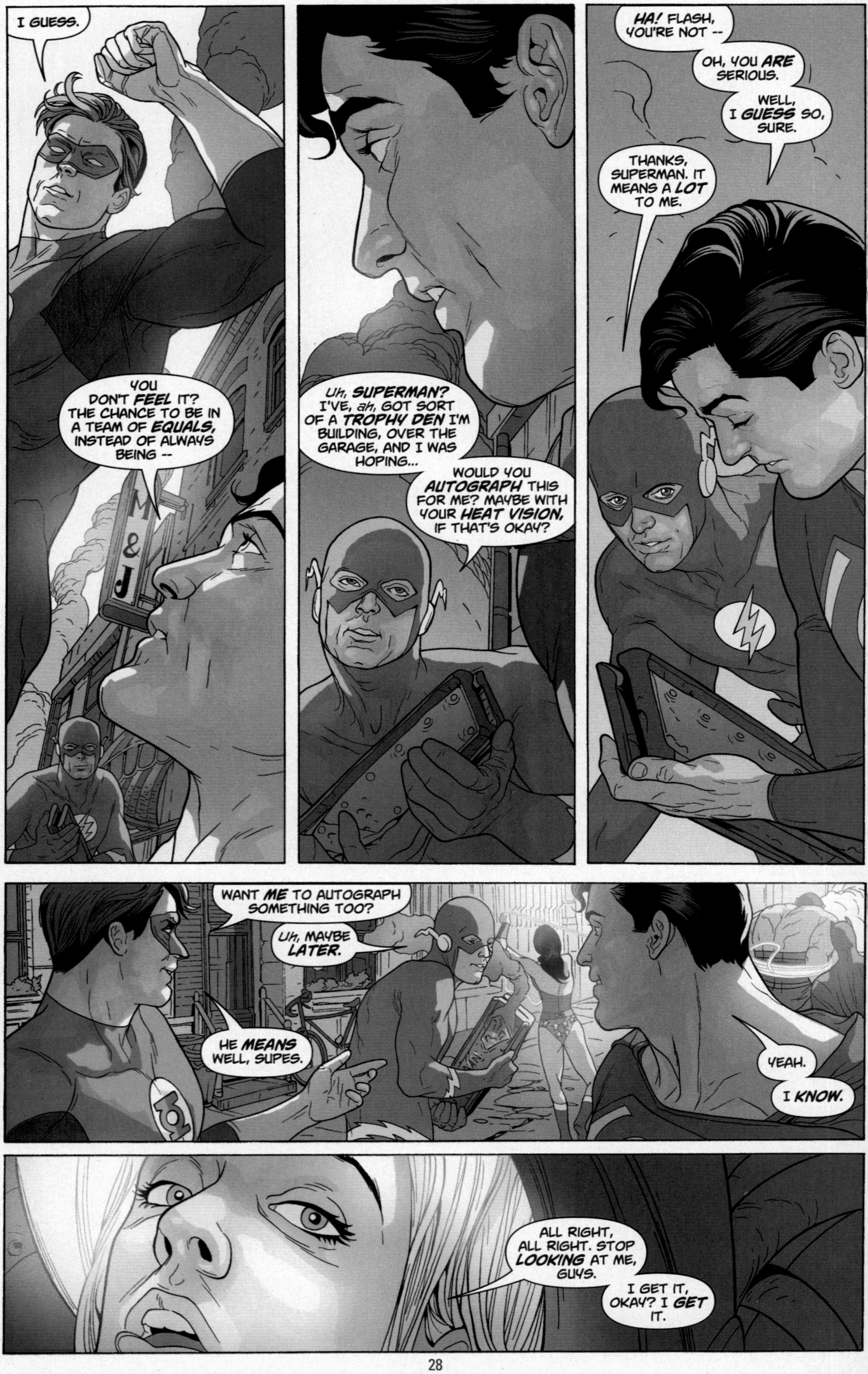
I GUESS.
YOU DON'T FEEL IT? THE CHANCE TO BE IN A TEAM OF EQUALS, INSTEAD OF ALWAYS BEING --
M & J
Uh, SUPERMAN? I'VE, ah, GOT SORT OF A TROPHY DEN I'M BUILDING, OVER THE GARAGE, AND I WAS HOPING...
WOULD YOU AUTOGRAPH THIS FOR ME? MAYBE WITH YOUR HEAT VISION, IF THAT'S OKAY?
HA! FLASH, YOU'RE NOT --
OH, YOU ARE SERIOUS.
WELL, I GUESS SO, SURE.
THANKS, SUPERMAN. IT MEANS A LOT TO ME.
WANT ME TO AUTOGRAPH SOMETHING TOO?
Uh, MAYBE LATER.
HE MEANS WELL, SUPES.
YEAH.
I KNOW.
ALL RIGHT, ALL RIGHT. STOP LOOKING AT ME, GUYS.
I GET IT, OKAY? I GET IT.

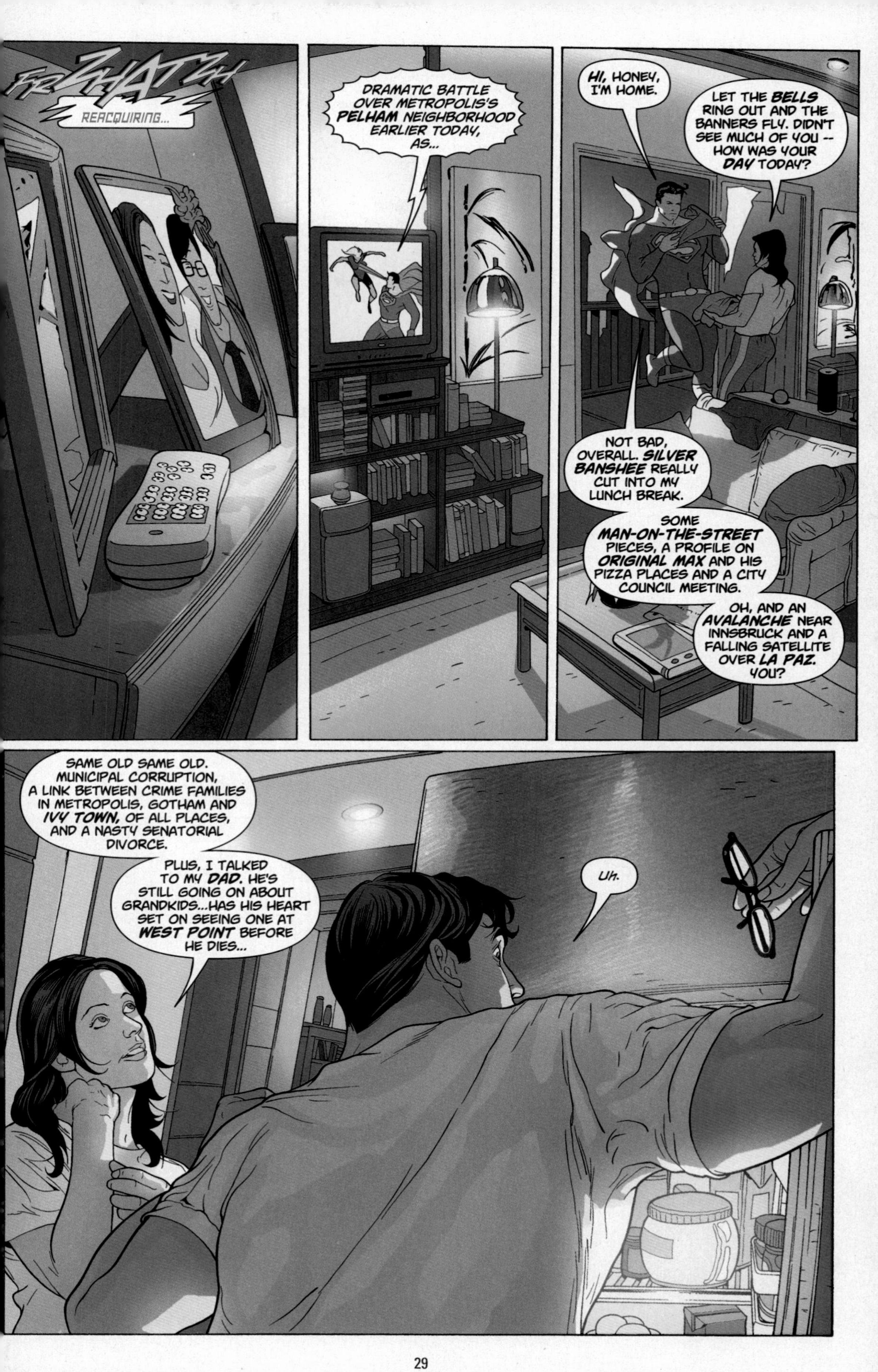
FRZHATZH
REACQUIRING...
DRAMATIC BATTLE OVER METROPOLIS'S PELHAM NEIGHBORHOOD EARLIER TODAY, AS...
HI, HONEY, I'M HOME.
LET THE BELLS RING OUT AND THE BANNERS FLY. DIDN'T SEE MUCH OF YOU -- HOW WAS YOUR DAY TODAY?
NOT BAD, OVERALL. SILVER BANSHEE REALLY CUT INTO MY LUNCH BREAK.
SOME MAN-ON-THE-STREET PIECES, A PROFILE ON ORIGINAL MAX AND HIS PIZZA PLACES AND A CITY COUNCIL MEETING.
OH, AND AN AVALANCHE NEAR INNSBRUCK AND A FALLING SATELLITE OVER LA PAZ. YOU?
SAME OLD SAME OLD. MUNICIPAL CORRUPTION, A LINK BETWEEN CRIME FAMILIES IN METROPOLIS, GOTHAM AND IVY TOWN, OF ALL PLACES, AND A NASTY SENATORIAL DIVORCE.
PLUS, I TALKED TO MY DAD. HE'S STILL GOING ON ABOUT GRANDKIDS...HAS HIS HEART SET ON SEEING ONE AT WEST POINT BEFORE HE DIES...
Uh.

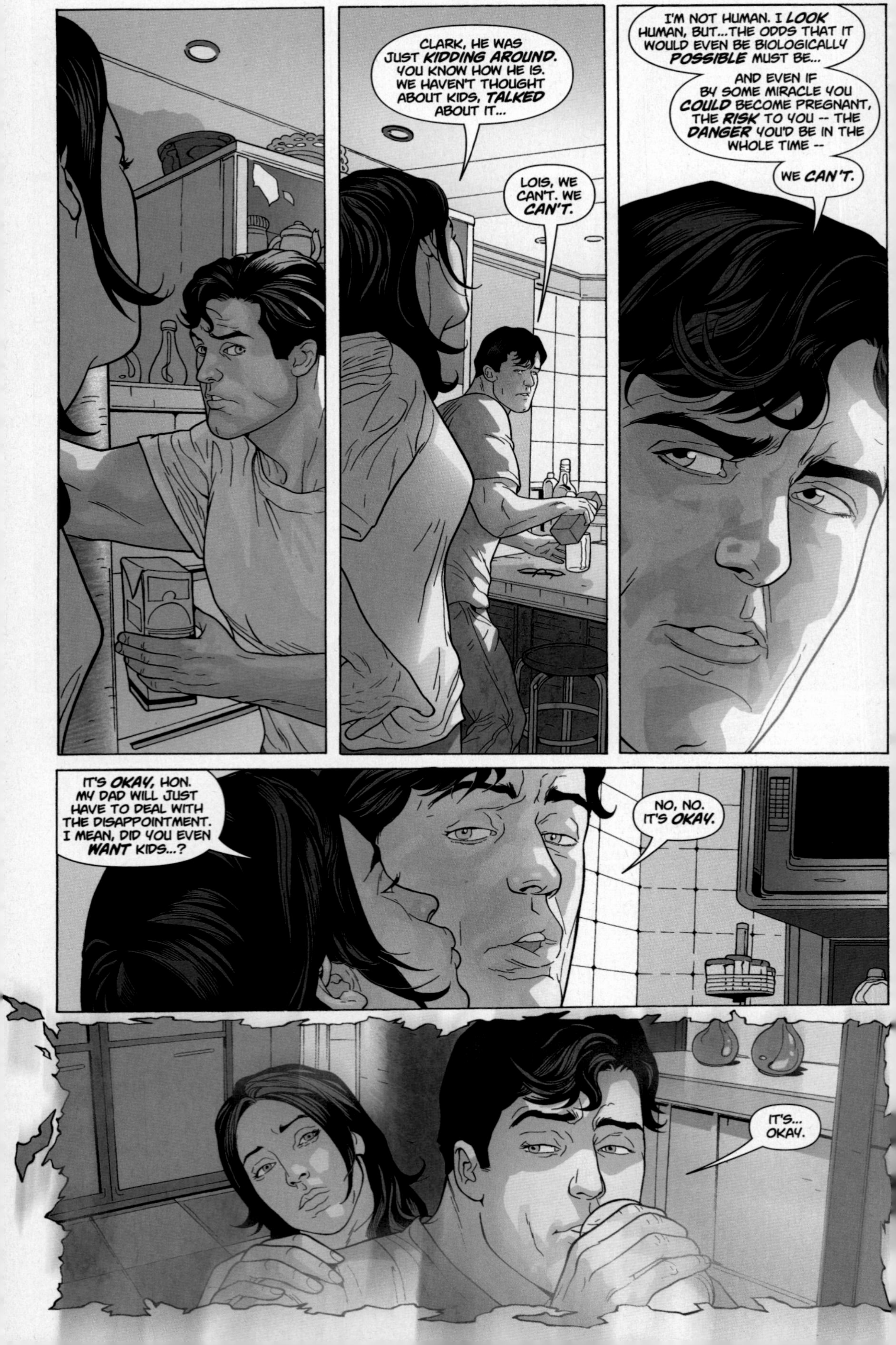
CLARK, HE WAS JUST KIDDING AROUND. YOU KNOW HOW HE IS. WE HAVEN'T THOUGHT ABOUT KIDS, TALKED ABOUT IT...
LOIS, WE CAN'T. WE CAN'T.
I'M NOT HUMAN. I LOOK HUMAN, BUT...THE ODDS THAT IT WOULD EVEN BE BIOLOGICALLY POSSIBLE MUST BE...
AND EVEN IF BY SOME MIRACLE YOU COULD BECOME PREGNANT, THE RISK TO YOU -- THE DANGER YOU'D BE IN THE WHOLE TIME --
WE CAN'T.
IT'S OKAY, HON. MY DAD WILL JUST HAVE TO DEAL WITH THE DISAPPOINTMENT. I MEAN, DID YOU EVEN WANT KIDS...?
NO, NO. IT'S OKAY.
IT'S... OKAY.

ZHATH

RETRACKING...

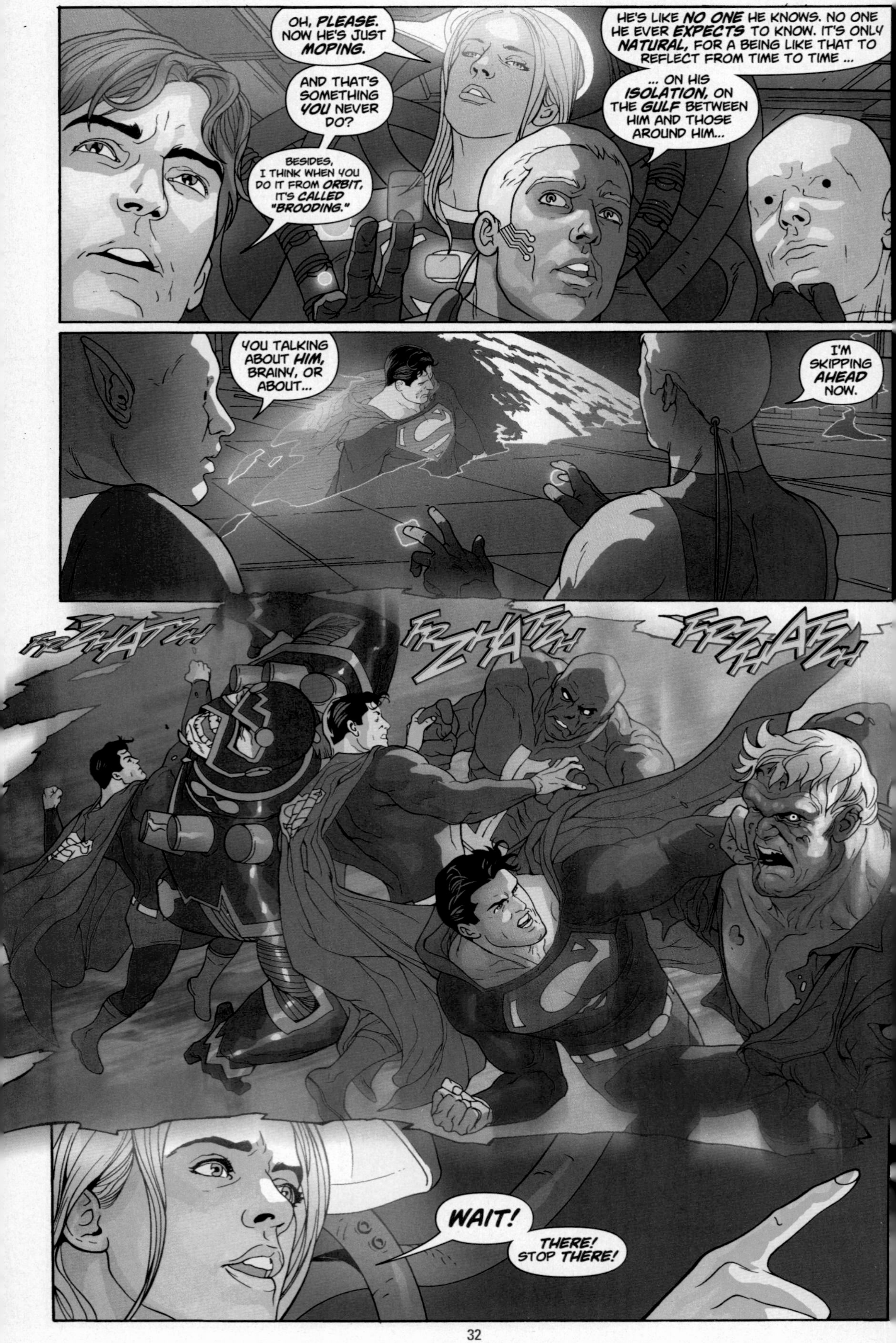
OH, PLEASE. NOW HE'S JUST MOPING.
HE'S LIKE NO ONE HE KNOWS. NO ONE HE EVER EXPECTS TO KNOW. IT'S ONLY NATURAL, FOR A BEING LIKE THAT TO REFLECT FROM TIME TO TIME ...
... ON HIS ISOLATION, ON THE GULF BETWEEN HIM AND THOSE AROUND HIM...
AND THAT'S SOMETHING YOU NEVER DO?
BESIDES, I THINK WHEN YOU DO IT FROM ORBIT, IT'S CALLED "BROODING."
YOU TALKING ABOUT HIM, BRAINY, OR ABOUT...
I'M SKIPPING AHEAD NOW.
FRZHATZH
FRZHATZH
FRZHATZH
WAIT!
THERE! STOP THERE!

I THOUGHT YOU DIDN'T WANT TO *SEE* YOUR OWN HISTORY.

OH, SHUT UP. THAT'S GOTHAM CITY -- THAT'S MY *FIRST DAY* ON EARTH!

NICE *OUTFIT* THERE, KARA.

OH, SHUT UP.

FRZHATH RETRACKING...

GRERR ARF ARF ARF

KRYPTO! NO! DOWN, BOY! DOWN!

WHAT'S WITH THE *DOG?* IT'S LIKE HE *HATES* YOU!

I...HAD ISSUES.

KAM KAM KAM

FRZHATH RETRACKING...

I'LL SAY!

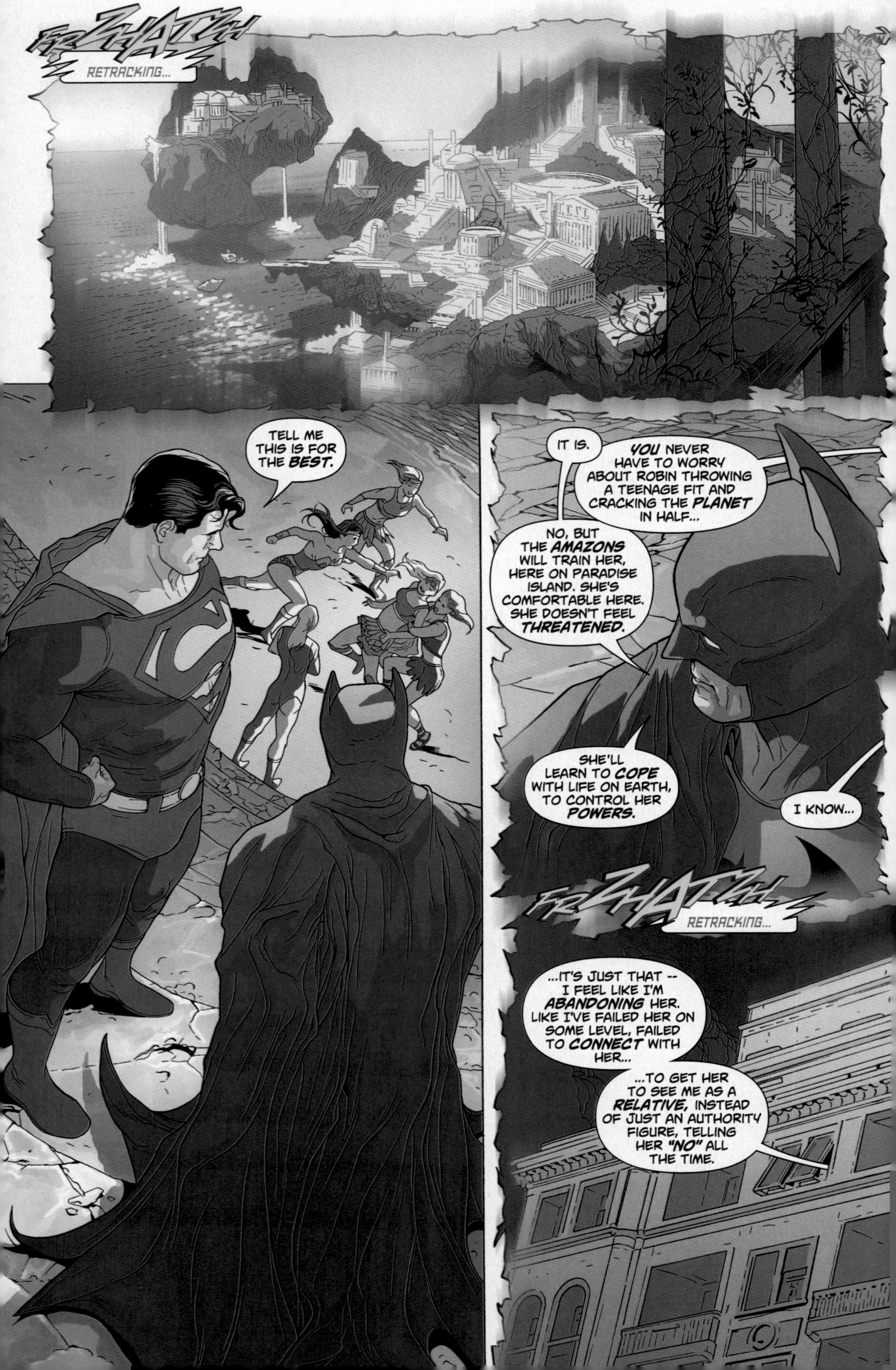
FRZHATZH
RETRACKING...
TELL ME THIS IS FOR THE BEST.
IT IS.
YOU NEVER HAVE TO WORRY ABOUT ROBIN THROWING A TEENAGE FIT AND CRACKING THE PLANET IN HALF...
NO, BUT THE AMAZONS WILL TRAIN HER, HERE ON PARADISE ISLAND. SHE'S COMFORTABLE HERE. SHE DOESN'T FEEL THREATENED.
SHE'LL LEARN TO COPE WITH LIFE ON EARTH, TO CONTROL HER POWERS.
I KNOW...
FRZHATZH
RETRACKING...
...IT'S JUST THAT -- I FEEL LIKE I'M ABANDONING HER. LIKE I'VE FAILED HER ON SOME LEVEL, FAILED TO CONNECT WITH HER...
...TO GET HER TO SEE ME AS A RELATIVE, INSTEAD OF JUST AN AUTHORITY FIGURE, TELLING HER "NO" ALL THE TIME.

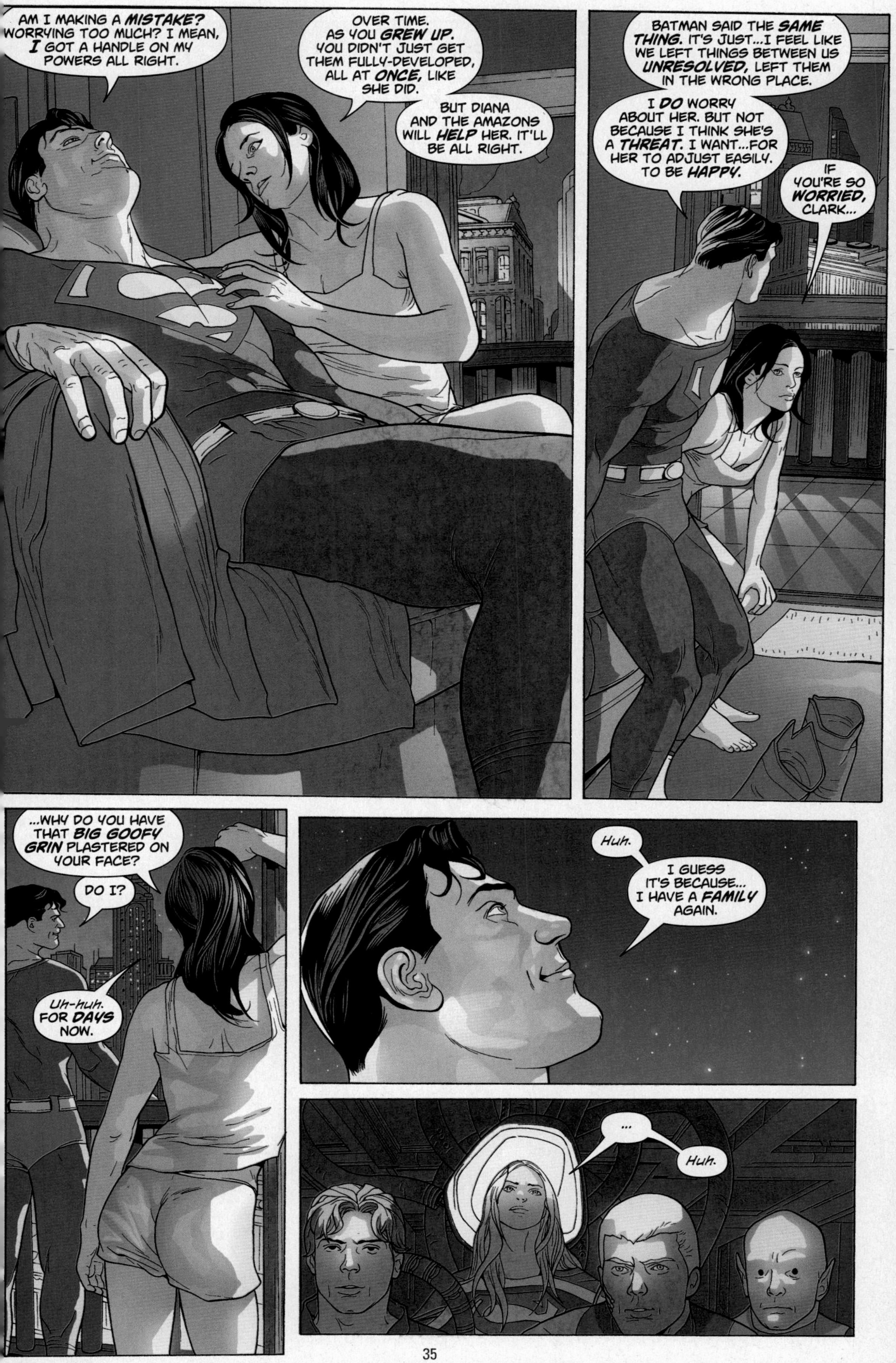
AM I MAKING A MISTAKE? WORRYING TOO MUCH? I MEAN, I GOT A HANDLE ON MY POWERS ALL RIGHT.
OVER TIME. AS YOU GREW UP. YOU DIDN'T JUST GET THEM FULLY-DEVELOPED, ALL AT ONCE, LIKE SHE DID.
BUT DIANA AND THE AMAZONS WILL HELP HER. IT'LL BE ALL RIGHT.
BATMAN SAID THE SAME THING. IT'S JUST...I FEEL LIKE WE LEFT THINGS BETWEEN US UNRESOLVED, LEFT THEM IN THE WRONG PLACE.
I DO WORRY ABOUT HER. BUT NOT BECAUSE I THINK SHE'S A THREAT. I WANT...FOR HER TO ADJUST EASILY. TO BE HAPPY.
IF YOU'RE SO WORRIED, CLARK...
...WHY DO YOU HAVE THAT BIG GOOFY GRIN PLASTERED ON YOUR FACE?
DO I?
Uh-huh. FOR DAYS NOW.
Huh.
I GUESS IT'S BECAUSE... I HAVE A FAMILY AGAIN.
...
Huh.

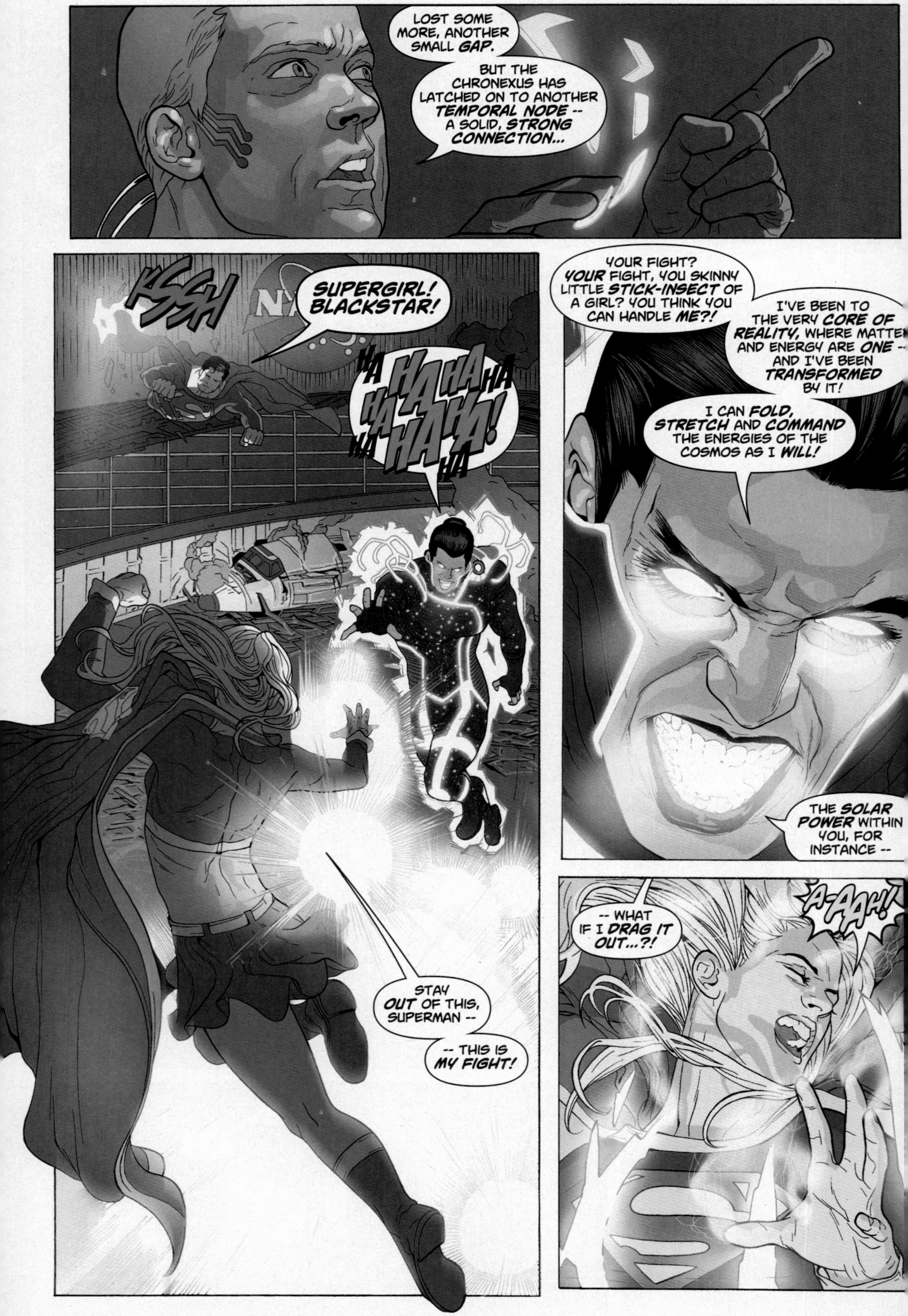
LOST SOME MORE, ANOTHER SMALL GAP.
BUT THE CHRONEXUS HAS LATCHED ON TO ANOTHER TEMPORAL NODE -- A SOLID, STRONG CONNECTION...
KSSH
SUPERGIRL! BLACKSTAR!
HA HA HA HA HA HA HA HA HA HA HA!
STAY OUT OF THIS, SUPERMAN --
-- THIS IS MY FIGHT!
YOUR FIGHT? YOUR FIGHT, YOU SKINNY LITTLE STICK-INSECT OF A GIRL? YOU THINK YOU CAN HANDLE ME?!
I'VE BEEN TO THE VERY CORE OF REALITY, WHERE MATTE AND ENERGY ARE ONE -- AND I'VE BEEN TRANSFORMED BY IT!
I CAN FOLD, STRETCH AND COMMAND THE ENERGIES OF THE COSMOS AS I WILL!
THE SOLAR POWER WITHIN YOU, FOR INSTANCE --
-- WHAT IF I DRAG IT OUT...?!
A-AAH!

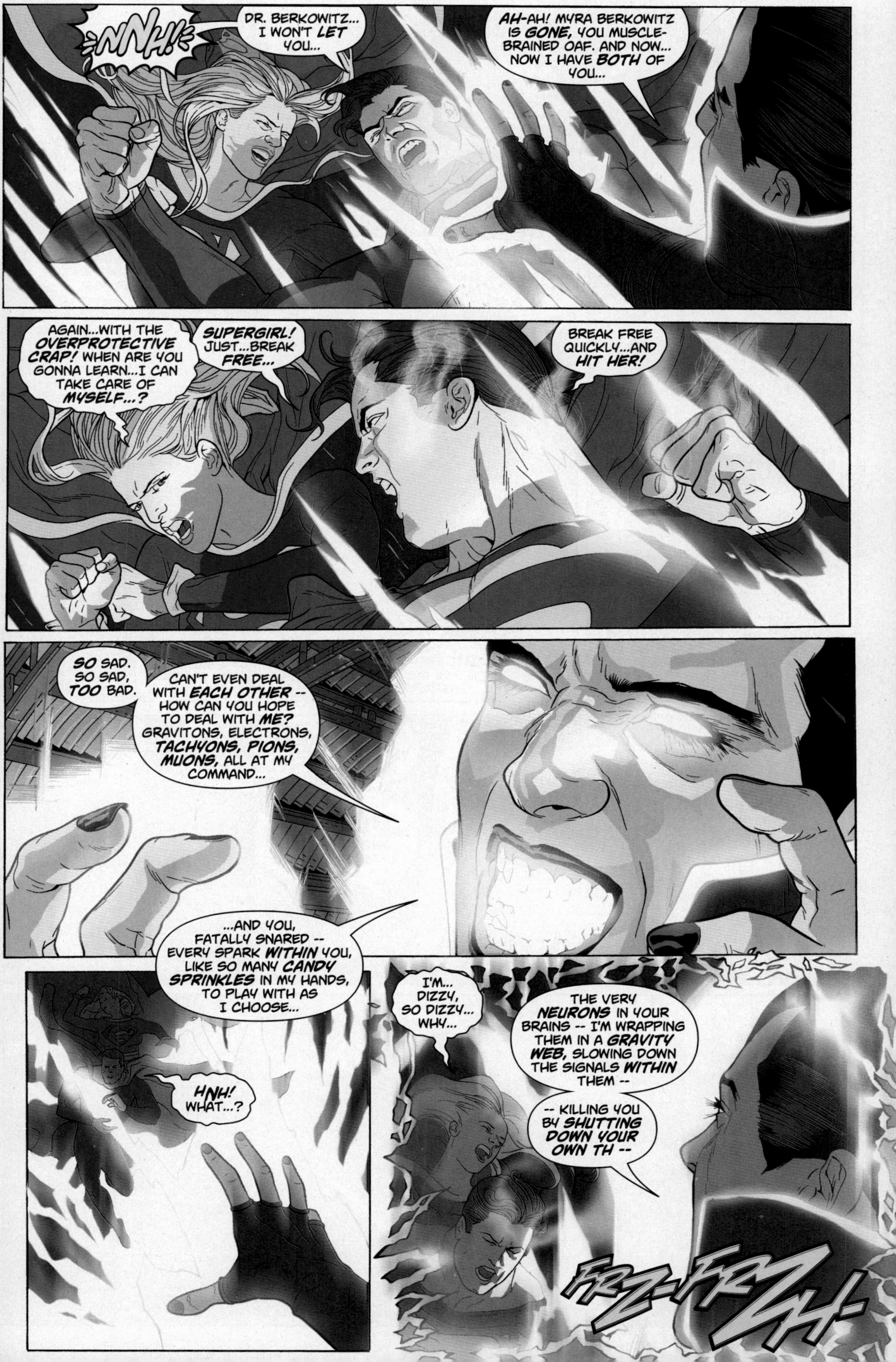
NNH!
DR. BERKOWITZ... I WON'T LET YOU...
AH-AH! MYRA BERKOWITZ IS GONE, YOU MUSCLE-BRAINED OAF. AND NOW... NOW I HAVE BOTH OF YOU...
AGAIN...WITH THE OVERPROTECTIVE CRAP! WHEN ARE YOU GONNA LEARN...I CAN TAKE CARE OF MYSELF...?
SUPERGIRL! JUST...BREAK FREE...
BREAK FREE QUICKLY...AND HIT HER!
SO SAD. SO SAD, TOO BAD.
CAN'T EVEN DEAL WITH EACH OTHER -- HOW CAN YOU HOPE TO DEAL WITH ME? GRAVITONS, ELECTRONS, TACHYONS, PIONS, MUONS, ALL AT MY COMMAND...
...AND YOU, FATALLY SNARED -- EVERY SPARK WITHIN YOU, LIKE SO MANY CANDY SPRINKLES IN MY HANDS, TO PLAY WITH AS I CHOOSE...
HNH! WHAT...?
I'M... DIZZY, SO DIZZY... WHY...
THE VERY NEURONS IN YOUR BRAINS -- I'M WRAPPING THEM IN A GRAVITY WEB, SLOWING DOWN THE SIGNALS WITHIN THEM --
-- KILLING YOU BY SHUTTING DOWN YOUR OWN TH --
FRZ-FRZZH-

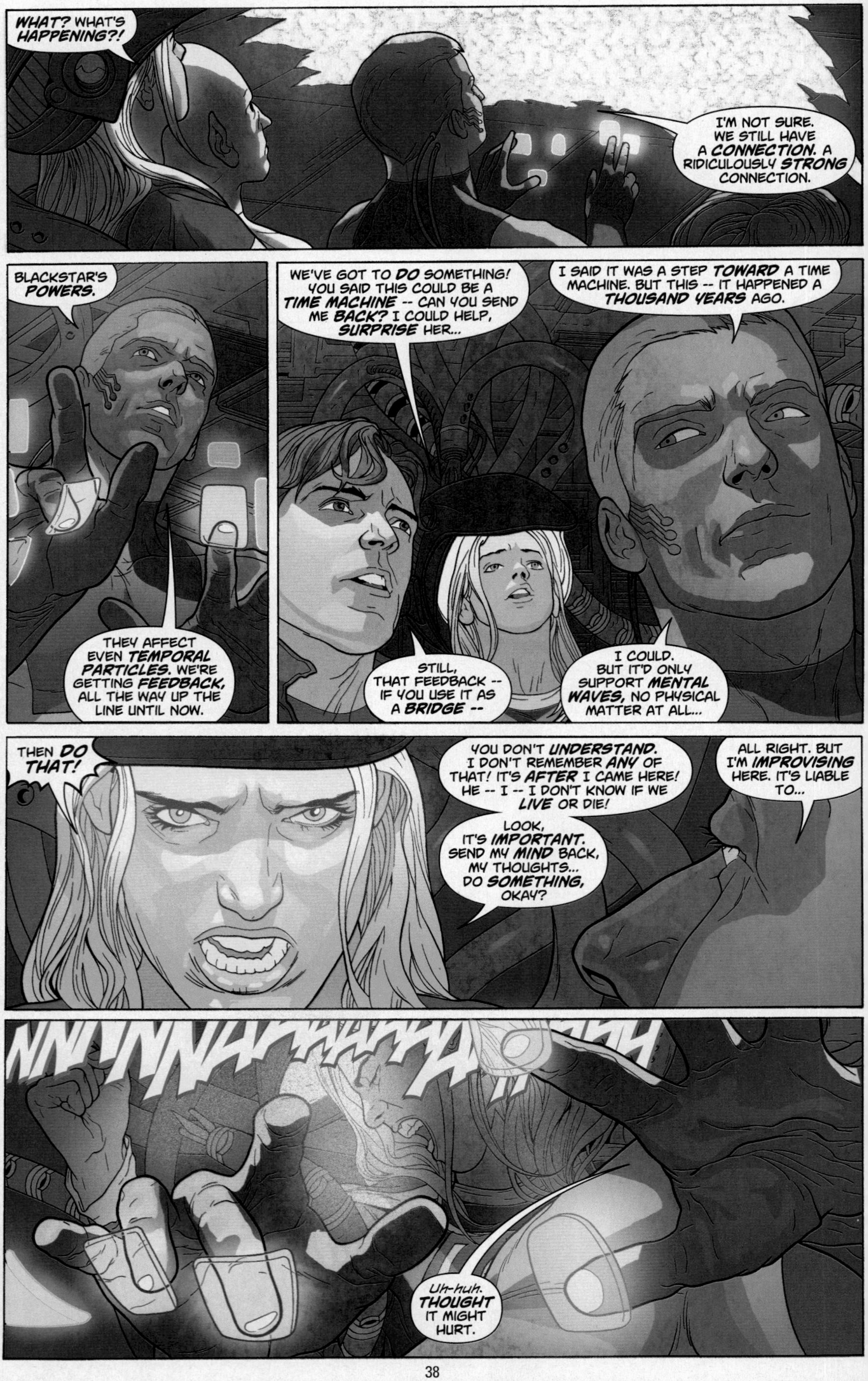
WHAT? WHAT'S HAPPENING?!
I'M NOT SURE. WE STILL HAVE A CONNECTION. A RIDICULOUSLY STRONG CONNECTION.
BLACKSTAR'S POWERS.
THEY AFFECT EVEN TEMPORAL PARTICLES. WE'RE GETTING FEEDBACK, ALL THE WAY UP THE LINE UNTIL NOW.
WE'VE GOT TO DO SOMETHING! YOU SAID THIS COULD BE A TIME MACHINE -- CAN YOU SEND ME BACK? I COULD HELP, SURPRISE HER...
I SAID IT WAS A STEP TOWARD A TIME MACHINE. BUT THIS -- IT HAPPENED A THOUSAND YEARS AGO.
STILL, THAT FEEDBACK -- IF YOU USE IT AS A BRIDGE --
I COULD. BUT IT'D ONLY SUPPORT MENTAL WAVES, NO PHYSICAL MATTER AT ALL...
THEN DO THAT!
YOU DON'T UNDERSTAND. I DON'T REMEMBER ANY OF THAT! IT'S AFTER I CAME HERE! HE -- I -- I DON'T KNOW IF WE LIVE OR DIE!
LOOK, IT'S IMPORTANT. SEND MY MIND BACK, MY THOUGHTS... DO SOMETHING, OKAY?
ALL RIGHT. BUT I'M IMPROVISING HERE. IT'S LIABLE TO...
NNNNNAAAAAAAAHHHH
Uh-huh. THOUGHT IT MIGHT HURT.

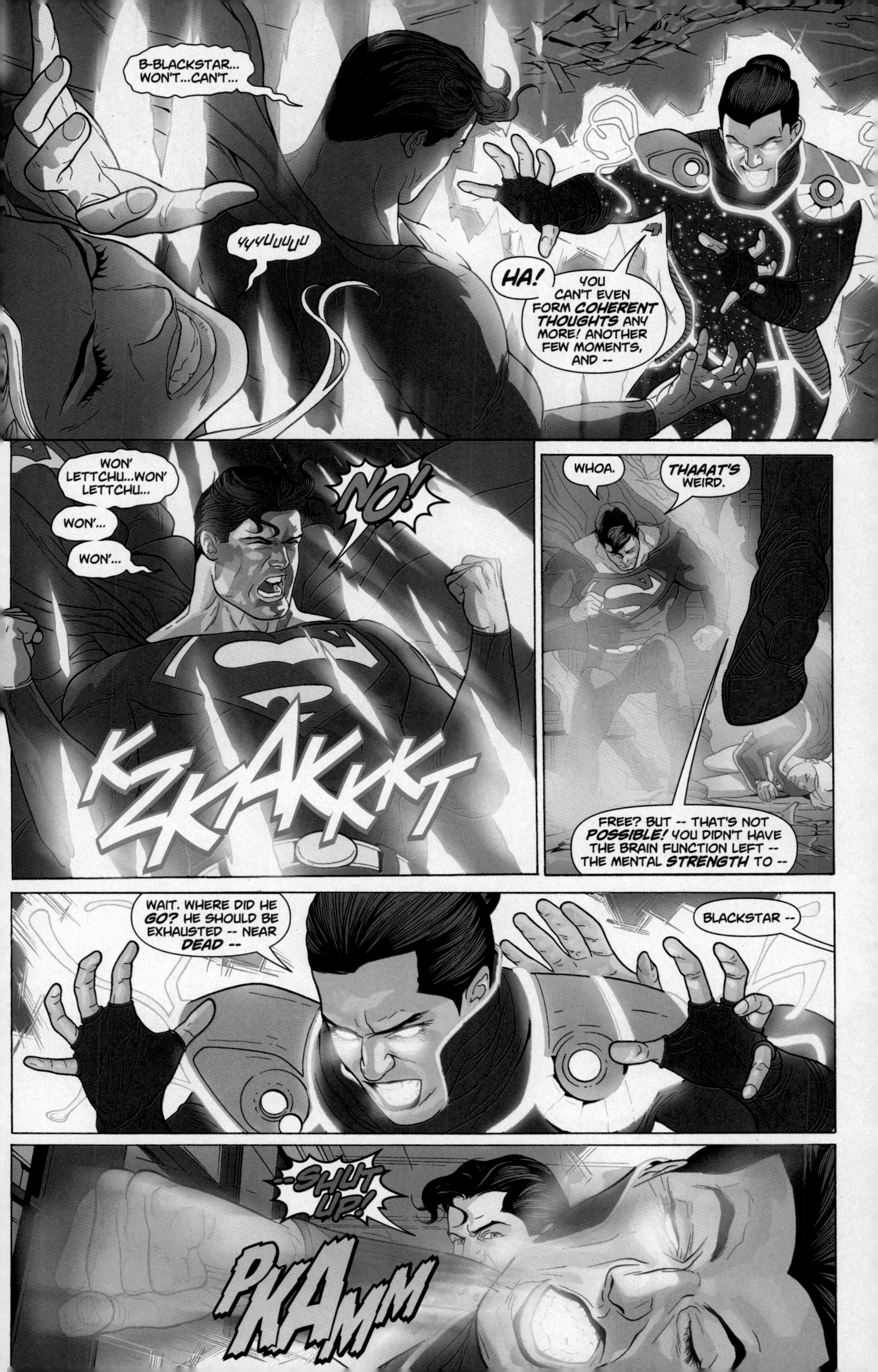
B-BLACKSTAR... WON'T...CAN'T...
YYYUUUUU
HA!
YOU CAN'T EVEN FORM COHERENT THOUGHTS ANY MORE! ANOTHER FEW MOMENTS, AND --
WON' LETTCHU...WON' LETTCHU...
WON'...
WON'...
NO!
KZKKAKKKT
WHOA.
THAAAT'S WEIRD.
FREE? BUT -- THAT'S NOT POSSIBLE! YOU DIDN'T HAVE THE BRAIN FUNCTION LEFT -- THE MENTAL STRENGTH TO --
WAIT. WHERE DID HE GO? HE SHOULD BE EXHAUSTED -- NEAR DEAD --
BLACKSTAR --
--SHUT UP!
PKAMM

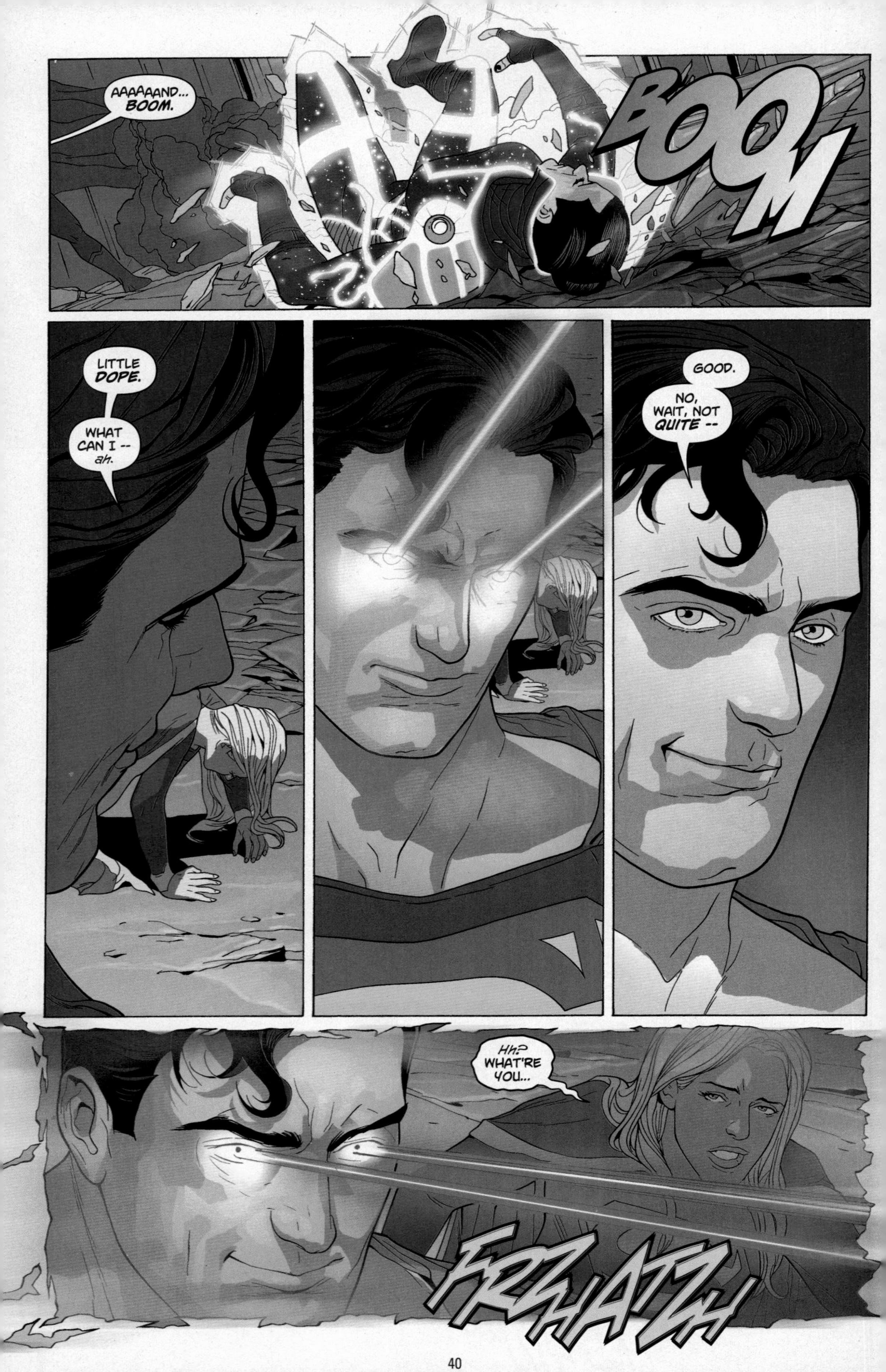
AAAAAAND...
BOOM.
BOOM
LITTLE
DOPE.
WHAT
CAN I --
ah.
GOOD.
NO,
WAIT, NOT
QUITE --
Hh?
WHAT'RE
YOU...
FRZHATZH

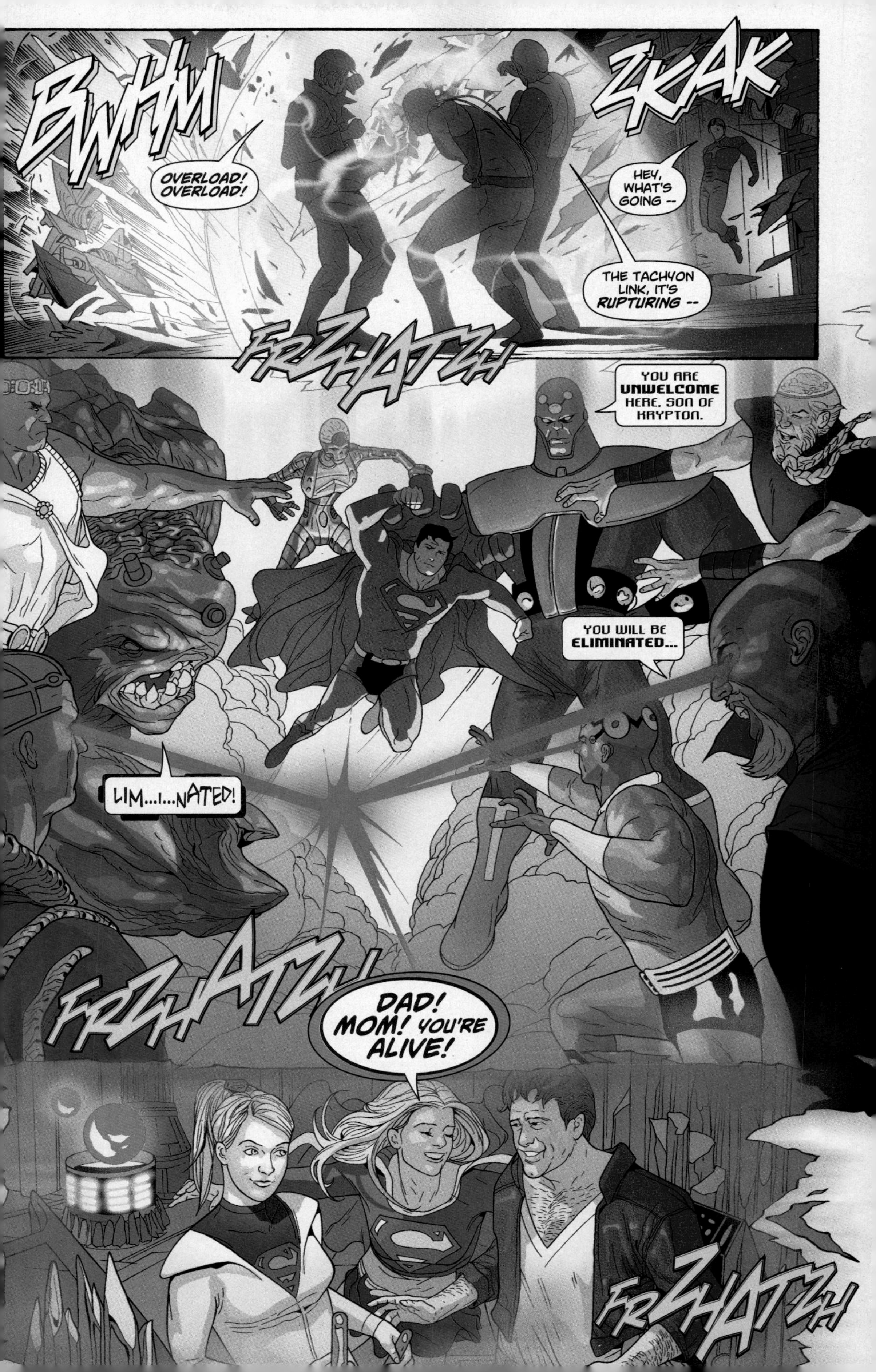
BWHM
OVERLOAD! OVERLOAD!
ZKAK
HEY, WHAT'S GOING --
THE TACHYON LINK, IT'S RUPTURING --
FRZHATZH
YOU ARE UNWELCOME HERE, SON OF KRYPTON.
YOU WILL BE ELIMINATED...
LIM...I...NATED!
FRZHATZH
DAD! MOM! YOU'RE ALIVE!
FRZHATZH

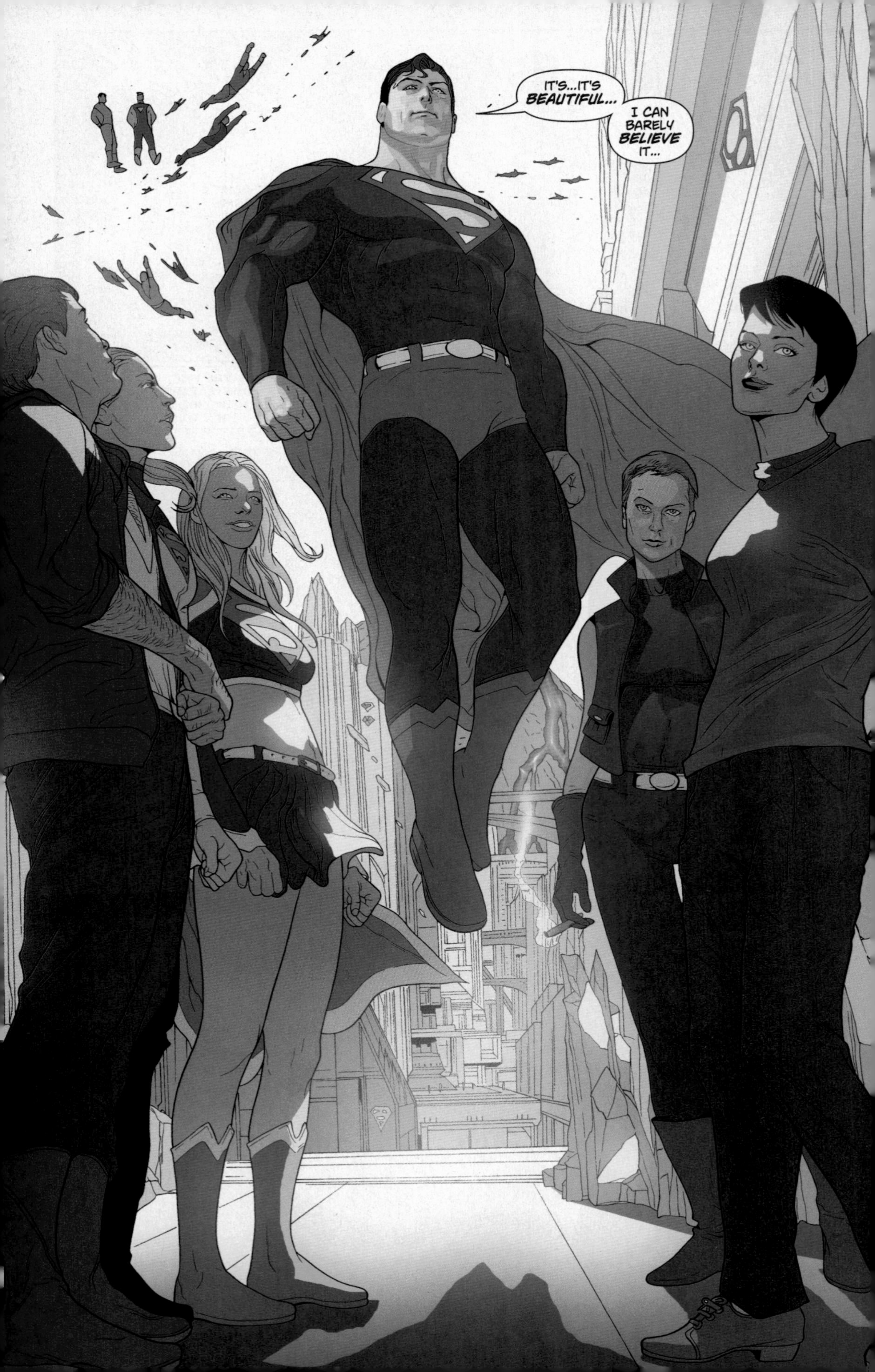
IT'S...IT'S BEAUTIFUL...
I CAN BARELY BELIEVE IT...

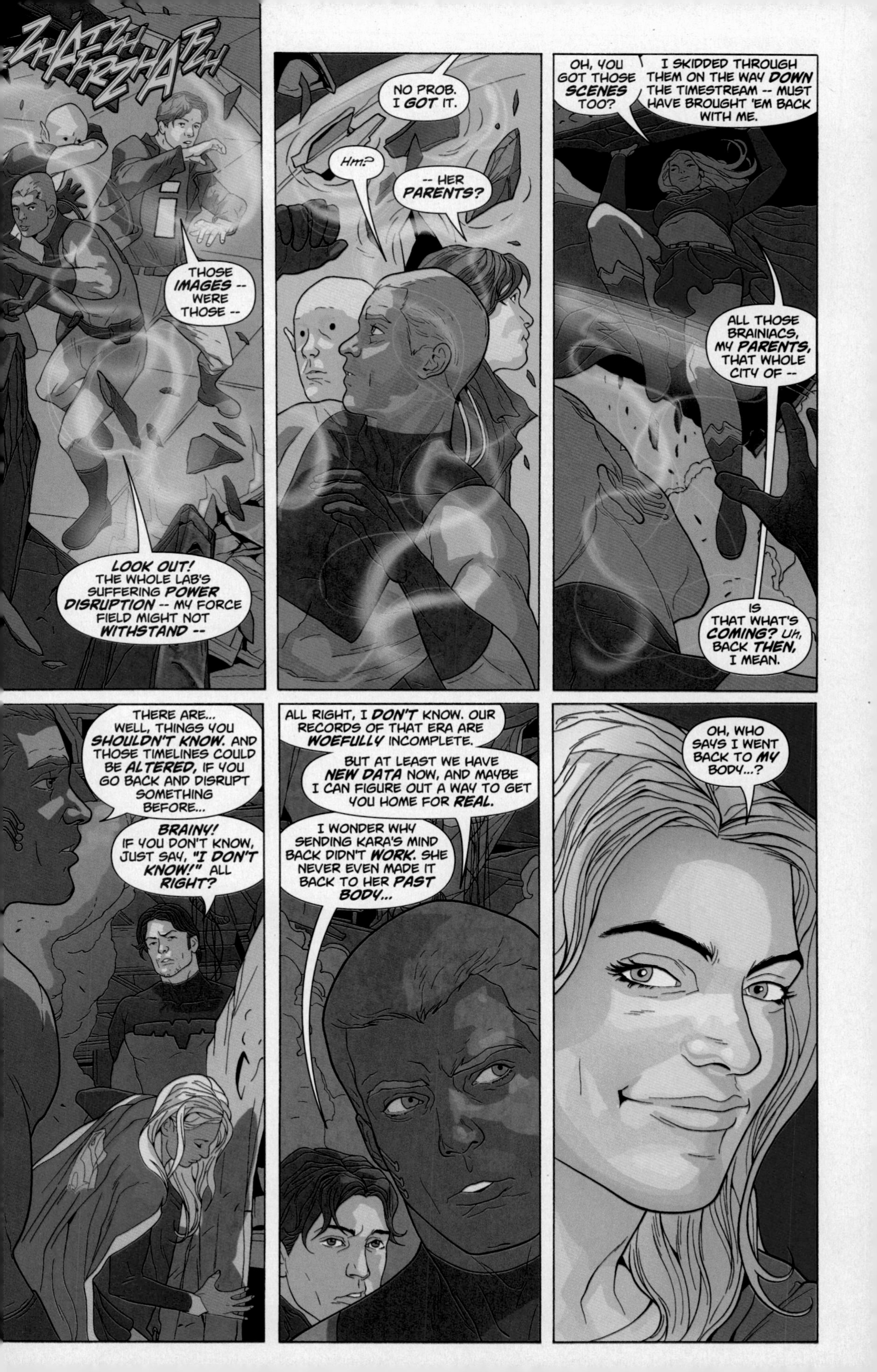
ZHATZH FRZHATZH
THOSE IMAGES -- WERE THOSE --
LOOK OUT! THE WHOLE LAB'S SUFFERING POWER DISRUPTION -- MY FORCE FIELD MIGHT NOT WITHSTAND --
NO PROB. I GOT IT.
Hm?
-- HER PARENTS?
OH, YOU GOT THOSE SCENES TOO?
I SKIDDED THROUGH THEM ON THE WAY DOWN THE TIMESTREAM -- MUST HAVE BROUGHT 'EM BACK WITH ME.
ALL THOSE BRAINIACS, MY PARENTS, THAT WHOLE CITY OF --
IS THAT WHAT'S COMING? Uh, BACK THEN, I MEAN.
THERE ARE... WELL, THINGS YOU SHOULDN'T KNOW. AND THOSE TIMELINES COULD BE ALTERED, IF YOU GO BACK AND DISRUPT SOMETHING BEFORE...
BRAINY! IF YOU DON'T KNOW, JUST SAY, "I DON'T KNOW!" ALL RIGHT?
ALL RIGHT, I DON'T KNOW. OUR RECORDS OF THAT ERA ARE WOEFULLY INCOMPLETE.
BUT AT LEAST WE HAVE NEW DATA NOW, AND MAYBE I CAN FIGURE OUT A WAY TO GET YOU HOME FOR REAL.
I WONDER WHY SENDING KARA'S MIND BACK DIDN'T WORK. SHE NEVER EVEN MADE IT BACK TO HER PAST BODY...
OH, WHO SAYS I WENT BACK TO MY BODY...?

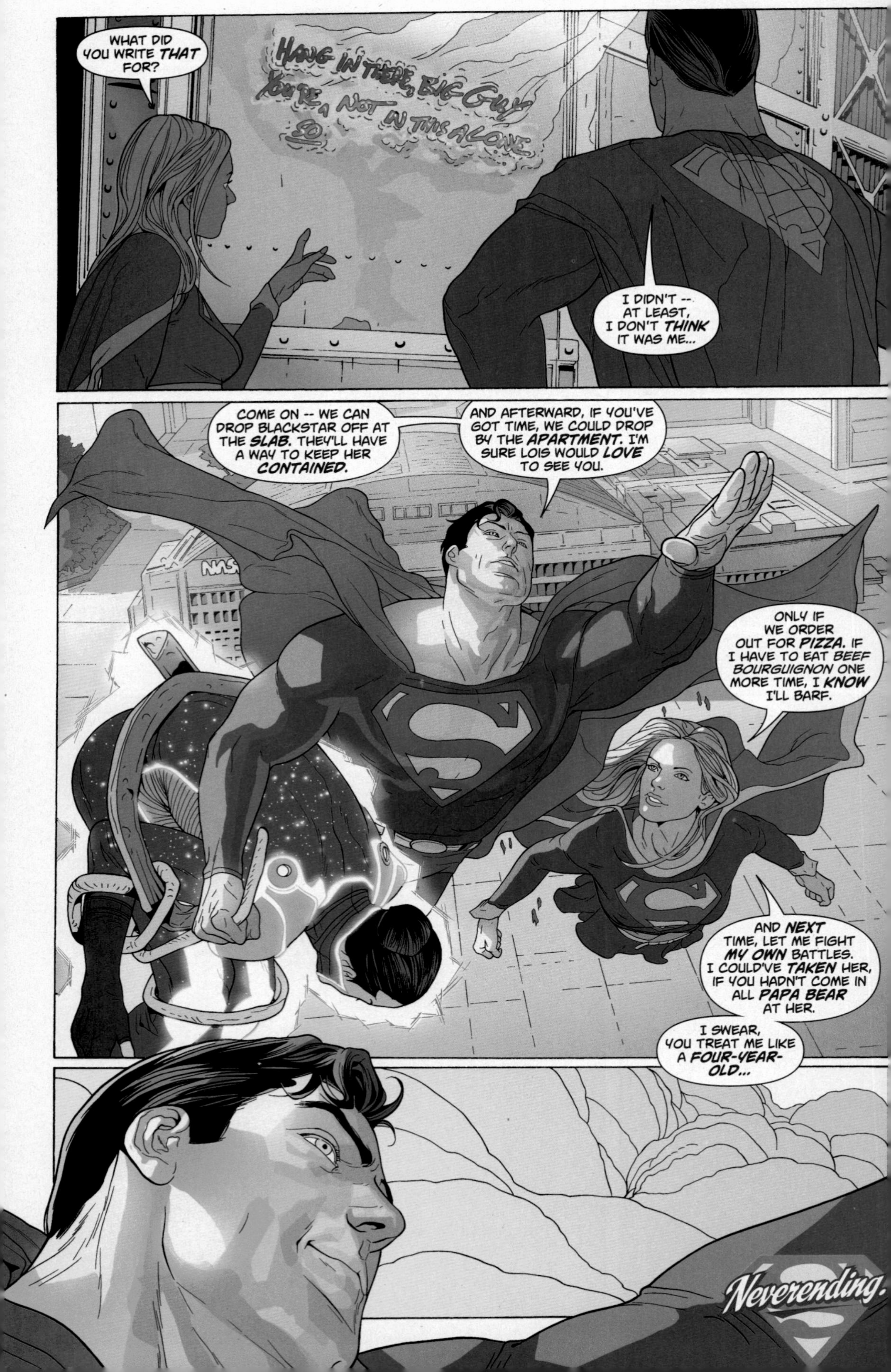
WHAT DID YOU WRITE THAT FOR?
HANG IN THERE, BIG GUY. YOU'RE NOT IN THIS ALONE.
SO
I DIDN'T -- AT LEAST, I DON'T THINK IT WAS ME...
COME ON -- WE CAN DROP BLACKSTAR OFF AT THE SLAB. THEY'LL HAVE A WAY TO KEEP HER CONTAINED.
AND AFTERWARD, IF YOU'VE GOT TIME, WE COULD DROP BY THE APARTMENT. I'M SURE LOIS WOULD LOVE TO SEE YOU.
ONLY IF WE ORDER OUT FOR PIZZA. IF I HAVE TO EAT BEEF BOURGUIGNON ONE MORE TIME, I KNOW I'LL BARF.
AND NEXT TIME, LET ME FIGHT MY OWN BATTLES. I COULD'VE TAKEN HER, IF YOU HADN'T COME IN ALL PAPA BEAR AT HER.
I SWEAR, YOU TREAT ME LIKE A FOUR-YEAR-OLD...
Neverending.

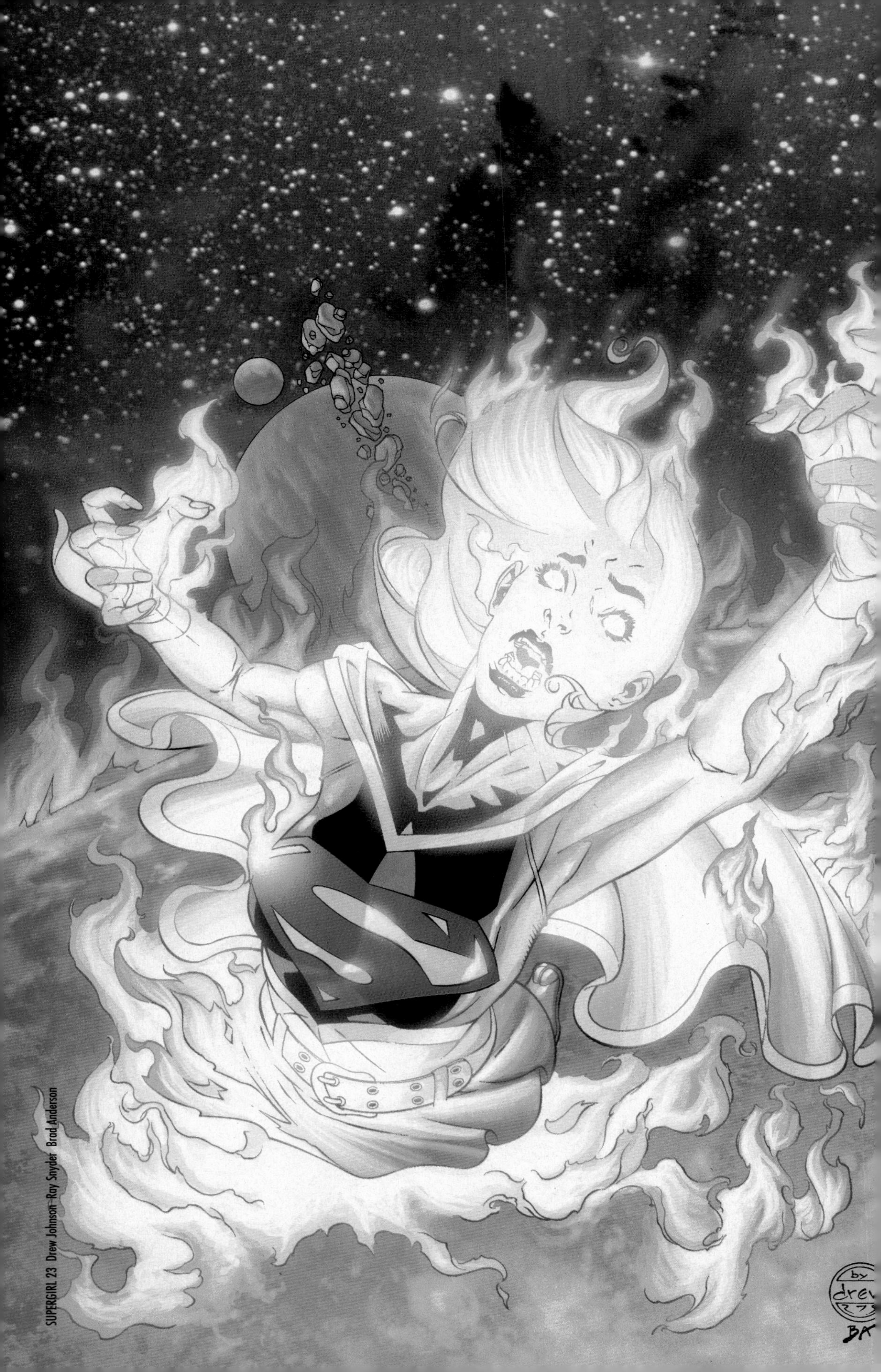
SUPERGIRL 23 Drew Johnson Ray Snyder Brad Anderson

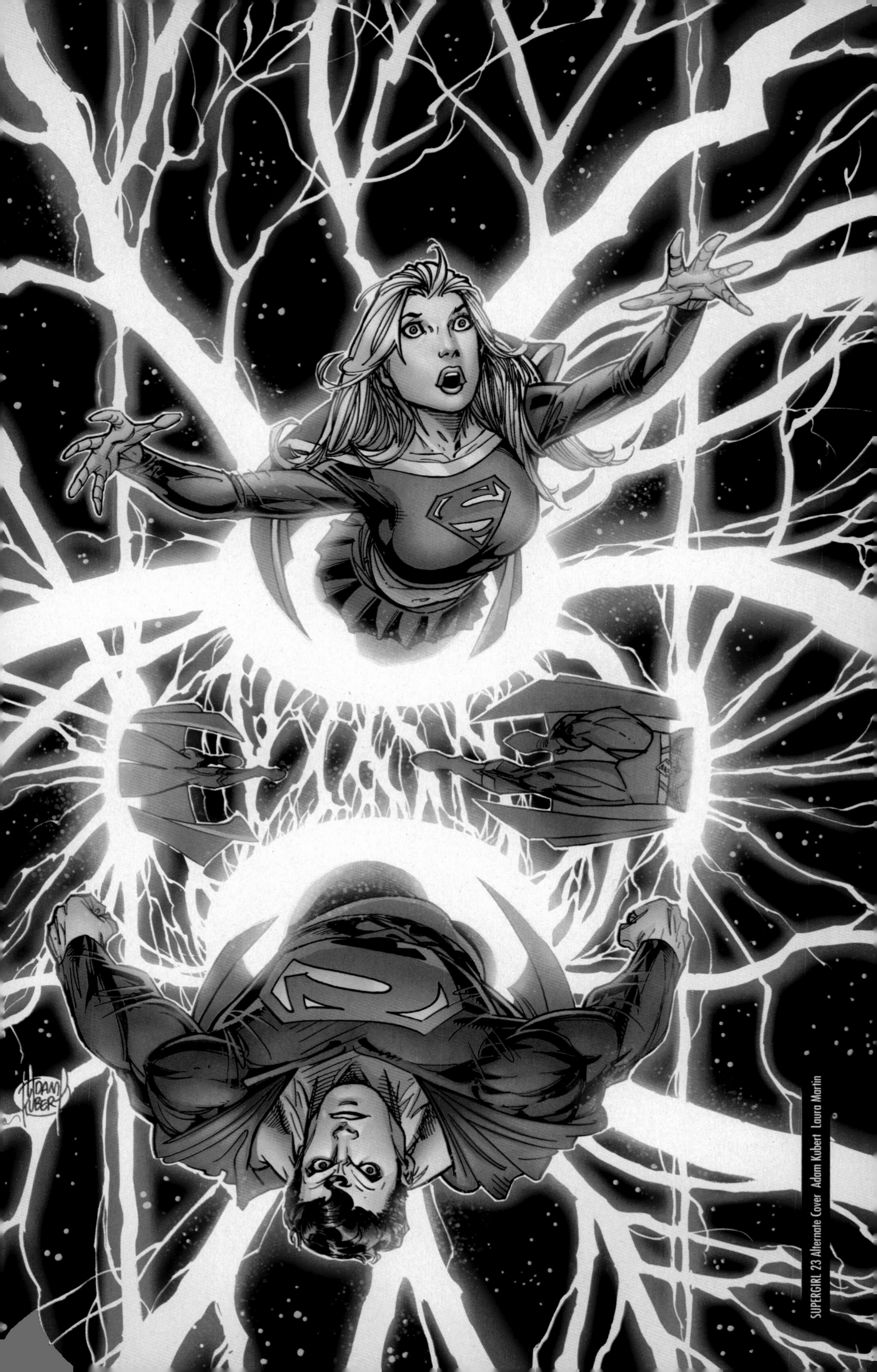

SUPERGIRL 23 Alternate Cover Adam Kubert Laura Martin

TESSERACT

KELLEY PUCKETT   WRITER
DREW JOHNSON   PENCILS
RAY SNYDER   INKS

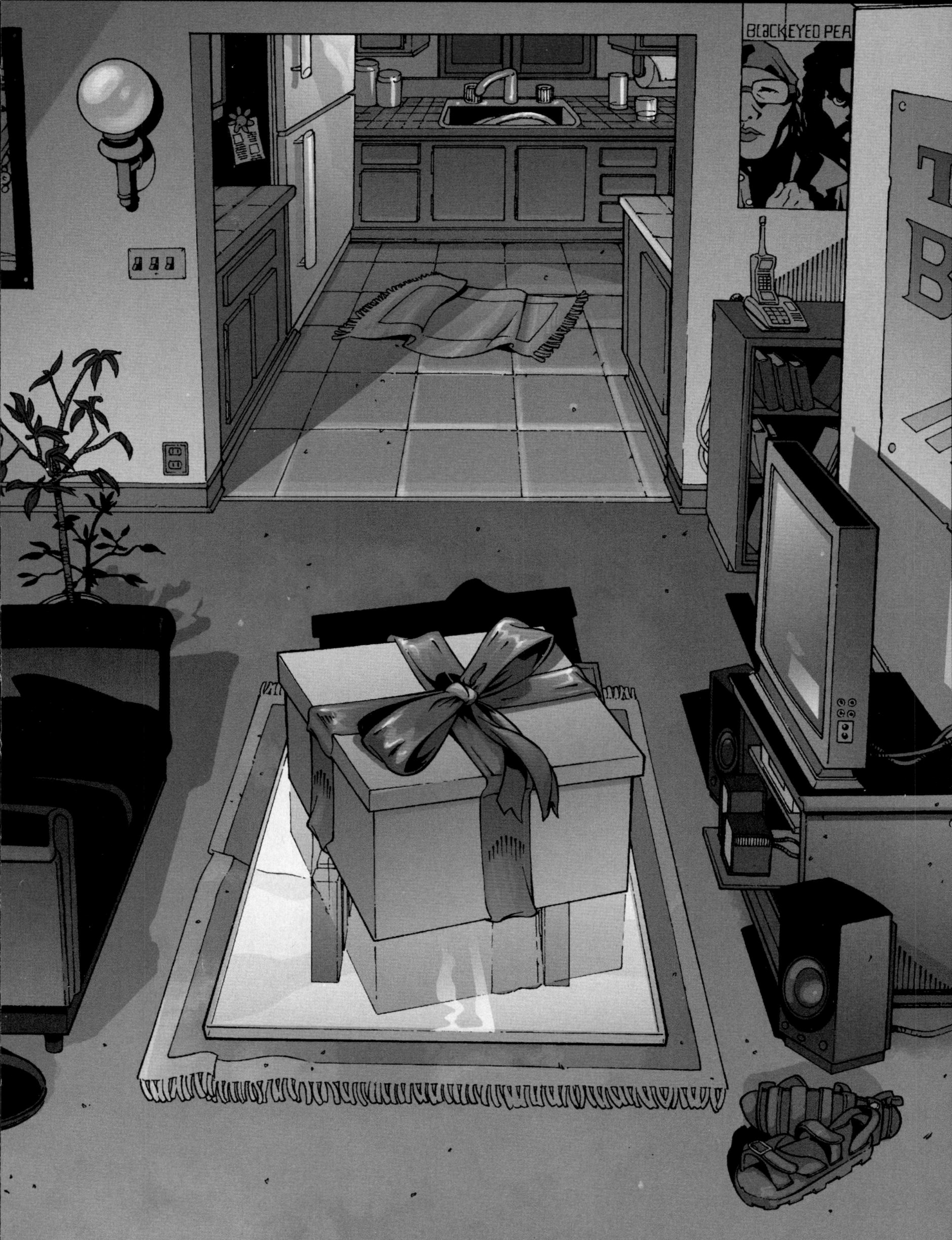
BLACKEYED PEA

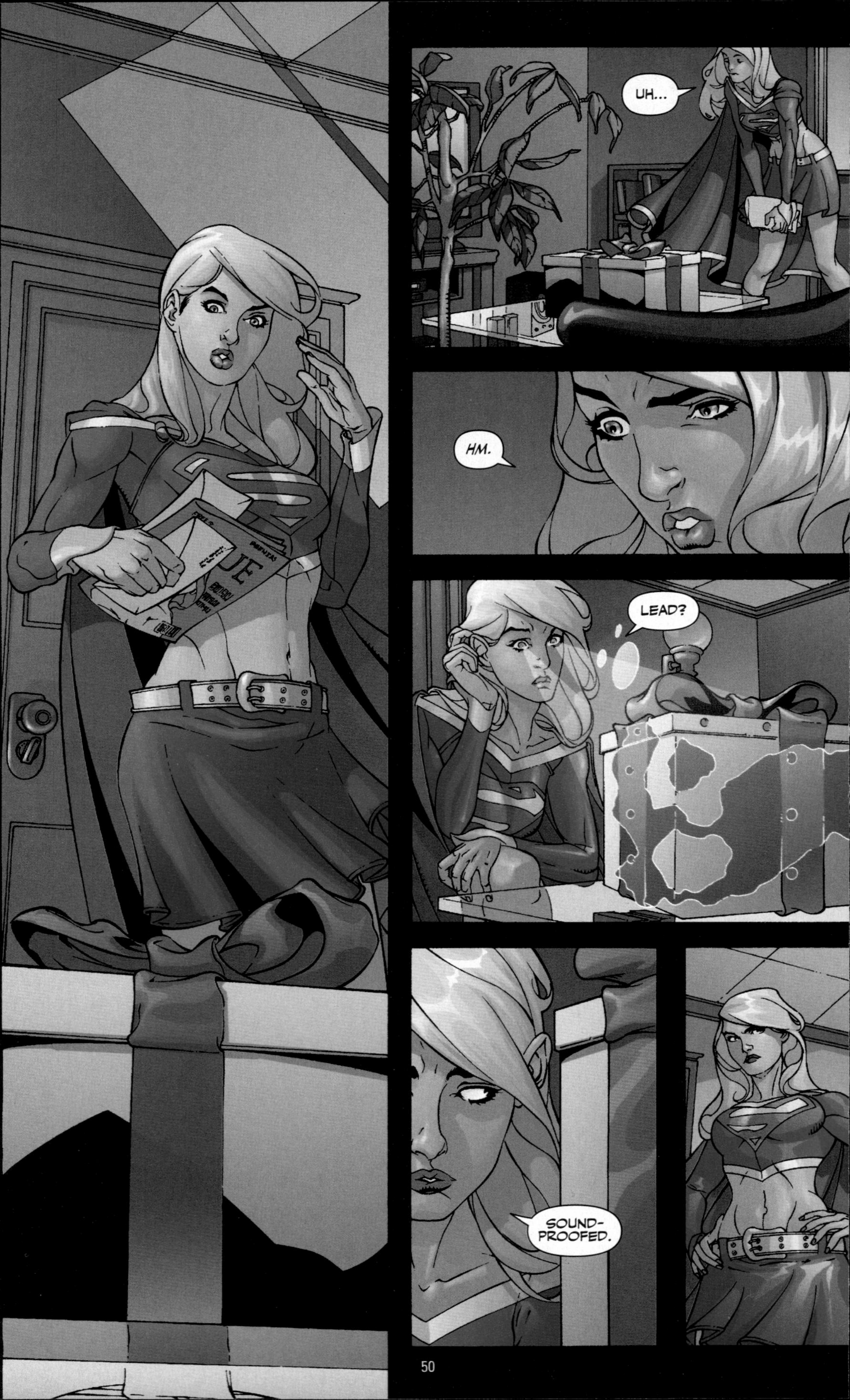
UH...
HM.
LEAD?
SOUND-PROOFED.

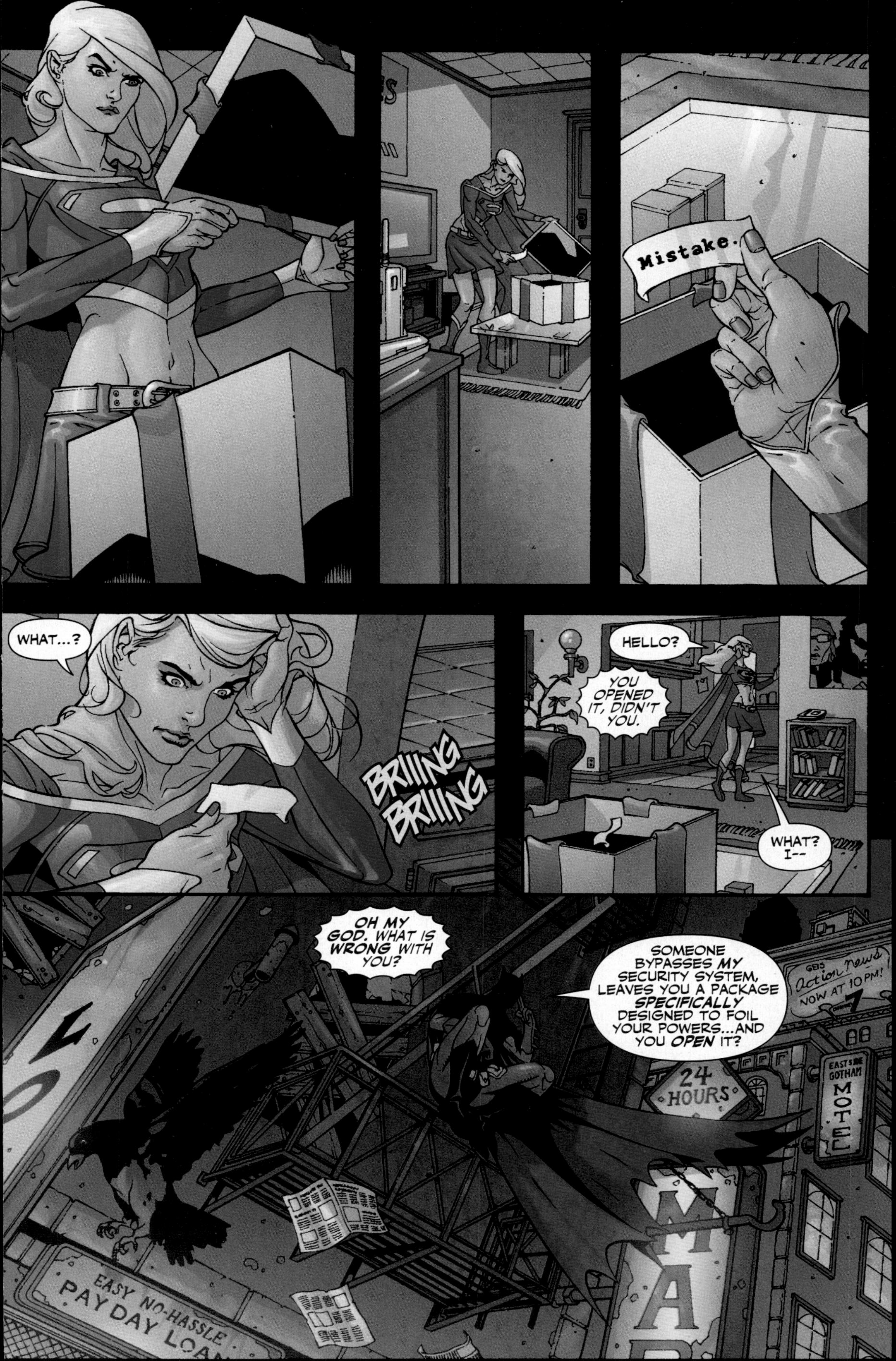
Mistake.
WHAT...?
BRIIING BRIIING
HELLO?
YOU OPENED IT, DIDN'T YOU.
WHAT? I--
OH MY GOD. WHAT IS WRONG WITH YOU?
SOMEONE BYPASSES MY SECURITY SYSTEM, LEAVES YOU A PACKAGE SPECIFICALLY DESIGNED TO FOIL YOUR POWERS...AND YOU OPEN IT?
GBS Action News NOW AT 10 PM!
24 HOURS
EASTSIDE GOTHAM MOTEL
EASY NO-HASSLE PAYDAY LOAN

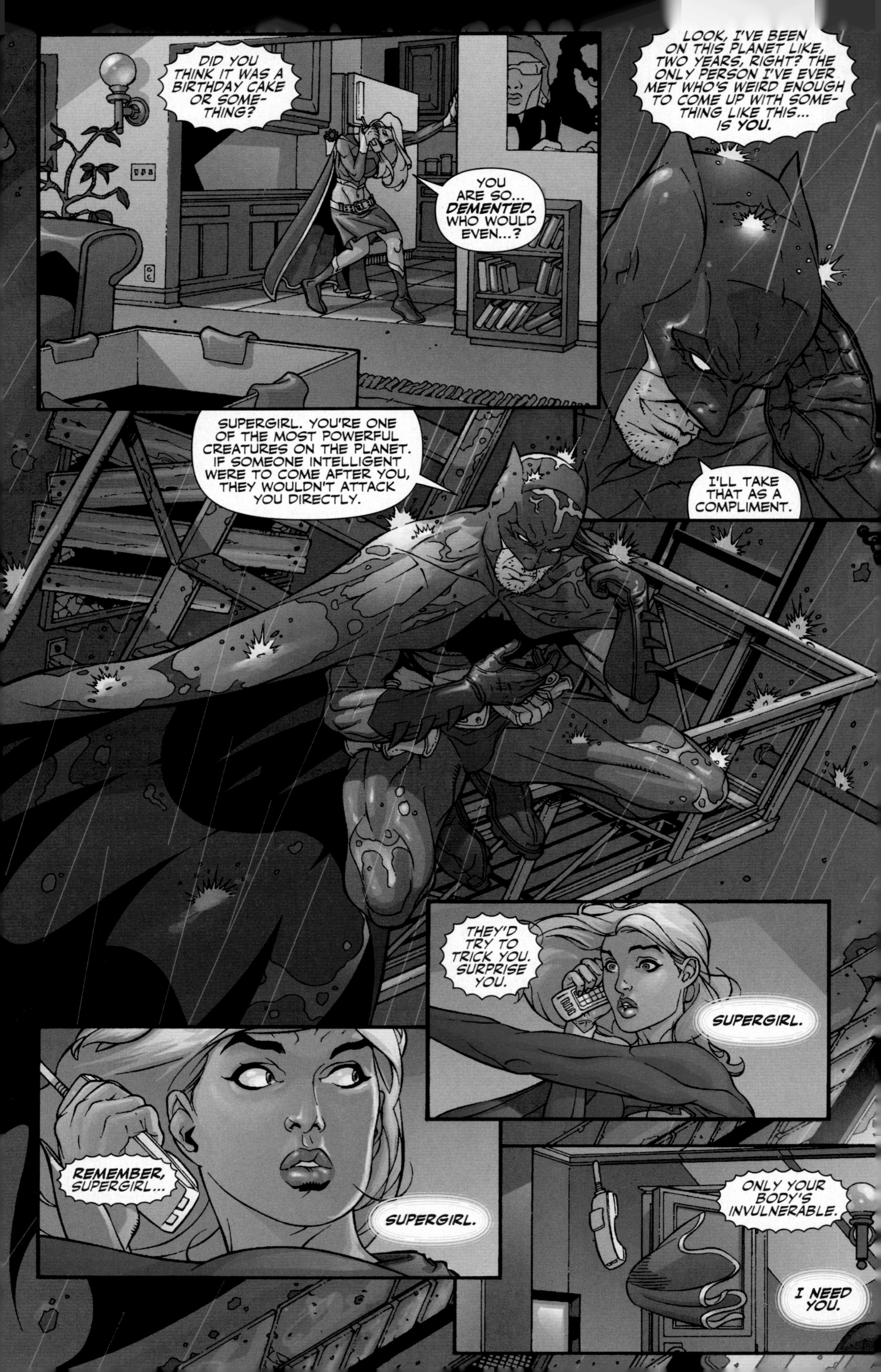
DID YOU THINK IT WAS A BIRTHDAY CAKE OR SOME-THING?
YOU ARE SO... DEMENTED. WHO WOULD EVEN...?
LOOK, I'VE BEEN ON THIS PLANET LIKE, TWO YEARS, RIGHT? THE ONLY PERSON I'VE EVER MET WHO'S WEIRD ENOUGH TO COME UP WITH SOME-THING LIKE THIS... IS YOU.
I'LL TAKE THAT AS A COMPLIMENT.
SUPERGIRL. YOU'RE ONE OF THE MOST POWERFUL CREATURES ON THE PLANET. IF SOMEONE INTELLIGENT WERE TO COME AFTER YOU, THEY WOULDN'T ATTACK YOU DIRECTLY.
THEY'D TRY TO TRICK YOU. SURPRISE YOU.
SUPERGIRL.
REMEMBER, SUPERGIRL...
SUPERGIRL.
ONLY YOUR BODY'S INVULNERABLE.
I NEED YOU.

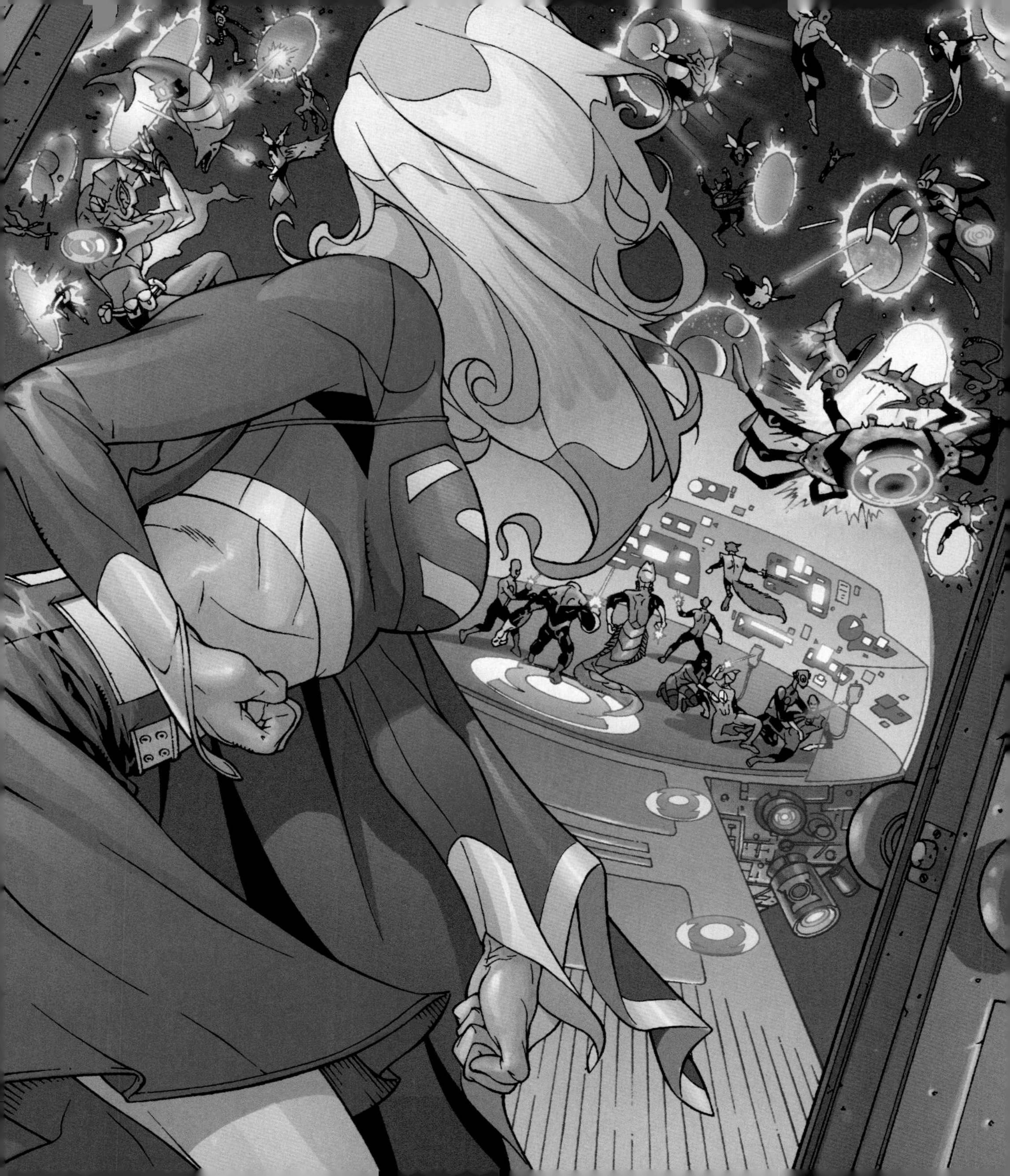

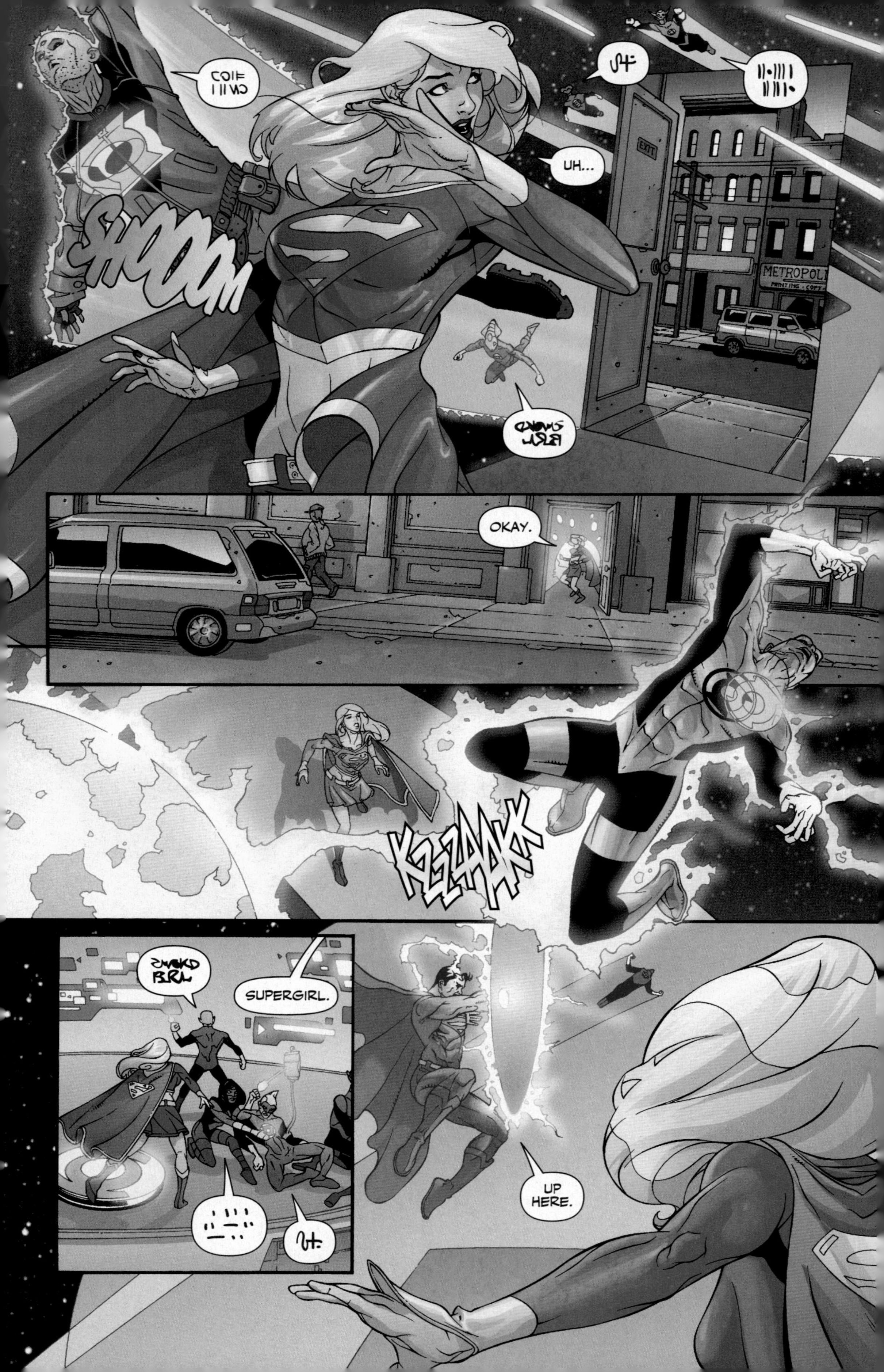
UH...
SHOOOM
OKAY.
KZZZAAKK
SUPERGIRL.
UP
HERE.

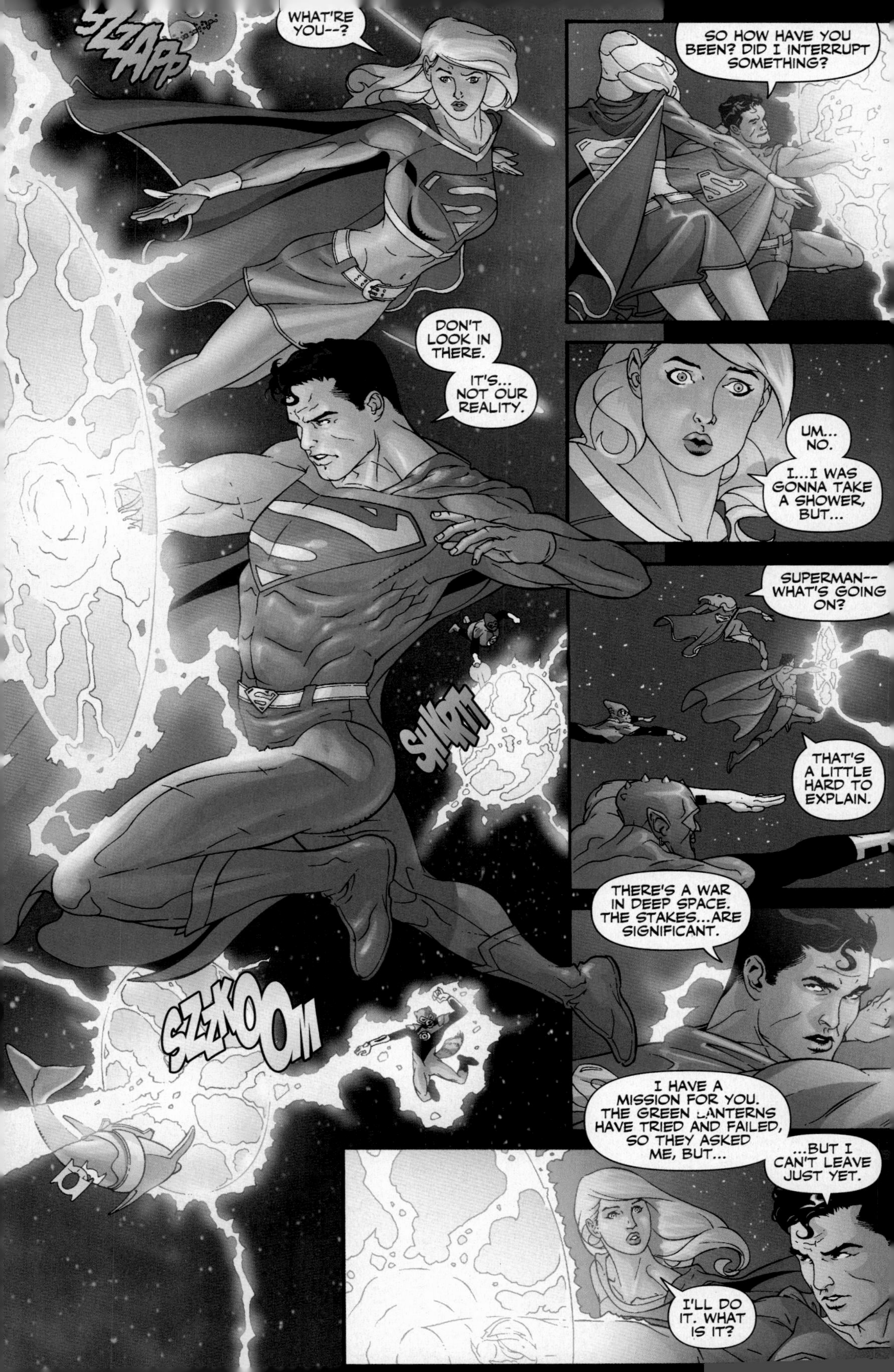
WHAT'RE YOU--?
SO HOW HAVE YOU BEEN? DID I INTERRUPT SOMETHING?
DON'T LOOK IN THERE.
IT'S... NOT OUR REALITY.
UM... NO.
I...I WAS GONNA TAKE A SHOWER, BUT...
SUPERMAN-- WHAT'S GOING ON?
THAT'S A LITTLE HARD TO EXPLAIN.
THERE'S A WAR IN DEEP SPACE. THE STAKES...ARE SIGNIFICANT.
I HAVE A MISSION FOR YOU. THE GREEN LANTERNS HAVE TRIED AND FAILED, SO THEY ASKED ME, BUT...
...BUT I CAN'T LEAVE JUST YET.
I'LL DO IT. WHAT IS IT?

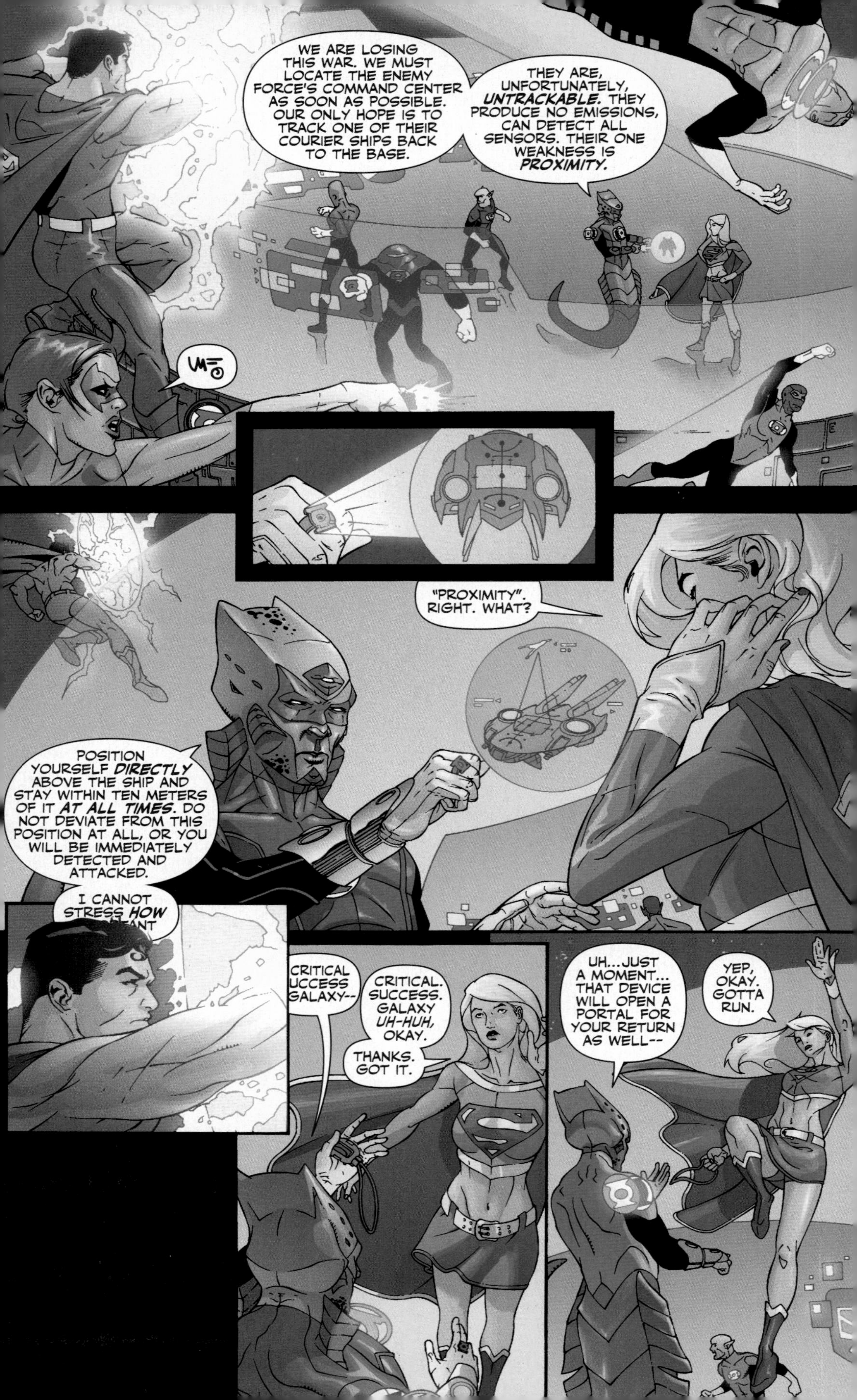
WE ARE LOSING THIS WAR. WE MUST LOCATE THE ENEMY FORCE'S COMMAND CENTER AS SOON AS POSSIBLE. OUR ONLY HOPE IS TO TRACK ONE OF THEIR COURIER SHIPS BACK TO THE BASE.
THEY ARE, UNFORTUNATELY, *UNTRACKABLE.* THEY PRODUCE NO EMISSIONS, CAN DETECT ALL SENSORS. THEIR ONE WEAKNESS IS *PROXIMITY.*
"PROXIMITY". RIGHT. WHAT?
POSITION YOURSELF *DIRECTLY* ABOVE THE SHIP AND STAY WITHIN TEN METERS OF IT *AT ALL TIMES.* DO NOT DEVIATE FROM THIS POSITION AT ALL, OR YOU WILL BE IMMEDIATELY DETECTED AND ATTACKED.
I CANNOT STRESS *HOW*
CRITICAL SUCCESS GALAXY--
CRITICAL. SUCCESS. GALAXY *UH-HUH,* OKAY.
THANKS. GOT IT.
UH...JUST A MOMENT... THAT DEVICE WILL OPEN A PORTAL FOR YOUR RETURN AS WELL--
YEP, OKAY. GOTTA RUN.

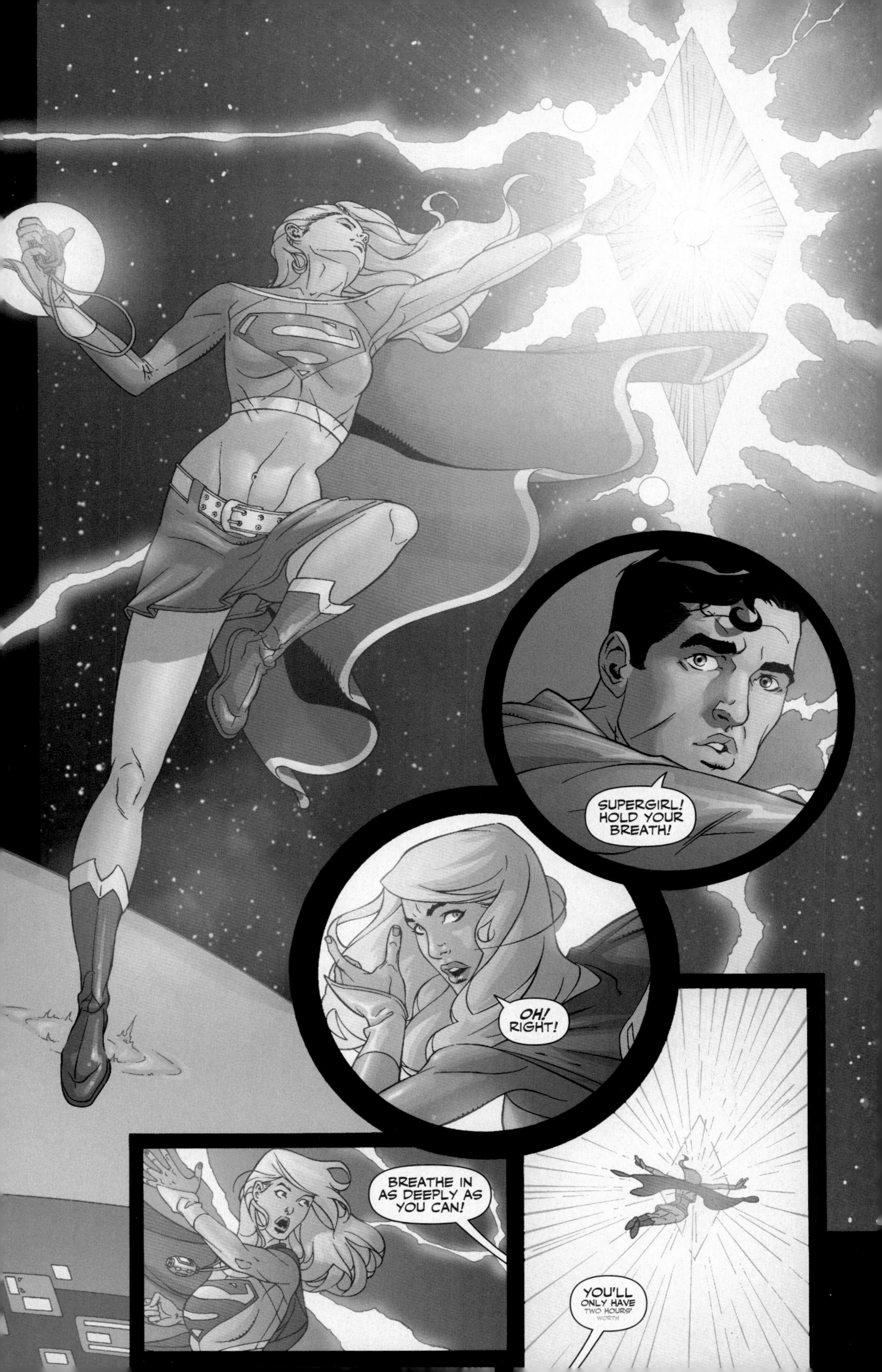
SUPERGIRL! HOLD YOUR BREATH!
OH! RIGHT!
BREATHE IN AS DEEPLY AS YOU CAN!
YOU'LL ONLY HAVE TWO HOURS' WORTH

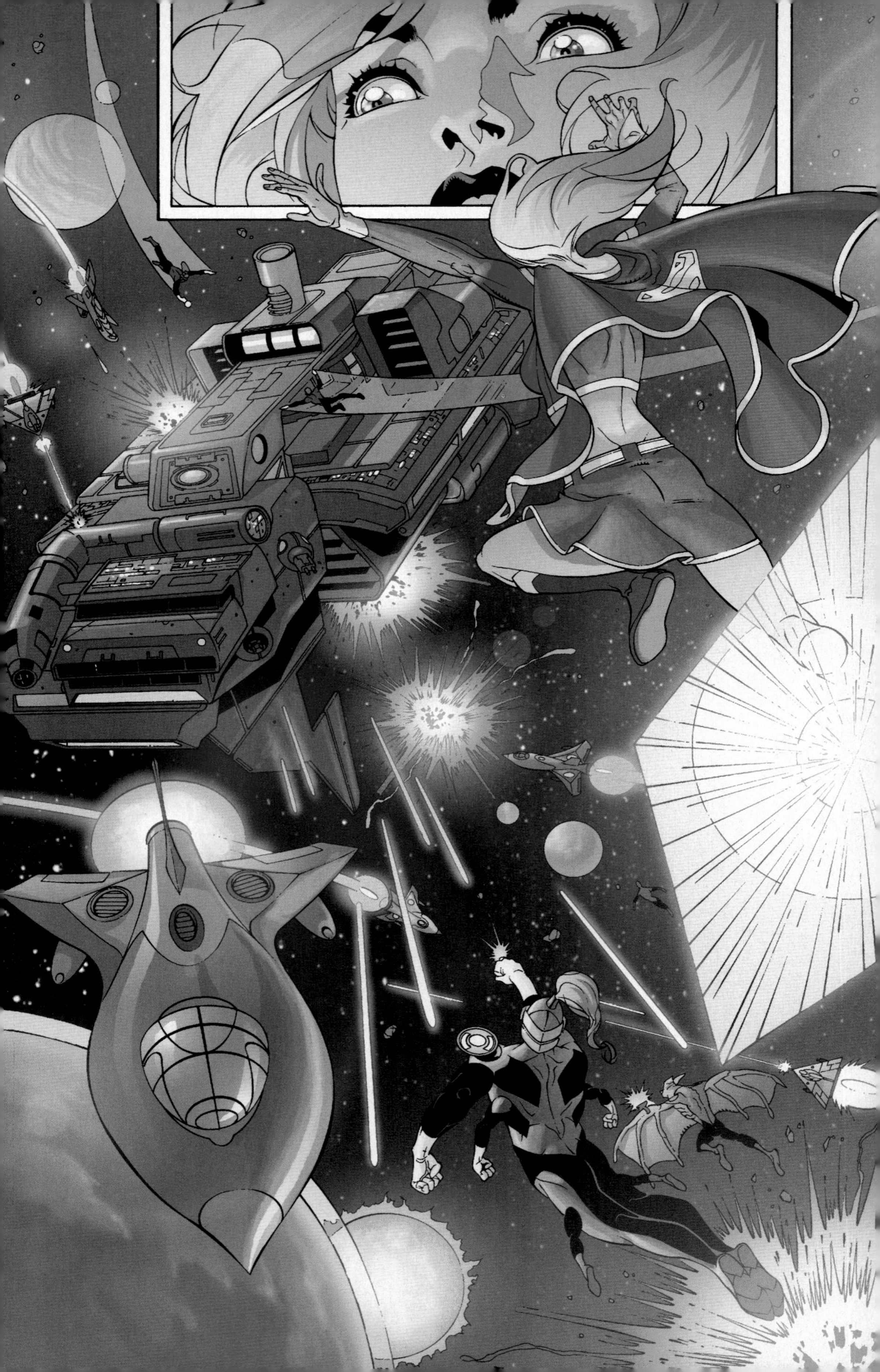

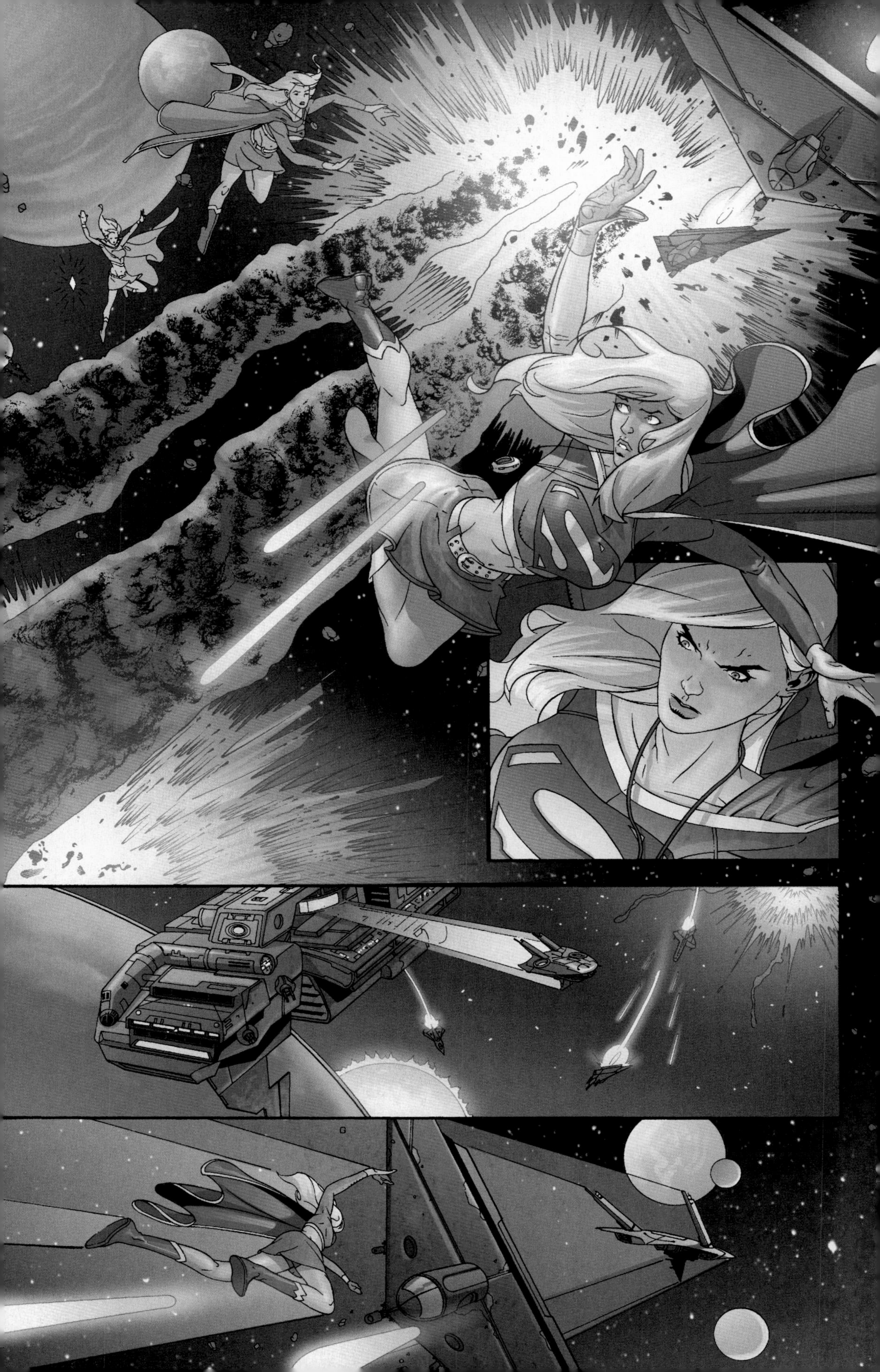

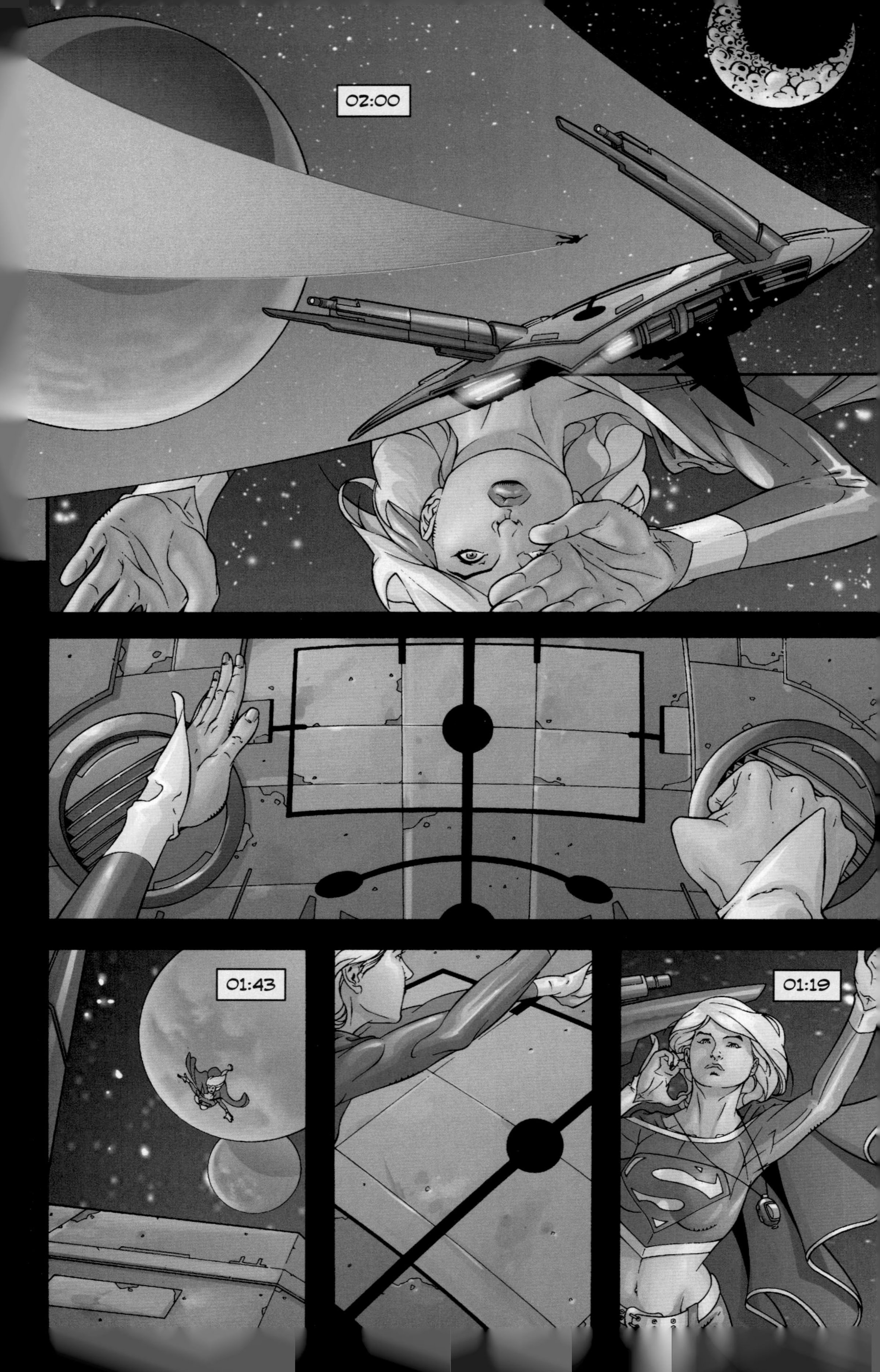
02:00
01:43
01:19

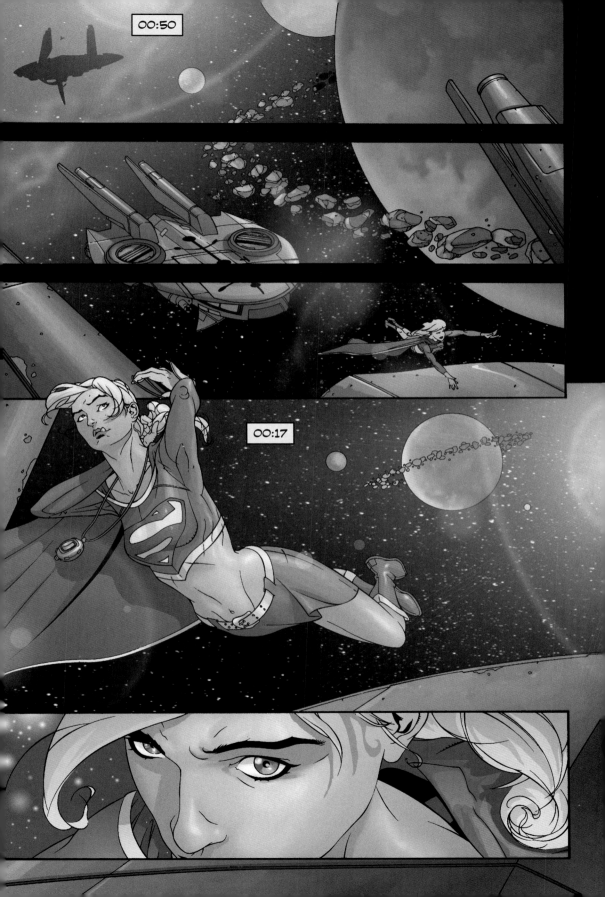

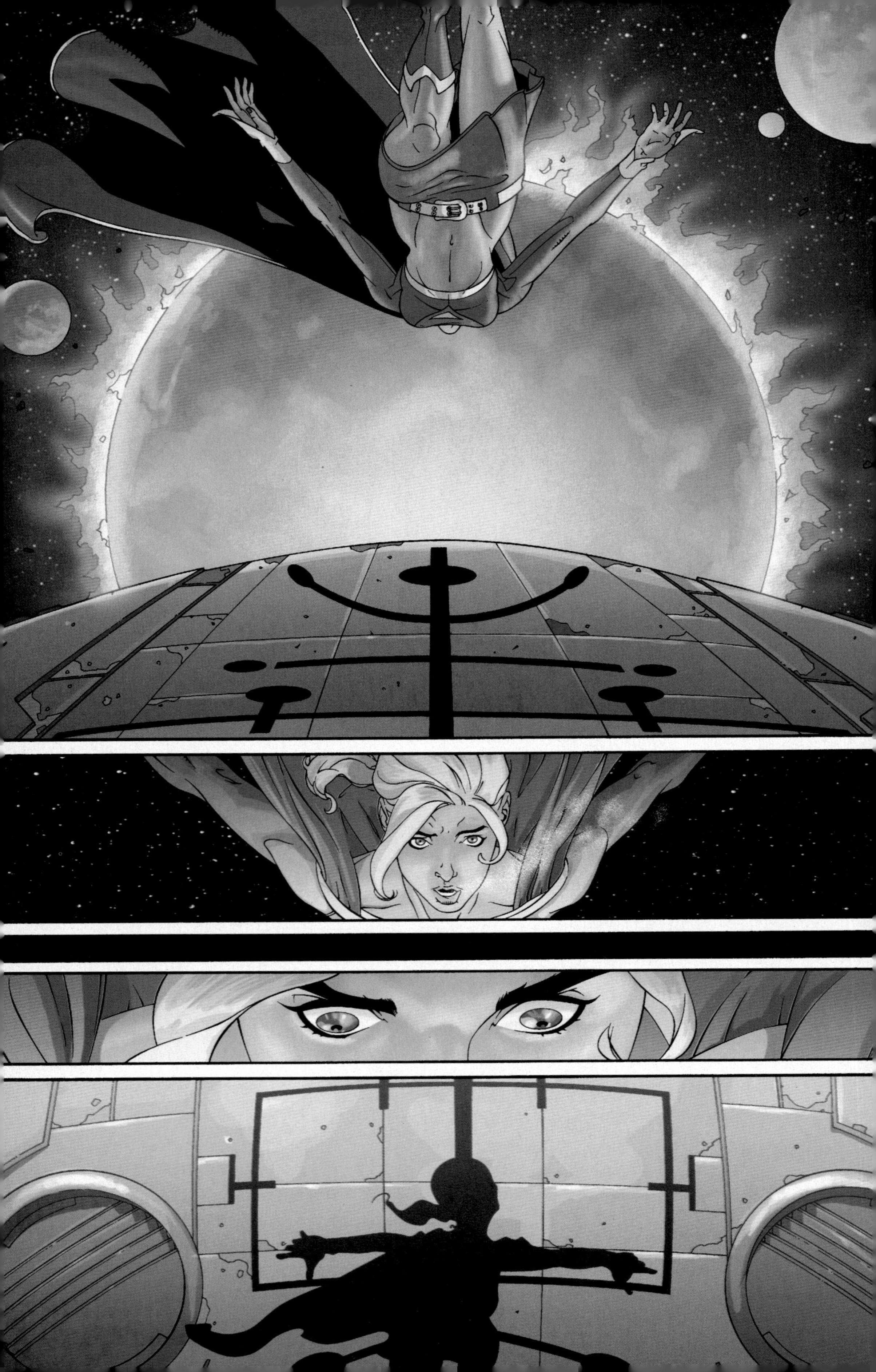

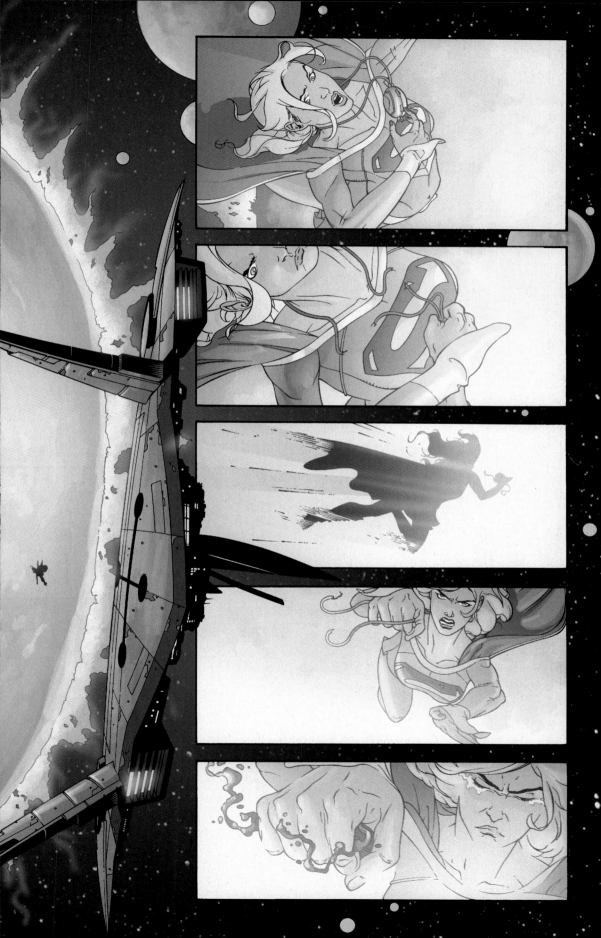

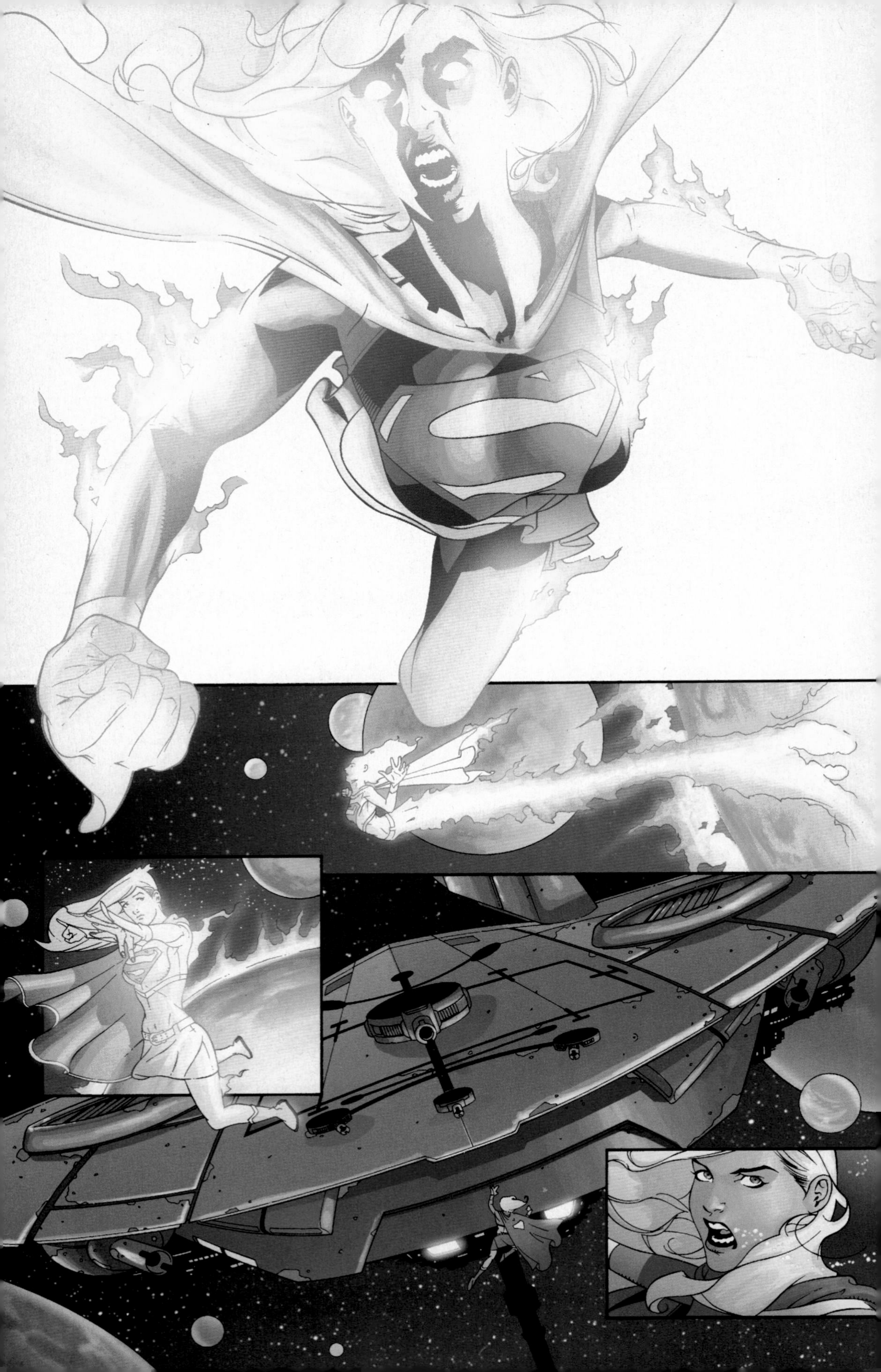

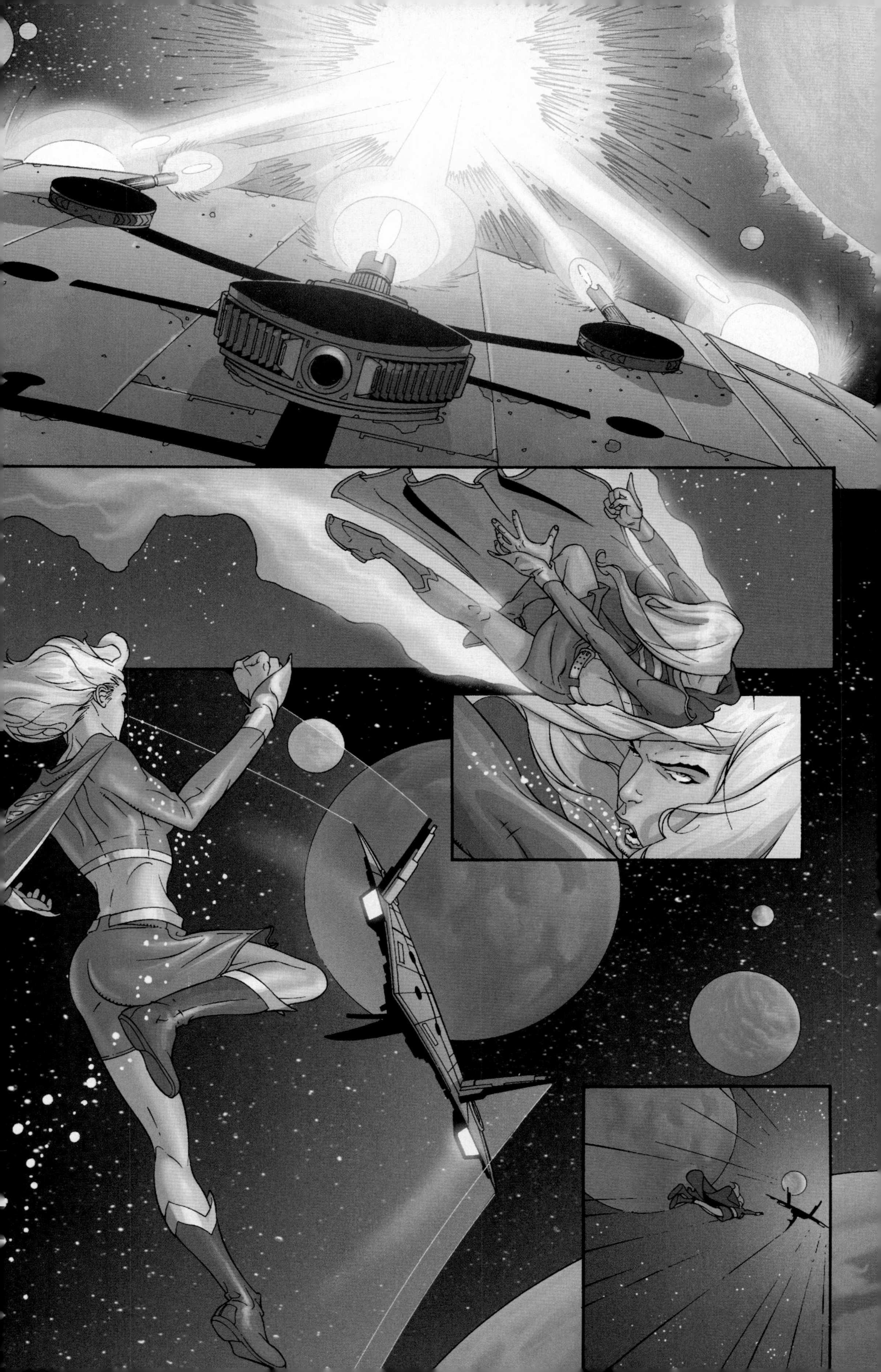

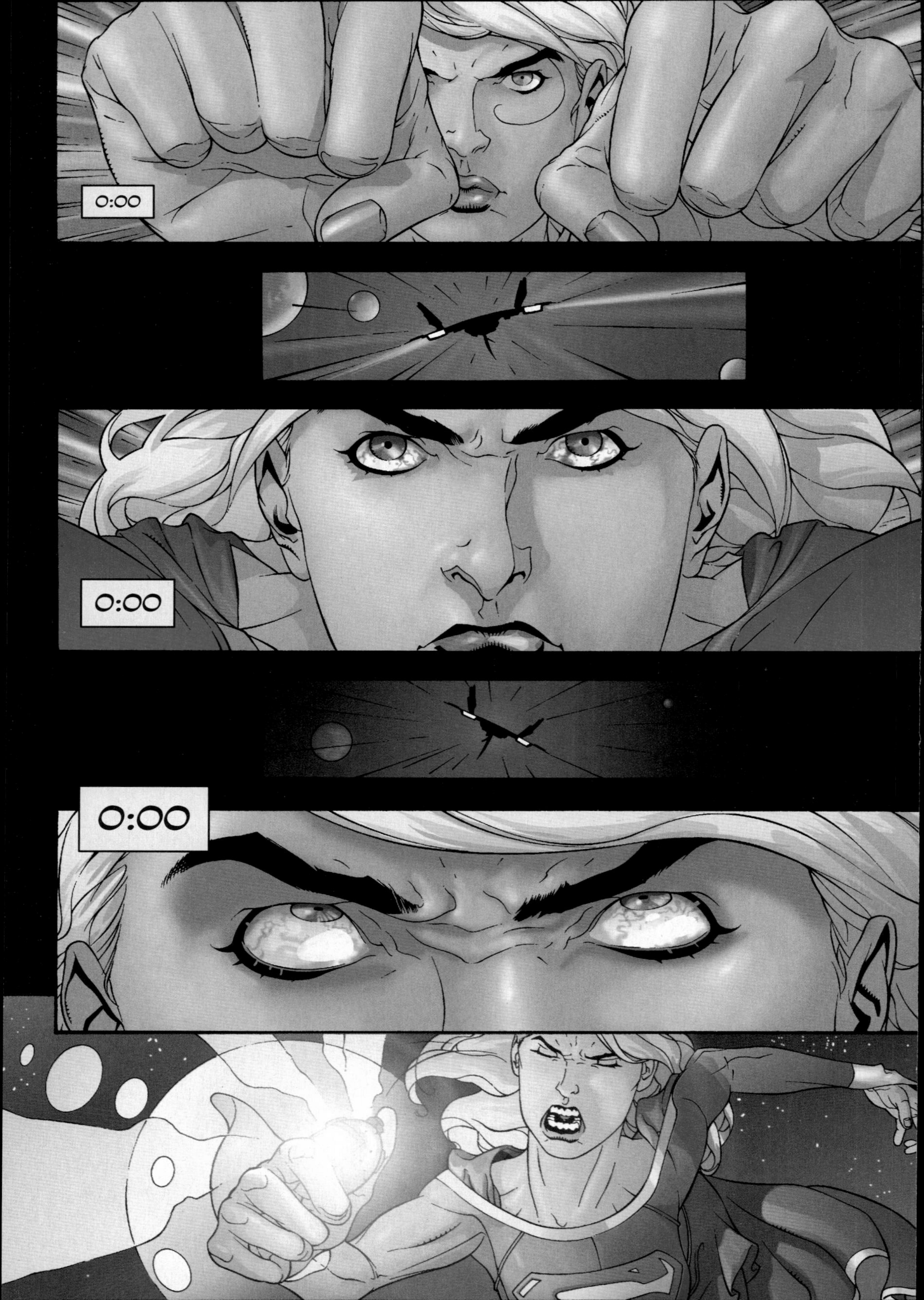
0:00
0:00
0:00

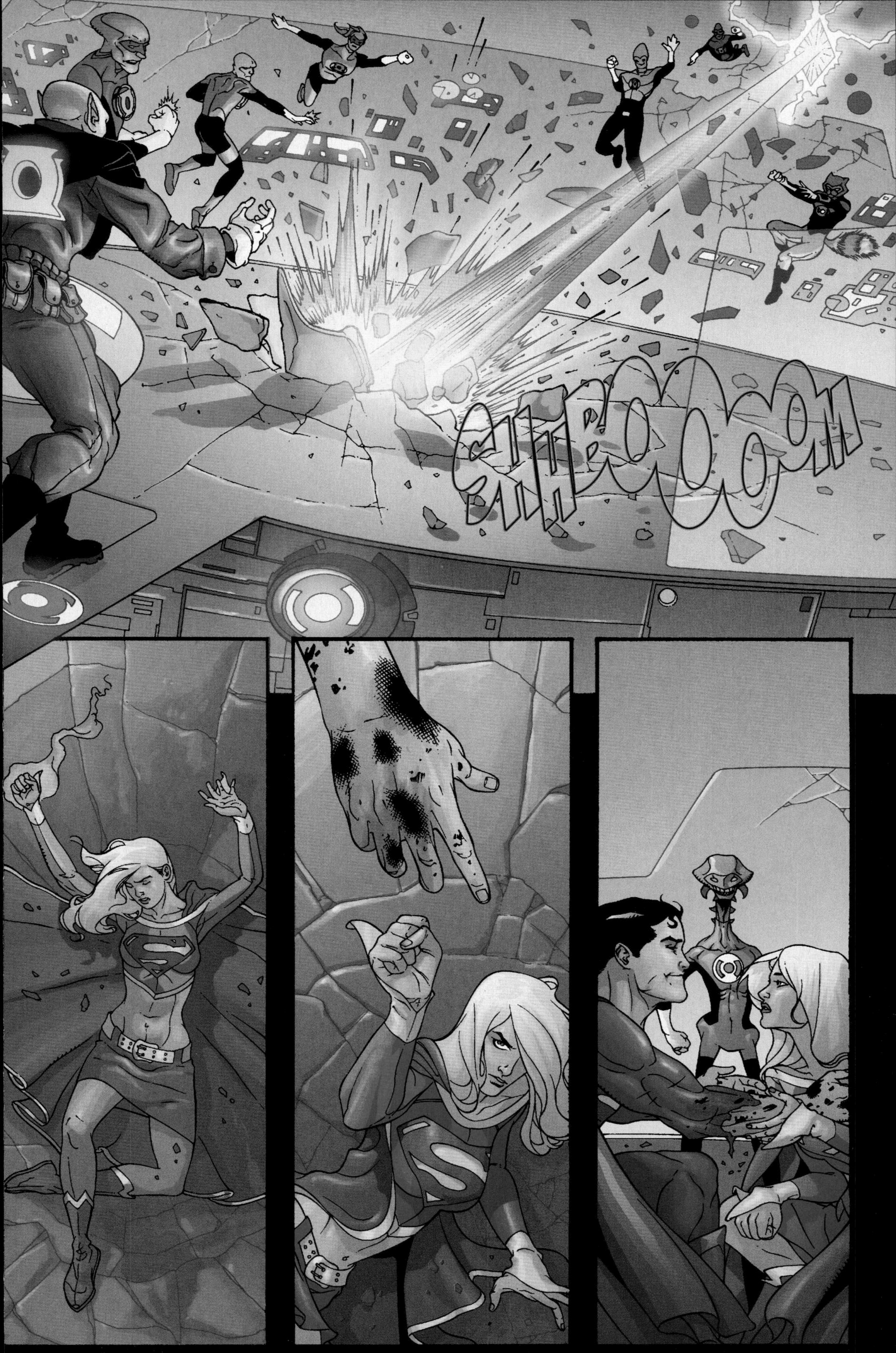
SHHROOOOOM

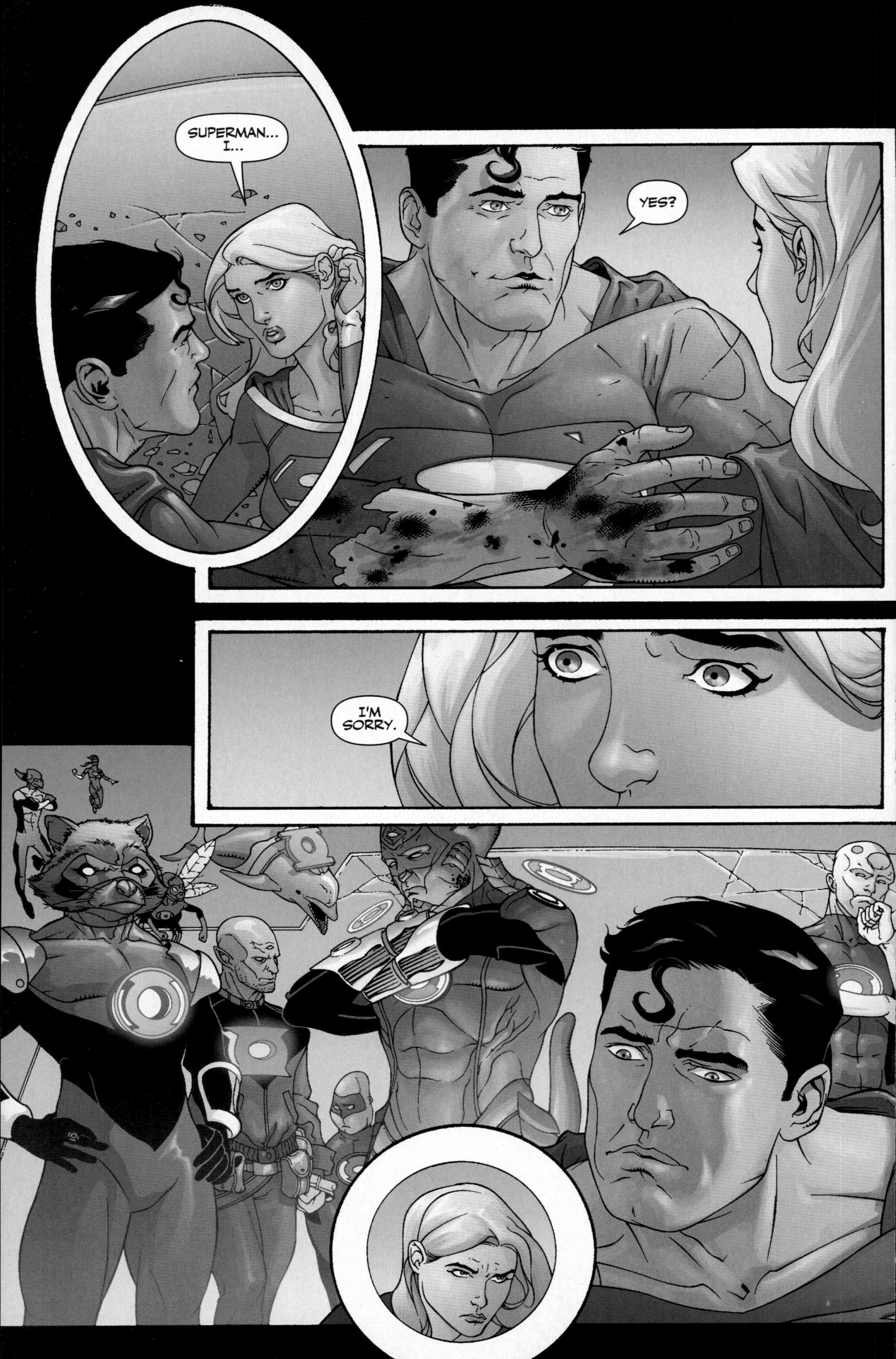
SUPERMAN... I...
YES?
I'M SORRY.

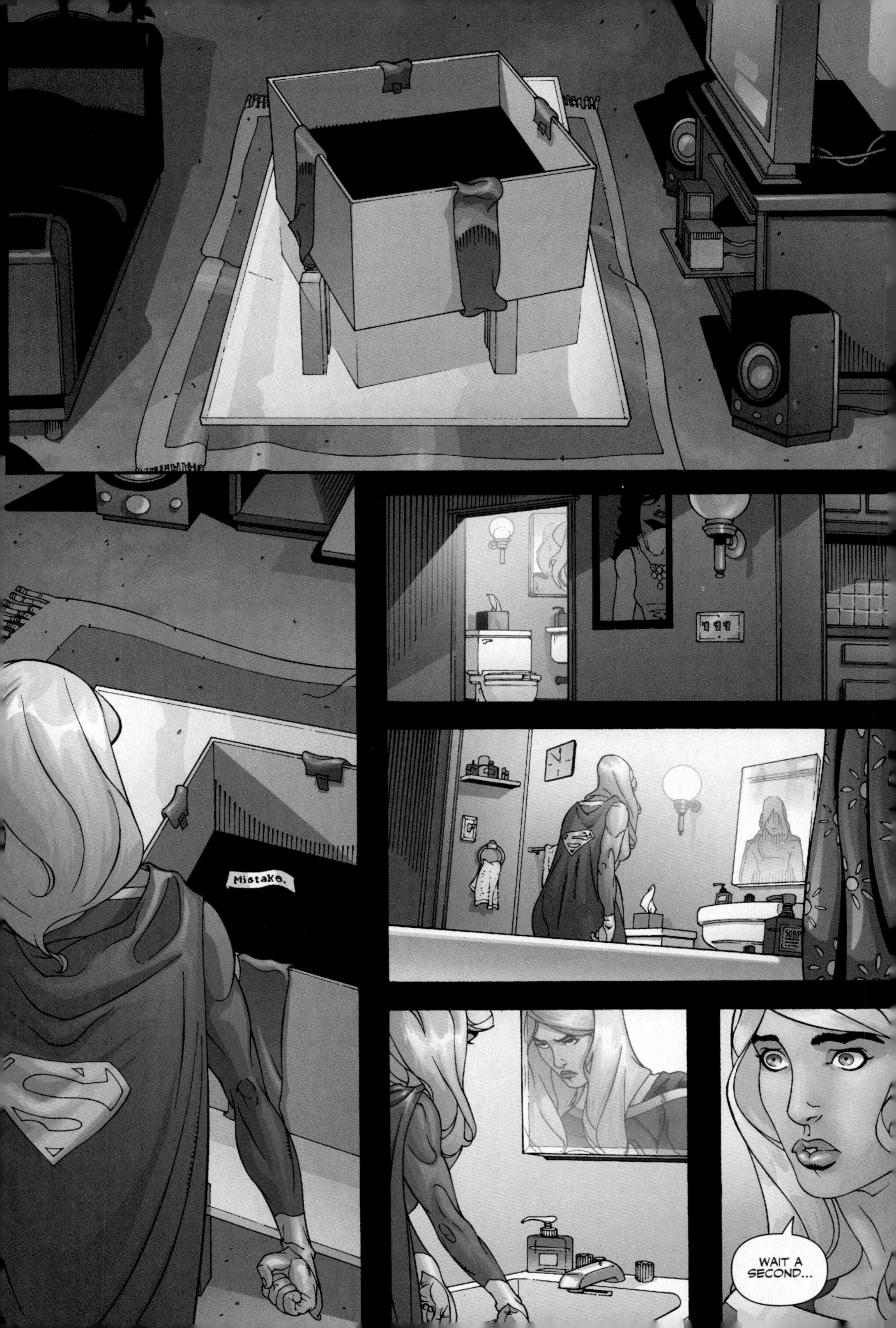
Mistake.
WAIT A SECOND...

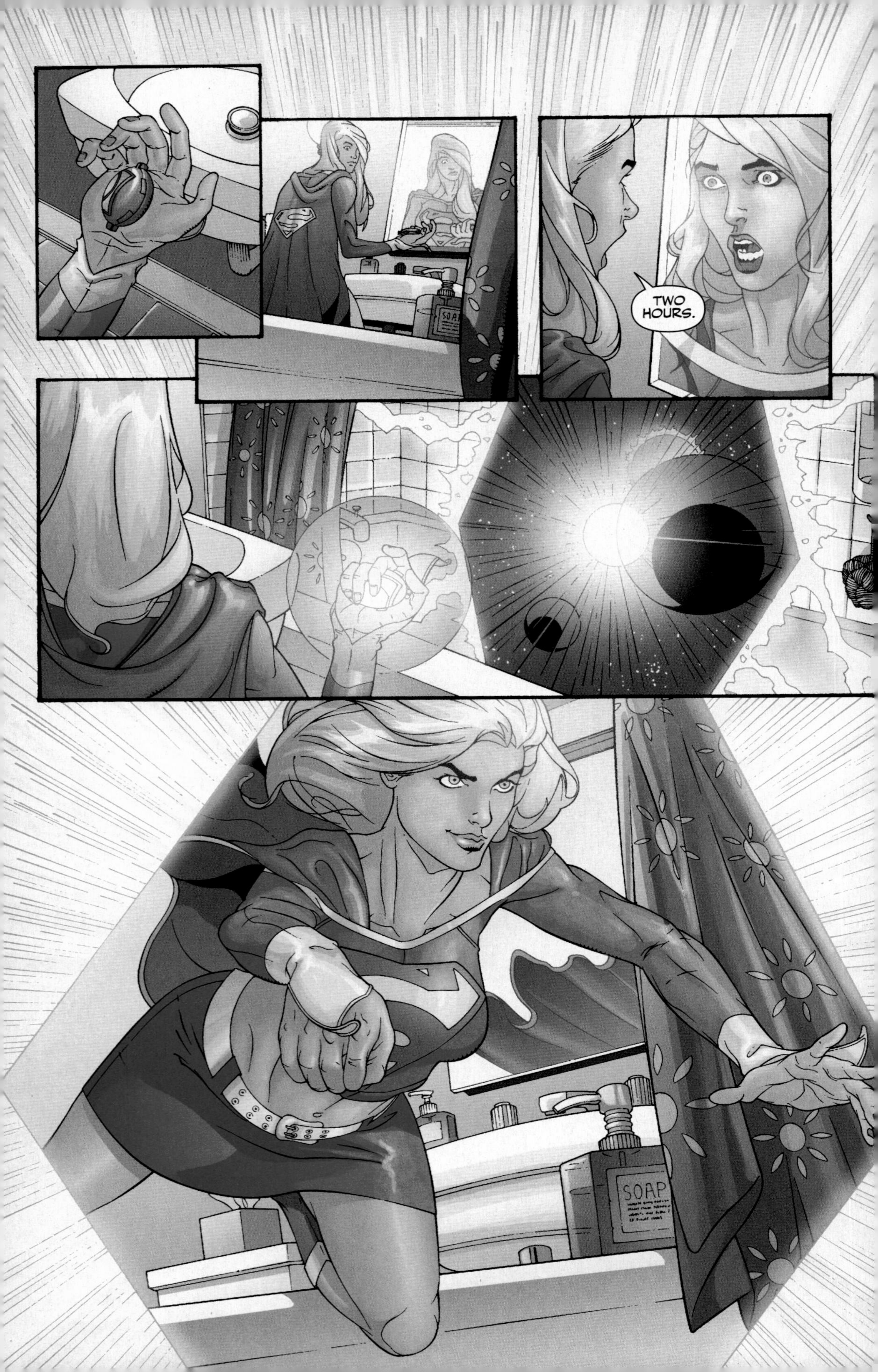
TWO HOURS.
SOAP

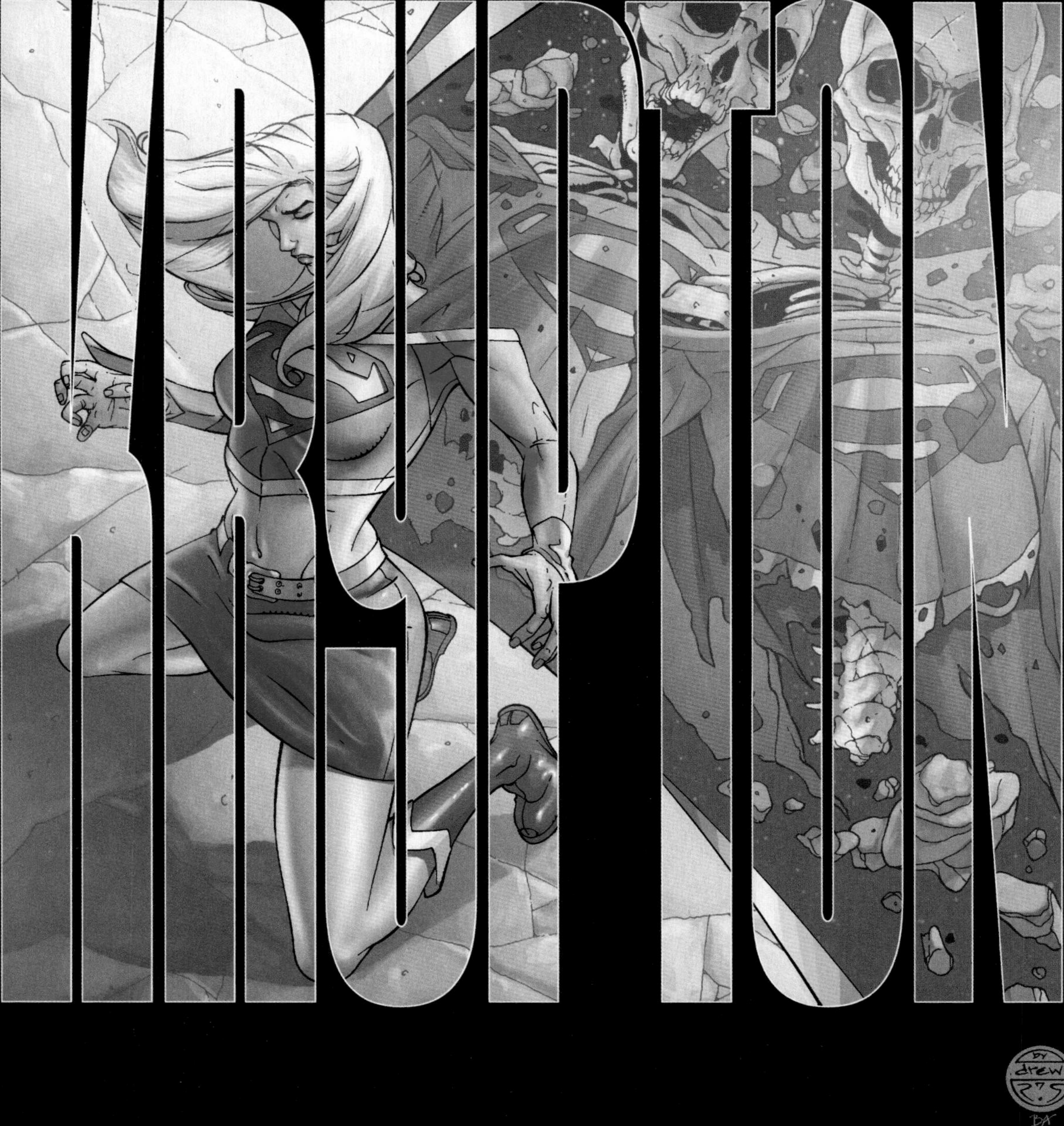
KRYPTON
by drew

STAR CHILD

KELLEY PUCKETT WRITER
DREW JOHNSON LEE FERGUSON PENCILS
RAY SNYDER INKS

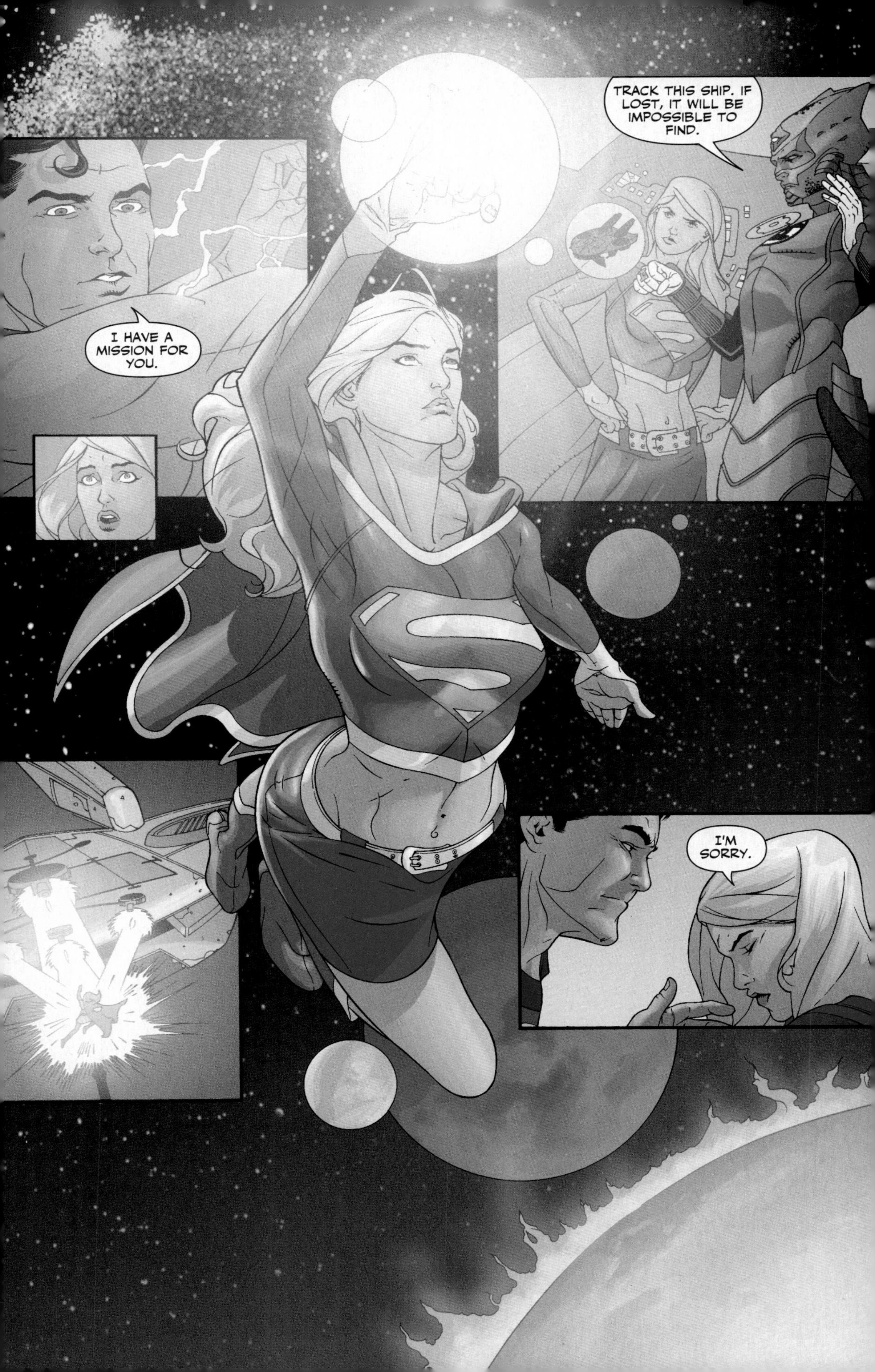

I HAVE A MISSION FOR YOU.
TRACK THIS SHIP. IF LOST, IT WILL BE IMPOSSIBLE TO FIND.
I'M SORRY.

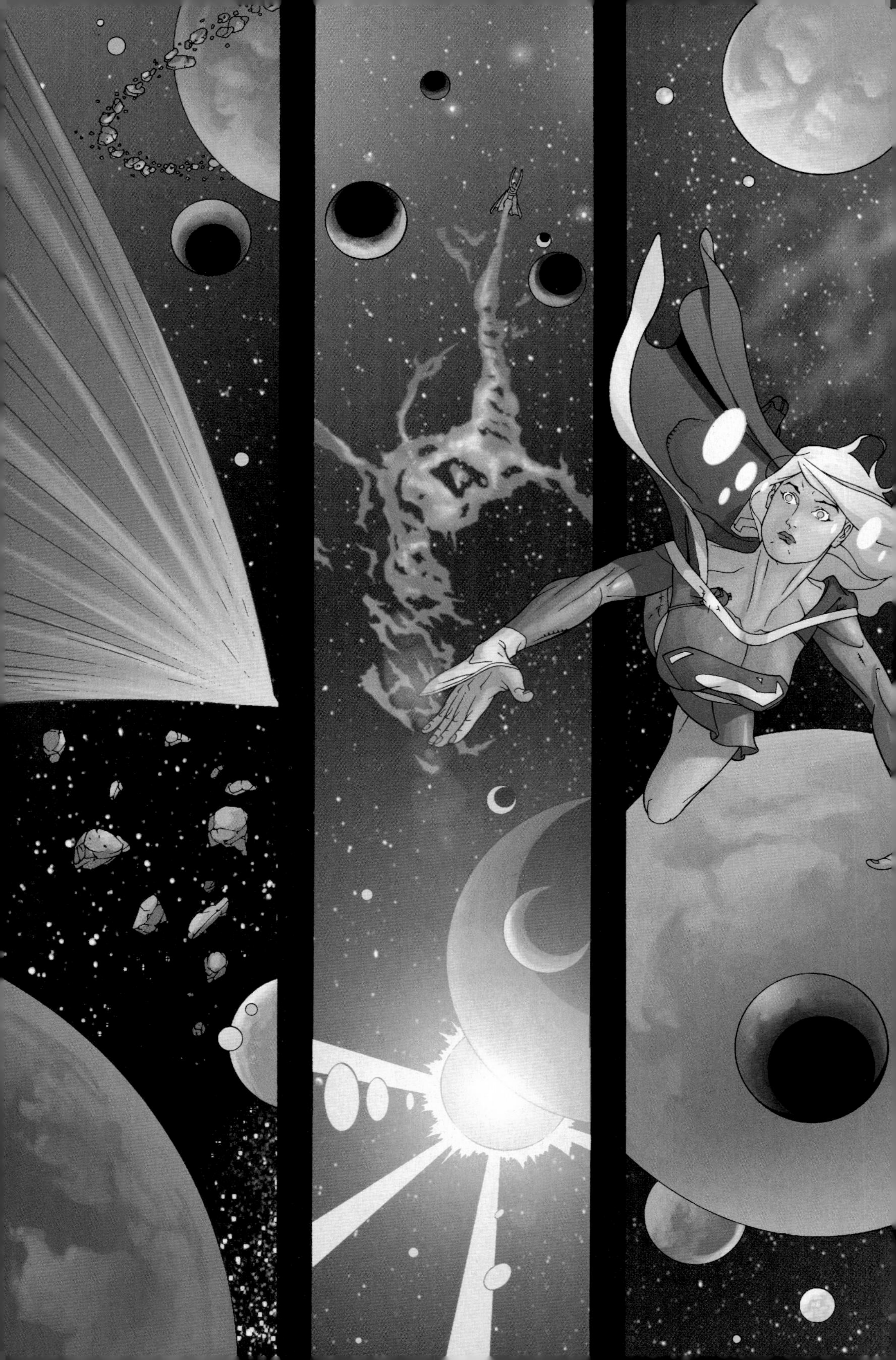

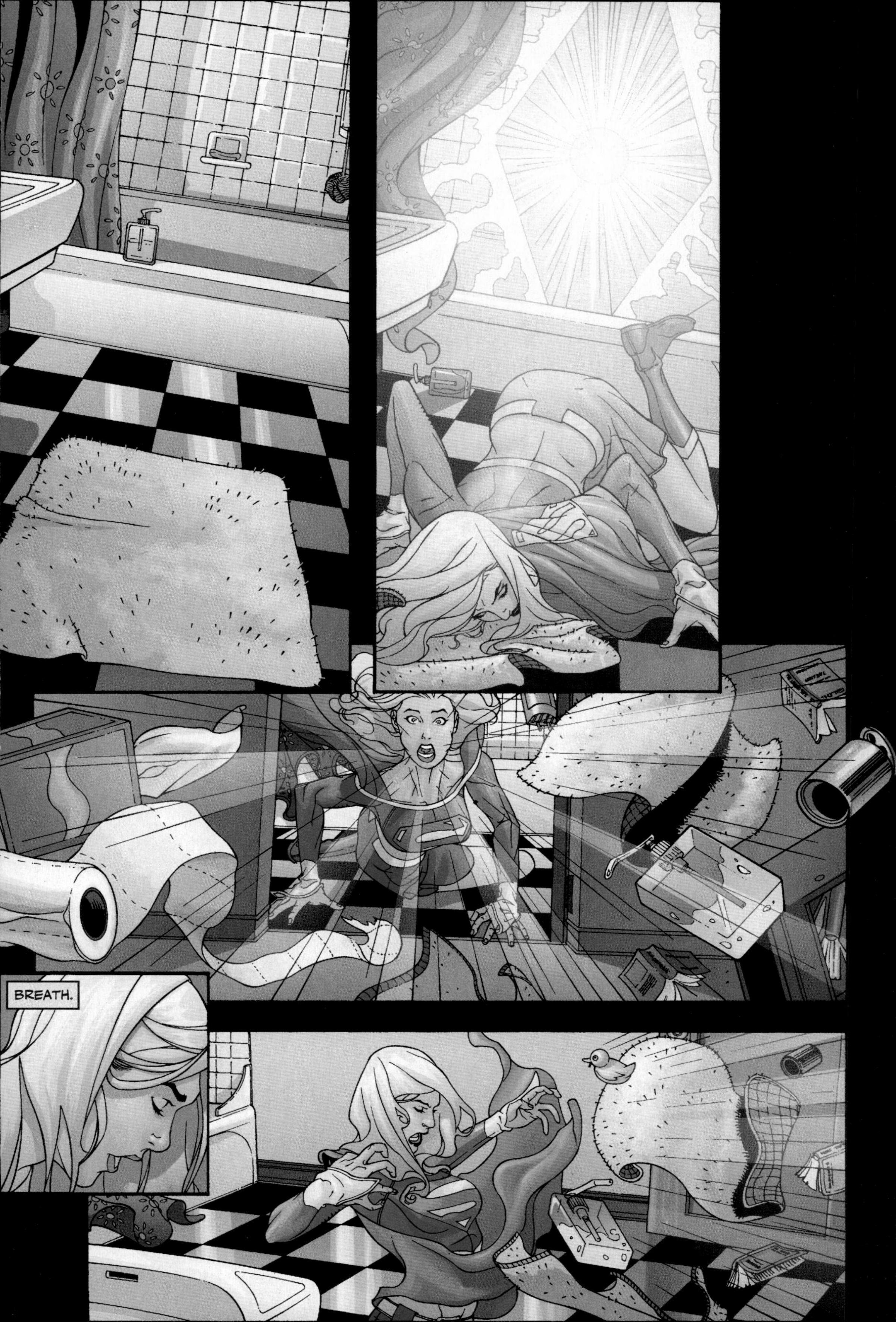
BREATH.

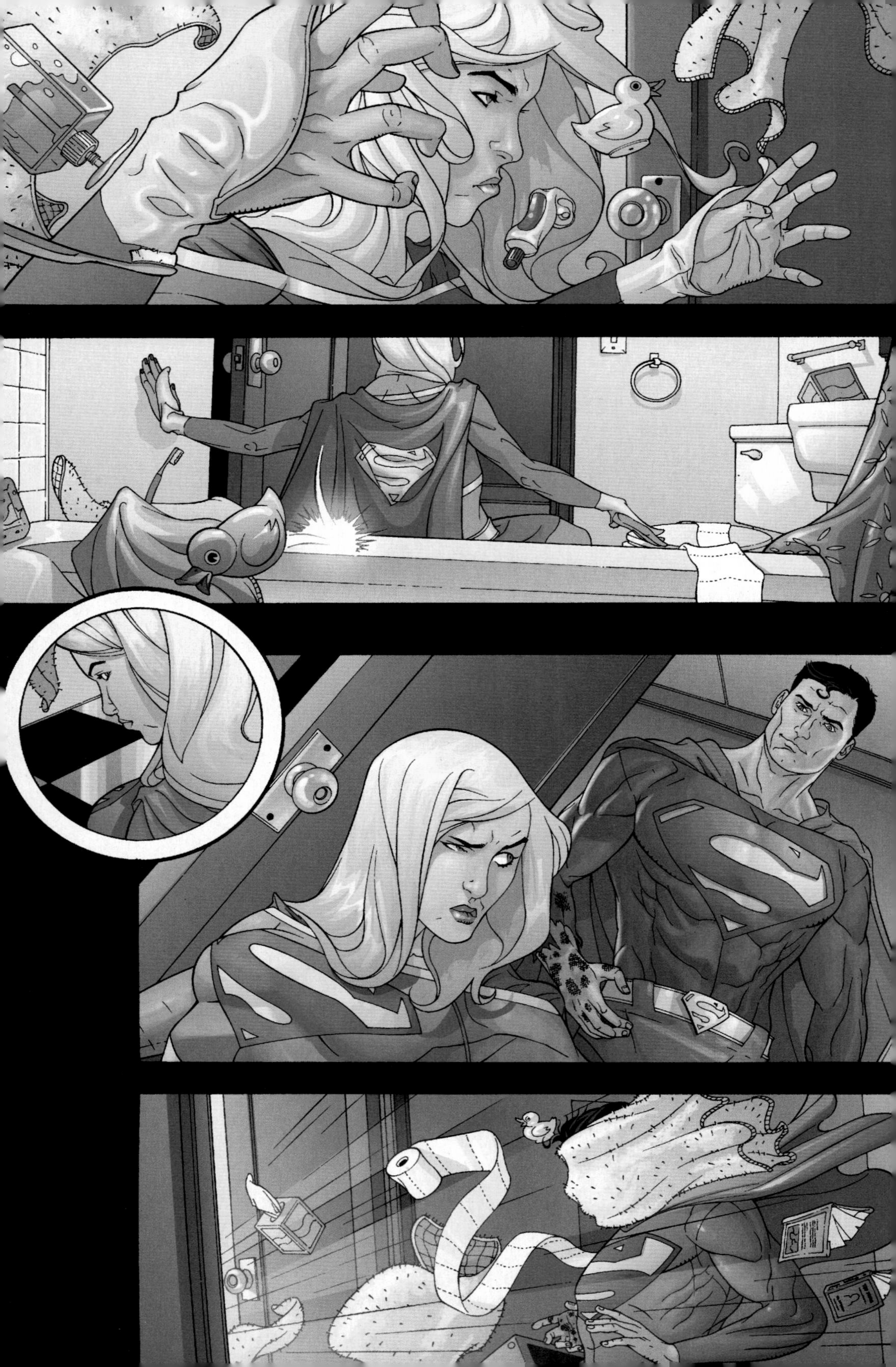

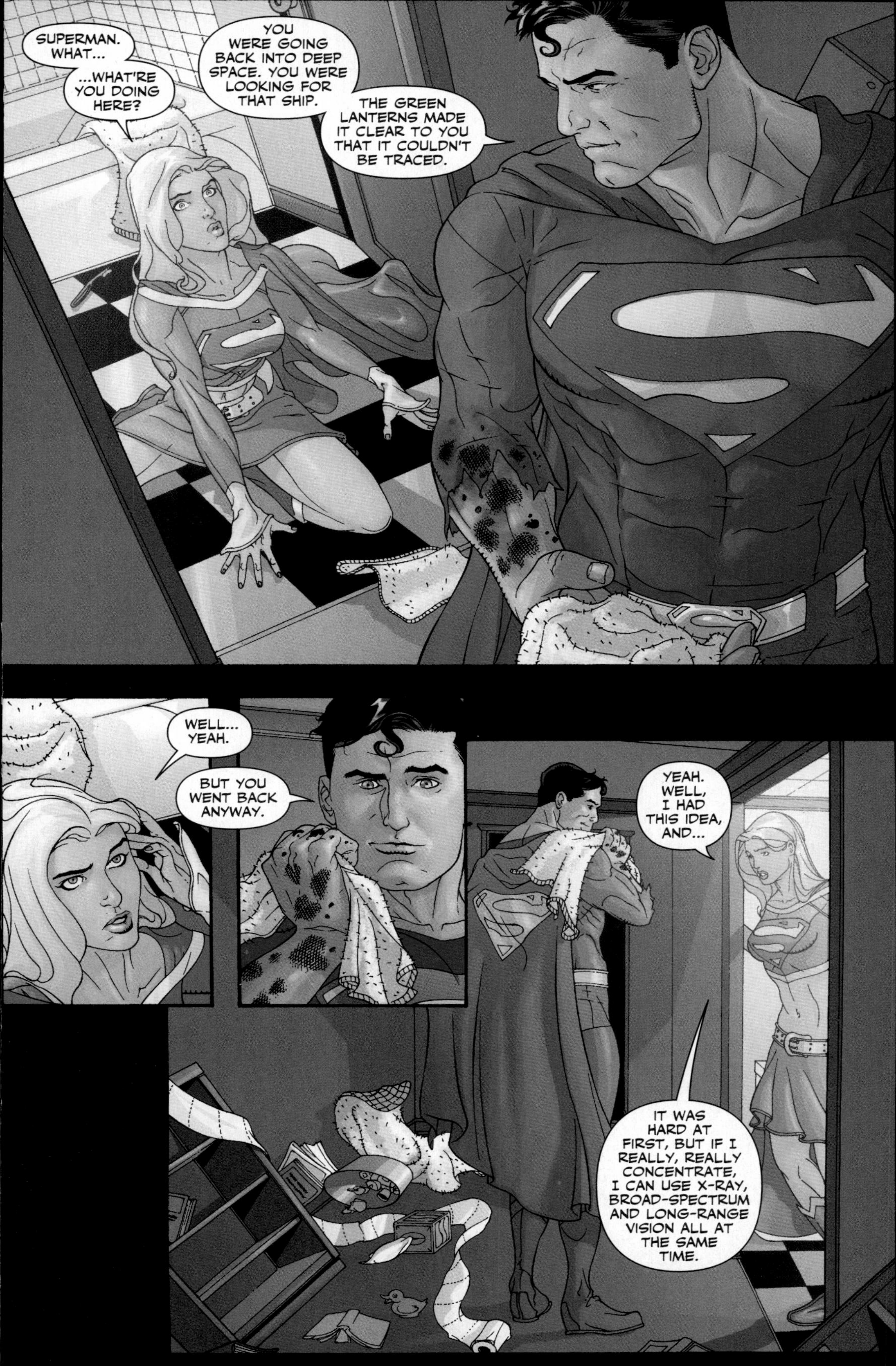

SUPERMAN. WHAT...
...WHAT'RE YOU DOING HERE?
YOU WERE GOING BACK INTO DEEP SPACE. YOU WERE LOOKING FOR THAT SHIP.
THE GREEN LANTERNS MADE IT CLEAR TO YOU THAT IT COULDN'T BE TRACED.
WELL... YEAH.
BUT YOU WENT BACK ANYWAY.
YEAH. WELL, I HAD THIS IDEA, AND...
IT WAS HARD AT FIRST, BUT IF I REALLY, REALLY CONCENTRATE, I CAN USE X-RAY, BROAD-SPECTRUM AND LONG-RANGE VISION ALL AT THE SAME TIME.

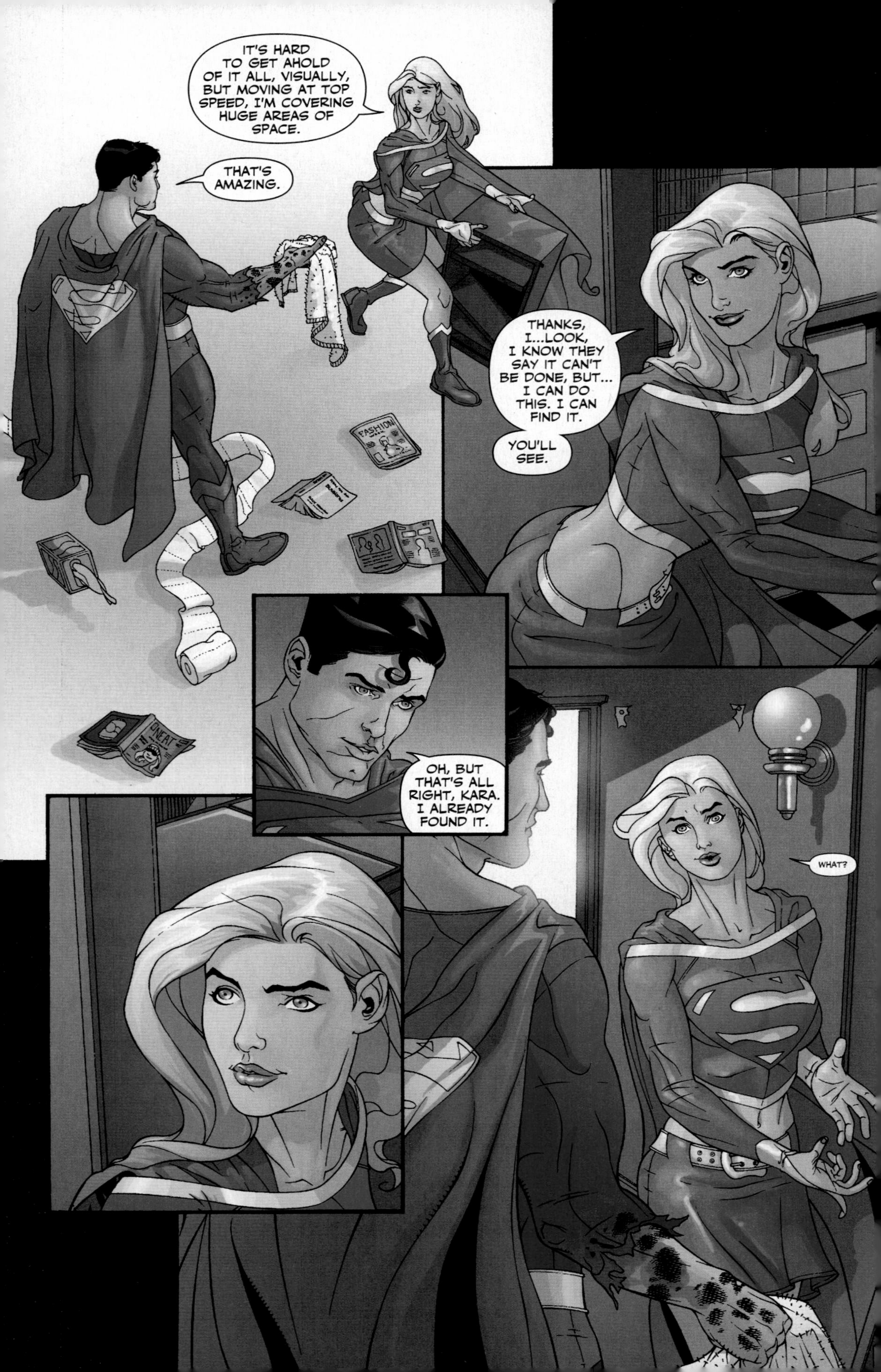
IT'S HARD TO GET AHOLD OF IT ALL, VISUALLY, BUT MOVING AT TOP SPEED, I'M COVERING HUGE AREAS OF SPACE.
THAT'S AMAZING.
THANKS, I...LOOK, I KNOW THEY SAY IT CAN'T BE DONE, BUT... I CAN DO THIS. I CAN FIND IT.
YOU'LL SEE.
OH, BUT THAT'S ALL RIGHT, KARA. I ALREADY FOUND IT.
WHAT?

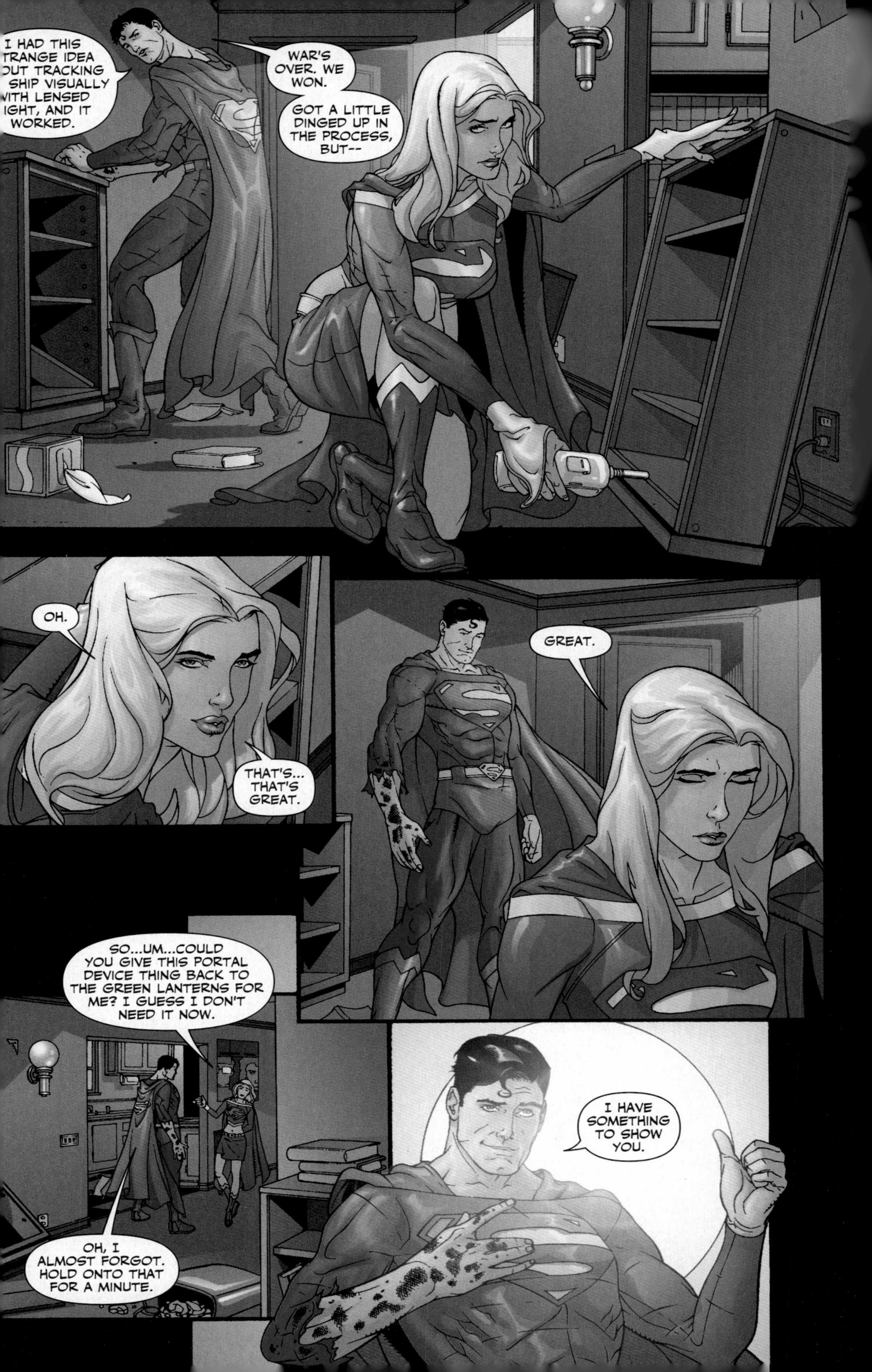
I HAD THIS
TRANGE IDEA
OUT TRACKING
SHIP VISUALLY
WITH LENSED
IGHT, AND IT
WORKED.
WAR'S OVER. WE WON.
GOT A LITTLE DINGED UP IN THE PROCESS, BUT--
OH.
THAT'S... THAT'S GREAT.
GREAT.
SO...UM...COULD YOU GIVE THIS PORTAL DEVICE THING BACK TO THE GREEN LANTERNS FOR ME? I GUESS I DON'T NEED IT NOW.
OH, I ALMOST FORGOT. HOLD ONTO THAT FOR A MINUTE.
I HAVE SOMETHING TO SHOW YOU.

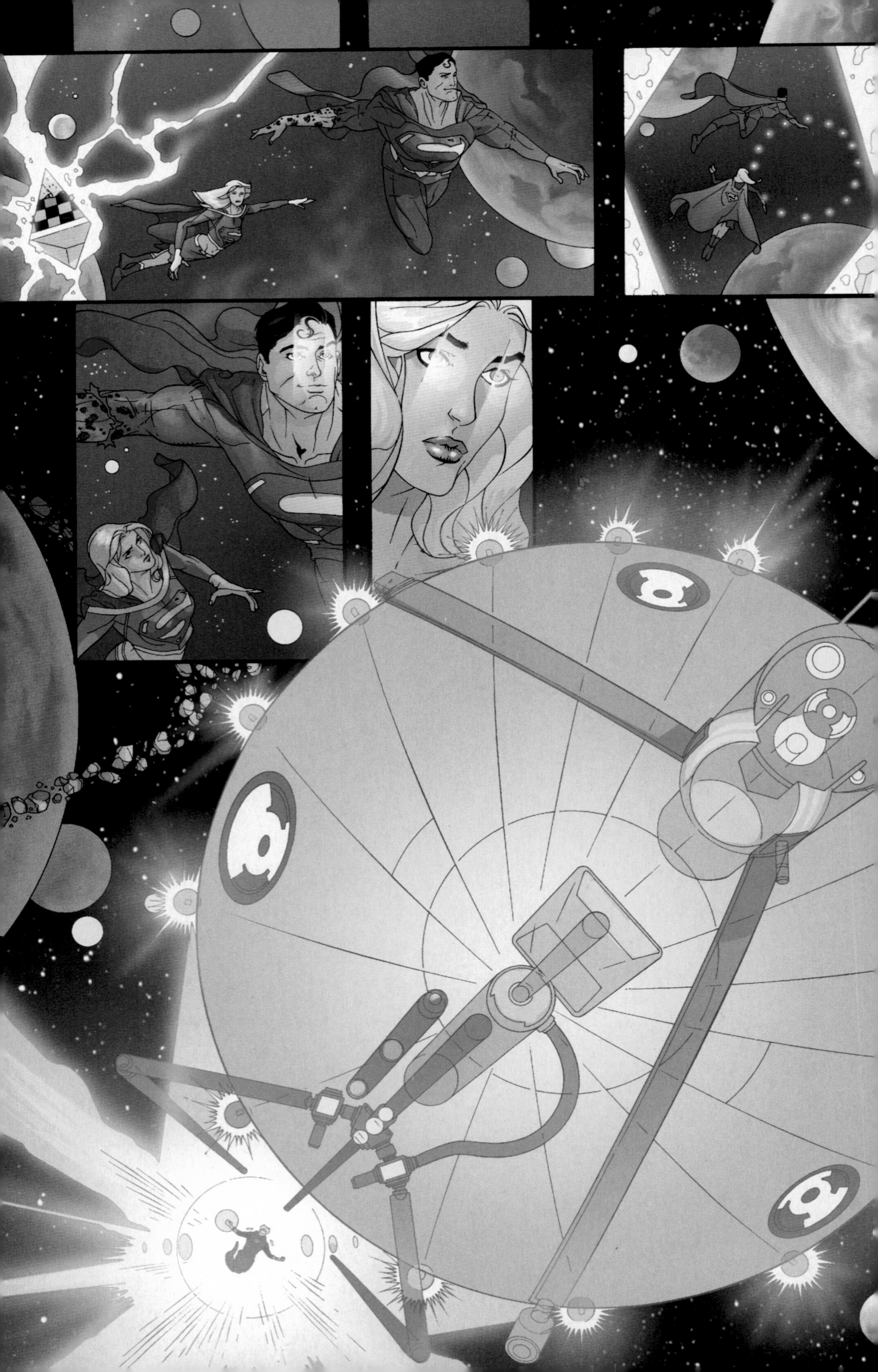

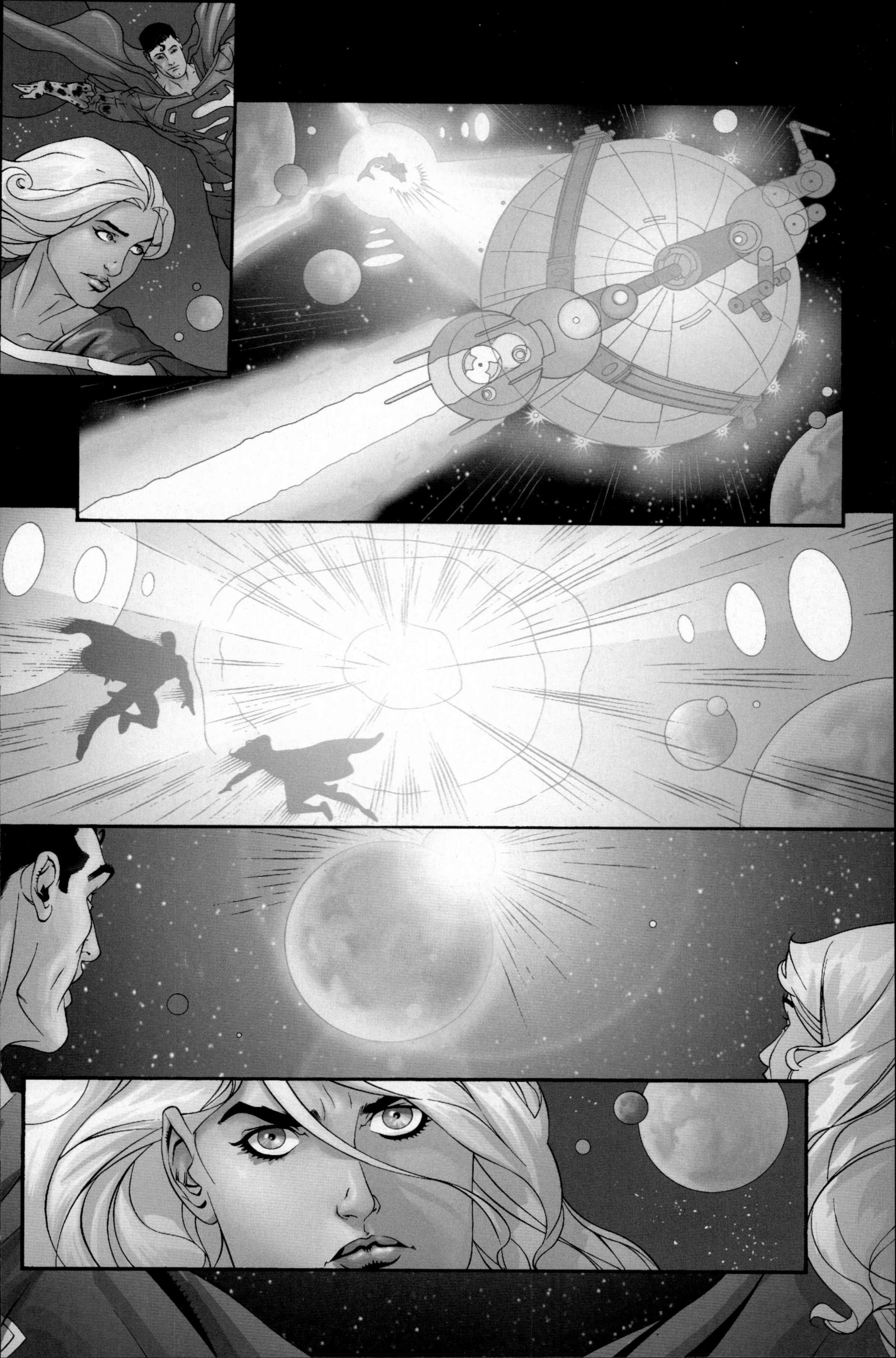

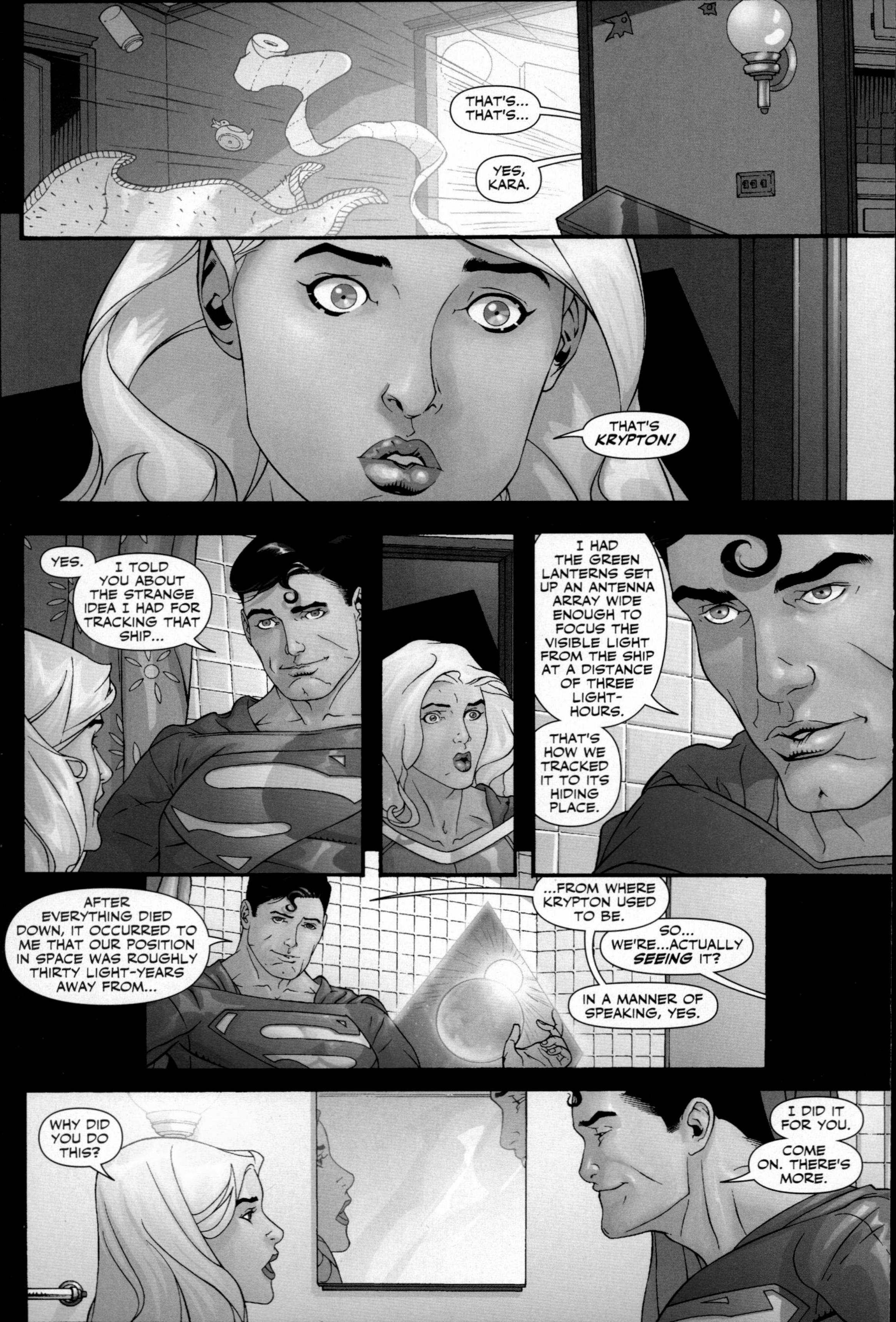
THAT'S... THAT'S...
YES, KARA.
THAT'S KRYPTON!
YES.
I TOLD YOU ABOUT THE STRANGE IDEA I HAD FOR TRACKING THAT SHIP...
I HAD THE GREEN LANTERNS SET UP AN ANTENNA ARRAY WIDE ENOUGH TO FOCUS THE VISIBLE LIGHT FROM THE SHIP AT A DISTANCE OF THREE LIGHT-HOURS.
THAT'S HOW WE TRACKED IT TO ITS HIDING PLACE.
AFTER EVERYTHING DIED DOWN, IT OCCURRED TO ME THAT OUR POSITION IN SPACE WAS ROUGHLY THIRTY LIGHT-YEARS AWAY FROM...
...FROM WHERE KRYPTON USED TO BE.
SO... WE'RE...ACTUALLY SEEING IT?
IN A MANNER OF SPEAKING, YES.
WHY DID YOU DO THIS?
I DID IT FOR YOU.
COME ON. THERE'S MORE.

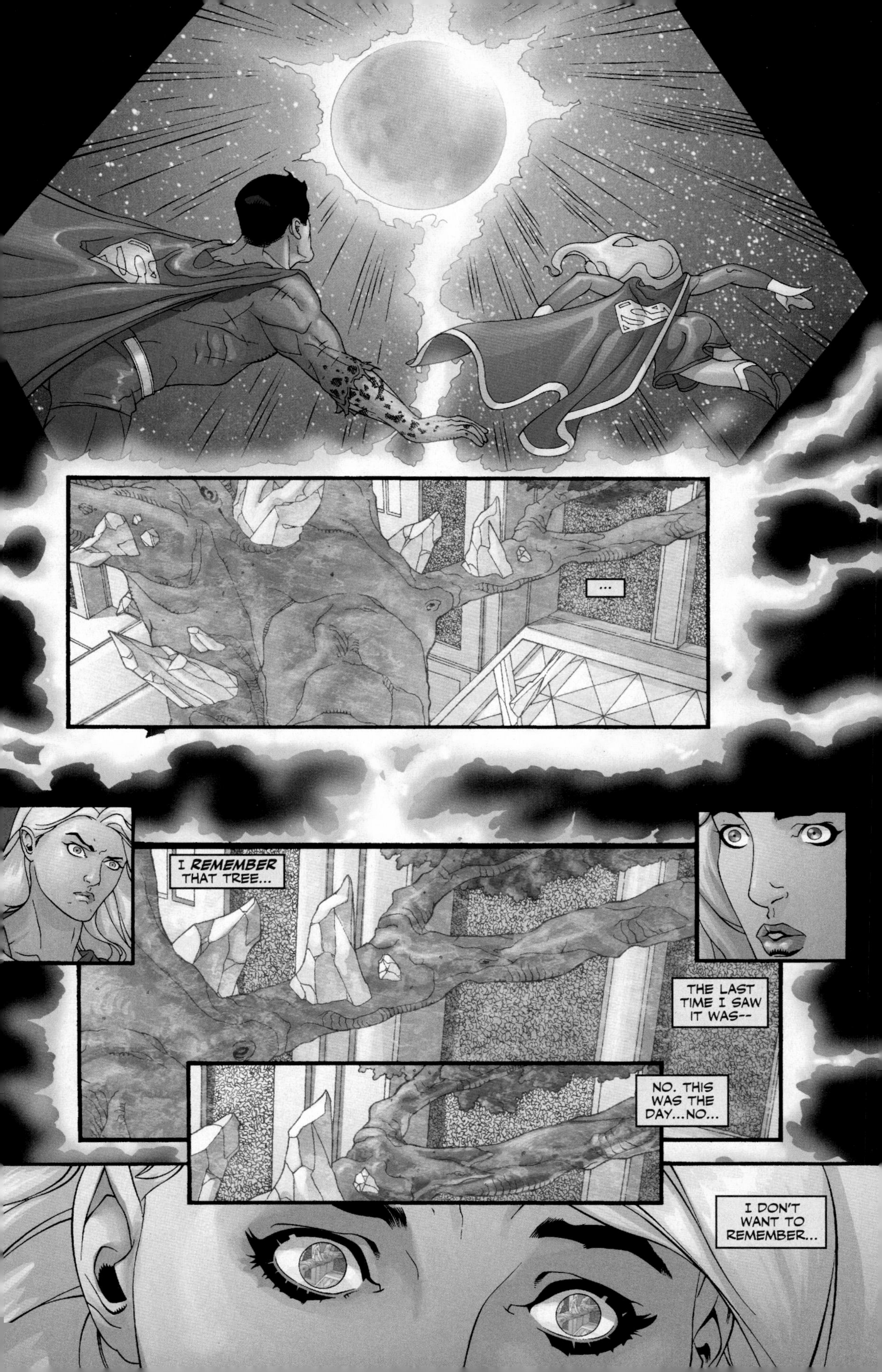
...
I REMEMBER THAT TREE...
THE LAST TIME I SAW IT WAS--
NO. THIS WAS THE DAY...NO...
I DON'T WANT TO REMEMBER...

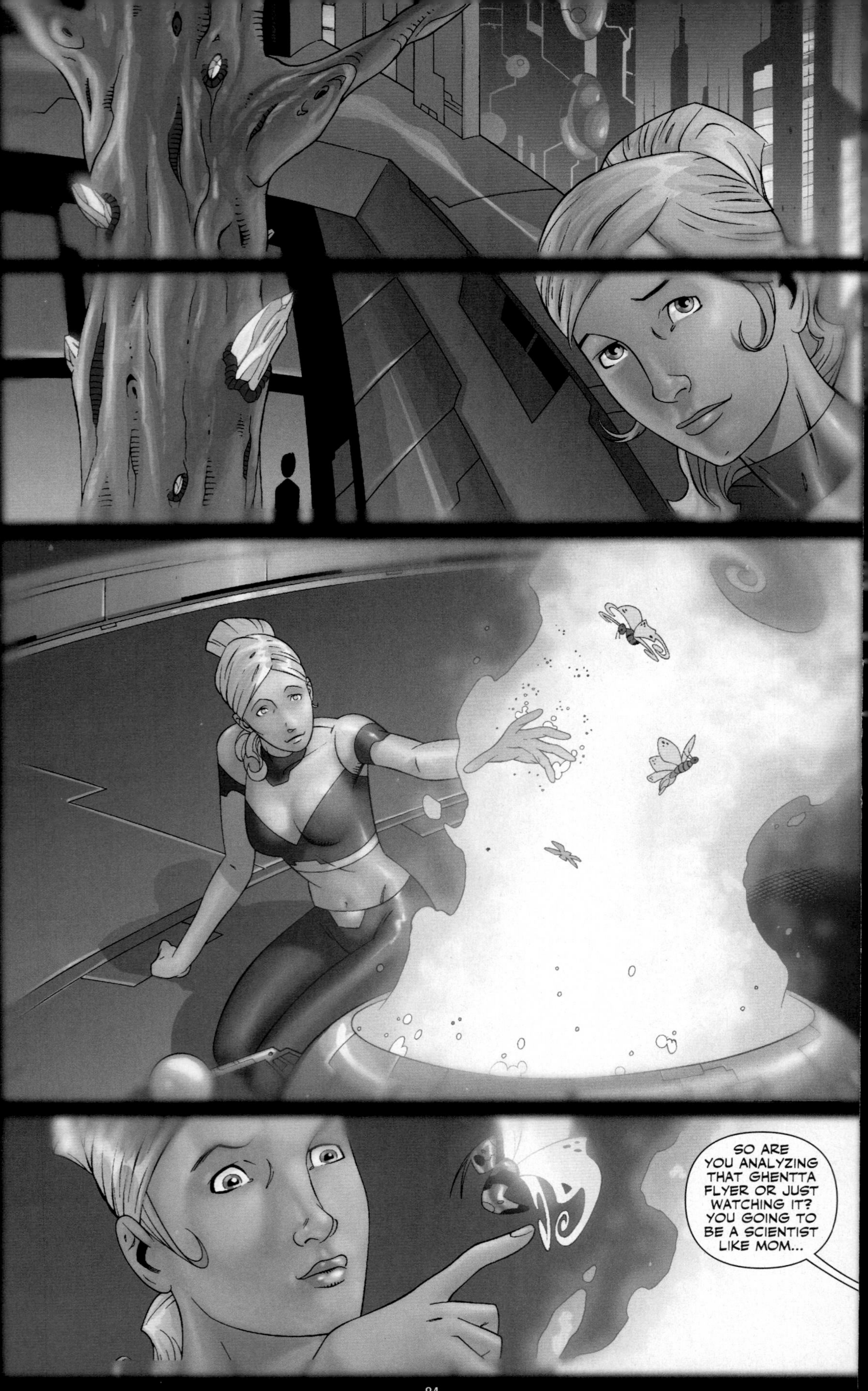
SO ARE YOU ANALYZING THAT GHENTTA FLYER OR JUST WATCHING IT? YOU GOING TO BE A SCIENTIST LIKE MOM...

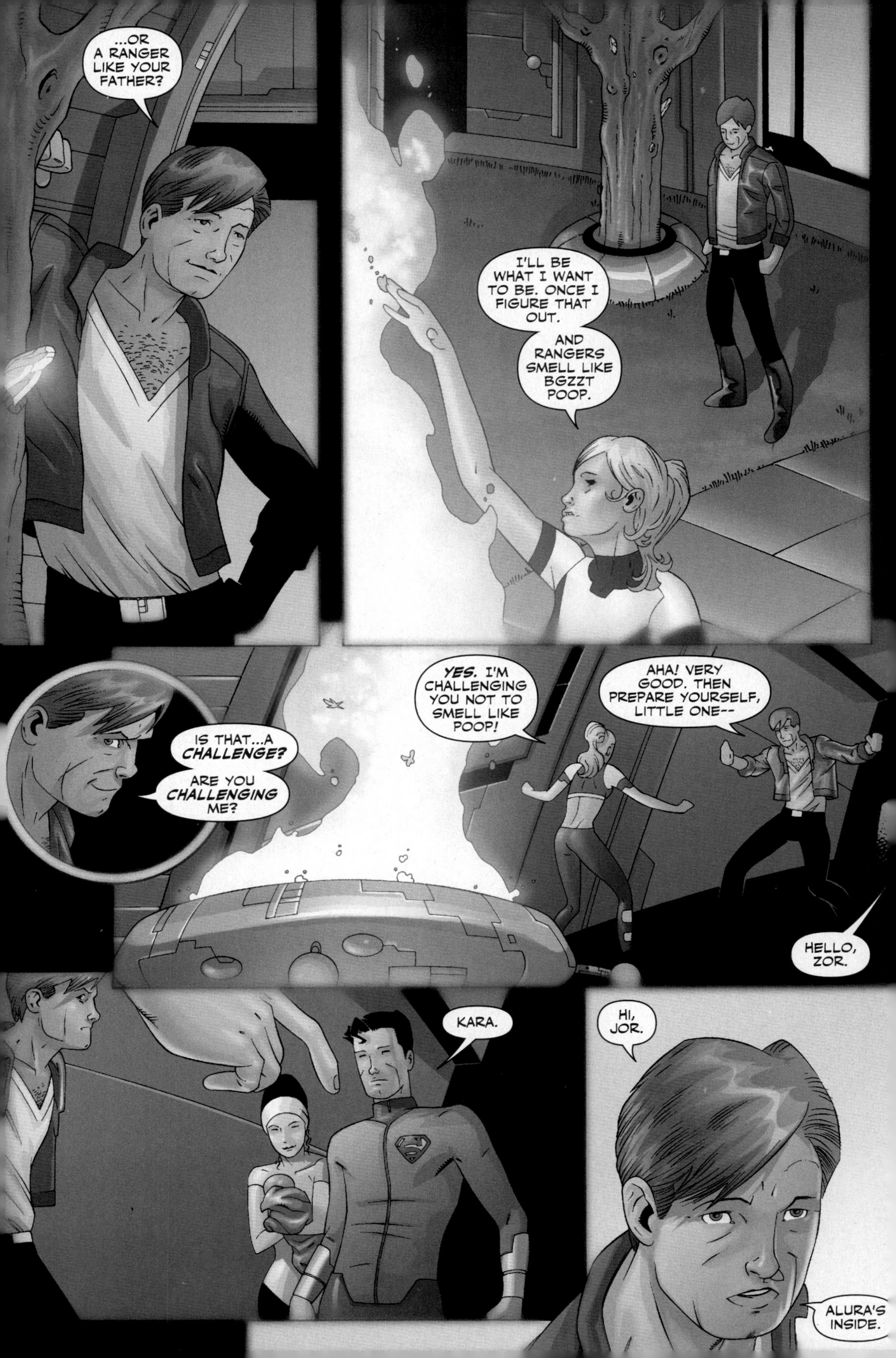
...OR A RANGER LIKE YOUR FATHER?
I'LL BE WHAT I WANT TO BE. ONCE I FIGURE THAT OUT.
AND RANGERS SMELL LIKE BGZZT POOP.
IS THAT...A CHALLENGE?
ARE YOU CHALLENGING ME?
YES. I'M CHALLENGING YOU NOT TO SMELL LIKE POOP!
AHA! VERY GOOD. THEN PREPARE YOURSELF, LITTLE ONE--
HELLO, ZOR.
KARA.
HI, JOR.
ALURA'S INSIDE.

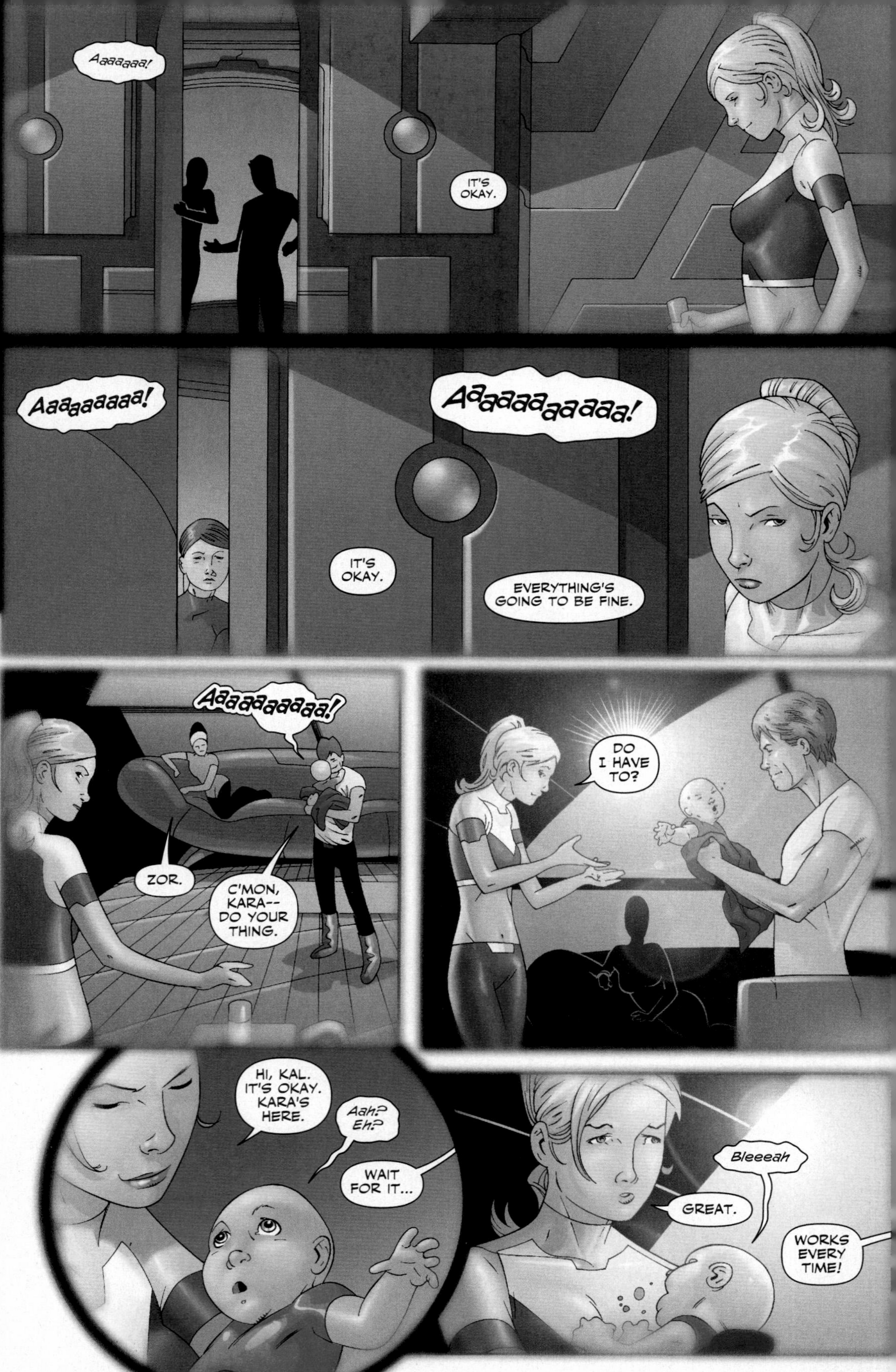

Aaaaaaa!
IT'S OKAY.
Aaaaaaaaa!
Aaaaaaaaaaaa!
IT'S OKAY.
EVERYTHING'S GOING TO BE FINE.
Aaaaaaaaaaa!
ZOR.
C'MON, KARA-- DO YOUR THING.
DO I HAVE TO?
HI, KAL. IT'S OKAY. KARA'S HERE.
Aah? Eh?
WAIT FOR IT...
Bleeeah
GREAT.
WORKS EVERY TIME!

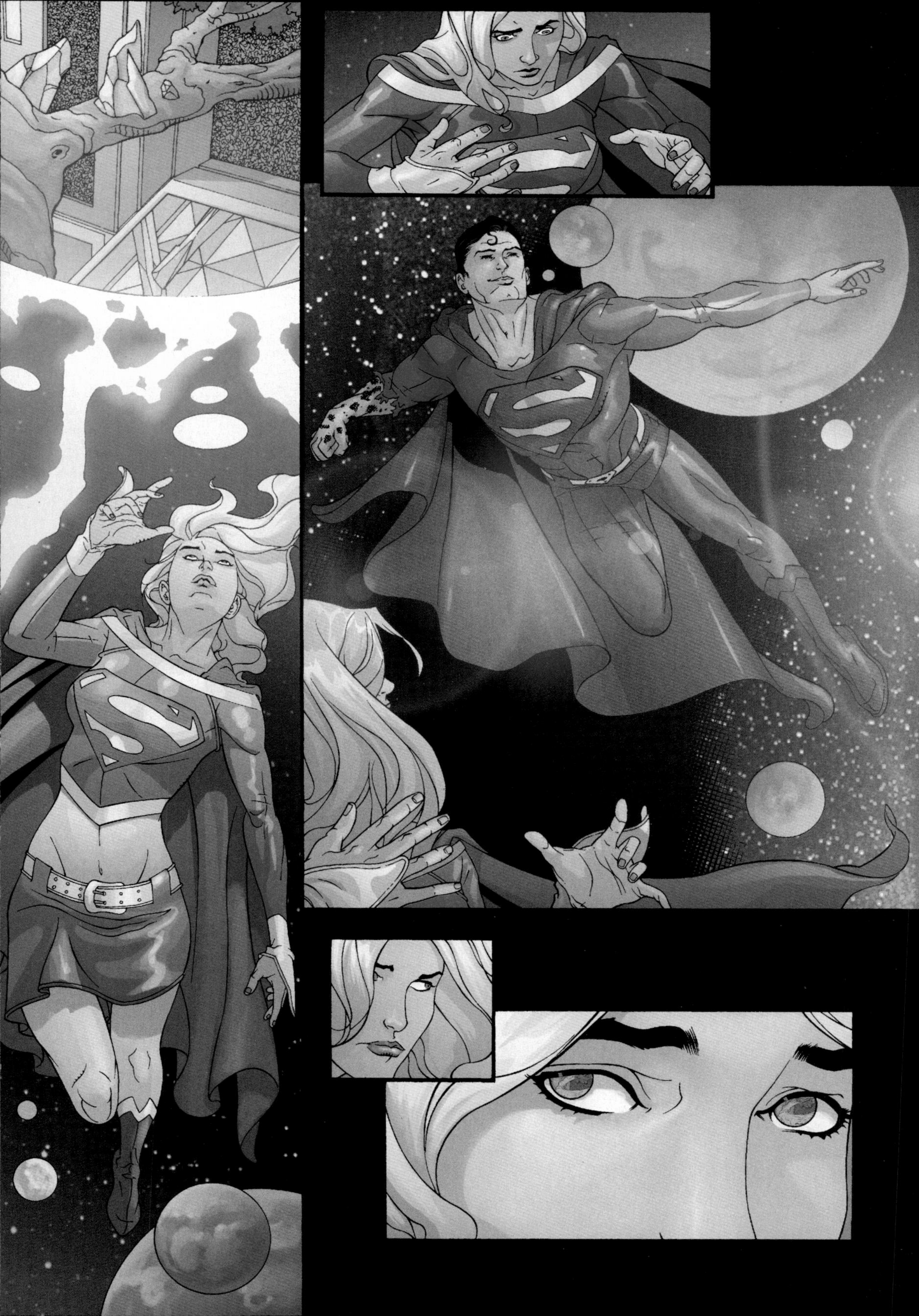

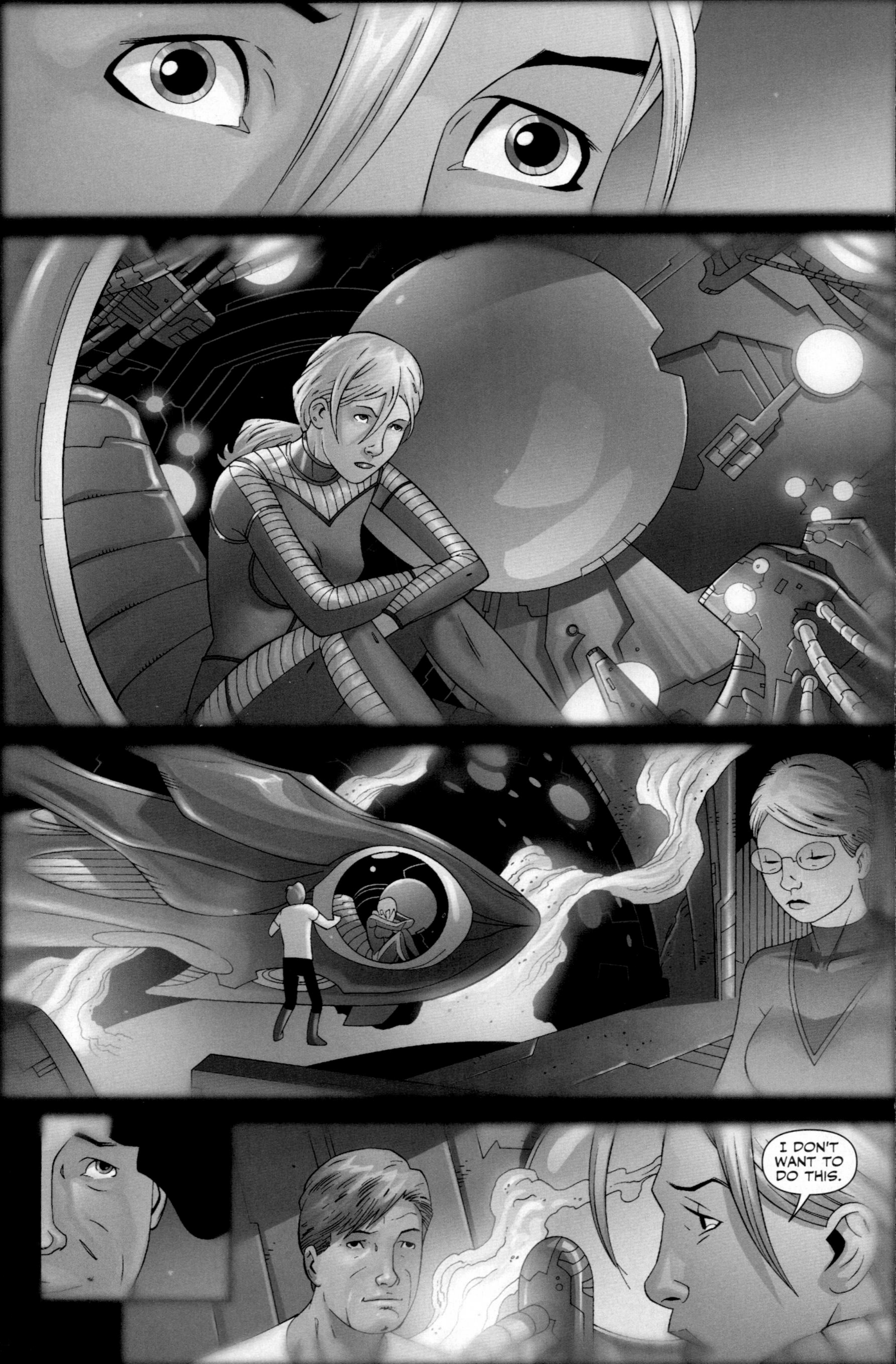
I DON'T WANT TO DO THIS.

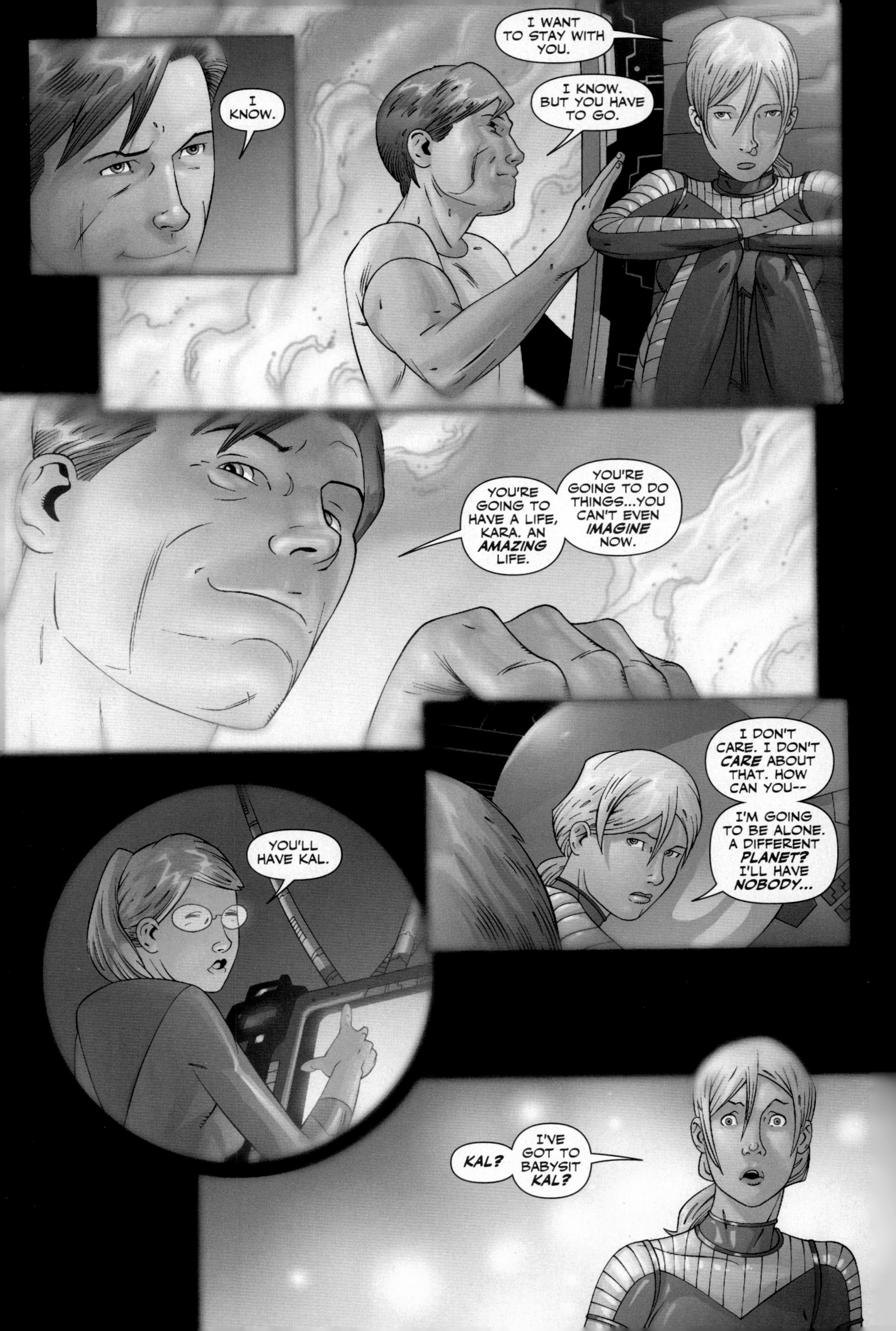
I WANT TO STAY WITH YOU.
I KNOW.
I KNOW. BUT YOU HAVE TO GO.
YOU'RE GOING TO HAVE A LIFE, KARA. AN *AMAZING* LIFE.
YOU'RE GOING TO DO THINGS...YOU CAN'T EVEN *IMAGINE* NOW.
I DON'T CARE. I DON'T *CARE* ABOUT THAT. HOW CAN YOU--
I'M GOING TO BE ALONE. A DIFFERENT *PLANET?* I'LL HAVE *NOBODY...*
YOU'LL HAVE KAL.
KAL?
I'VE GOT TO BABYSIT *KAL?*

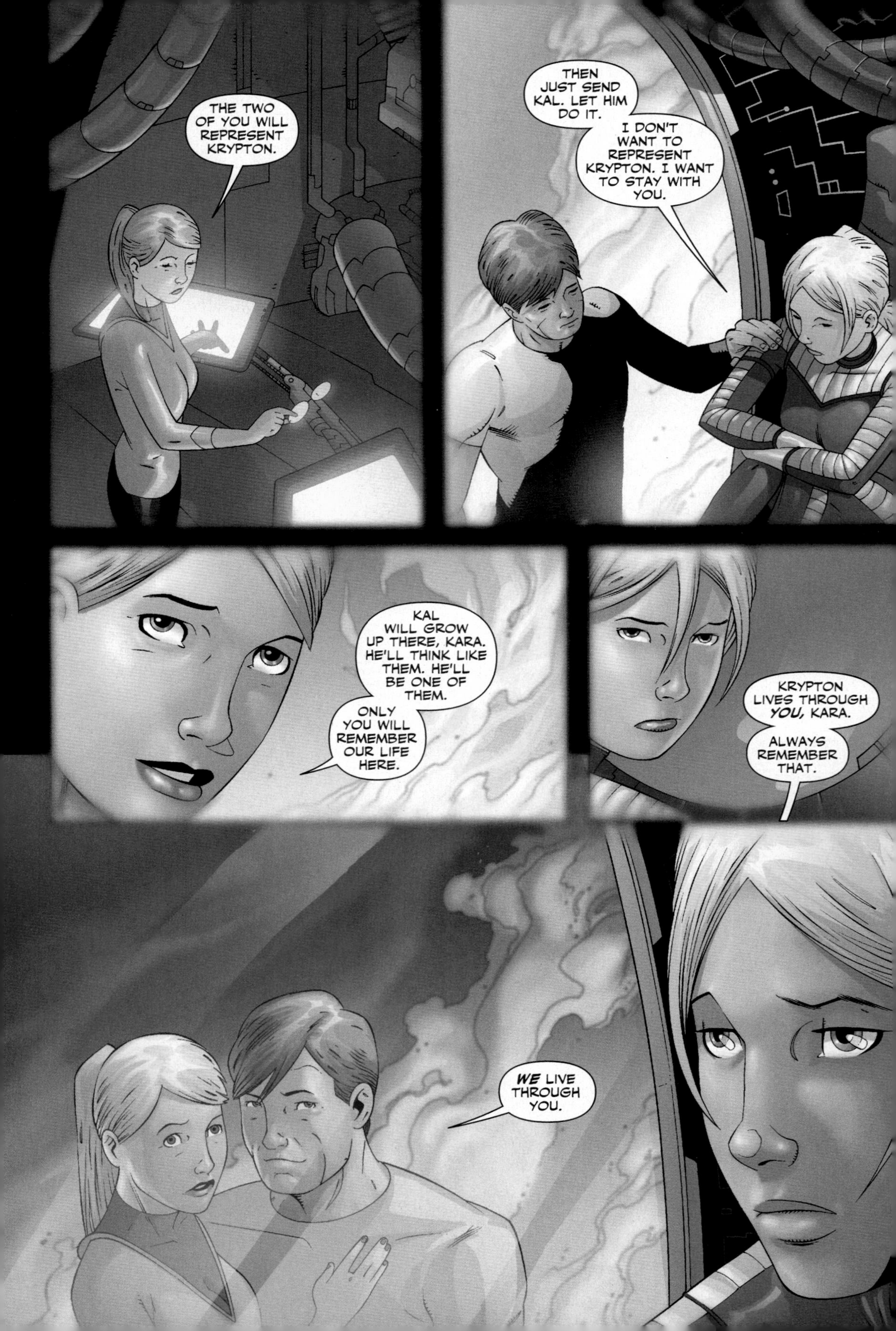
THE TWO OF YOU WILL REPRESENT KRYPTON.
THEN JUST SEND KAL. LET HIM DO IT.
I DON'T WANT TO REPRESENT KRYPTON. I WANT TO STAY WITH YOU.
KAL WILL GROW UP THERE, KARA. HE'LL THINK LIKE THEM. HE'LL BE ONE OF THEM.
ONLY YOU WILL REMEMBER OUR LIFE HERE.
KRYPTON LIVES THROUGH *YOU,* KARA.
ALWAYS REMEMBER THAT.
WE LIVE THROUGH YOU.

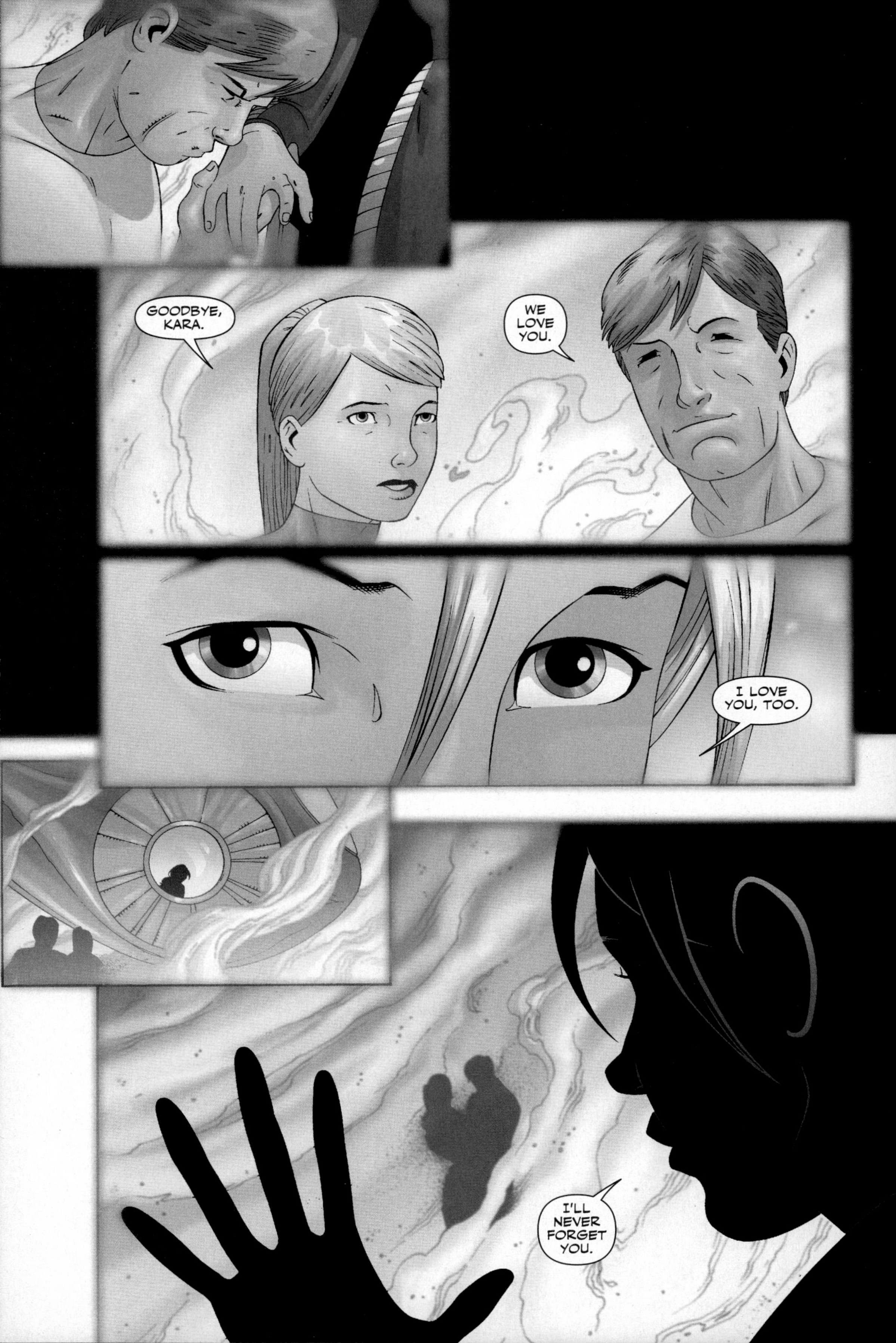
GOODBYE, KARA.
WE LOVE YOU.
I LOVE YOU, TOO.
I'LL NEVER FORGET YOU.

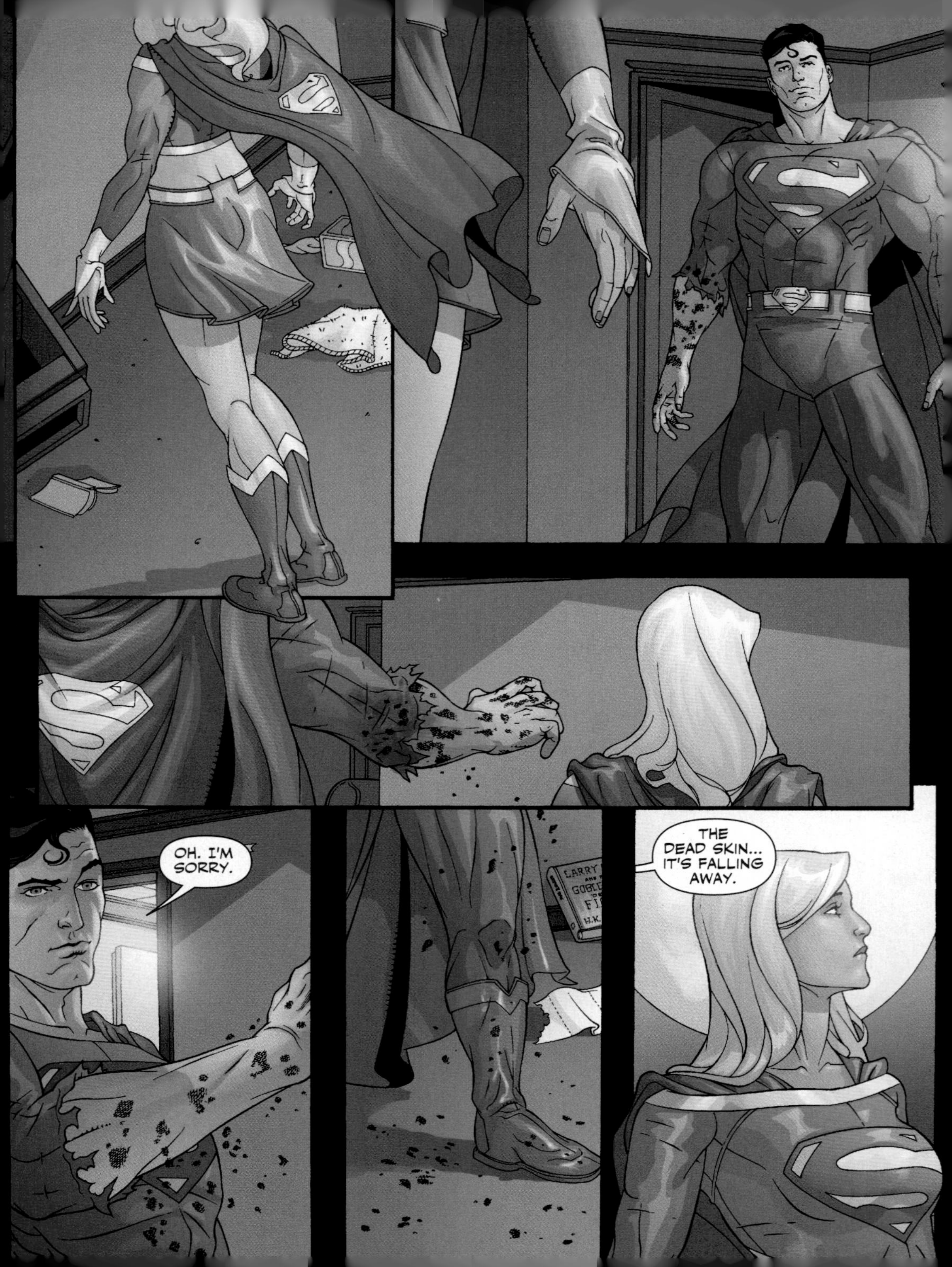
OH. I'M SORRY.
THE DEAD SKIN... IT'S FALLING AWAY.

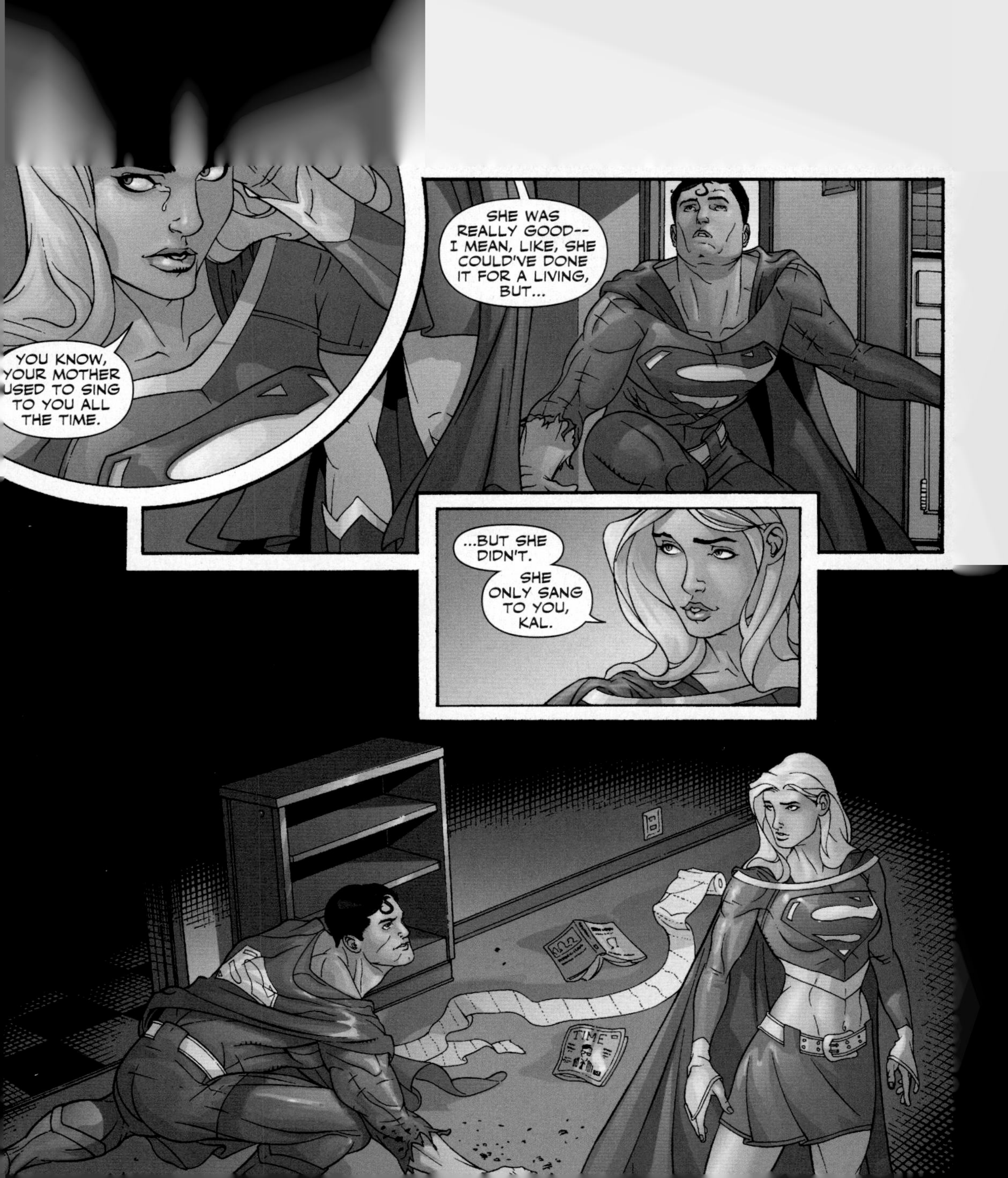
YOU KNOW, YOUR MOTHER USED TO SING TO YOU ALL THE TIME.
SHE WAS REALLY GOOD-- I MEAN, LIKE, SHE COULD'VE DONE IT FOR A LIVING, BUT...
...BUT SHE DIDN'T.
SHE ONLY SANG TO YOU, KAL.
TIME

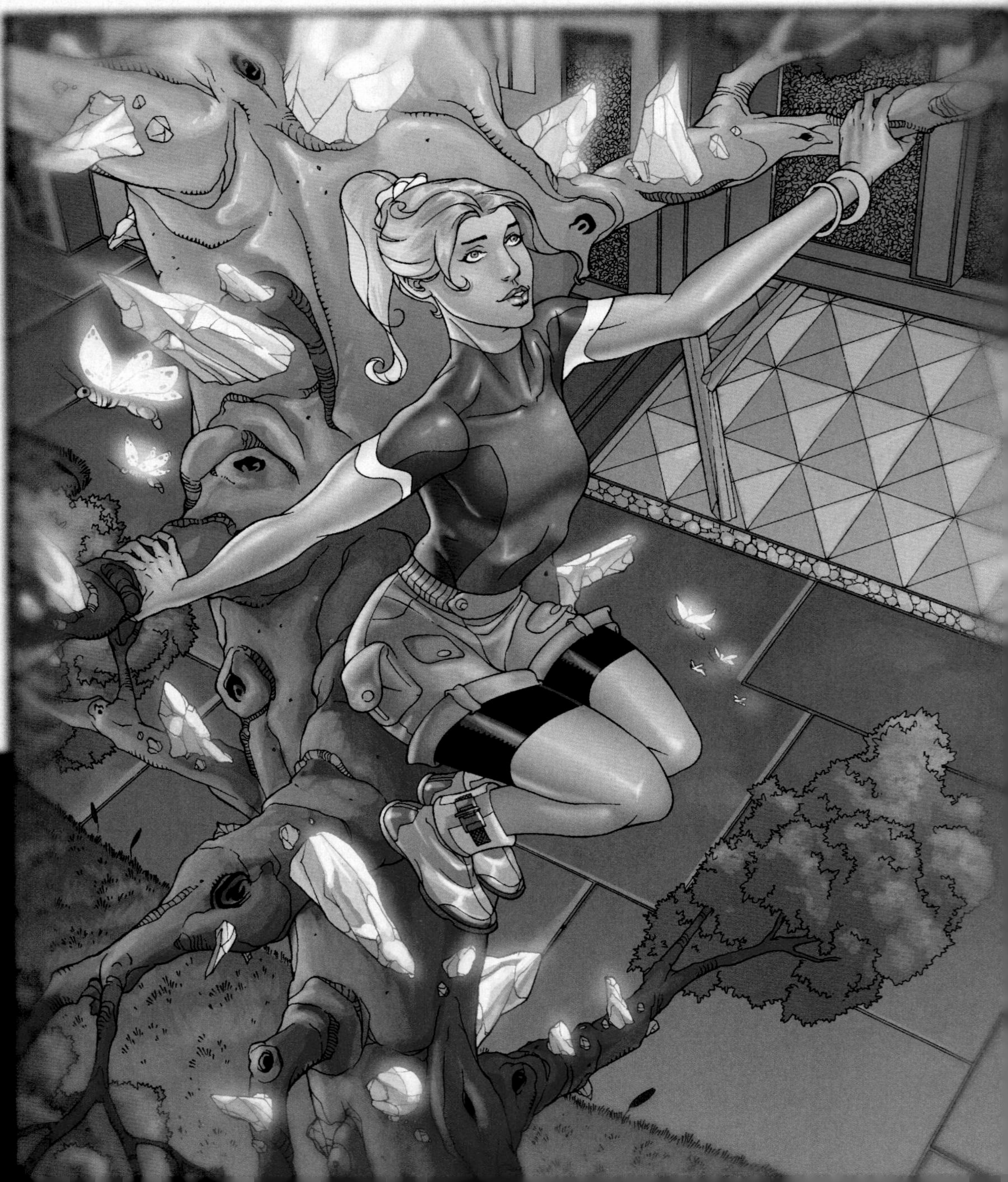

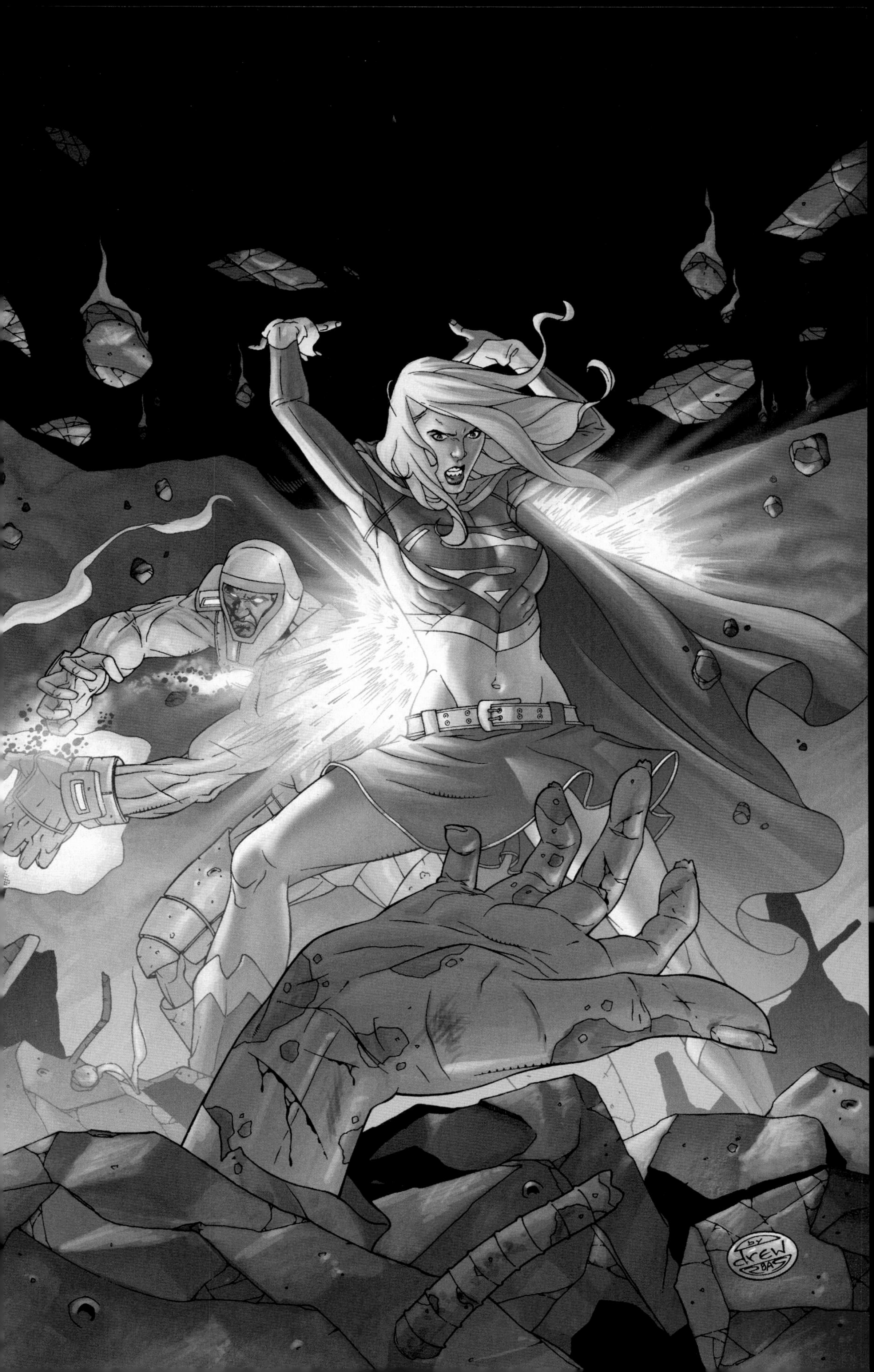
by drew

BOOM

KELLEY PUCKETT WRITER
DREW JOHNSON LEE FERGUSON PENCILS
RAY SNYDER INKS

YOU ALWAYS STOOD BY ME, NO MATTER WHAT, KARA. FRIENDS FOREVER!

MY CEILING CRUSHED MY SKULL WHILE I SLEPT.

YOU WANTED TO KISS ME THAT TIME BY THE SPIRE. I WANTED TO KISS YOU, TOO.

I MADE IT THROUGH THE QUAKES AND WAS FLASH-ROASTED BY A STEAM GEYSER.

WE LOVE YOU, DEAR. WE ALWAYS WILL.

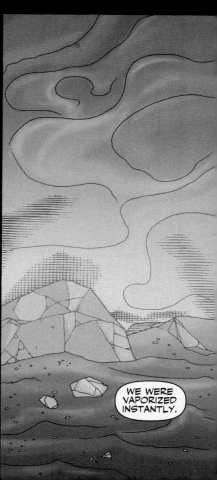

WE WERE VAPORIZED INSTANTLY.

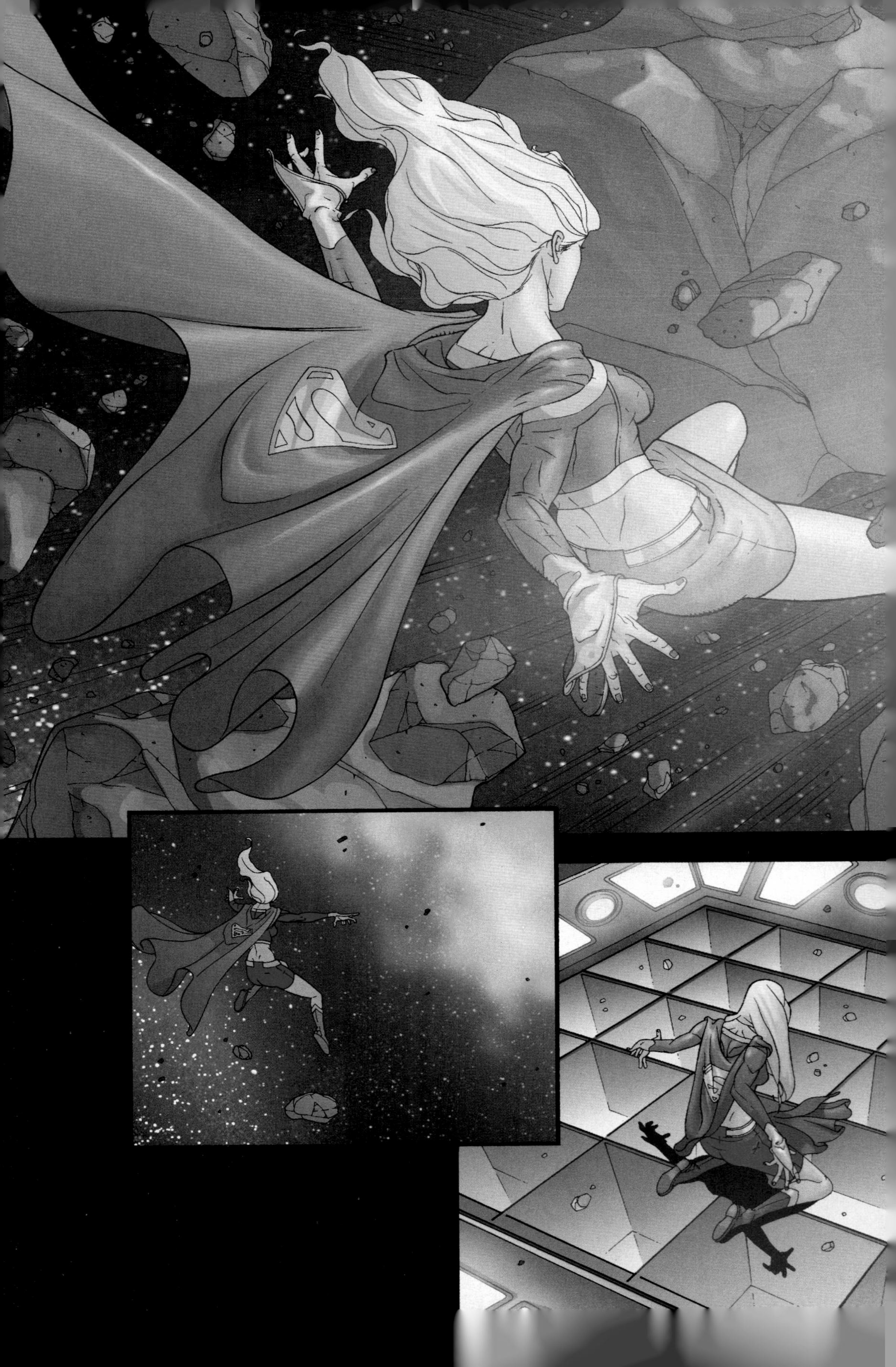

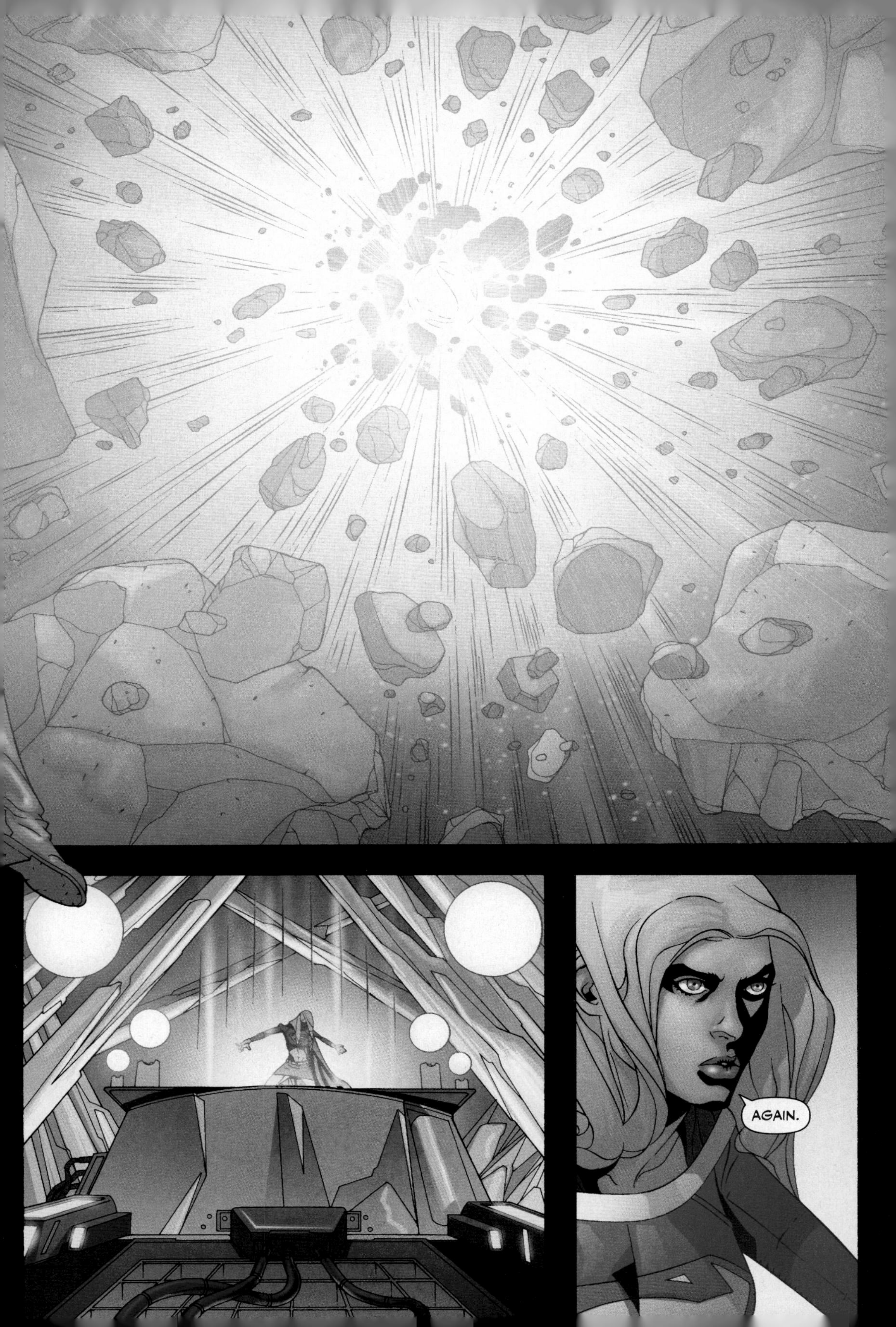
AGAIN.

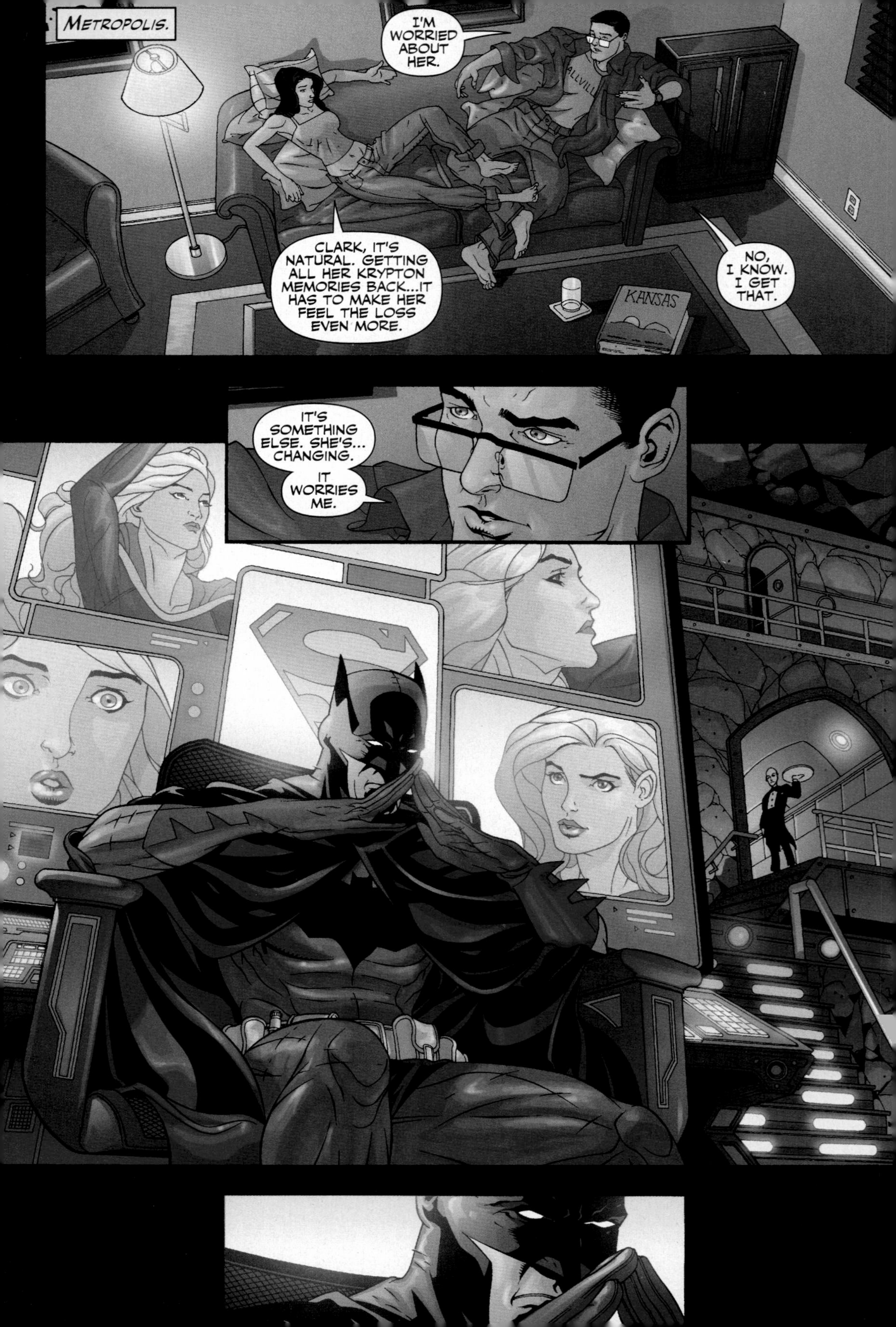
METROPOLIS.
I'M WORRIED ABOUT HER.
CLARK, IT'S NATURAL. GETTING ALL HER KRYPTON MEMORIES BACK...IT HAS TO MAKE HER FEEL THE LOSS EVEN MORE.
NO, I KNOW. I GET THAT.
KANSAS
IT'S SOMETHING ELSE. SHE'S... CHANGING.
IT WORRIES ME.

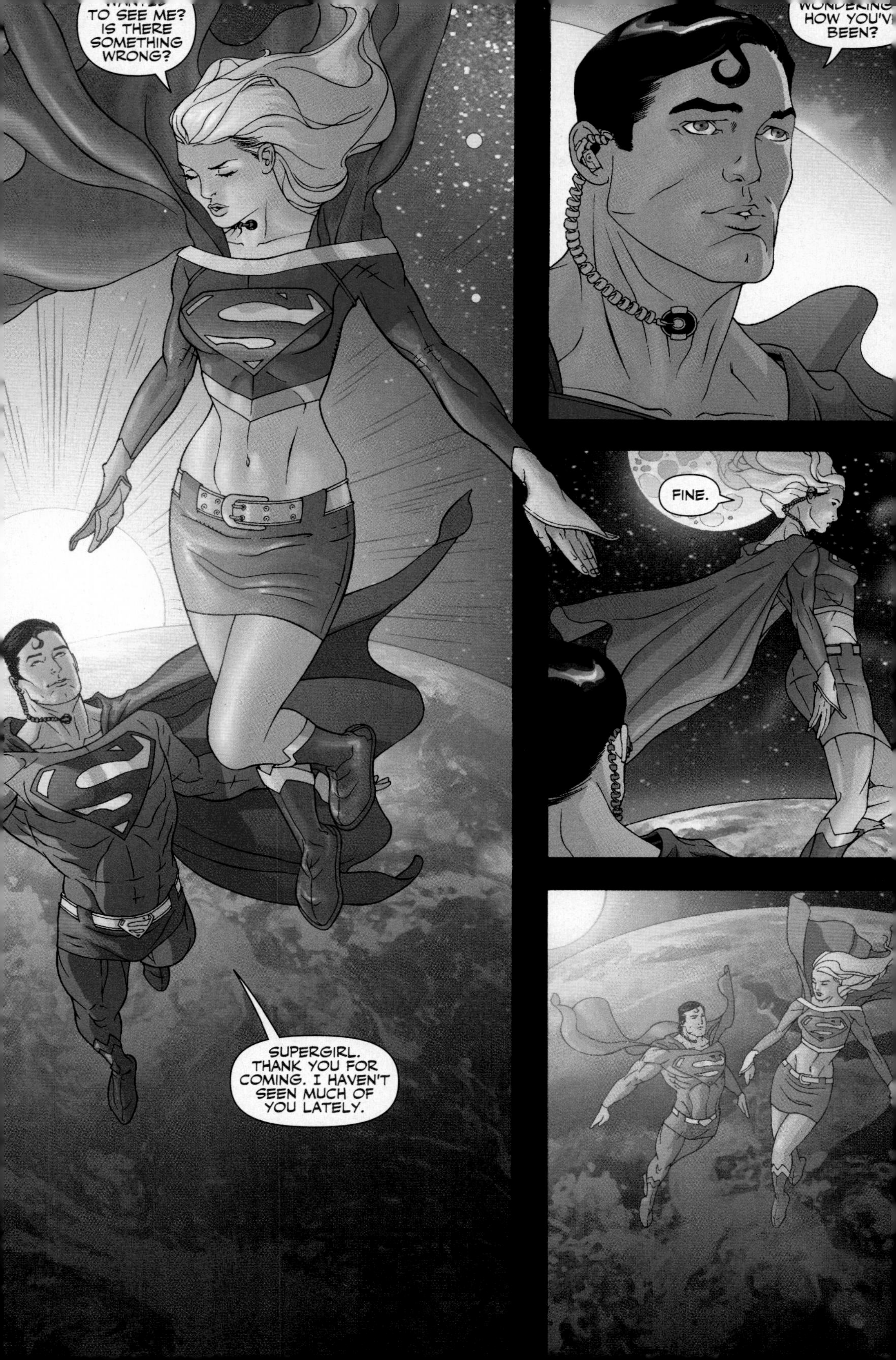
SUPERGIRL. THANK YOU FOR COMING. I HAVEN'T SEEN MUCH OF YOU LATELY.
TO SEE ME? IS THERE SOMETHING WRONG?
HOW YOU'V BEEN?
FINE.

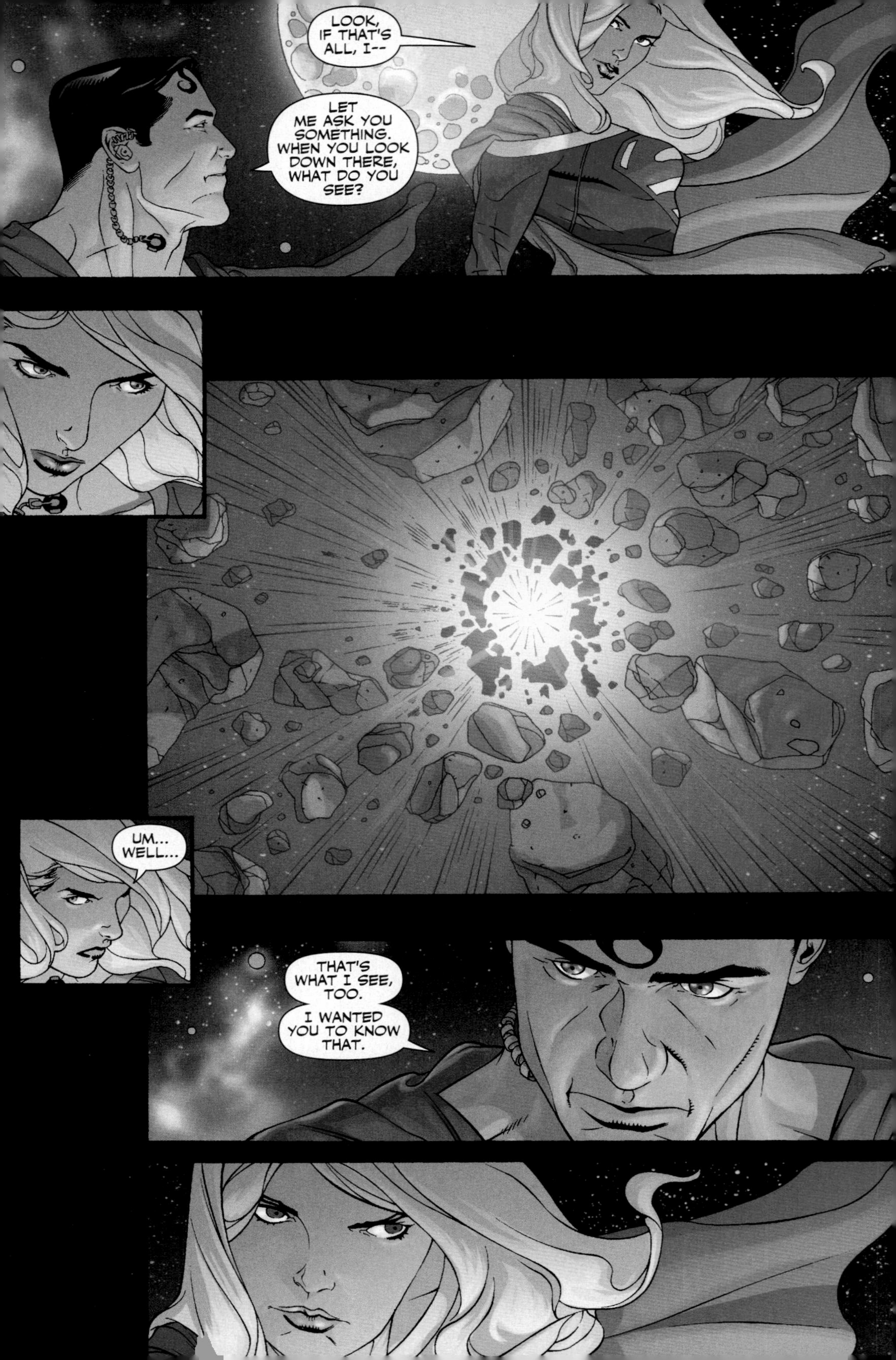
LOOK, IF THAT'S ALL, I--
LET ME ASK YOU SOMETHING. WHEN YOU LOOK DOWN THERE, WHAT DO YOU SEE?
UM... WELL...
THAT'S WHAT I SEE, TOO.
I WANTED YOU TO KNOW THAT.

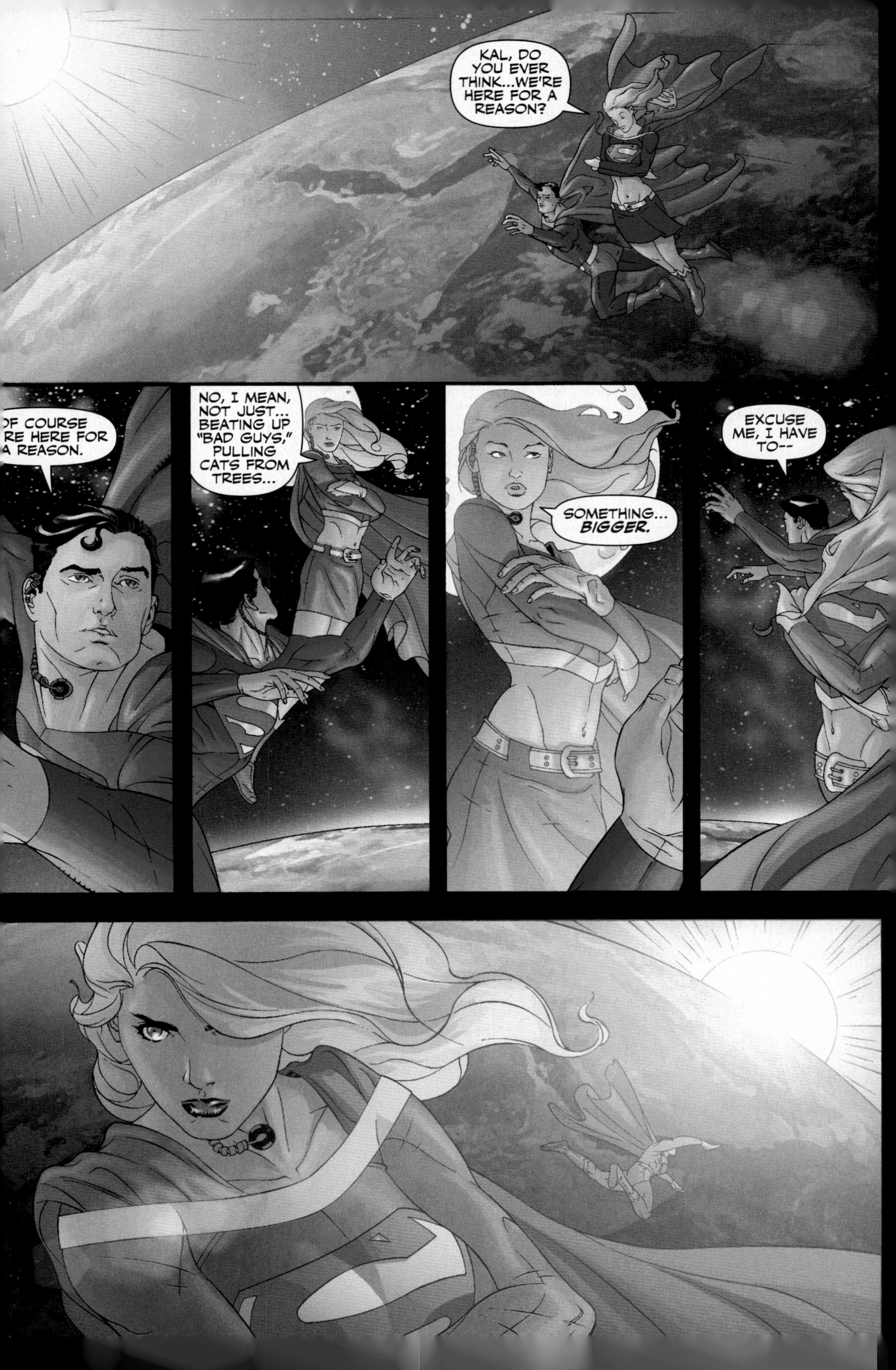
KAL, DO YOU EVER THINK...WE'RE HERE FOR A REASON?
OF COURSE RE HERE FOR A REASON.
NO, I MEAN, NOT JUST... BEATING UP "BAD GUYS," PULLING CATS FROM TREES...
SOMETHING... BIGGER.
EXCUSE ME, I HAVE TO--

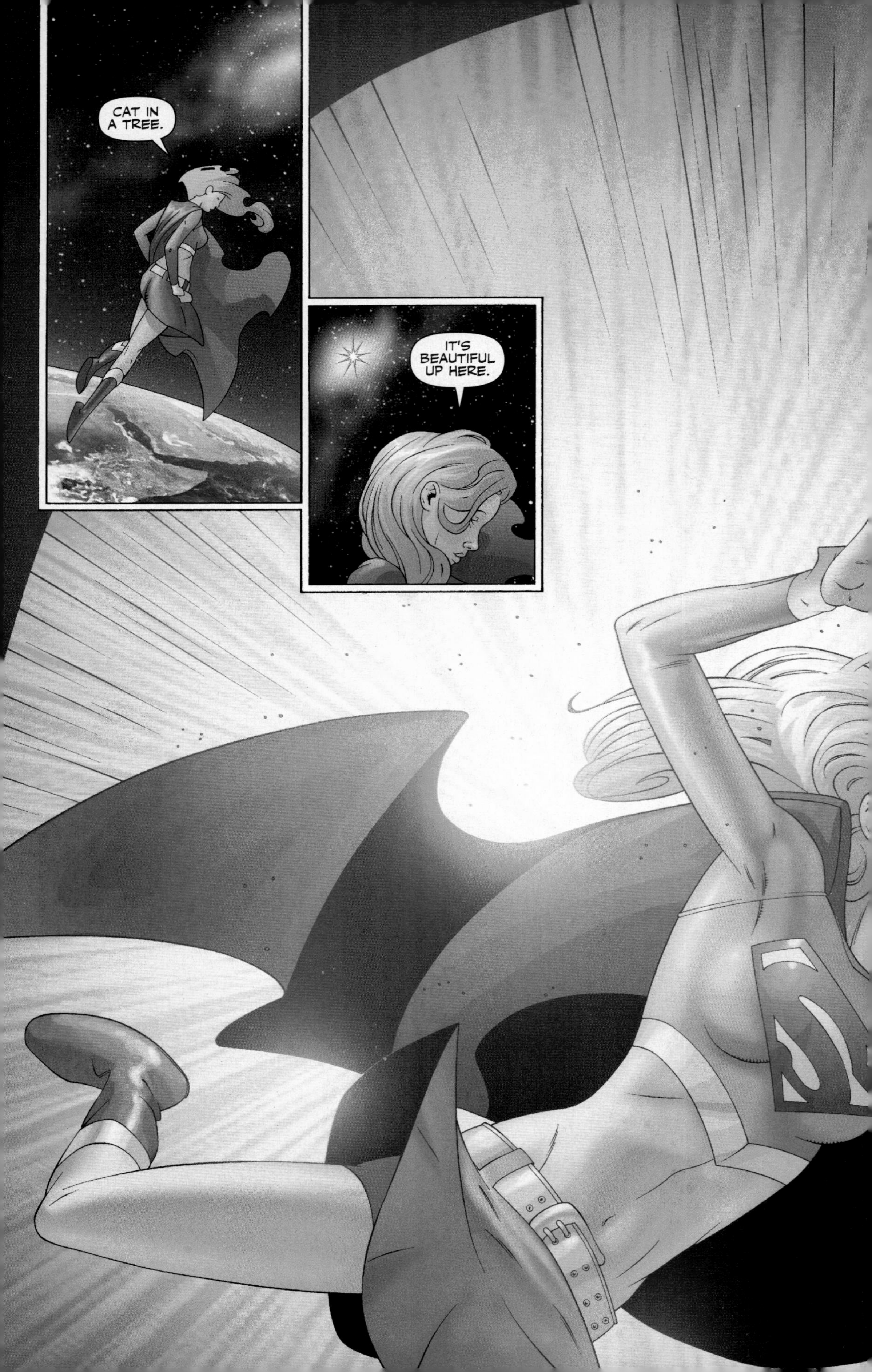
CAT IN A TREE.
IT'S BEAUTIFUL UP HERE.

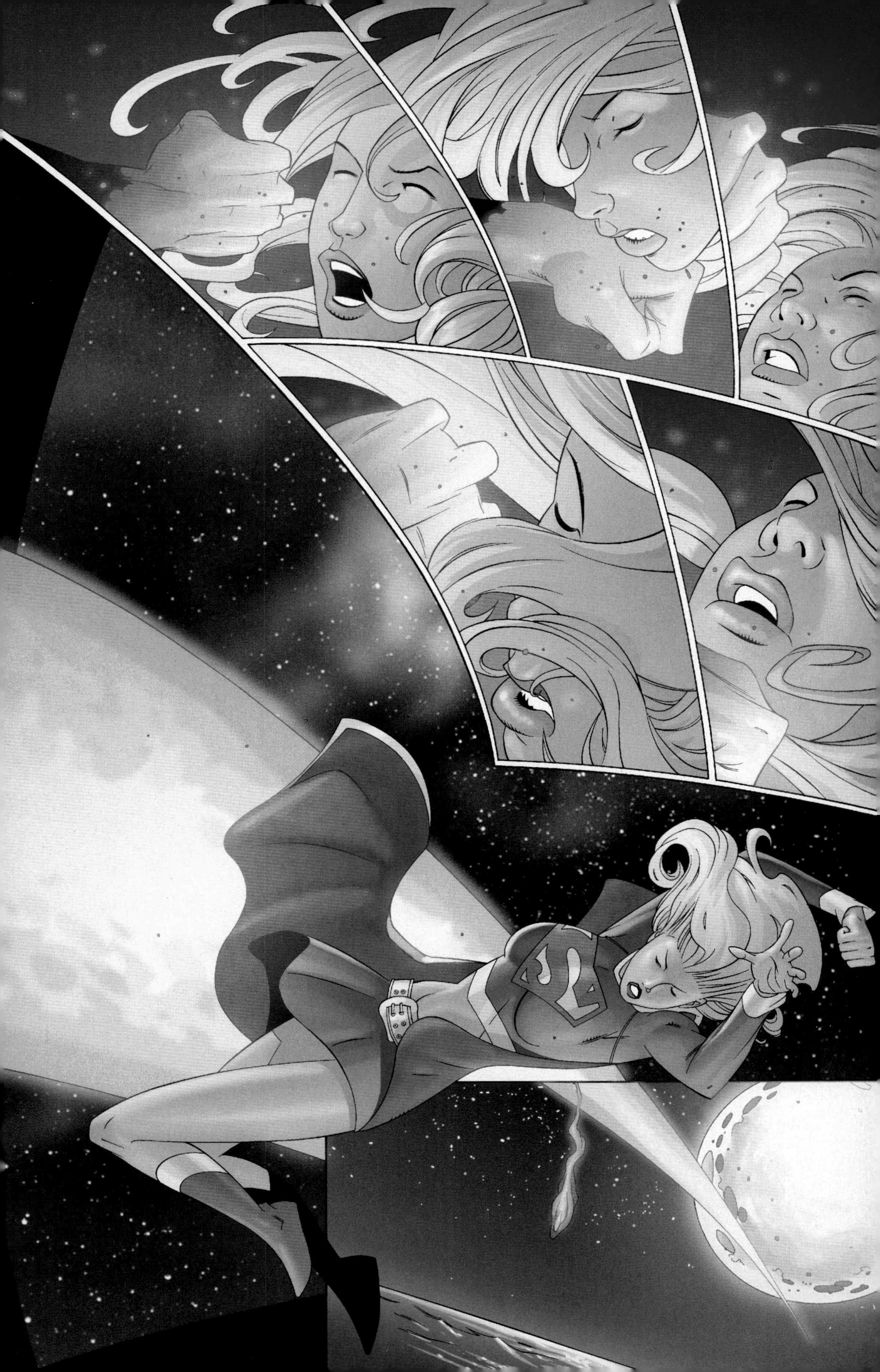

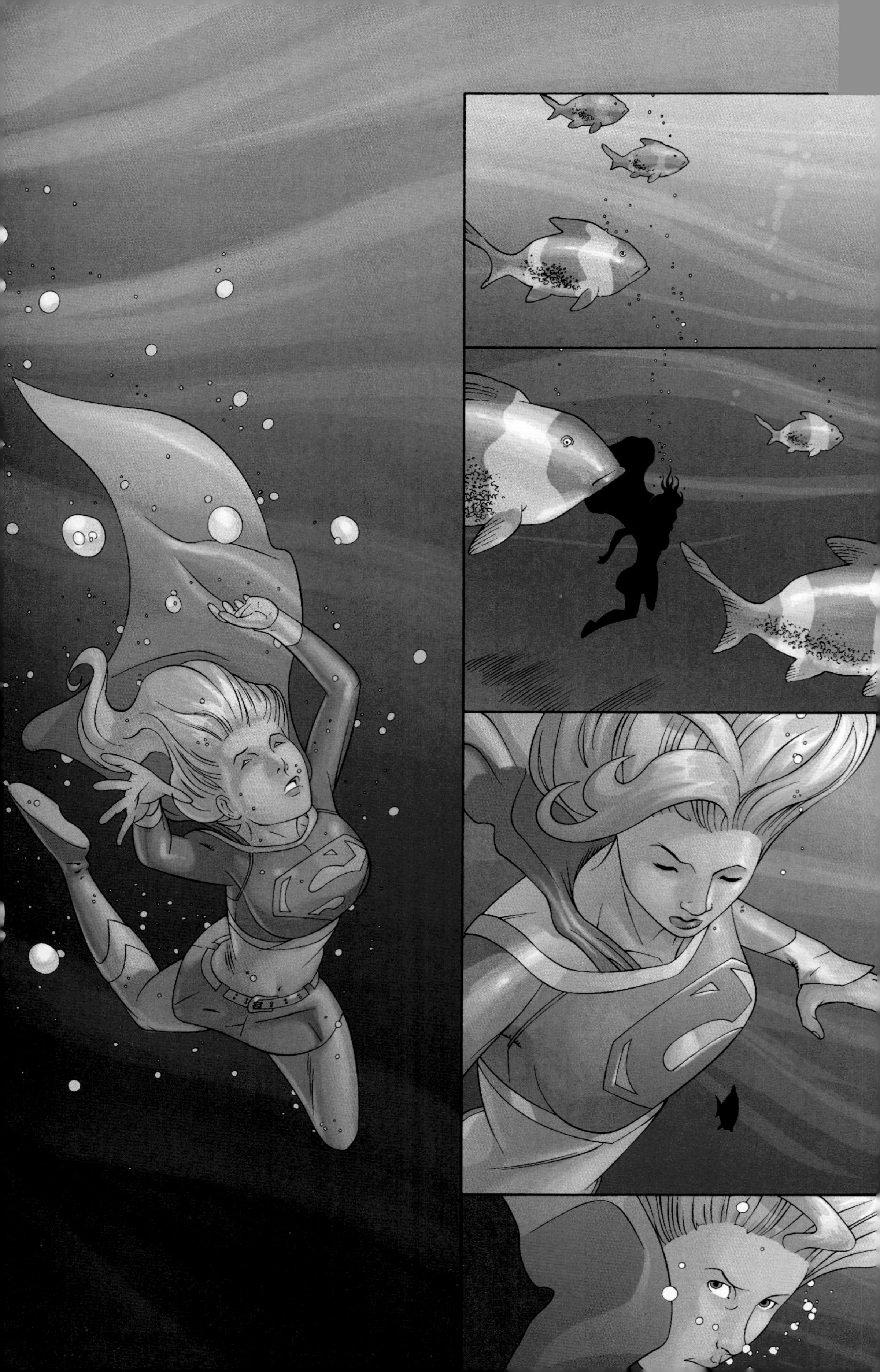

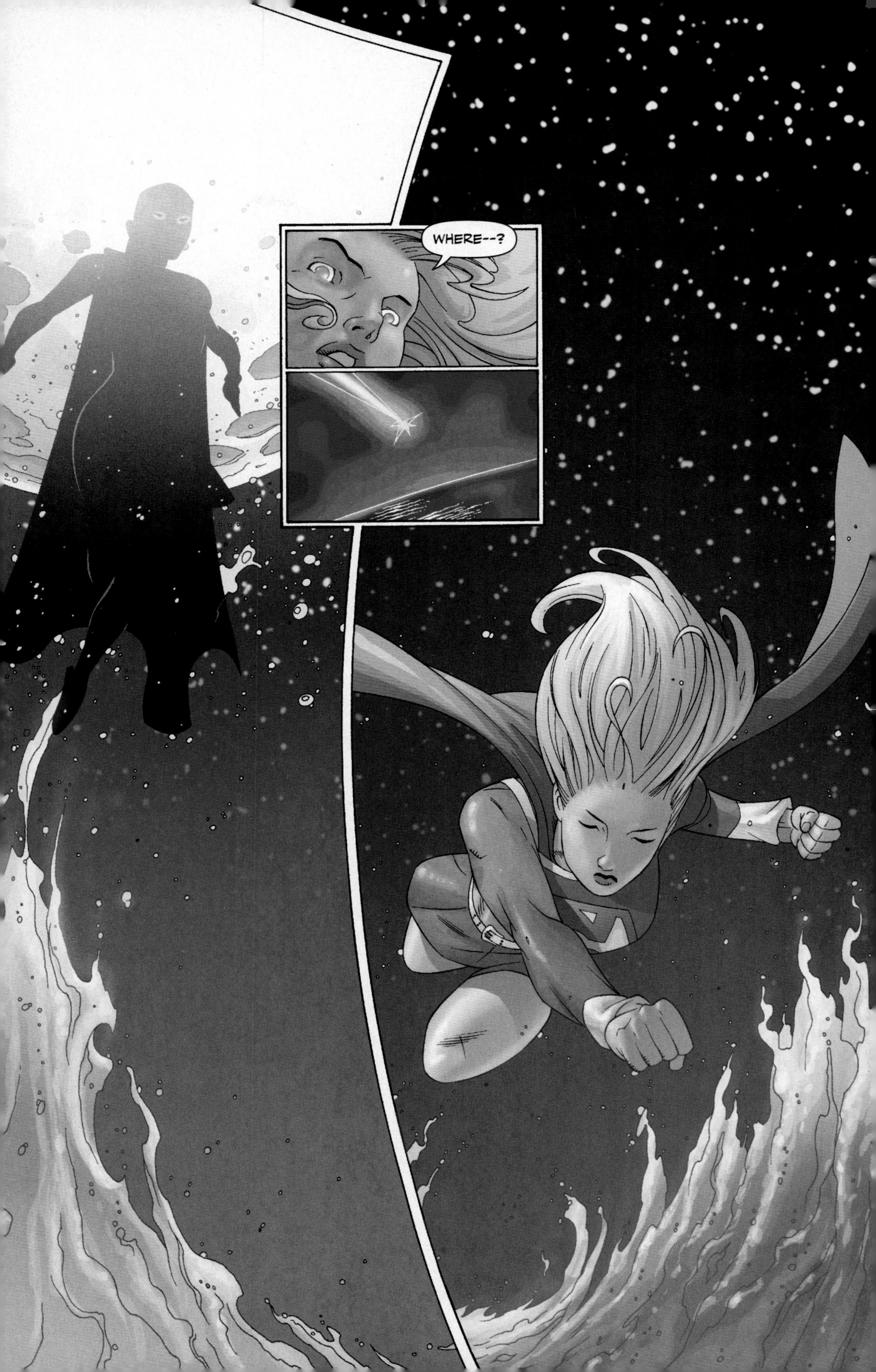
WHERE--?

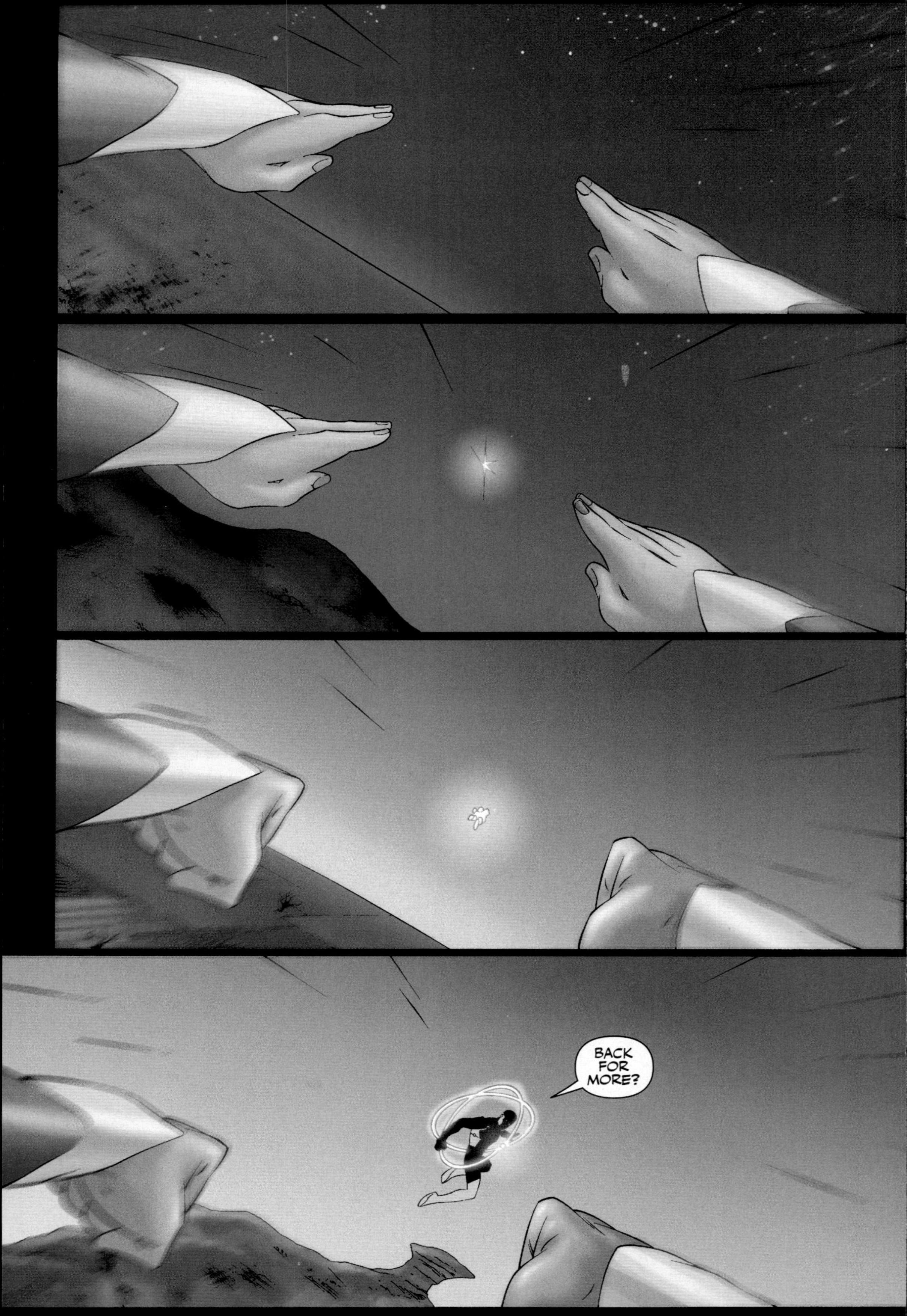
BACK FOR MORE?

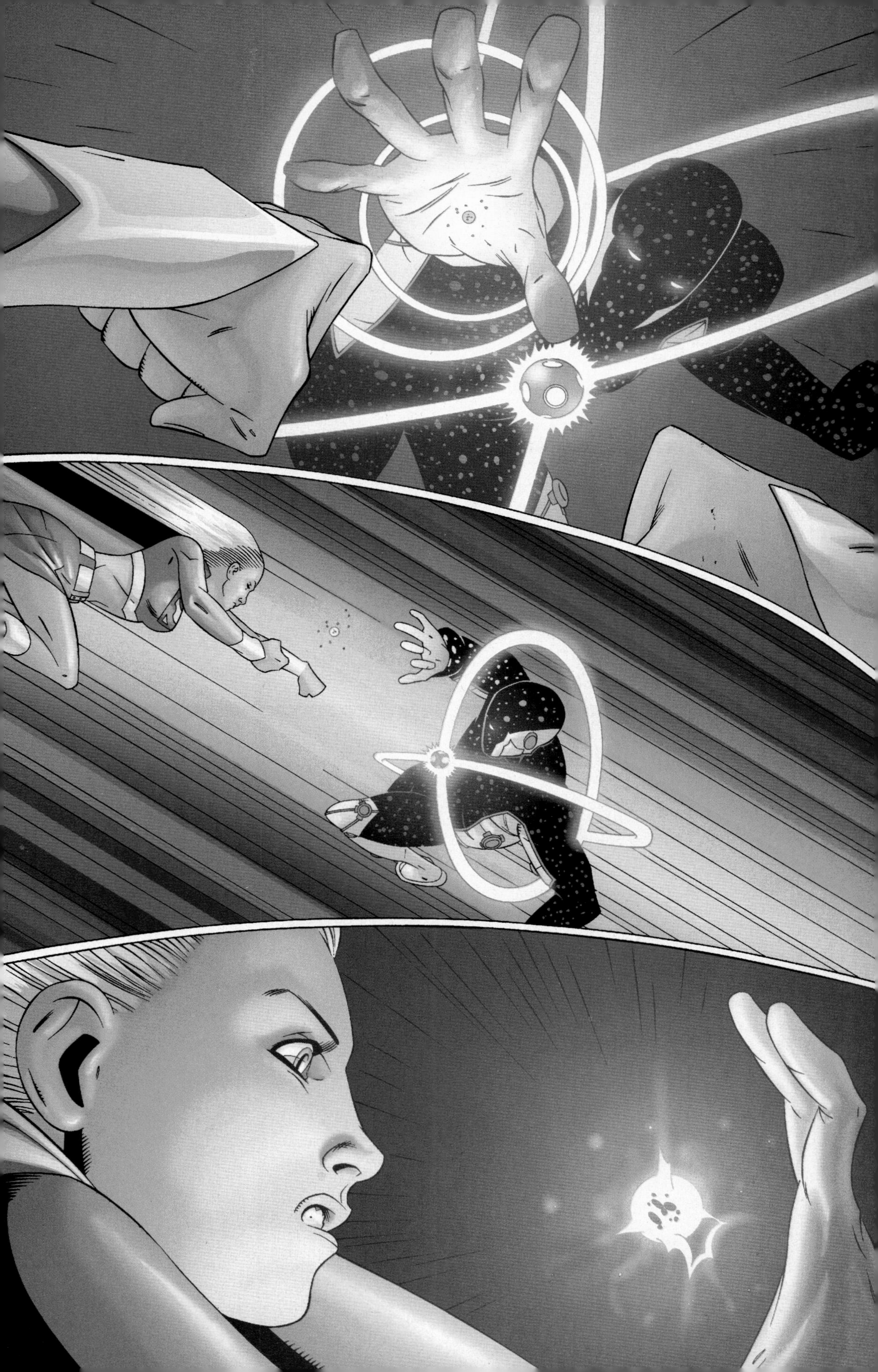

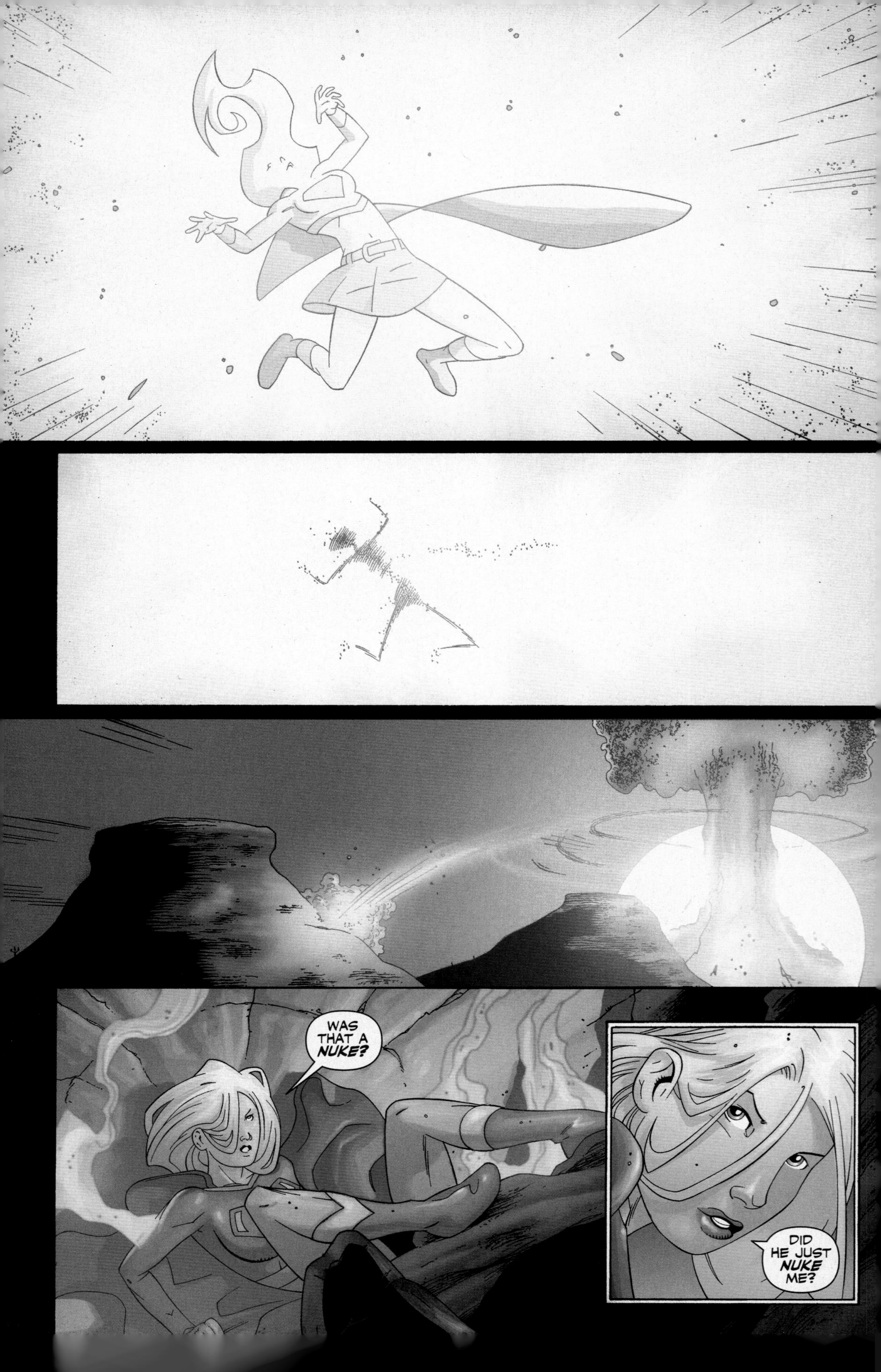
WAS THAT A NUKE?
DID HE JUST NUKE ME?

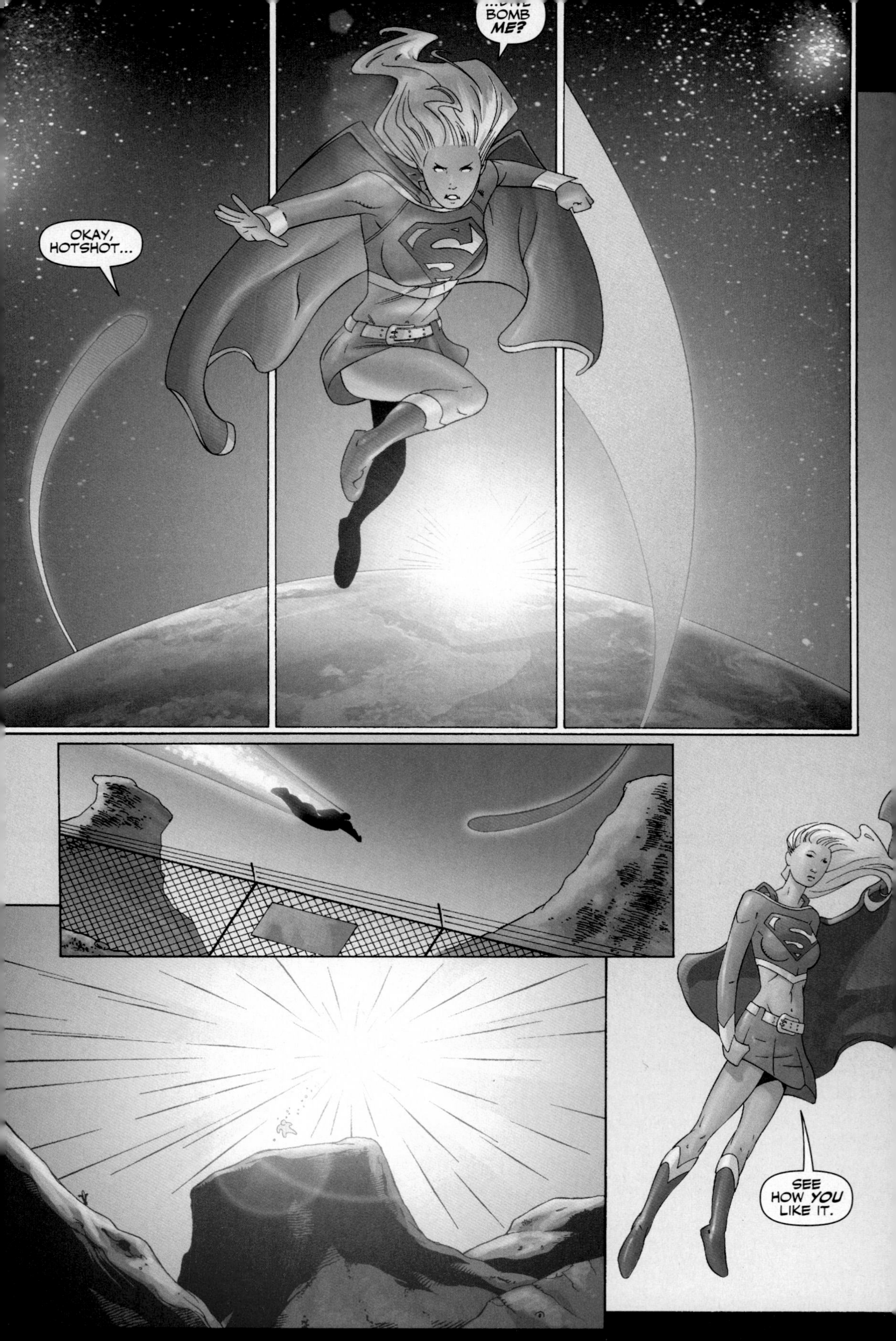
OKAY, HOTSHOT...
...DIVE BOMB ME?
SEE HOW YOU LIKE IT.

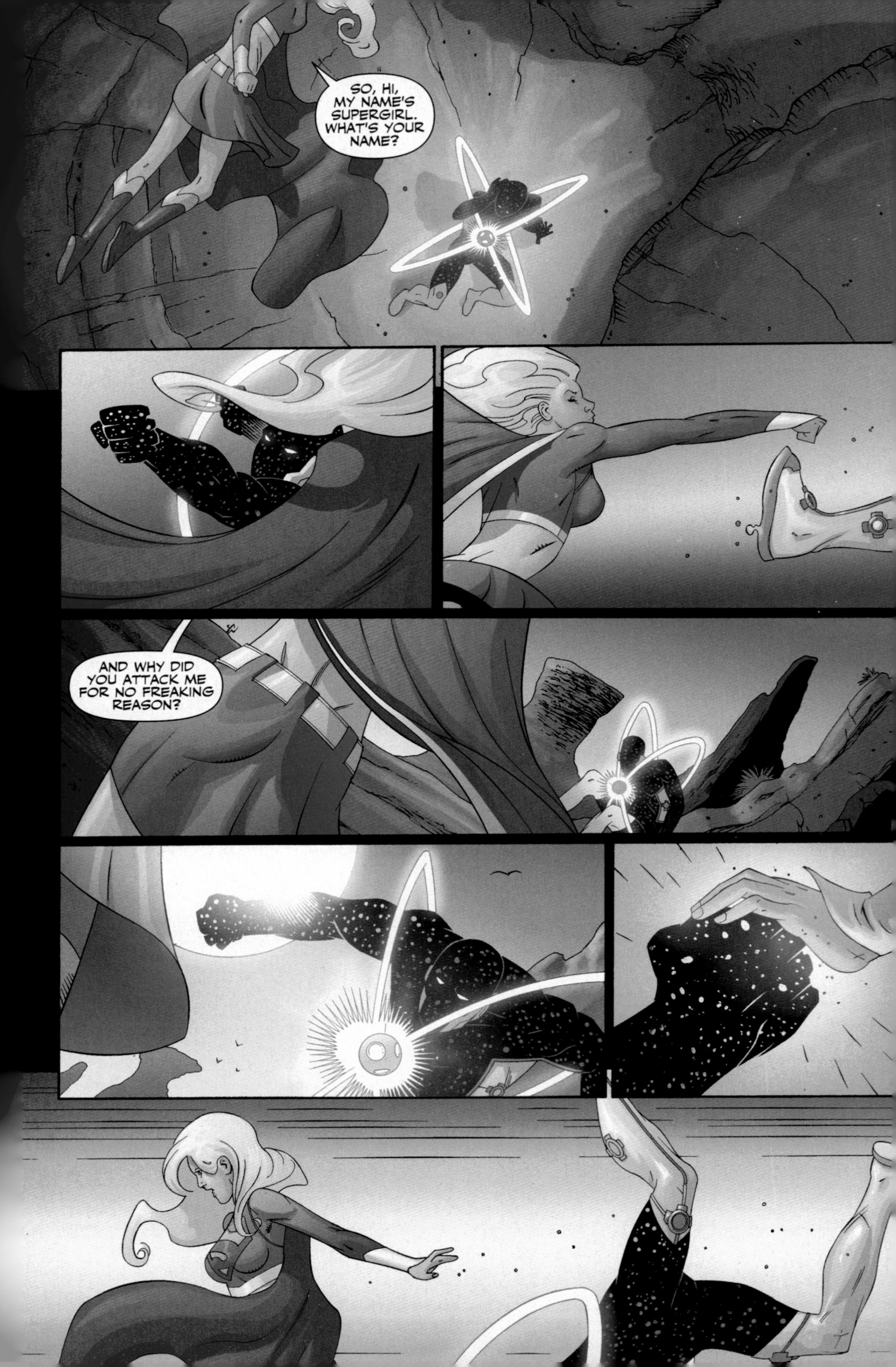
SO, HI, MY NAME'S SUPERGIRL. WHAT'S YOUR NAME?
AND WHY DID YOU ATTACK ME FOR NO FREAKING REASON?

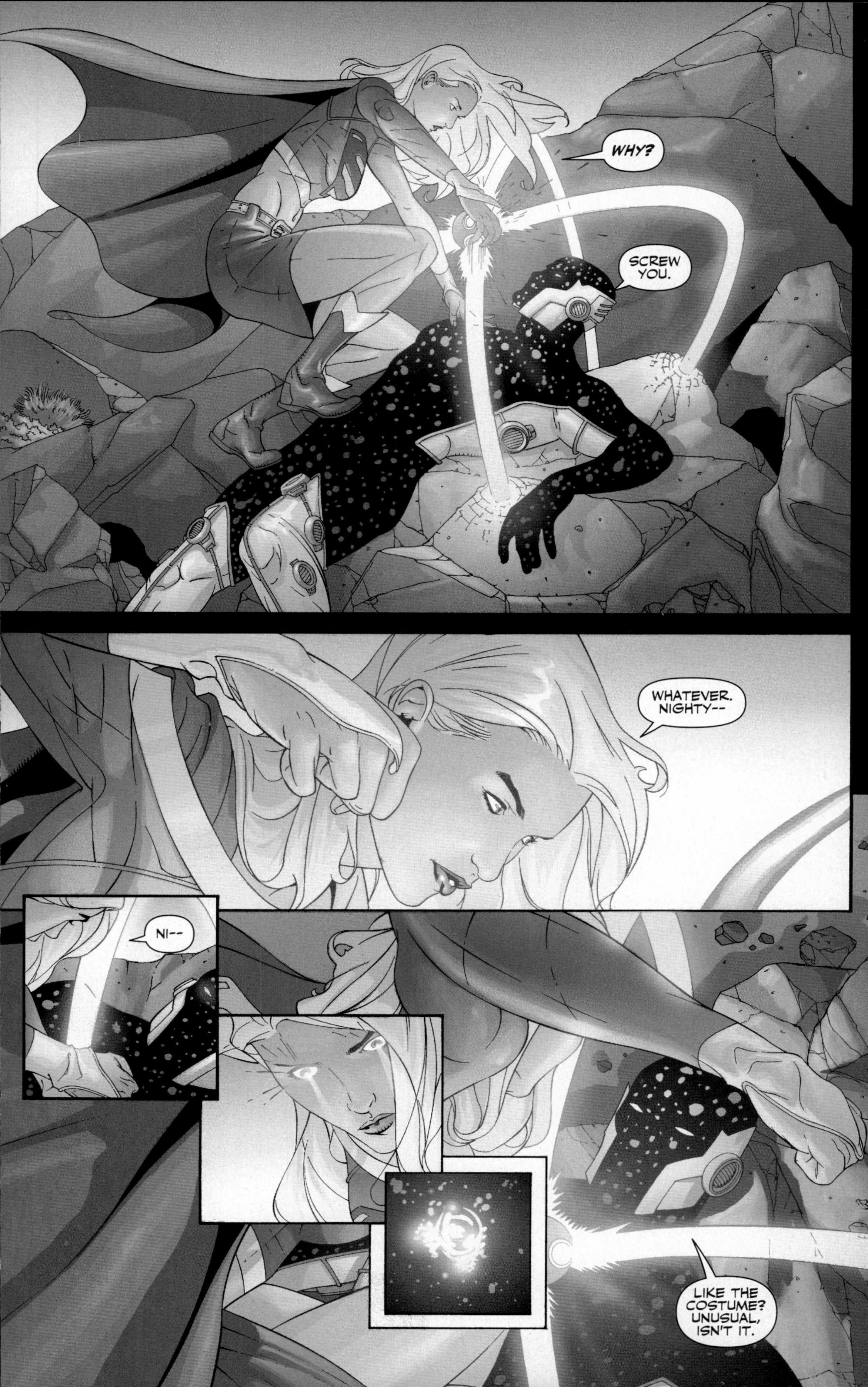
WHY?
SCREW YOU.
WHATEVER. NIGHTY--
NI--
LIKE THE COSTUME? UNUSUAL, ISN'T IT.

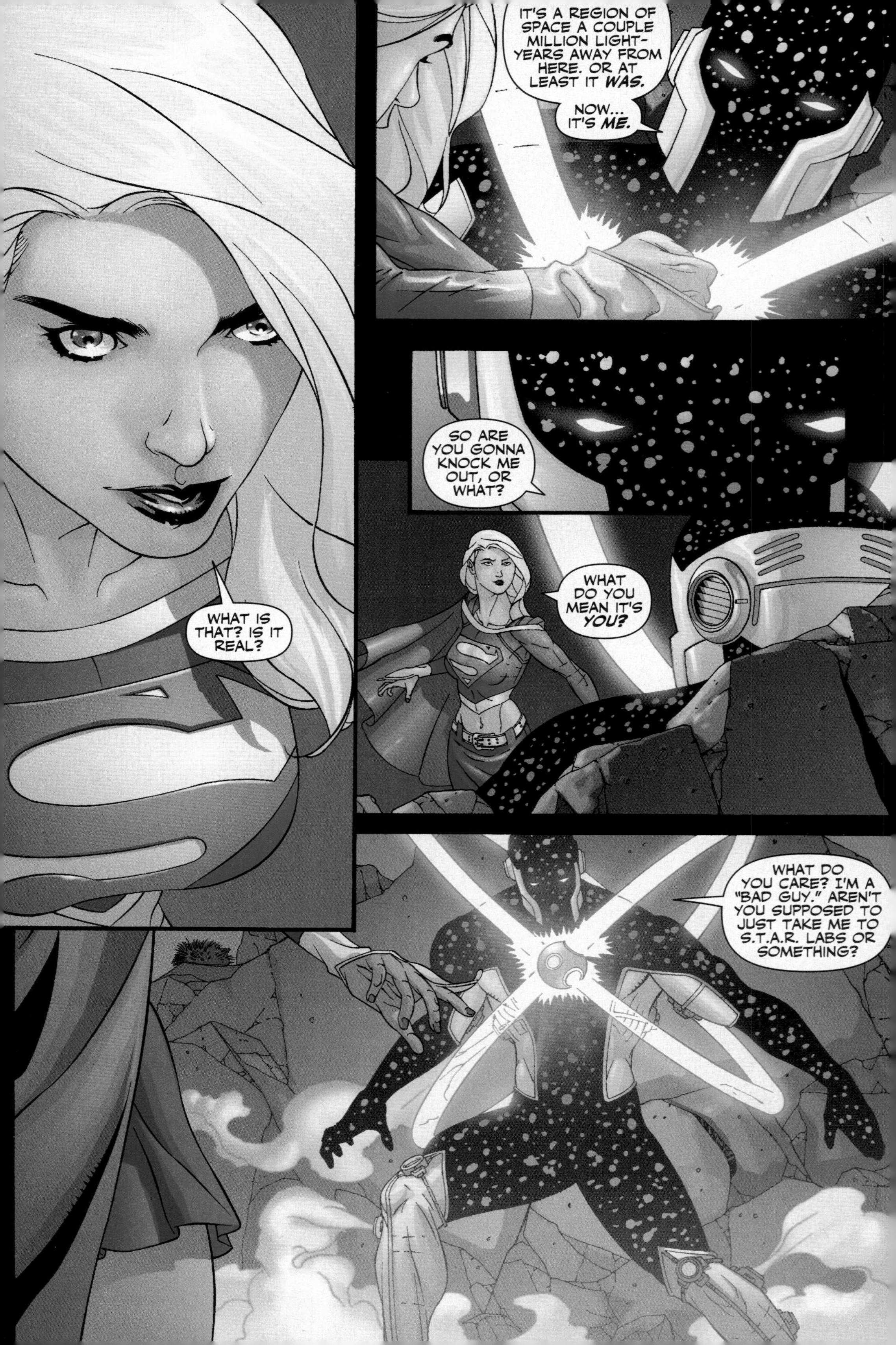

IT'S A REGION OF SPACE A COUPLE MILLION LIGHT-YEARS AWAY FROM HERE. OR AT LEAST IT *WAS.*
NOW... IT'S *ME.*
WHAT IS THAT? IS IT REAL?
SO ARE YOU GONNA KNOCK ME OUT, OR WHAT?
WHAT DO YOU MEAN IT'S *YOU?*
WHAT DO YOU CARE? I'M A "BAD GUY." AREN'T YOU SUPPOSED TO JUST TAKE ME TO S.T.A.R. LABS OR SOMETHING?

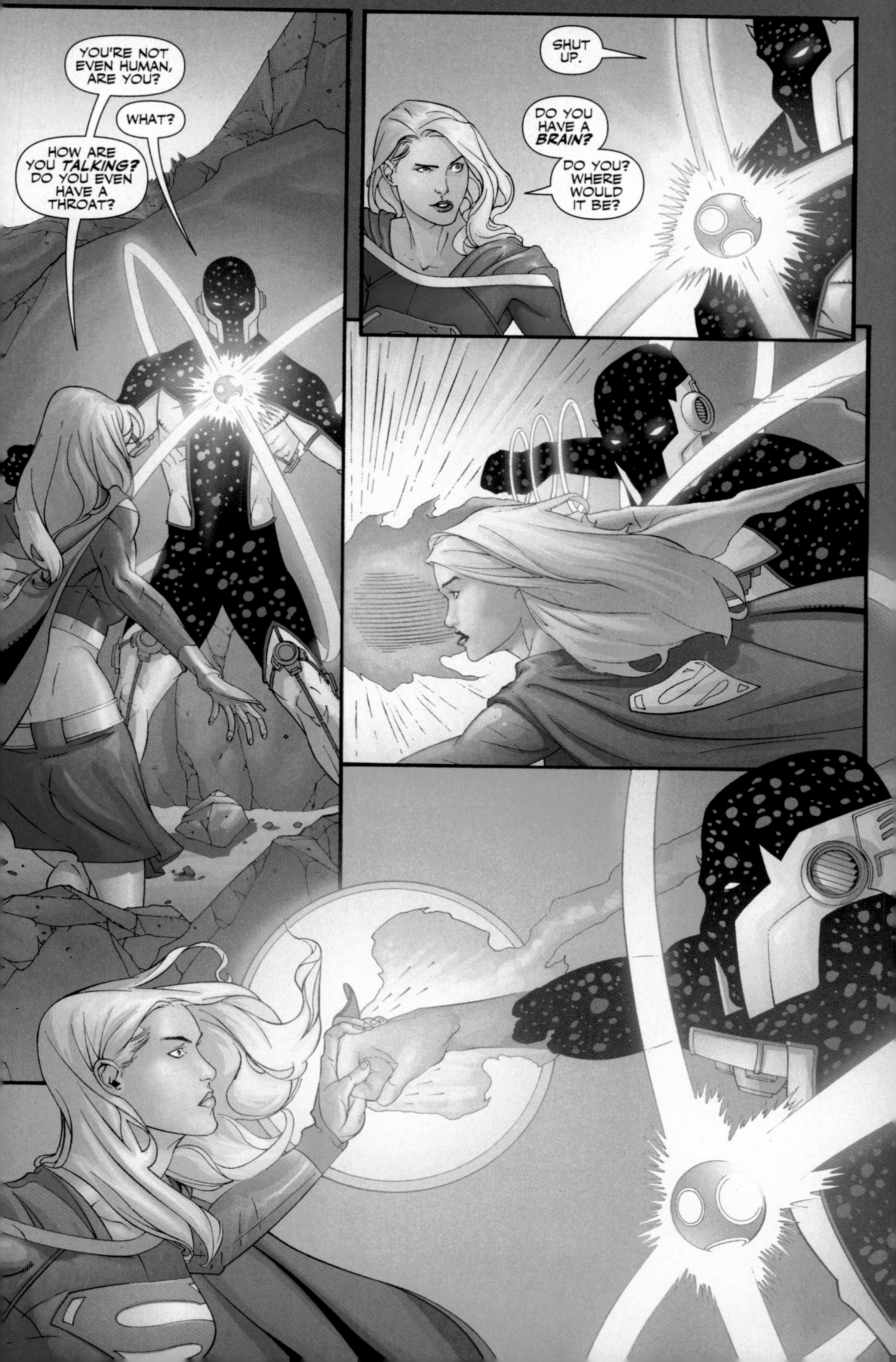
YOU'RE NOT EVEN HUMAN, ARE YOU?
WHAT?
HOW ARE YOU *TALKING?* DO YOU EVEN HAVE A THROAT?
SHUT UP.
DO YOU HAVE A *BRAIN?*
DO YOU? WHERE WOULD IT BE?

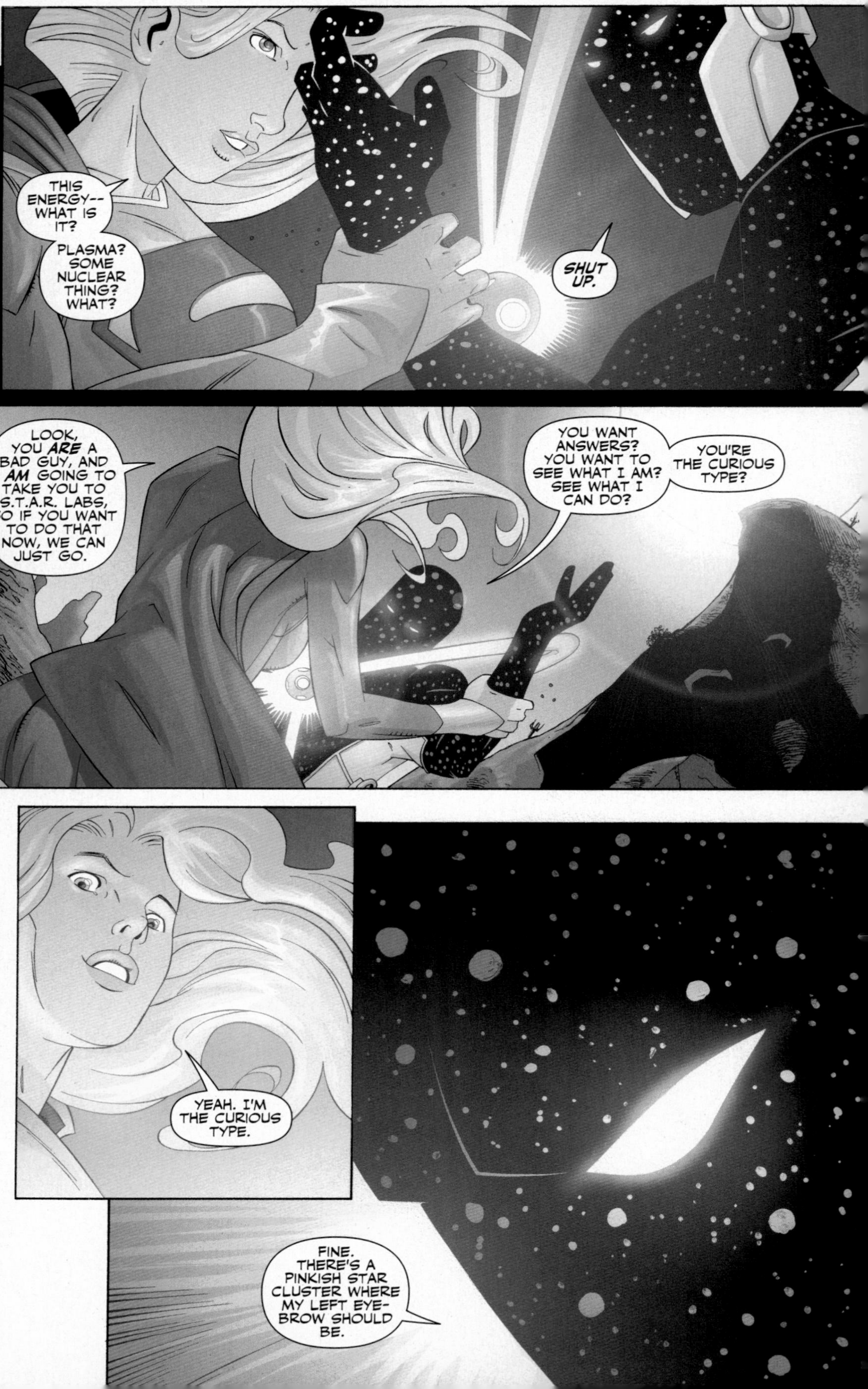
THIS ENERGY-- WHAT IS IT?
PLASMA? SOME NUCLEAR THING? WHAT?
SHUT UP.
LOOK, YOU ARE A BAD GUY, AND I AM GOING TO TAKE YOU TO S.T.A.R. LABS, SO IF YOU WANT TO DO THAT NOW, WE CAN JUST GO.
YOU WANT ANSWERS? YOU WANT TO SEE WHAT I AM? SEE WHAT I CAN DO?
YOU'RE THE CURIOUS TYPE?
YEAH. I'M THE CURIOUS TYPE.
FINE. THERE'S A PINKISH STAR CLUSTER WHERE MY LEFT EYE-BROW SHOULD BE.

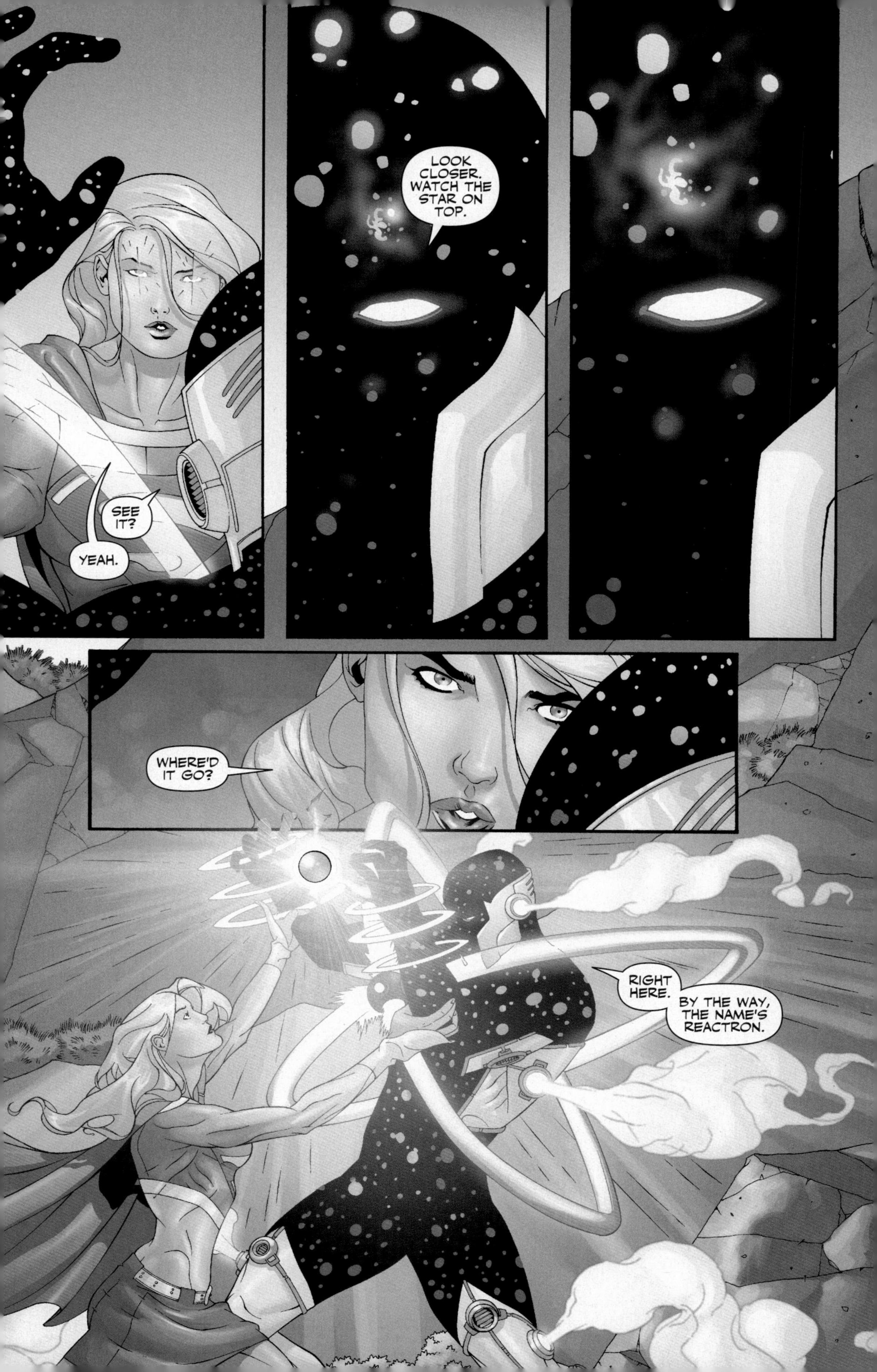
SEE IT?
YEAH.
LOOK CLOSER. WATCH THE STAR ON TOP.
WHERE'D IT GO?
RIGHT HERE.
BY THE WAY, THE NAME'S REACTRON.

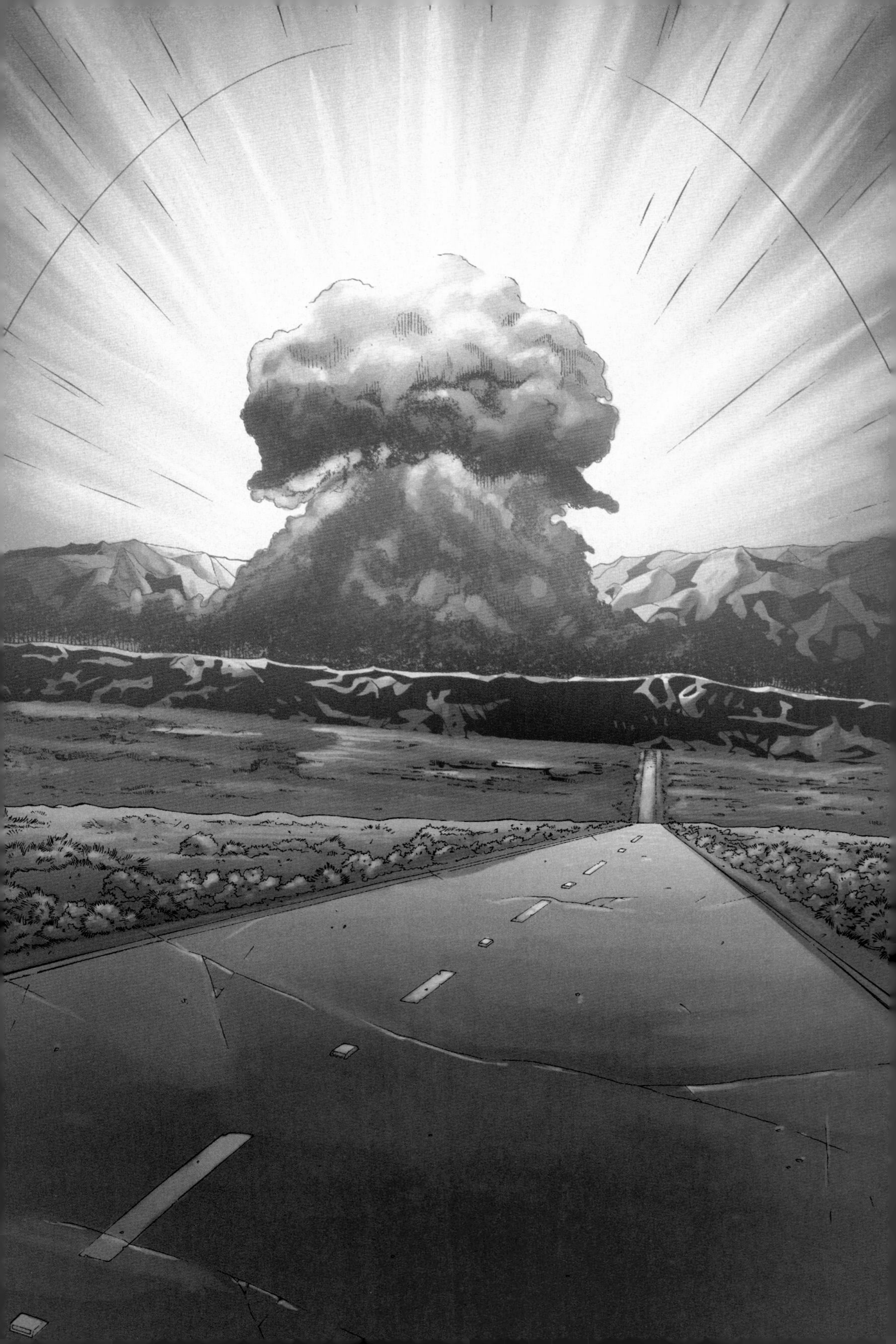

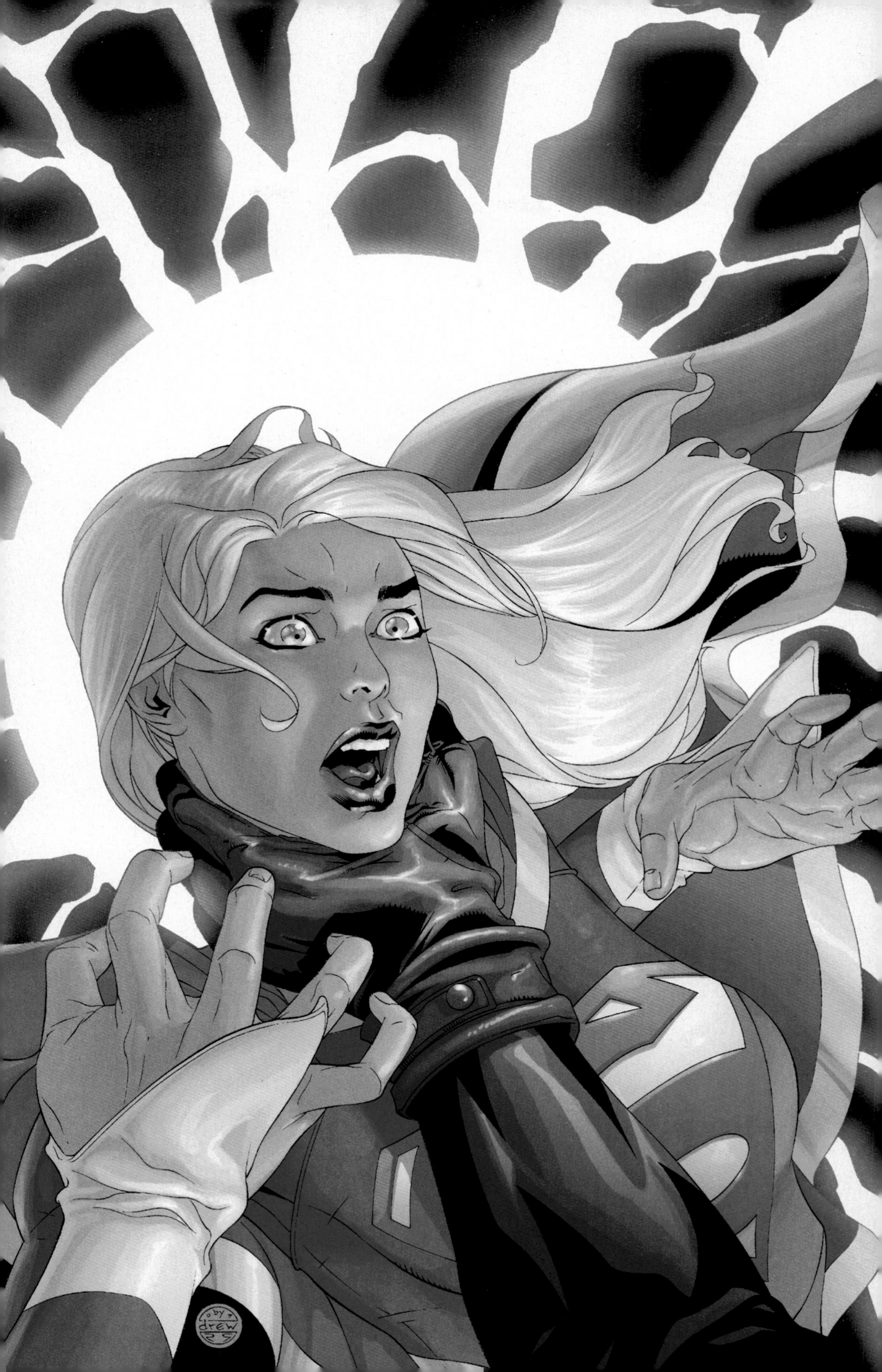

BREAK POINT

KELLEY PUCKETT WRITER

DREW JOHNSON LEE FERGUSON PENCILS

RAY SNYDER MARC DEERING INKS

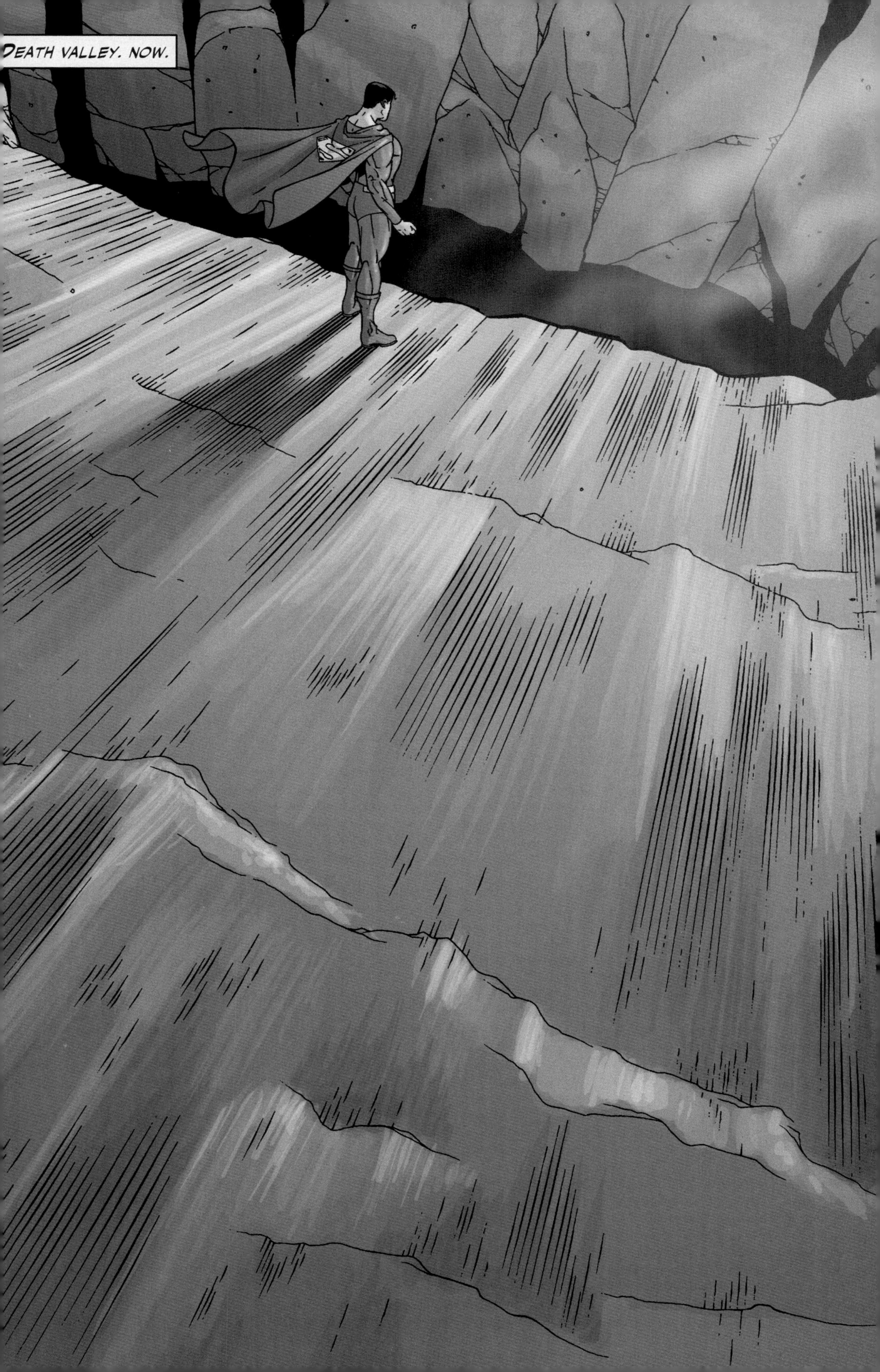
DEATH VALLEY. NOW.

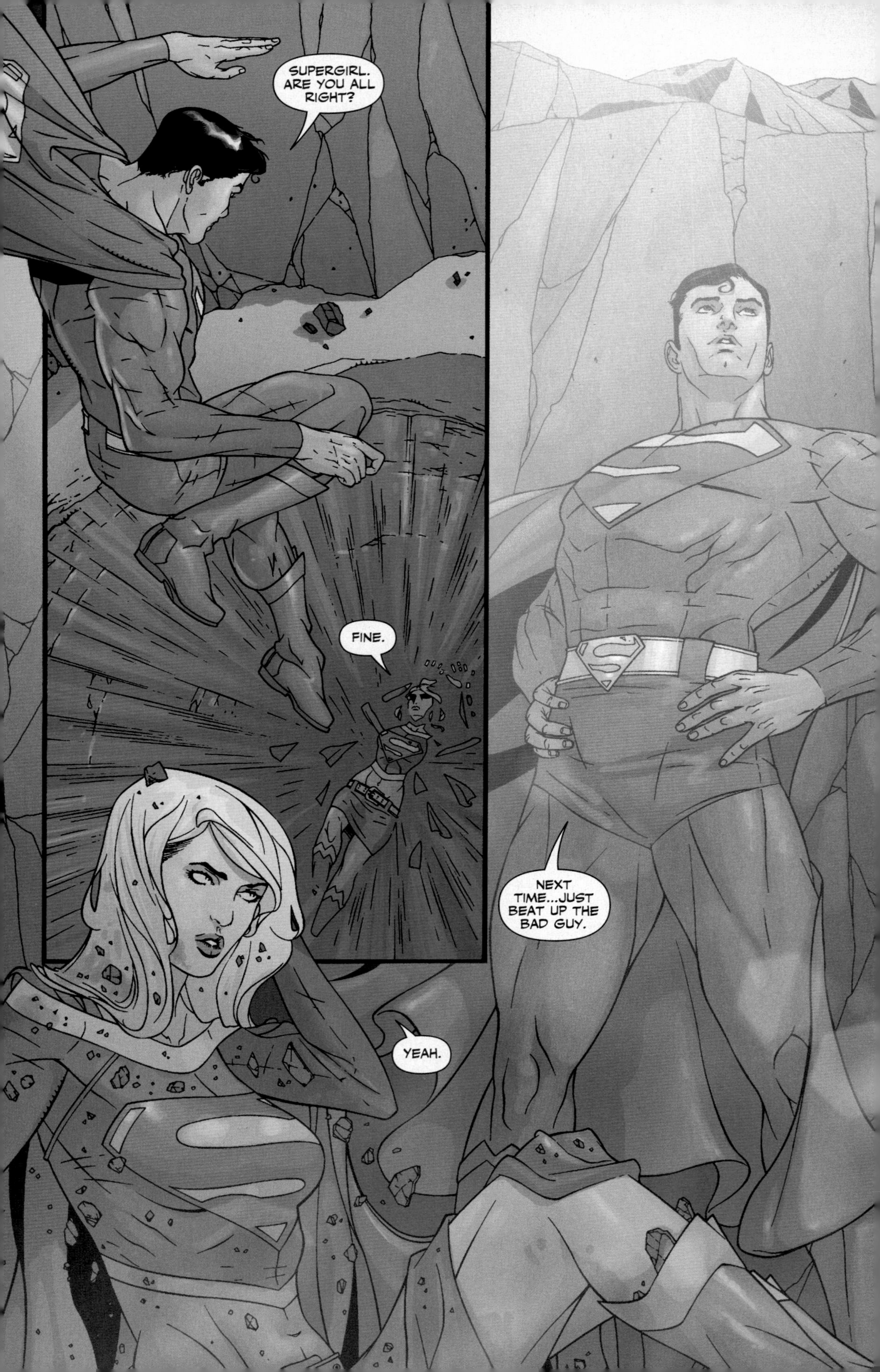
SUPERGIRL. ARE YOU ALL RIGHT?
FINE.
YEAH.
NEXT TIME...JUST BEAT UP THE BAD GUY.

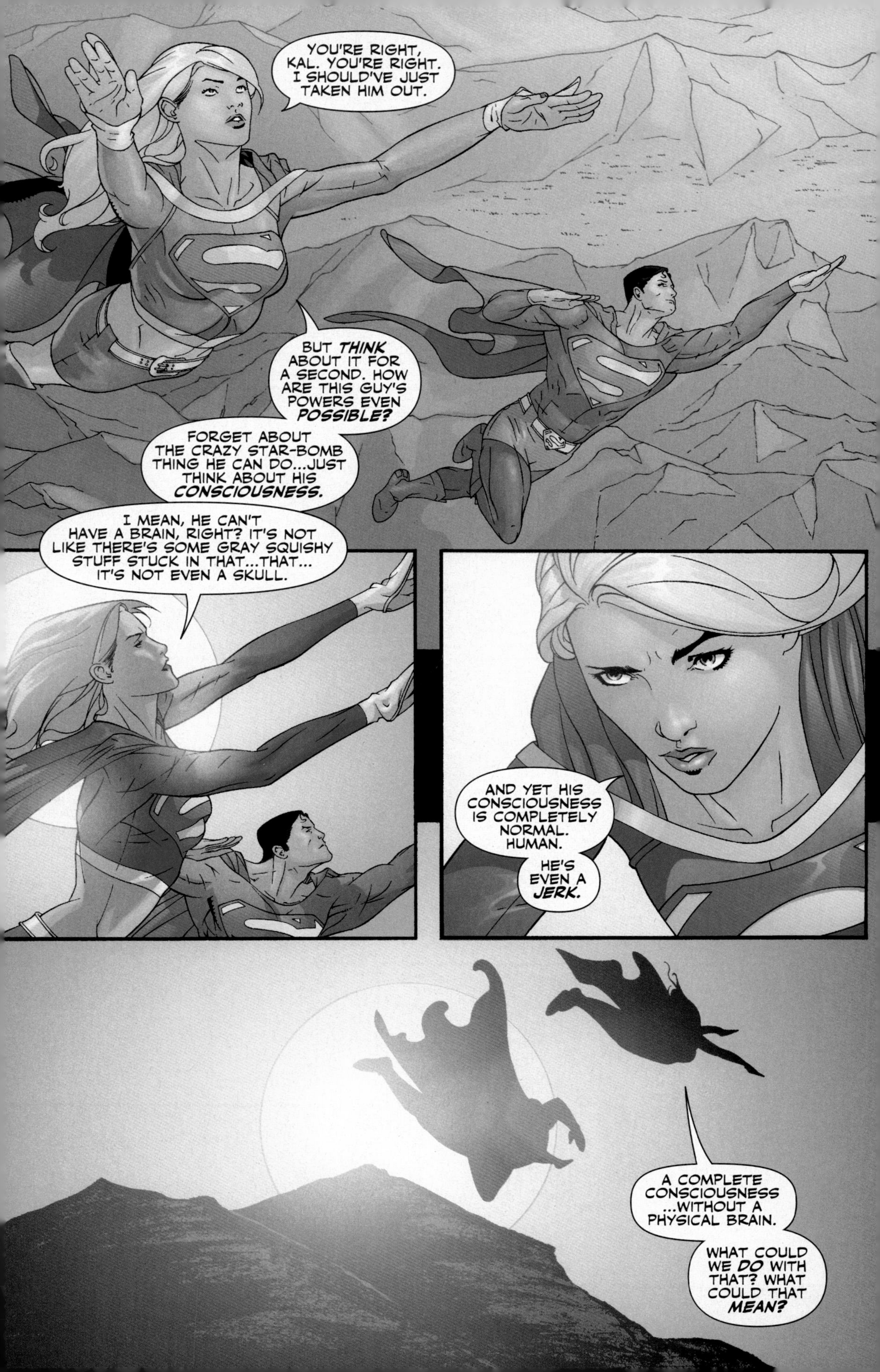
YOU'RE RIGHT, KAL. YOU'RE RIGHT. I SHOULD'VE JUST TAKEN HIM OUT.
BUT THINK ABOUT IT FOR A SECOND. HOW ARE THIS GUY'S POWERS EVEN POSSIBLE?
FORGET ABOUT THE CRAZY STAR-BOMB THING HE CAN DO...JUST THINK ABOUT HIS CONSCIOUSNESS.
I MEAN, HE CAN'T HAVE A BRAIN, RIGHT? IT'S NOT LIKE THERE'S SOME GRAY SQUISHY STUFF STUCK IN THAT...THAT... IT'S NOT EVEN A SKULL.
AND YET HIS CONSCIOUSNESS IS COMPLETELY NORMAL. HUMAN.
HE'S EVEN A JERK.
A COMPLETE CONSCIOUSNESS ...WITHOUT A PHYSICAL BRAIN.
WHAT COULD WE DO WITH THAT? WHAT COULD THAT MEAN?

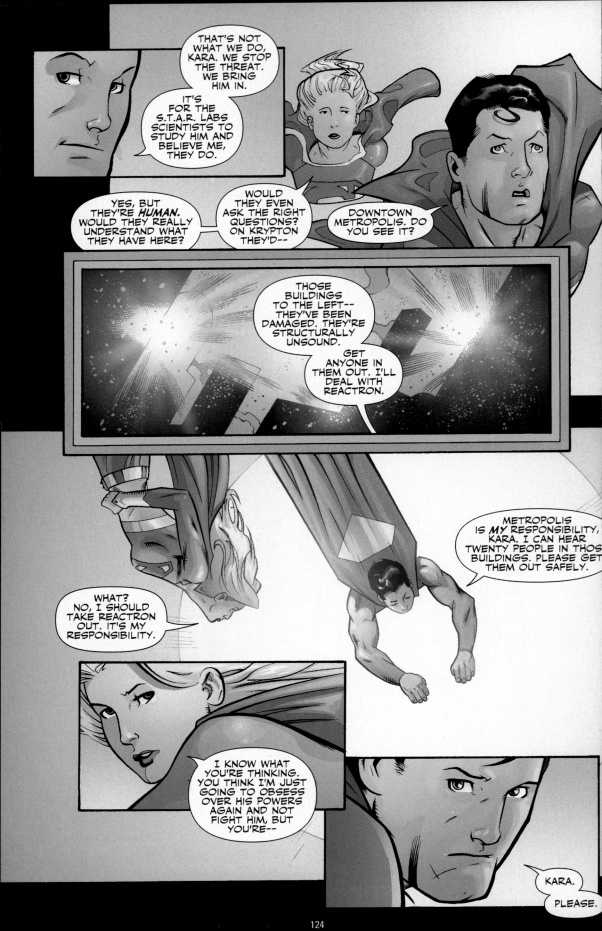

THAT'S NOT WHAT WE DO, KARA. WE STOP THE THREAT. WE BRING HIM IN.

IT'S FOR THE S.T.A.R. LABS SCIENTISTS TO STUDY HIM AND BELIEVE ME, THEY DO.

YES, BUT THEY'RE *HUMAN.* WOULD THEY REALLY UNDERSTAND WHAT THEY HAVE HERE?

WOULD THEY EVEN ASK THE RIGHT QUESTIONS? ON KRYPTON THEY'D--

DOWNTOWN METROPOLIS. DO YOU SEE IT?

THOSE BUILDINGS TO THE LEFT-- THEY'VE BEEN DAMAGED. THEY'RE STRUCTURALLY UNSOUND.

GET ANYONE IN THEM OUT. I'LL DEAL WITH REACTRON.

METROPOLIS IS *MY* RESPONSIBILITY, KARA. I CAN HEAR TWENTY PEOPLE IN THOS BUILDINGS. PLEASE GET THEM OUT SAFELY.

WHAT? NO, I SHOULD TAKE REACTRON OUT. IT'S MY RESPONSIBILITY.

I KNOW WHAT YOU'RE THINKING. YOU THINK I'M JUST GOING TO OBSESS OVER HIS POWERS AGAIN AND NOT FIGHT HIM, BUT YOU'RE--

KARA.

PLEASE.

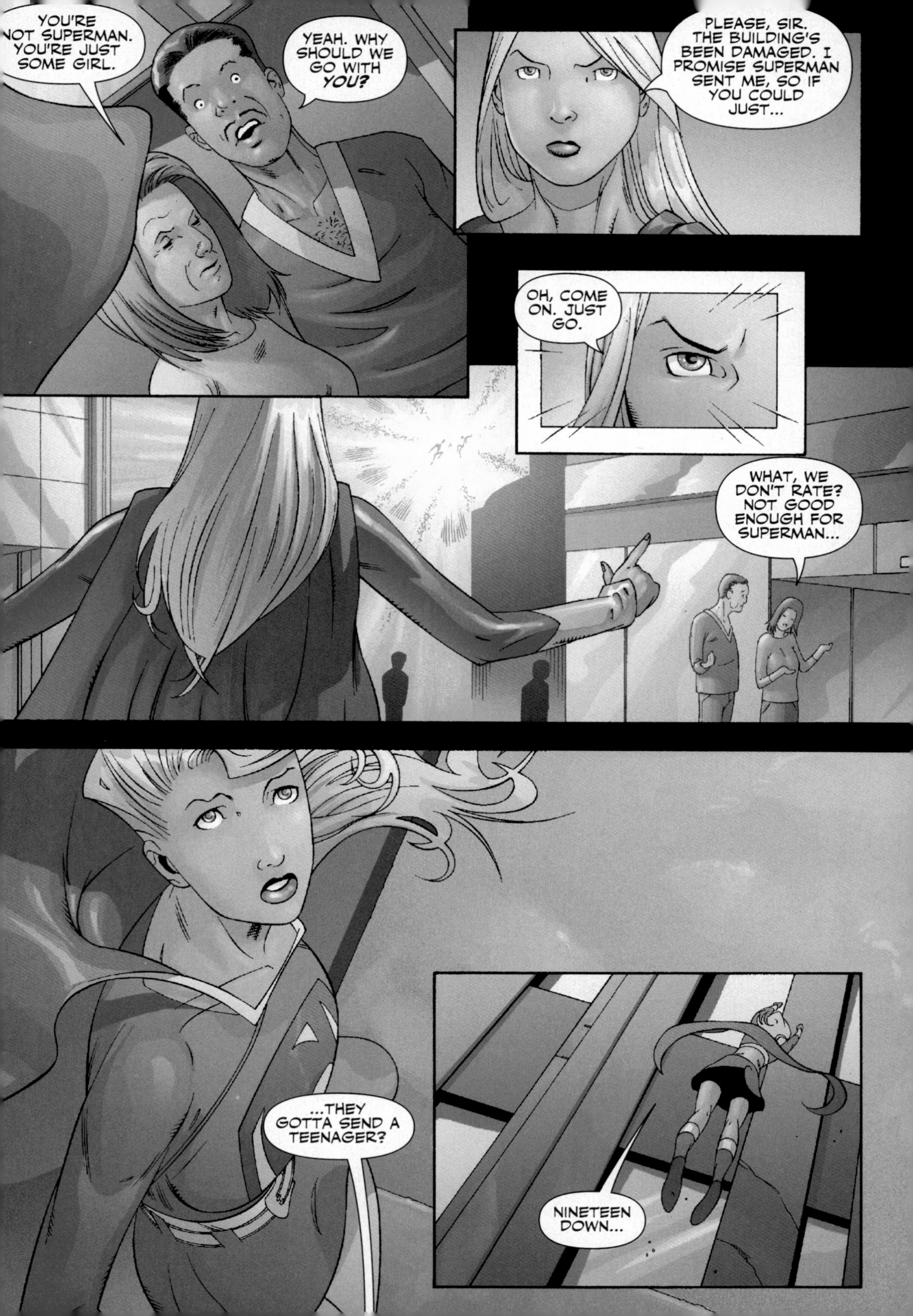
YOU'RE NOT SUPERMAN. YOU'RE JUST SOME GIRL.
YEAH. WHY SHOULD WE GO WITH *YOU?*
PLEASE, SIR. THE BUILDING'S BEEN DAMAGED. I PROMISE SUPERMAN SENT ME, SO IF YOU COULD JUST...
OH, COME ON. JUST GO.
WHAT, WE DON'T RATE? NOT GOOD ENOUGH FOR SUPERMAN...
...THEY GOTTA SEND A TEENAGER?
NINETEEN DOWN...

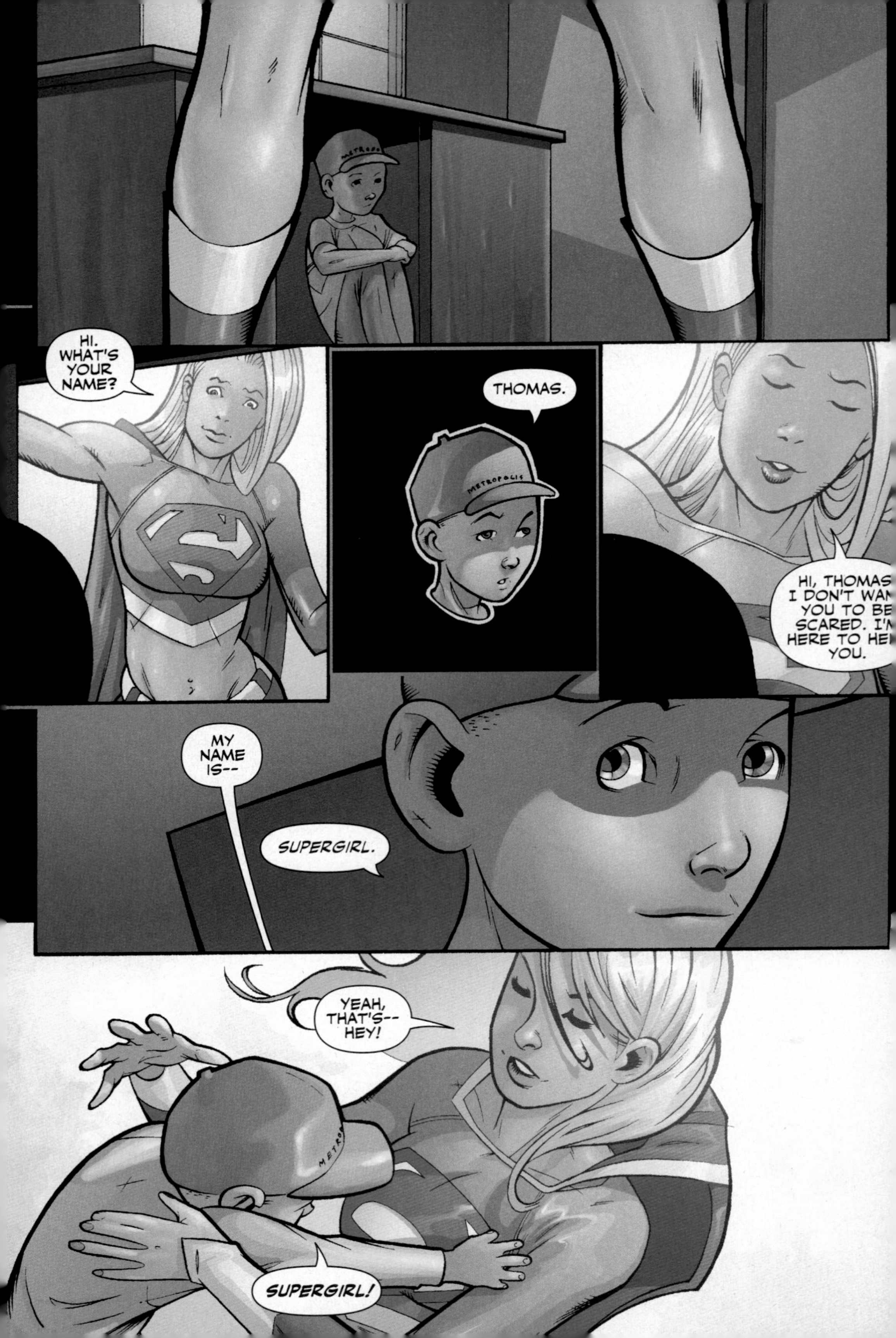
HI. WHAT'S YOUR NAME?
THOMAS.
HI, THOMAS I DON'T WAN YOU TO BE SCARED. I'M HERE TO HE YOU.
MY NAME IS--
SUPERGIRL.
YEAH, THAT'S-- HEY!
SUPERGIRL!

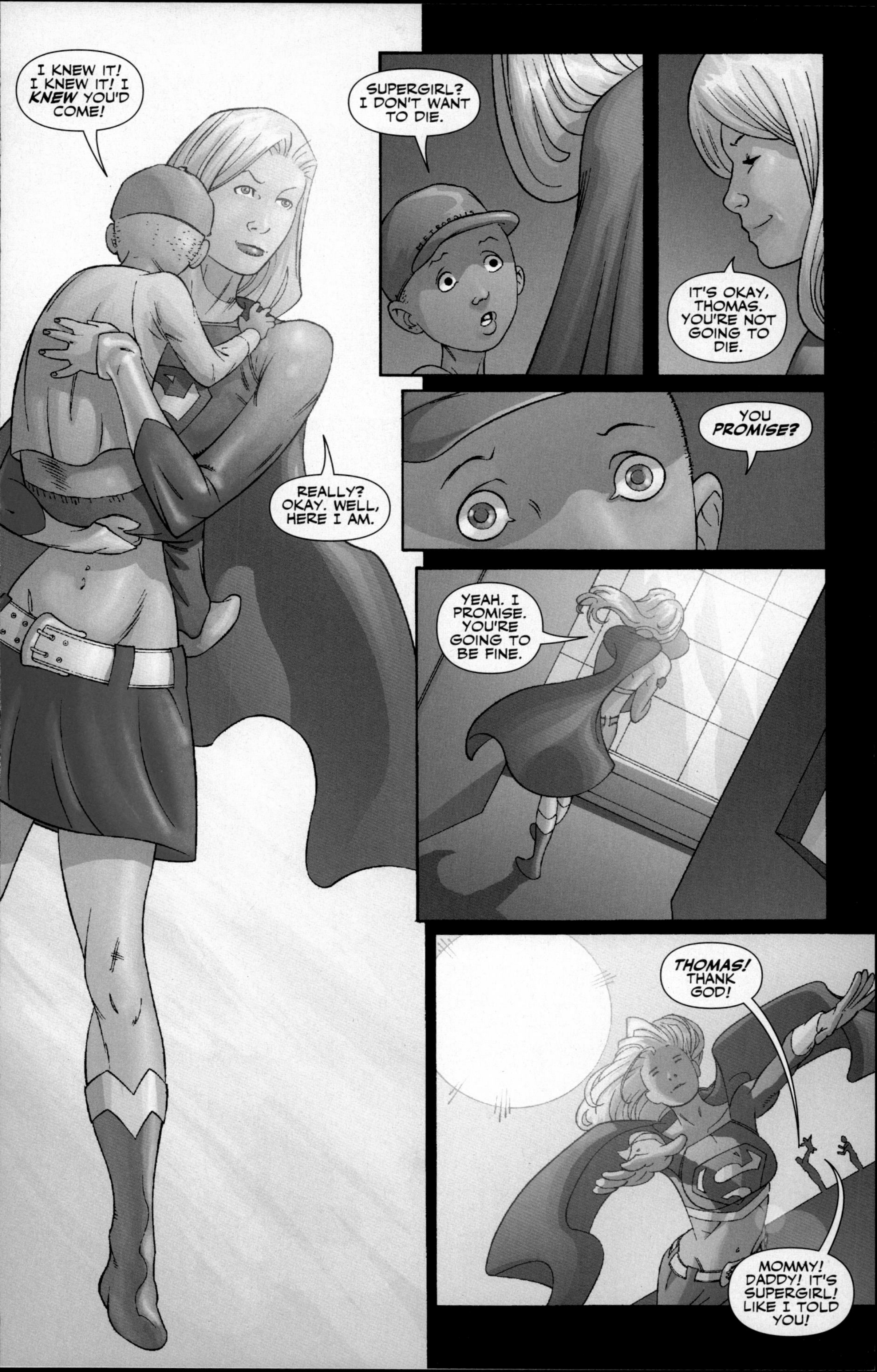
I KNEW IT! I KNEW IT! I KNEW YOU'D COME!
REALLY? OKAY. WELL, HERE I AM.
SUPERGIRL? I DON'T WANT TO DIE.
IT'S OKAY, THOMAS. YOU'RE NOT GOING TO DIE.
YOU PROMISE?
YEAH. I PROMISE. YOU'RE GOING TO BE FINE.
THOMAS! THANK GOD!
MOMMY! DADDY! IT'S SUPERGIRL! LIKE I TOLD YOU!

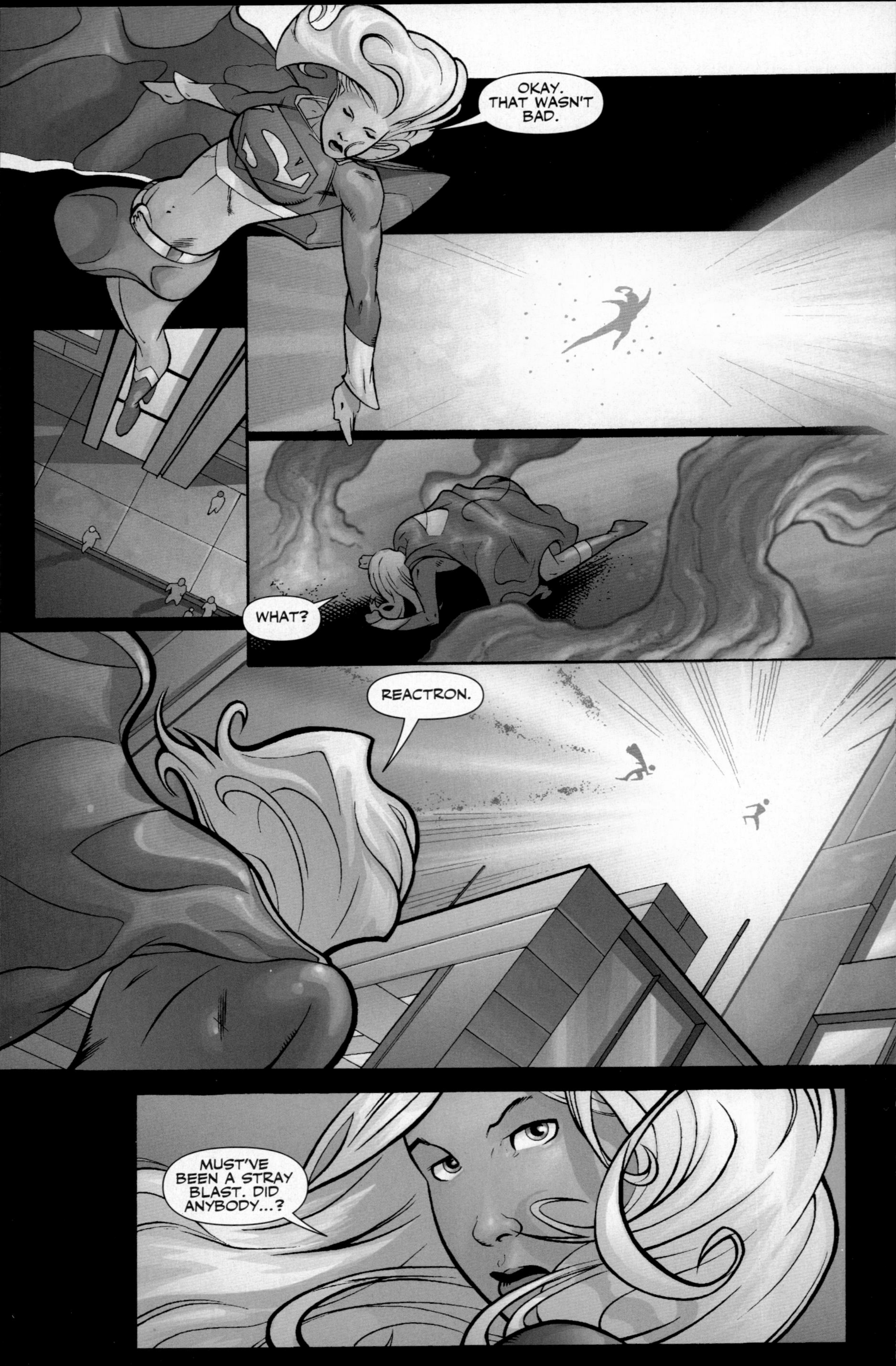
OKAY. THAT WASN'T BAD.
WHAT?
REACTRON.
MUST'VE BEEN A STRAY BLAST. DID ANYBODY...?

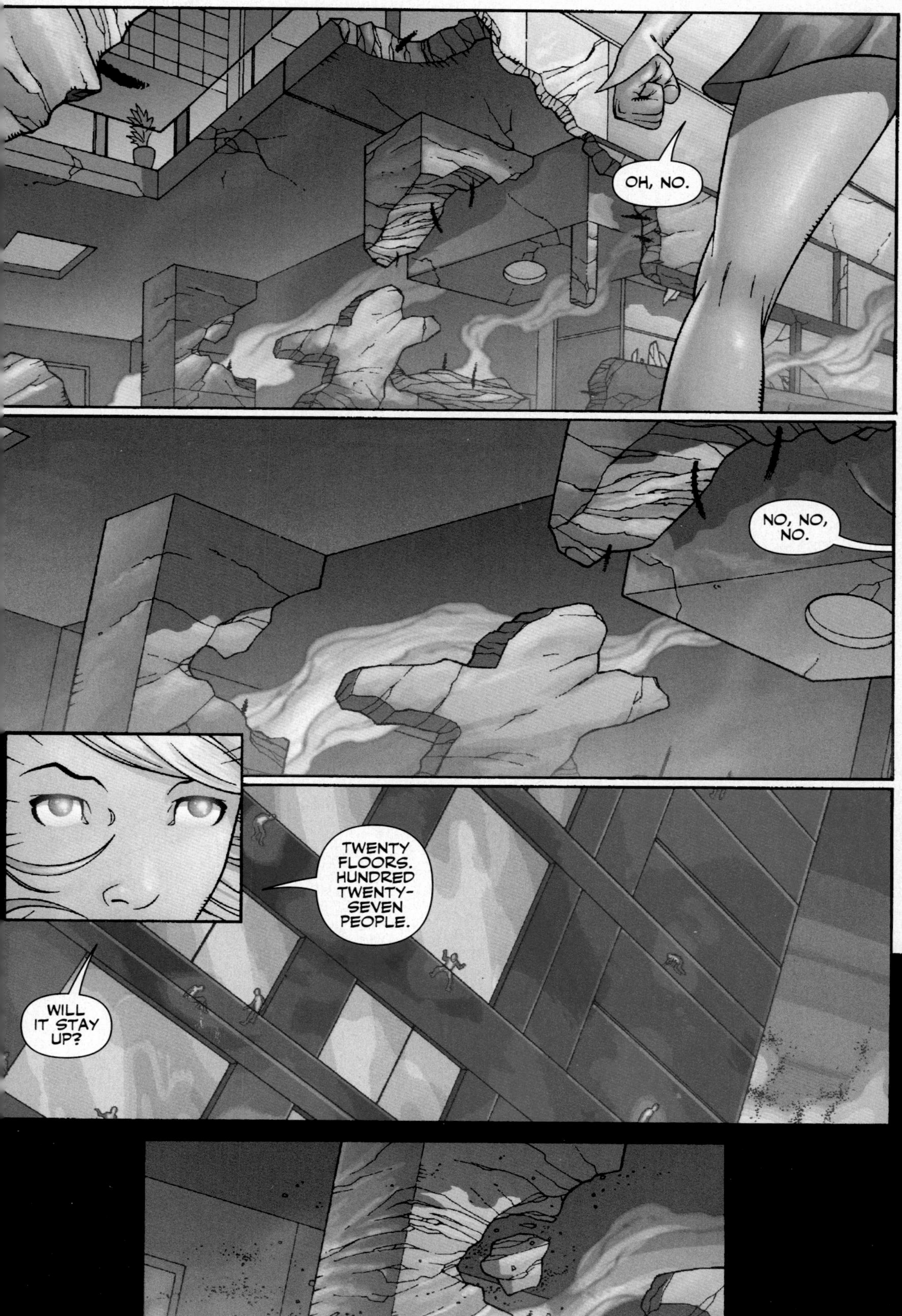
OH, NO.
NO, NO, NO.
TWENTY FLOORS. HUNDRED TWENTY-SEVEN PEOPLE.
WILL IT STAY UP?

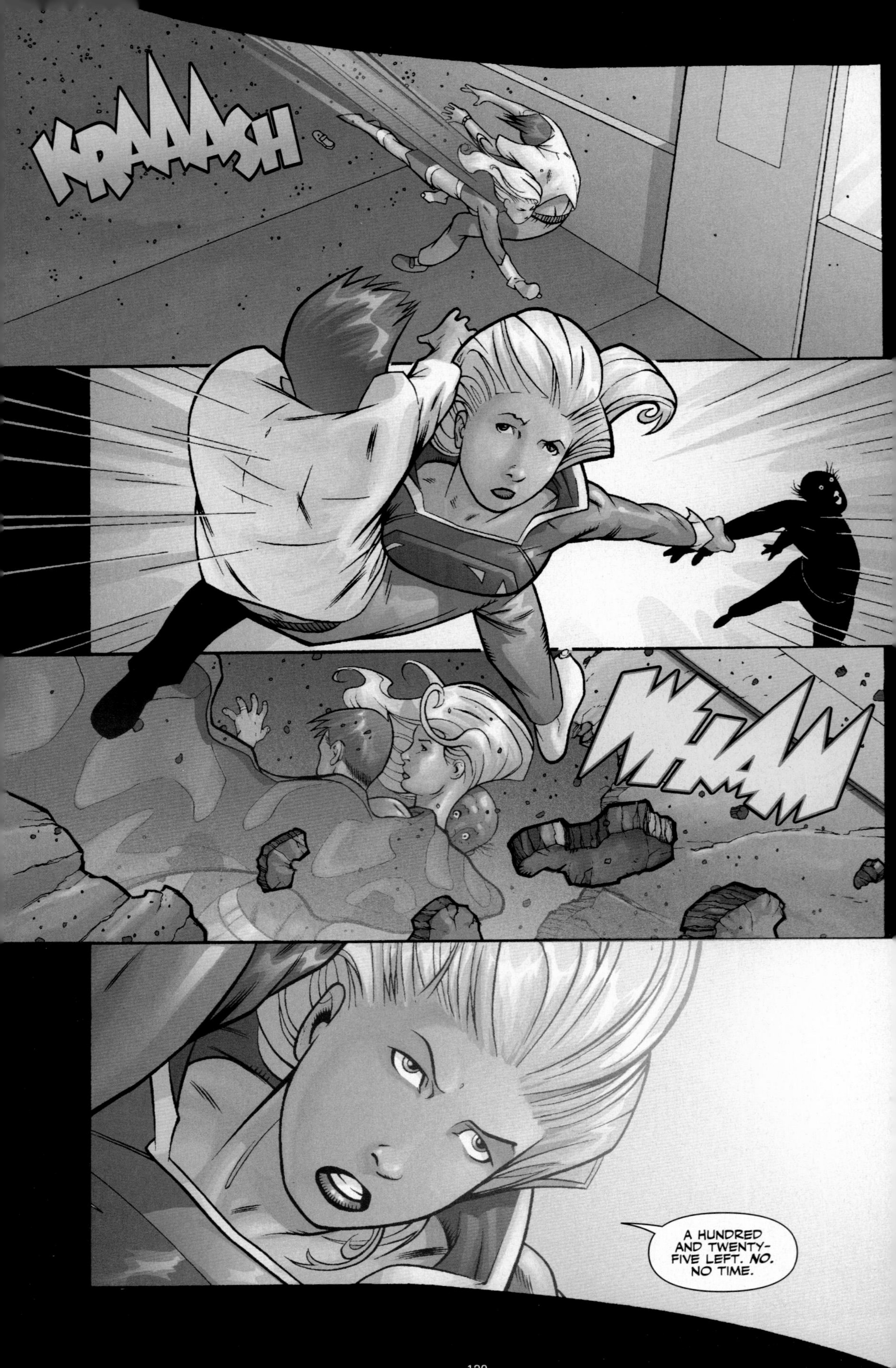
KRAAASH
WHAM
A HUNDRED AND TWENTY-FIVE LEFT. NO. NO TIME.

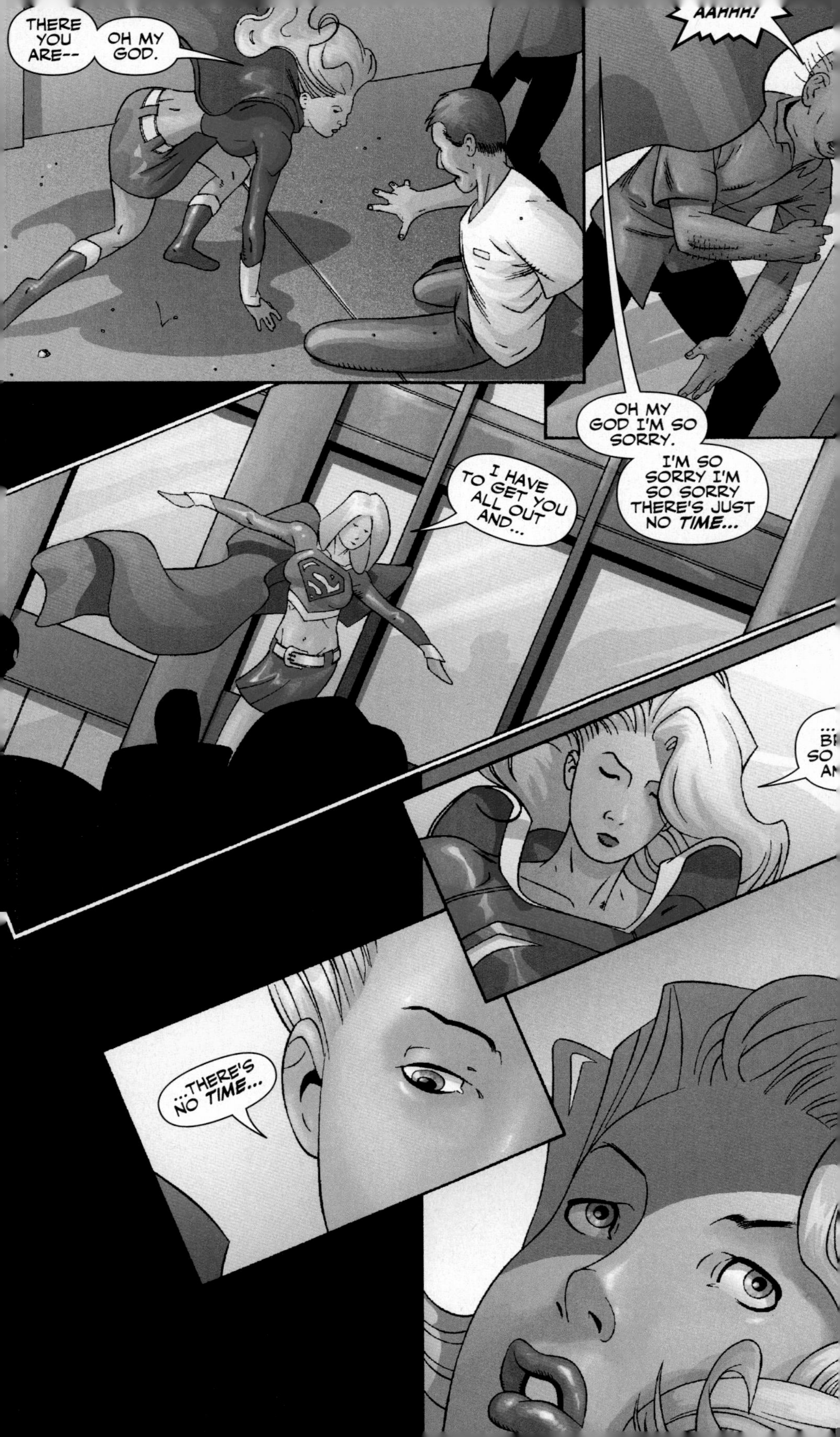
THERE YOU ARE--
OH MY GOD.
AAHHH!
OH MY GOD I'M SO SORRY.
I'M SO SORRY I'M SO SORRY THERE'S JUST NO *TIME*...
I HAVE TO GET YOU ALL OUT AND...
...THERE'S NO *TIME*...

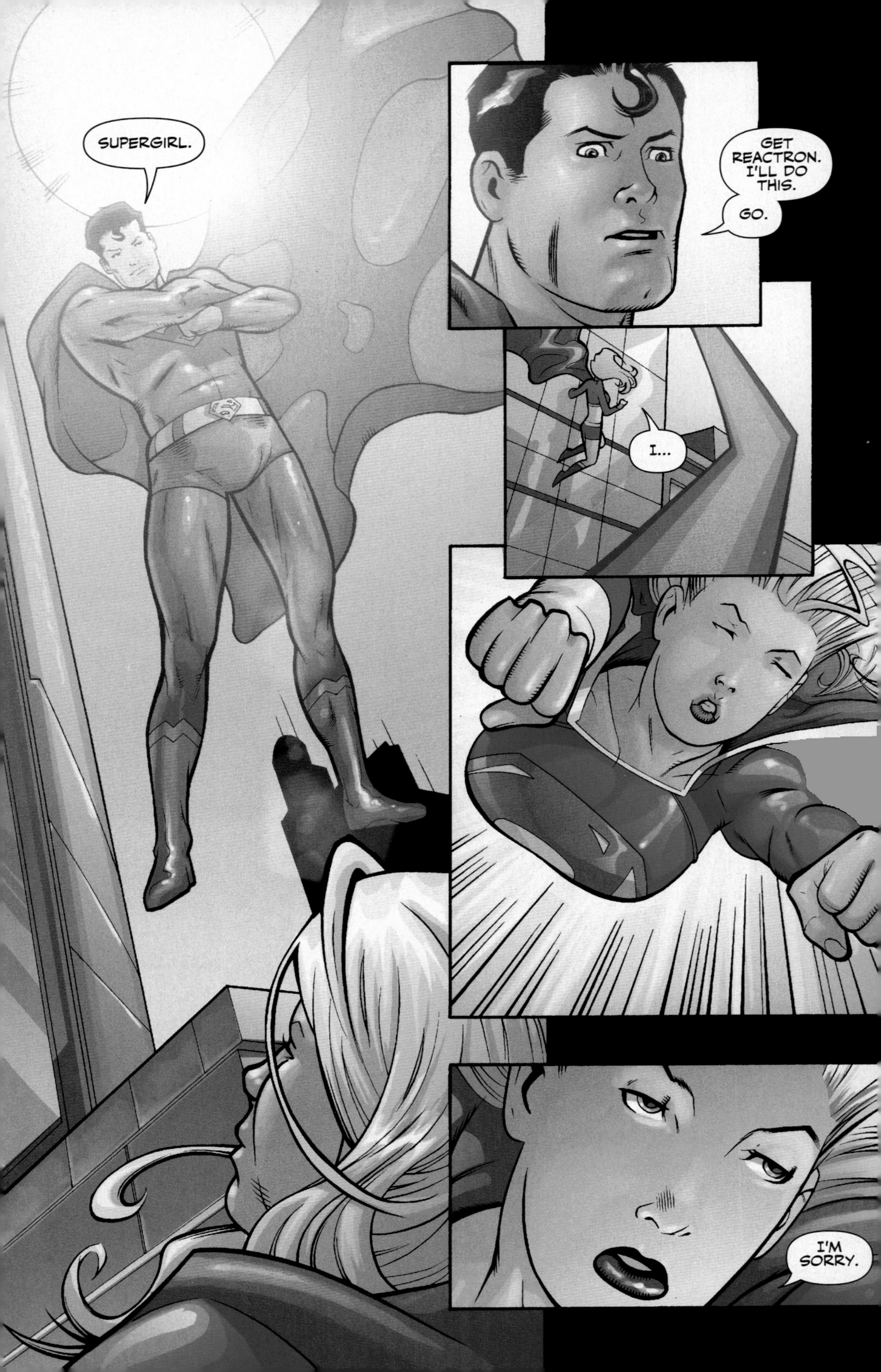
SUPERGIRL.
GET REACTRON. I'LL DO THIS.
GO.
I...
I'M SORRY.

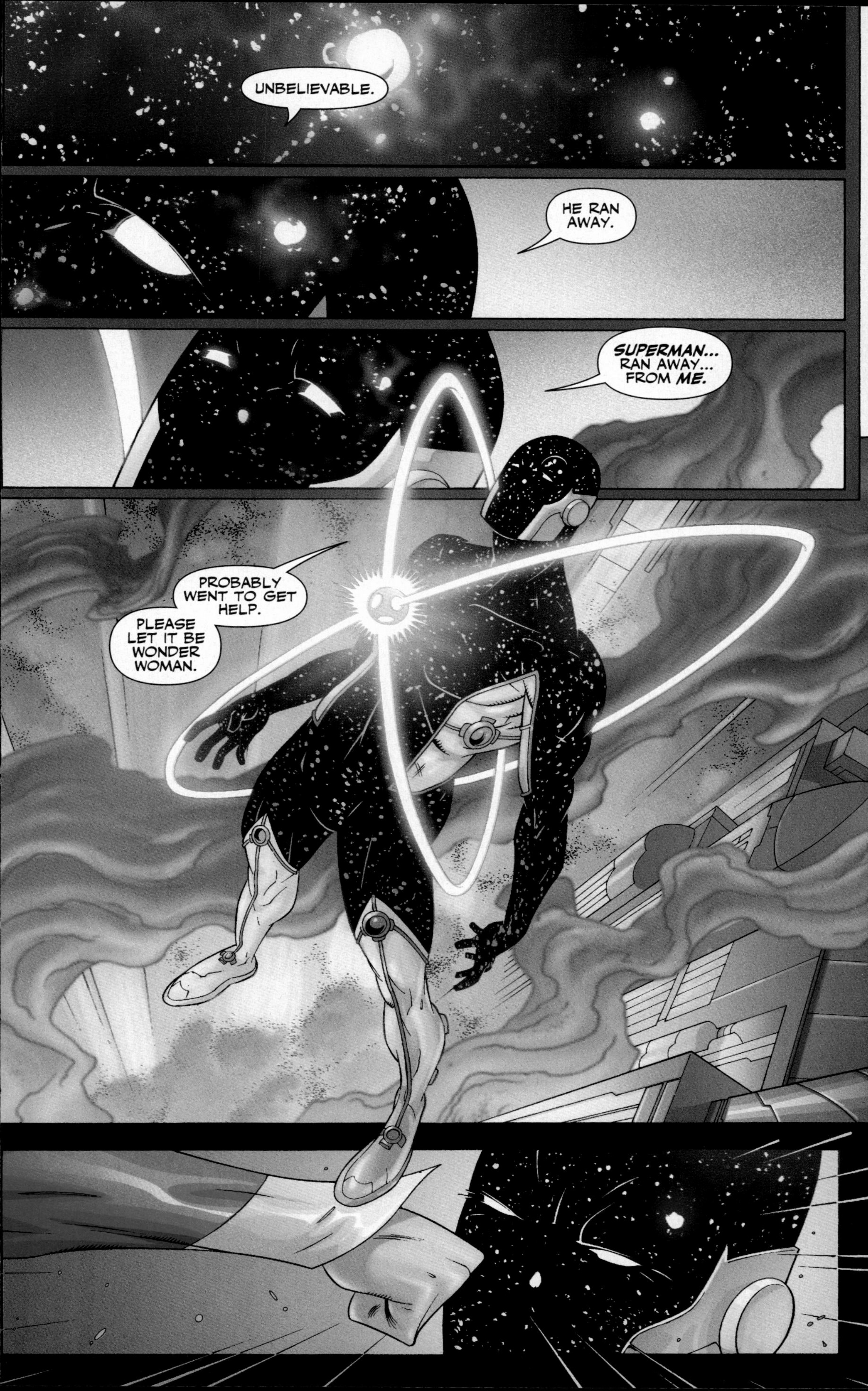
UNBELIEVABLE.
HE RAN AWAY.
SUPERMAN... RAN AWAY... FROM ME.
PROBABLY WENT TO GET HELP.
PLEASE LET IT BE WONDER WOMAN.

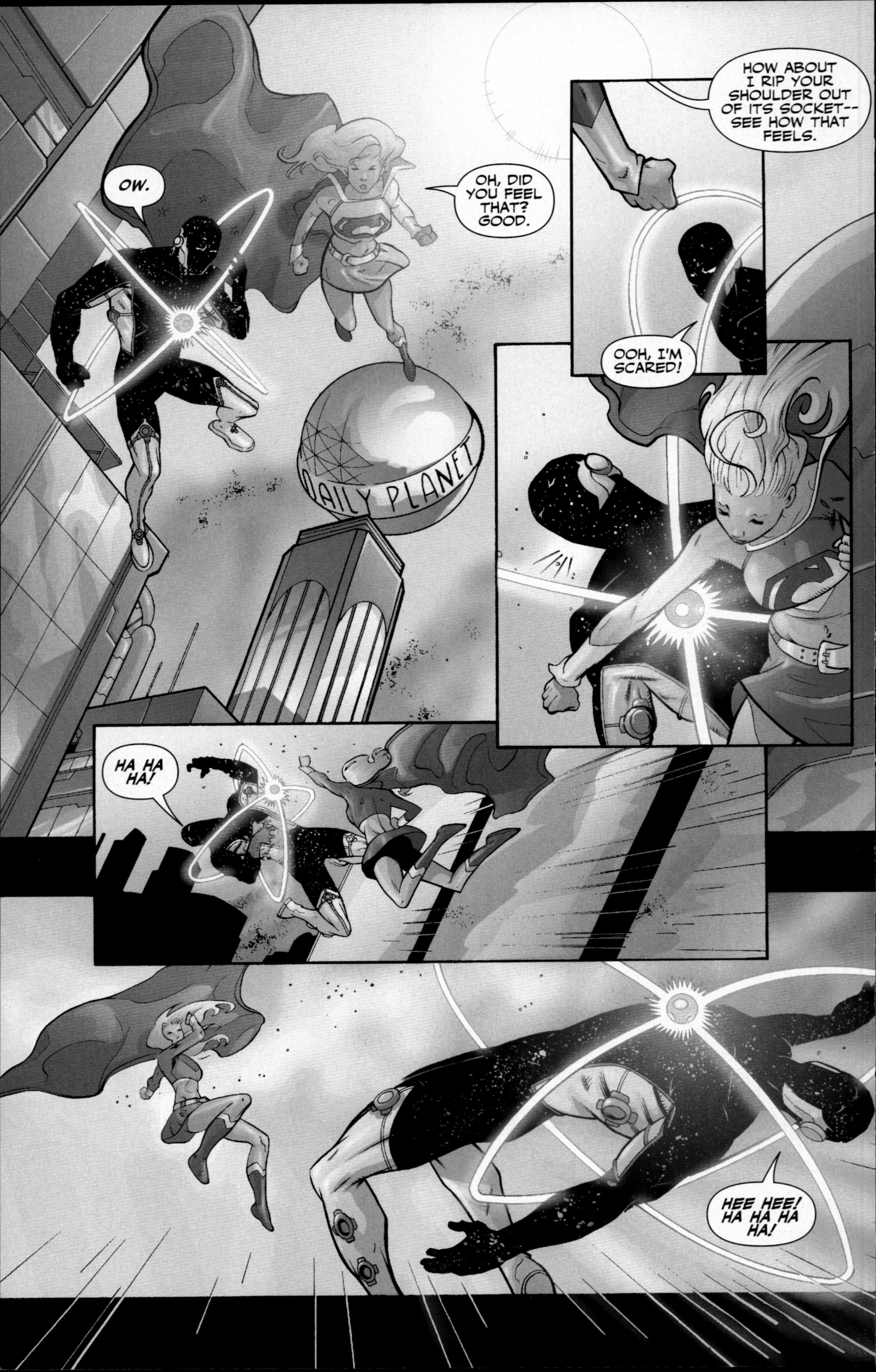
OW.
OH, DID YOU FEEL THAT? GOOD.
HOW ABOUT I RIP YOUR SHOULDER OUT OF ITS SOCKET-- SEE HOW THAT FEELS.
OOH, I'M SCARED!
DAILY PLANET
HA HA HA!
HEE HEE! HA HA HA HA!

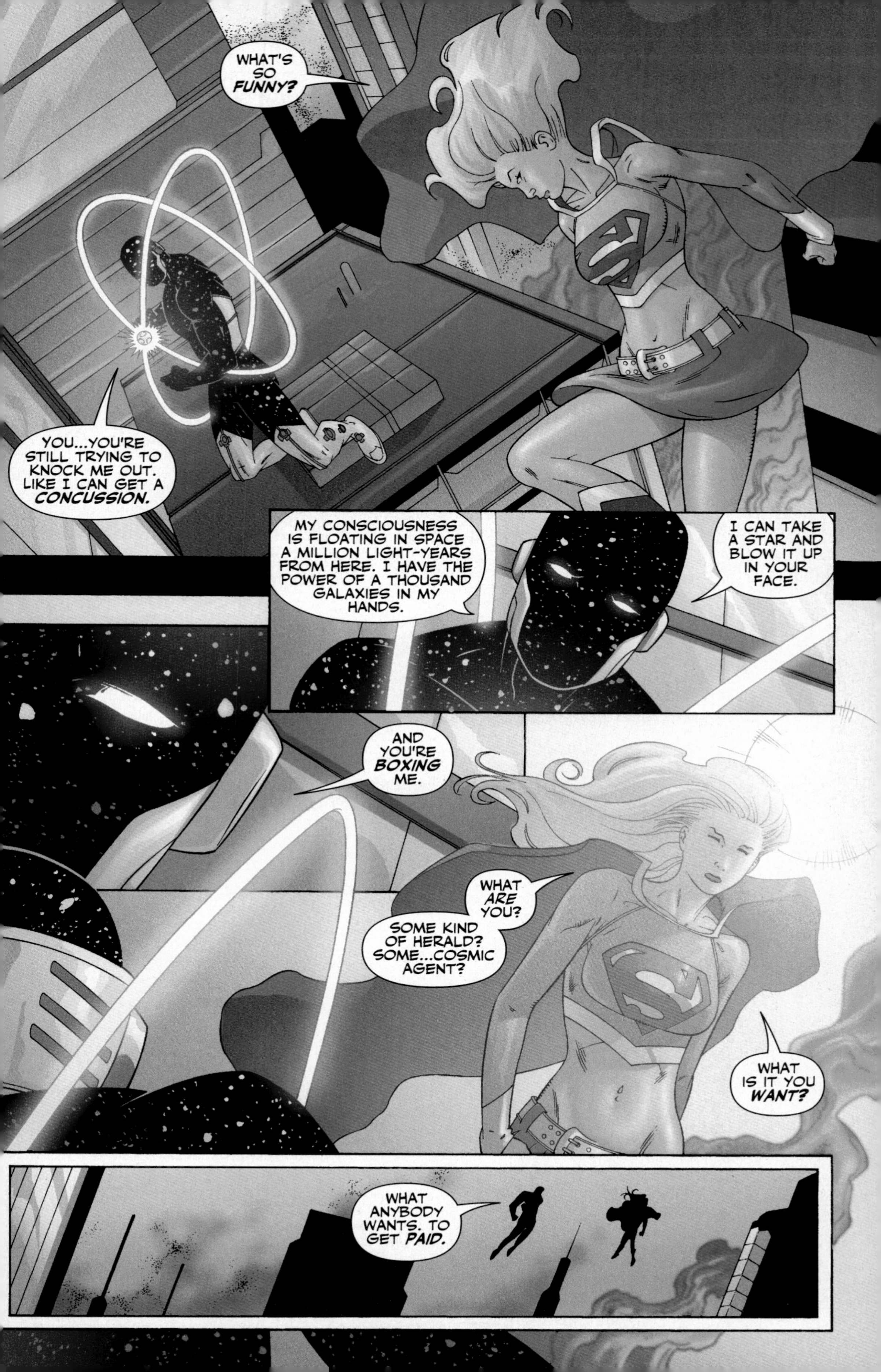
WHAT'S SO FUNNY?
YOU...YOU'RE STILL TRYING TO KNOCK ME OUT. LIKE I CAN GET A CONCUSSION.
MY CONSCIOUSNESS IS FLOATING IN SPACE A MILLION LIGHT-YEARS FROM HERE. I HAVE THE POWER OF A THOUSAND GALAXIES IN MY HANDS.
I CAN TAKE A STAR AND BLOW IT UP IN YOUR FACE.
AND YOU'RE BOXING ME.
WHAT ARE YOU?
SOME KIND OF HERALD? SOME...COSMIC AGENT?
WHAT IS IT YOU WANT?
WHAT ANYBODY WANTS. TO GET PAID.

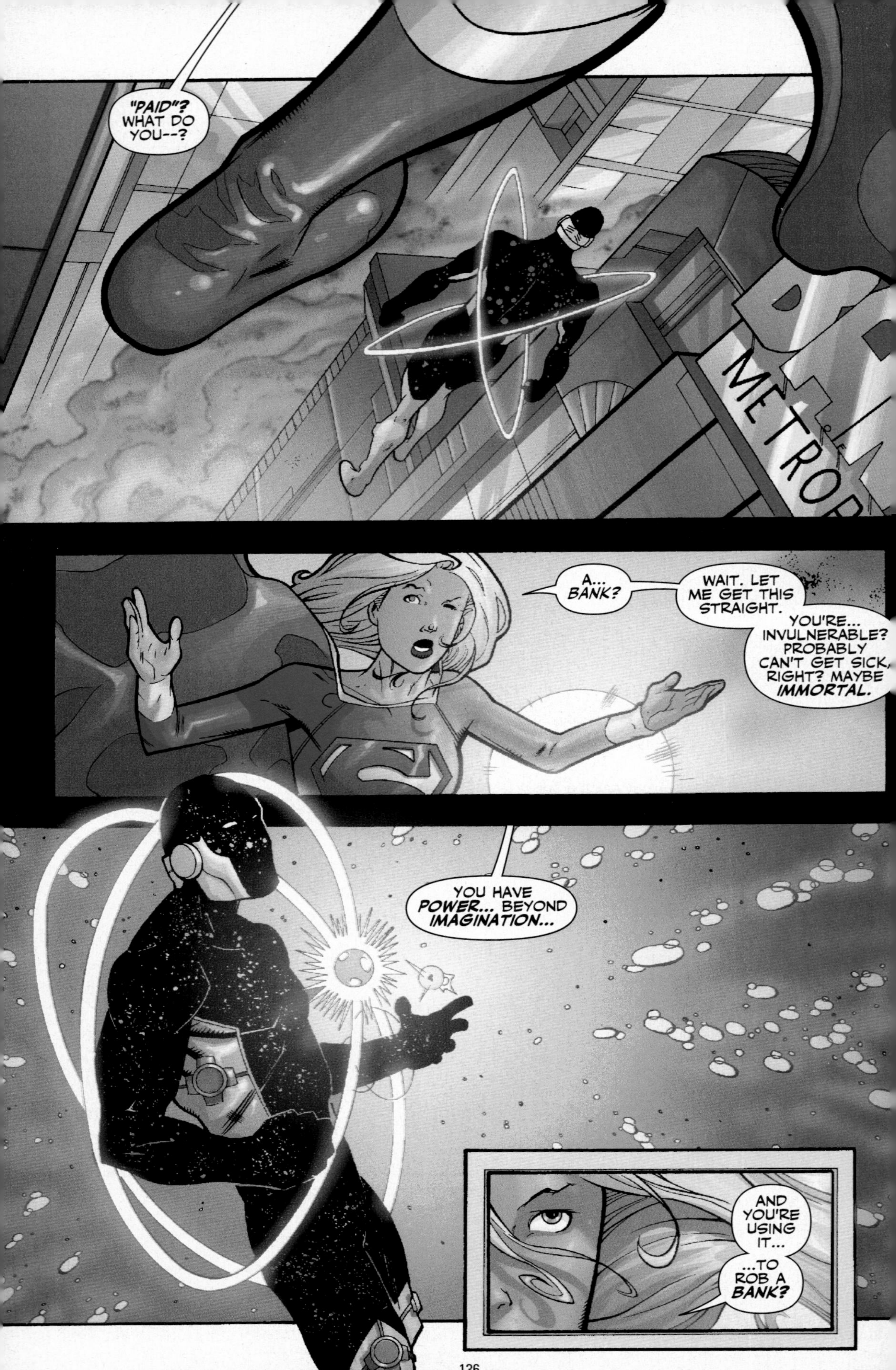
"PAID"? WHAT DO YOU--?
METRO
A... BANK?
WAIT. LET ME GET THIS STRAIGHT.
YOU'RE... INVULNERABLE? PROBABLY CAN'T GET SICK, RIGHT? MAYBE IMMORTAL.
YOU HAVE POWER... BEYOND IMAGINATION...
AND YOU'RE USING IT...
...TO ROB A BANK?

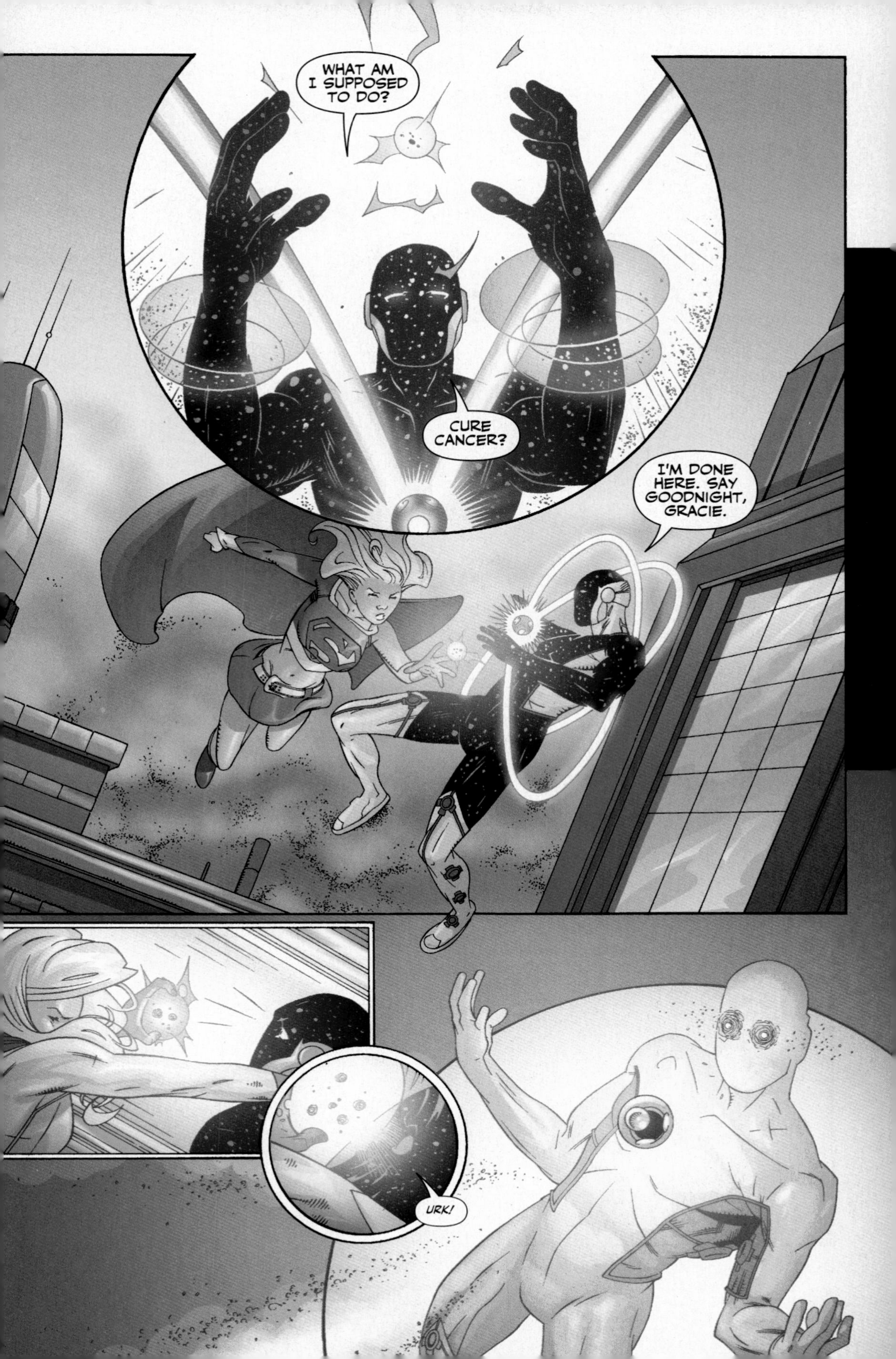
WHAT AM I SUPPOSED TO DO?
CURE CANCER?
I'M DONE HERE. SAY GOODNIGHT, GRACIE.
URK!

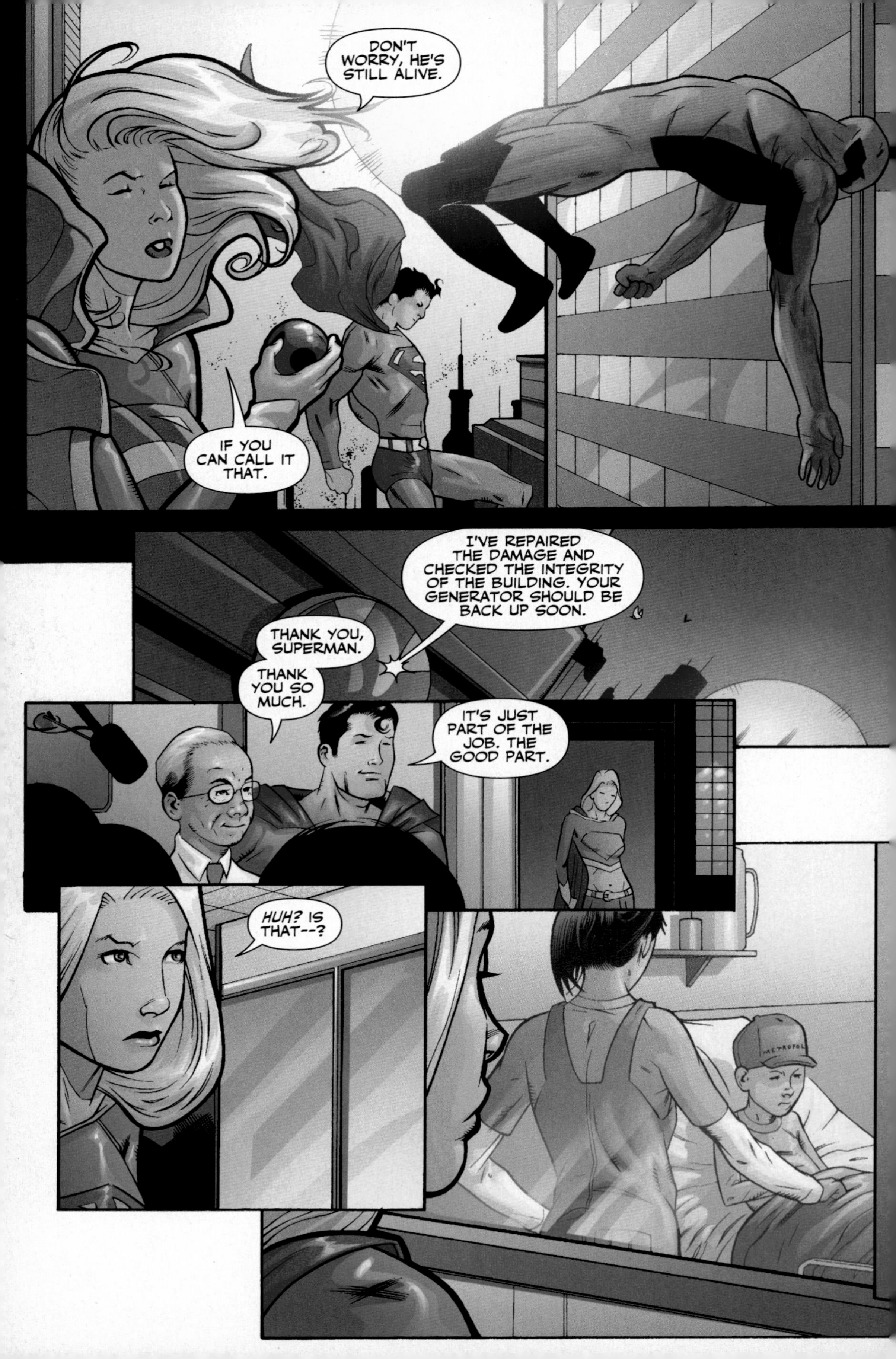
DON'T WORRY, HE'S STILL ALIVE.
IF YOU CAN CALL IT THAT.
I'VE REPAIRED THE DAMAGE AND CHECKED THE INTEGRITY OF THE BUILDING. YOUR GENERATOR SHOULD BE BACK UP SOON.
THANK YOU, SUPERMAN.
THANK YOU SO MUCH.
IT'S JUST PART OF THE JOB. THE GOOD PART.
HUH? IS THAT--?

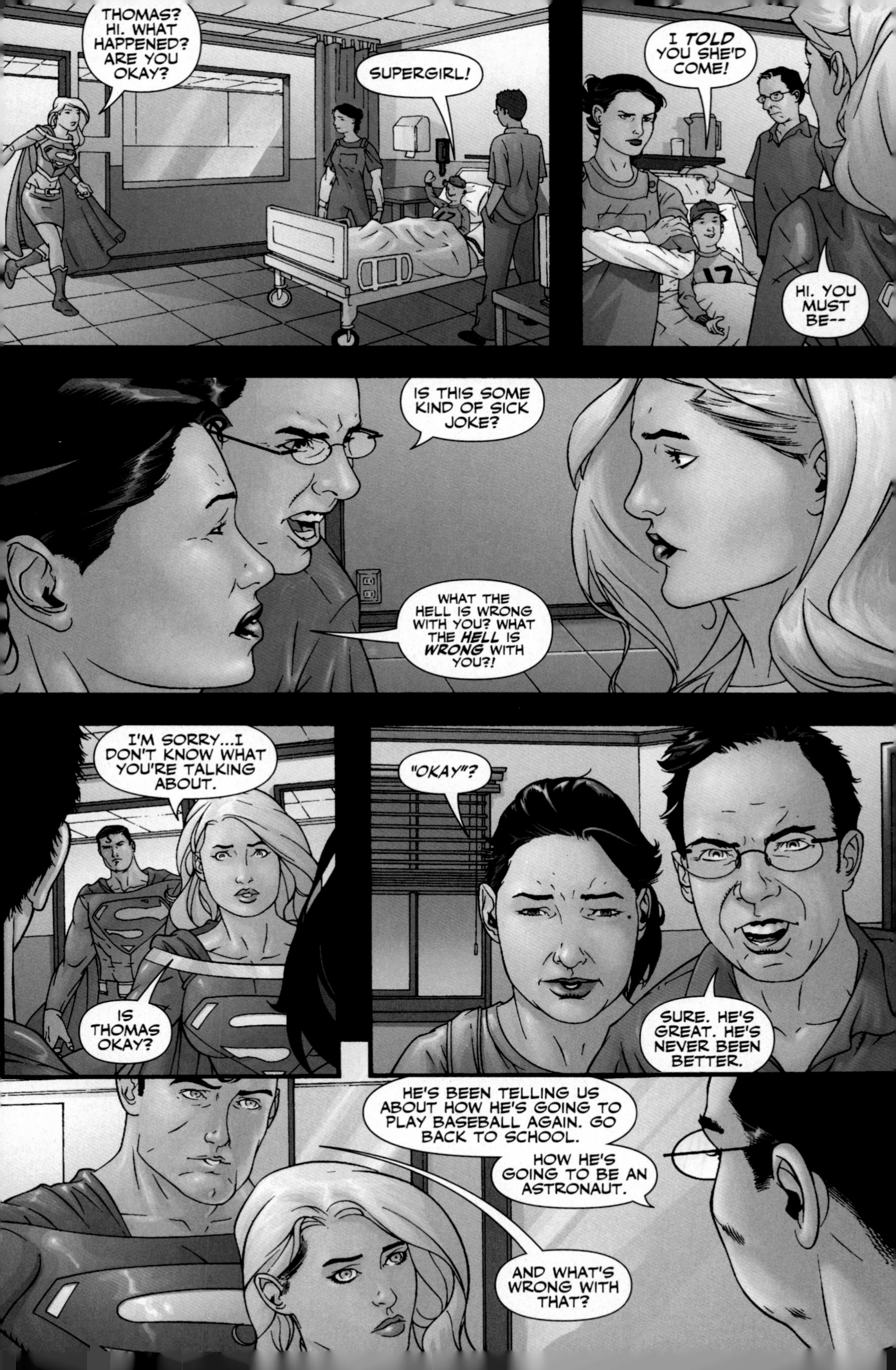
THOMAS? HI. WHAT HAPPENED? ARE YOU OKAY?
SUPERGIRL!
I *TOLD* YOU SHE'D COME!
HI. YOU MUST BE--
IS THIS SOME KIND OF SICK JOKE?
WHAT THE HELL IS WRONG WITH YOU? WHAT THE ***HELL*** IS ***WRONG*** WITH YOU?!
I'M SORRY...I DON'T KNOW WHAT YOU'RE TALKING ABOUT.
IS THOMAS OKAY?
"OKAY"?
SURE. HE'S GREAT. HE'S NEVER BEEN BETTER.
HE'S BEEN TELLING US ABOUT HOW HE'S GOING TO PLAY BASEBALL AGAIN. GO BACK TO SCHOOL.
HOW HE'S GOING TO BE AN ASTRONAUT.
AND WHAT'S WRONG WITH THAT?

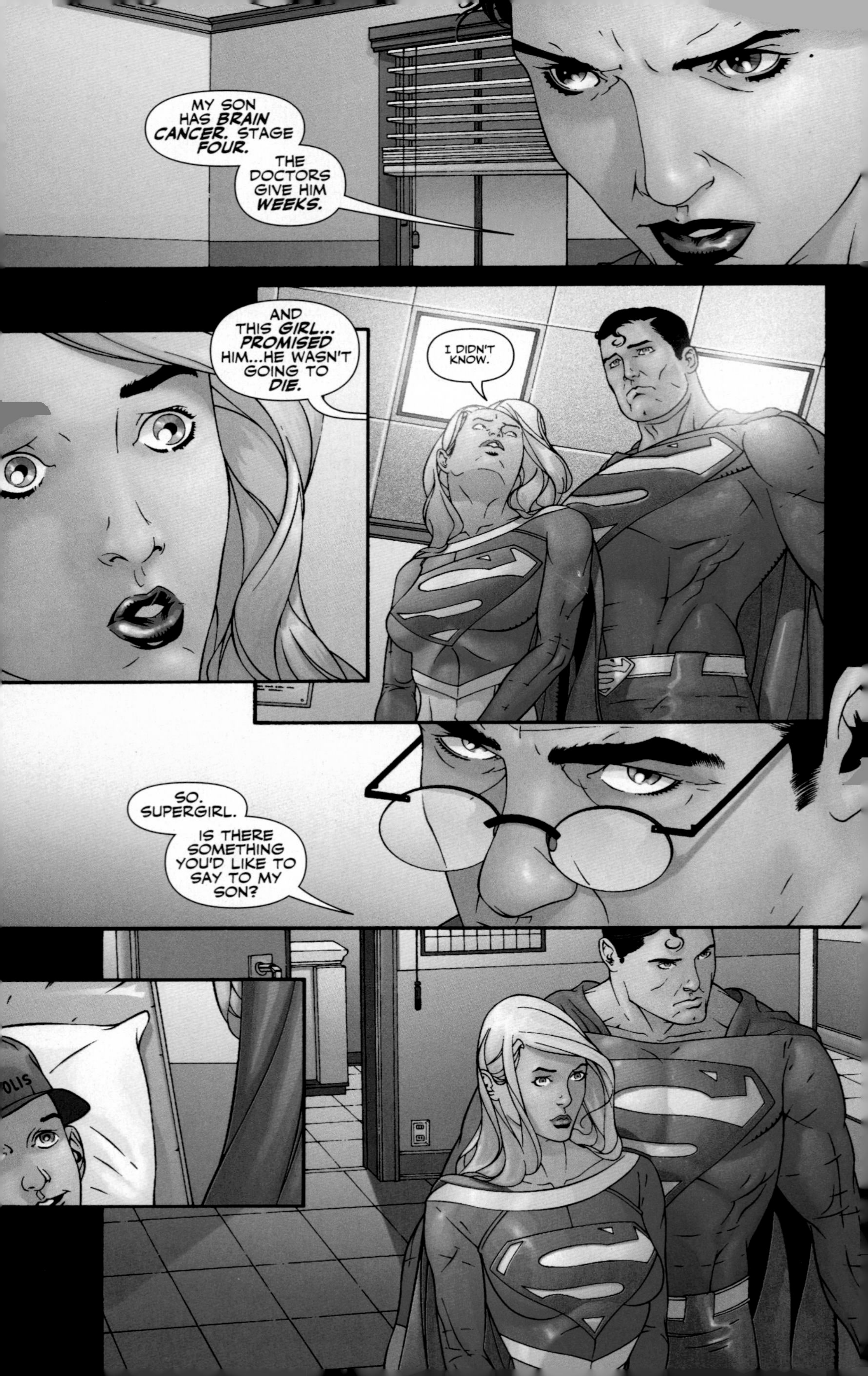
MY SON HAS BRAIN CANCER. STAGE FOUR.
THE DOCTORS GIVE HIM WEEKS.
AND THIS GIRL... PROMISED HIM...HE WASN'T GOING TO DIE.
I DIDN'T KNOW.
SO. SUPERGIRL.
IS THERE SOMETHING YOU'D LIKE TO SAY TO MY SON?
OLIS

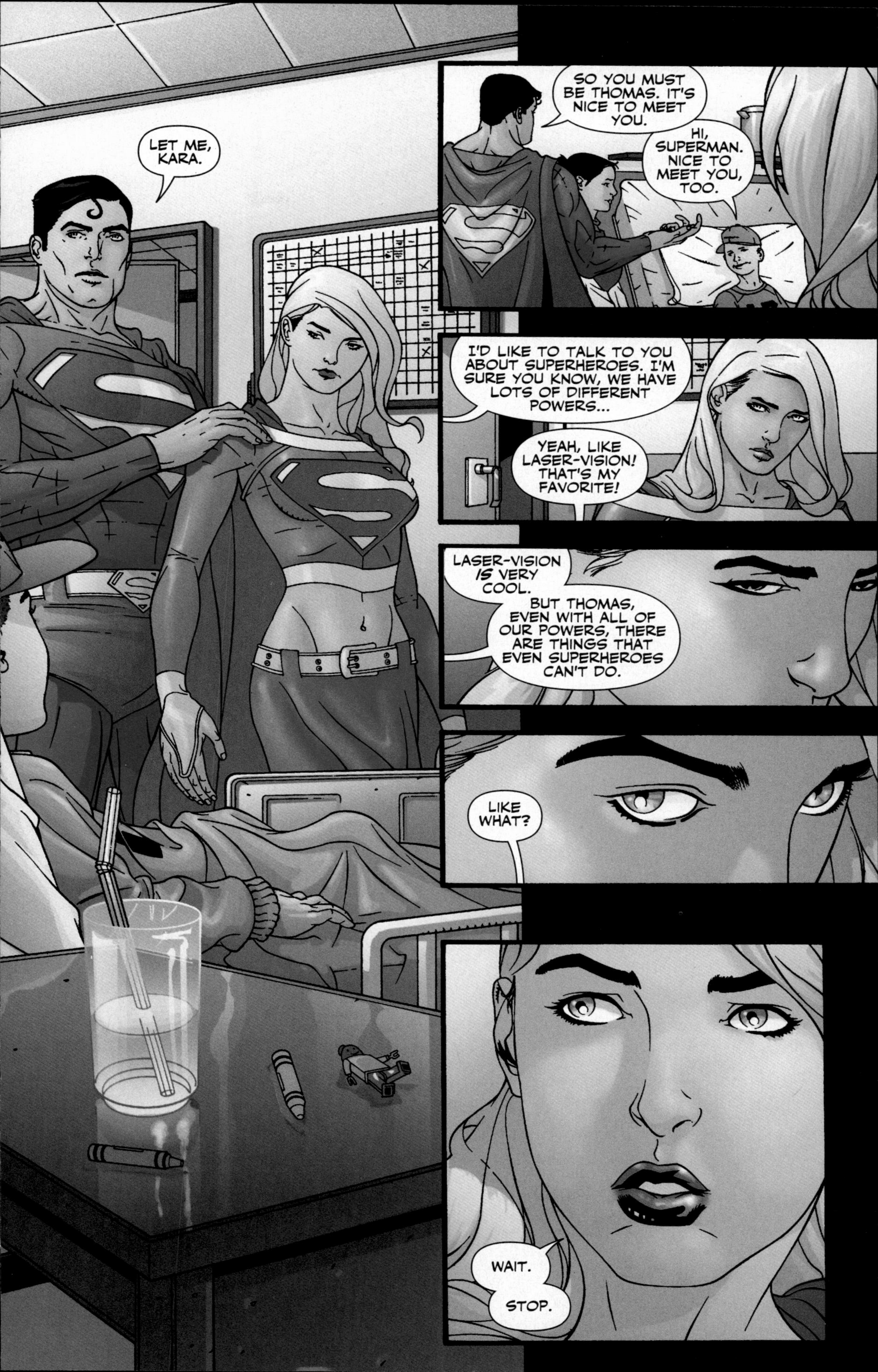
LET ME, KARA.
SO YOU MUST BE THOMAS. IT'S NICE TO MEET YOU.
HI, SUPERMAN. NICE TO MEET YOU, TOO.
I'D LIKE TO TALK TO YOU ABOUT SUPERHEROES. I'M SURE YOU KNOW, WE HAVE LOTS OF DIFFERENT POWERS...
YEAH, LIKE LASER-VISION! THAT'S MY FAVORITE!
LASER-VISION IS VERY COOL.
BUT THOMAS, EVEN WITH ALL OF OUR POWERS, THERE ARE THINGS THAT EVEN SUPERHEROES CAN'T DO.
LIKE WHAT?
WAIT.
STOP.

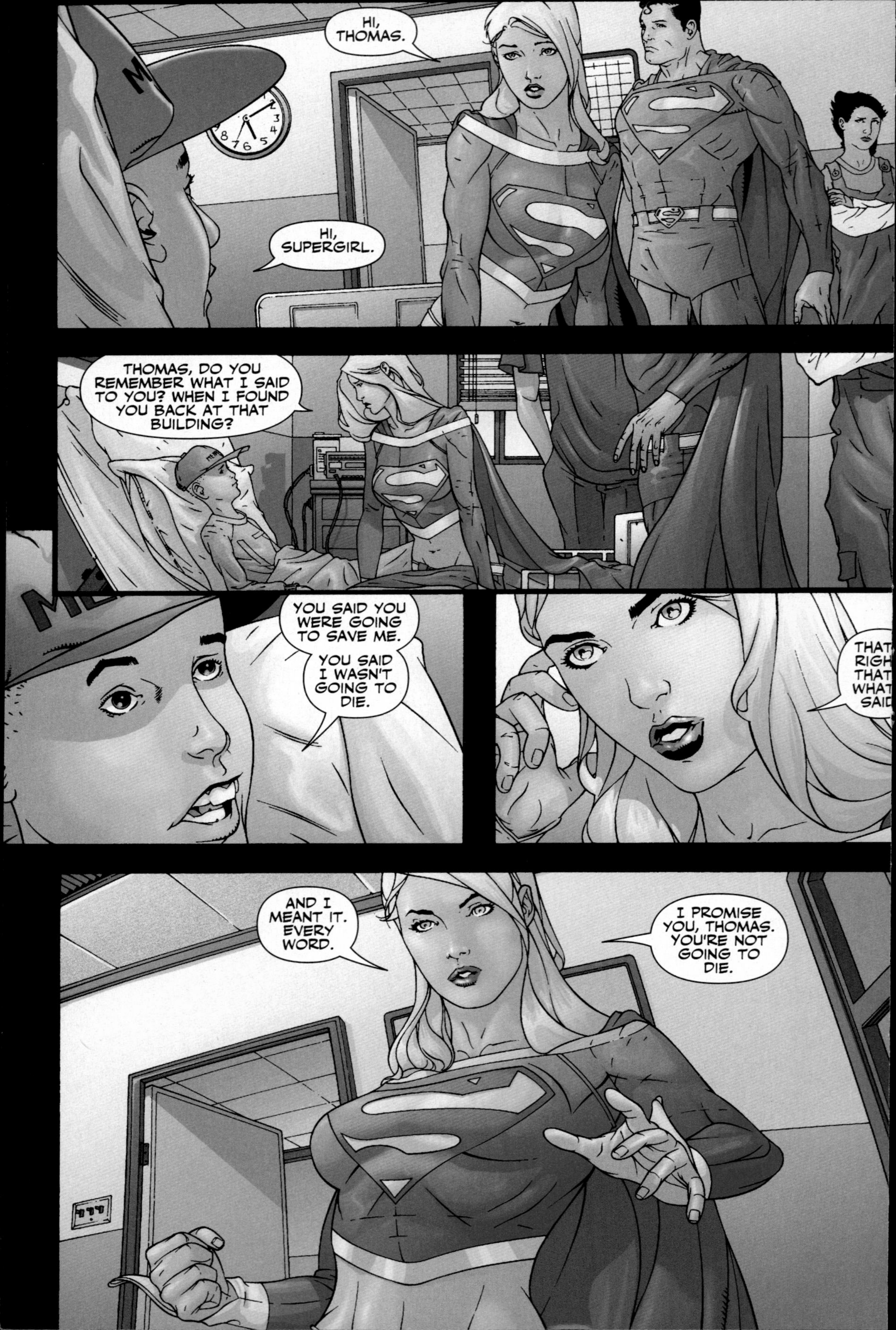
HI, THOMAS.
HI, SUPERGIRL.
THOMAS, DO YOU REMEMBER WHAT I SAID TO YOU? WHEN I FOUND YOU BACK AT THAT BUILDING?
YOU SAID YOU WERE GOING TO SAVE ME.
YOU SAID I WASN'T GOING TO DIE.
AND I MEANT IT. EVERY WORD.
I PROMISE YOU, THOMAS. YOU'RE NOT GOING TO DIE.

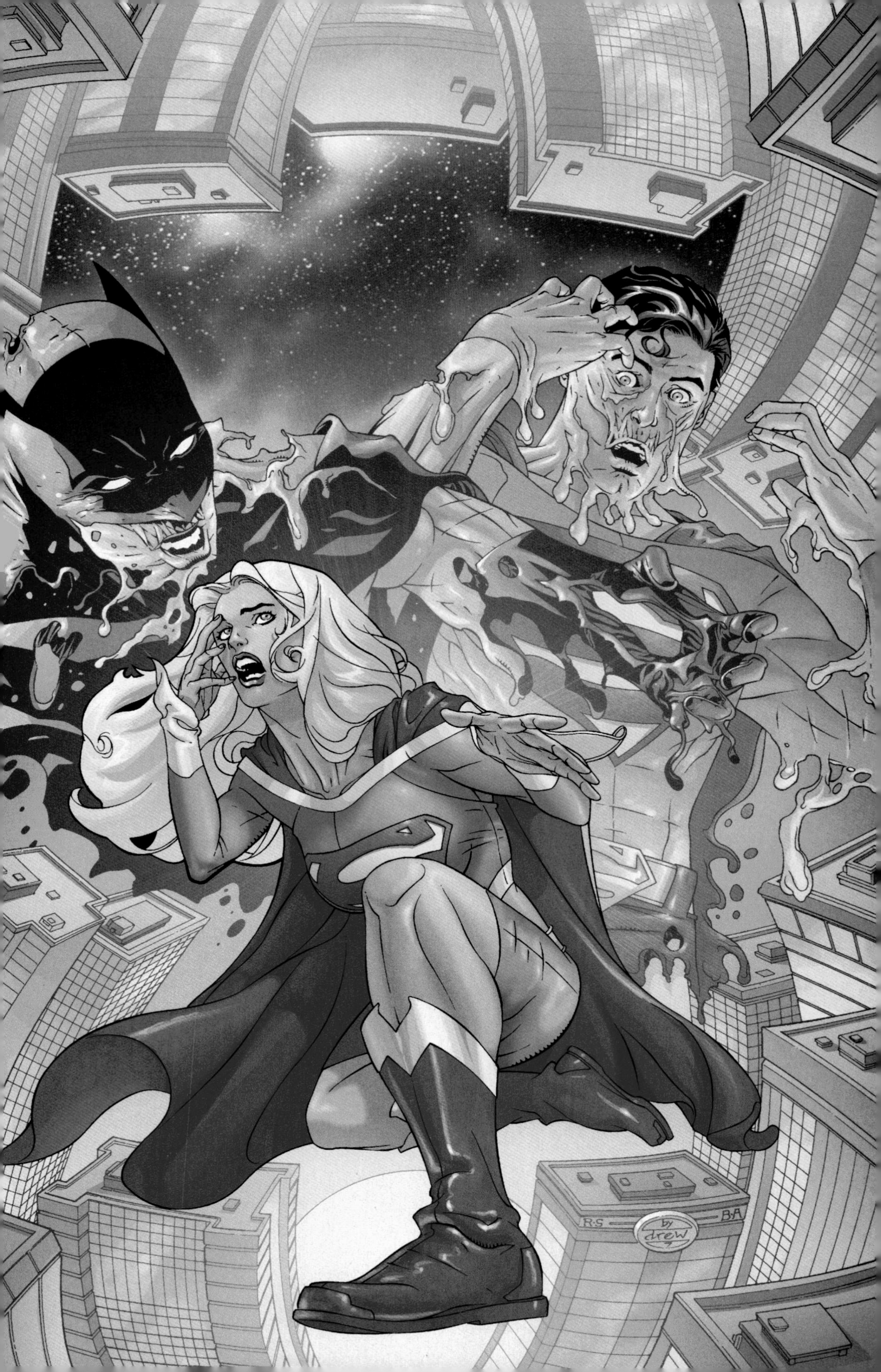
R·S
by drew
B·A

THE GIRL OF TOMORROW

KELLEY PUCKETT WRITER
RICK LEONARDI DREW JOHNSON PENCILS
DAN GREEN RAY SNYDER INKS

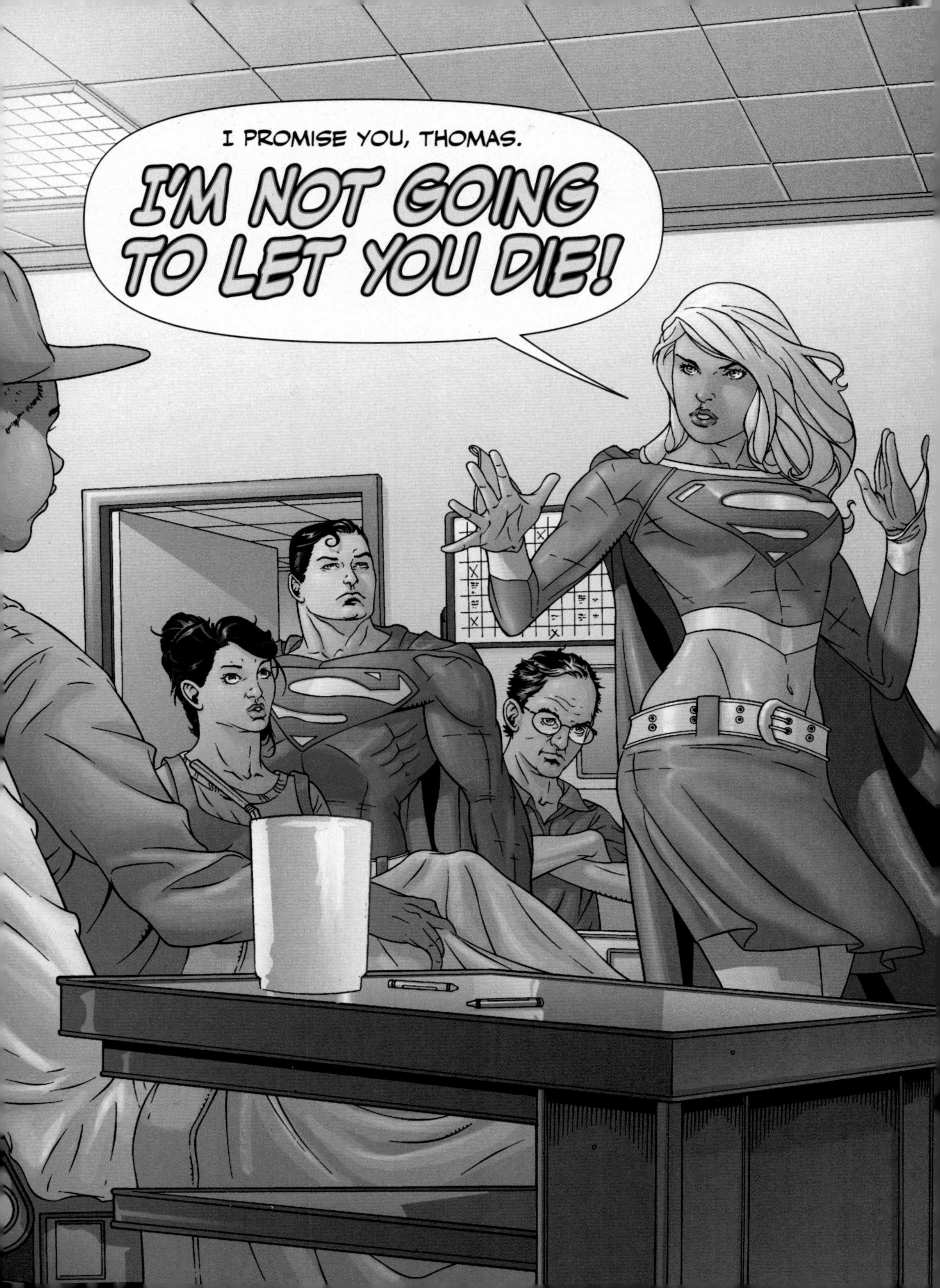
I PROMISE YOU, THOMAS.
I'M NOT GOING TO LET YOU DIE!

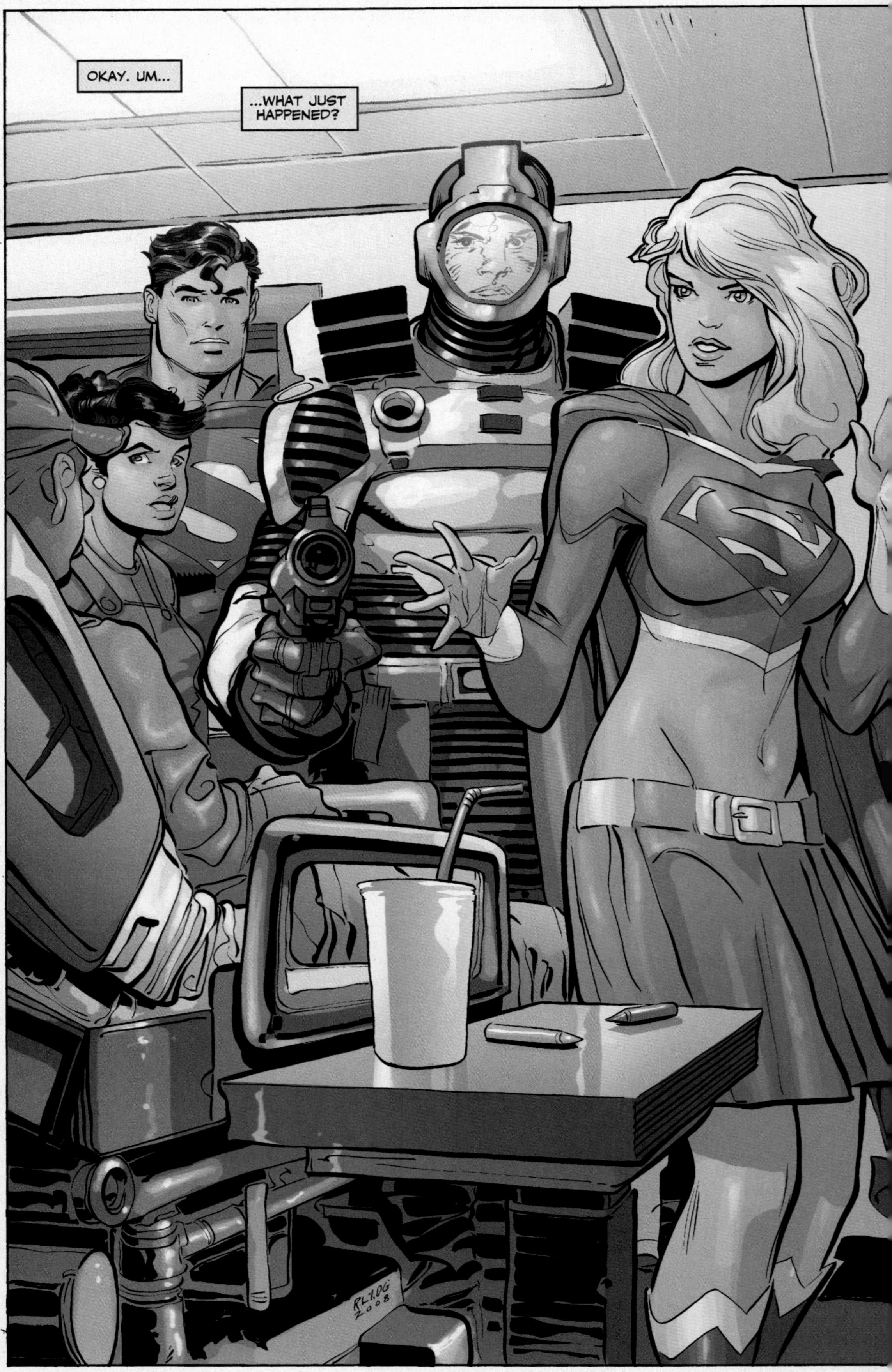
OKAY. UM...
...WHAT JUST HAPPENED?
RL/DG 2008

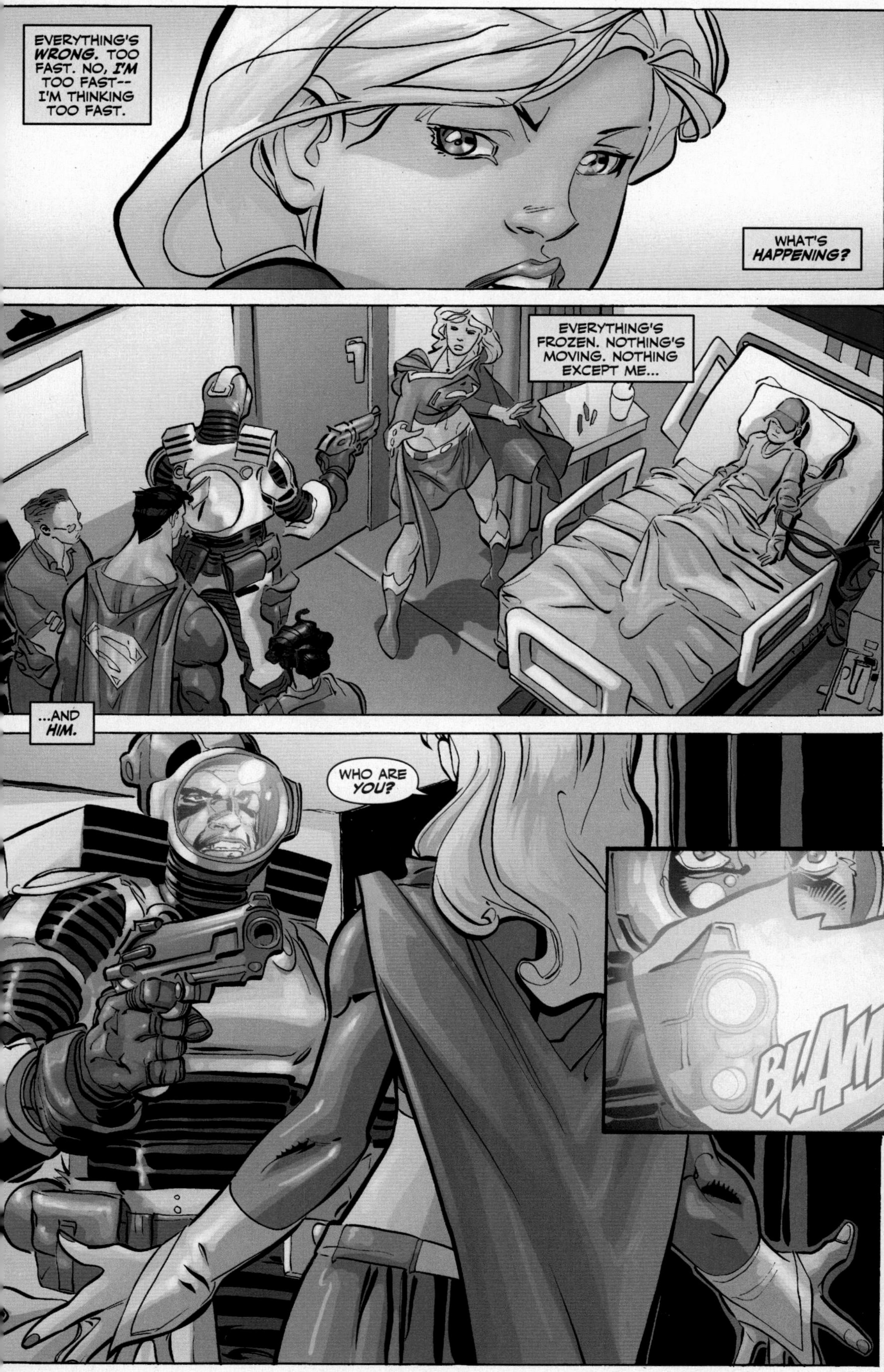
EVERYTHING'S *WRONG*. TOO FAST. NO, *I'M* TOO FAST-- I'M THINKING TOO FAST.
WHAT'S *HAPPENING?*
EVERYTHING'S FROZEN. NOTHING'S MOVING. NOTHING EXCEPT ME...
...AND *HIM*.
WHO ARE *YOU?*
BLAM

PLEASE.

WHAT'S GOING ON? ARE *YOU* DOING THIS?

YOU SHOULD JUST TELL--

THAT FEELING.

I KNOW THAT FEELING.

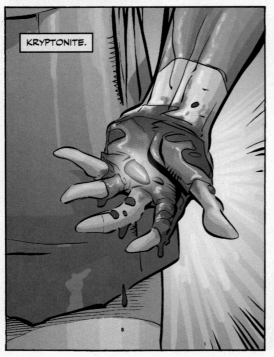

KRYPTONITE.

OH.

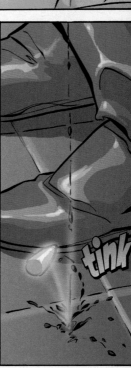

tink

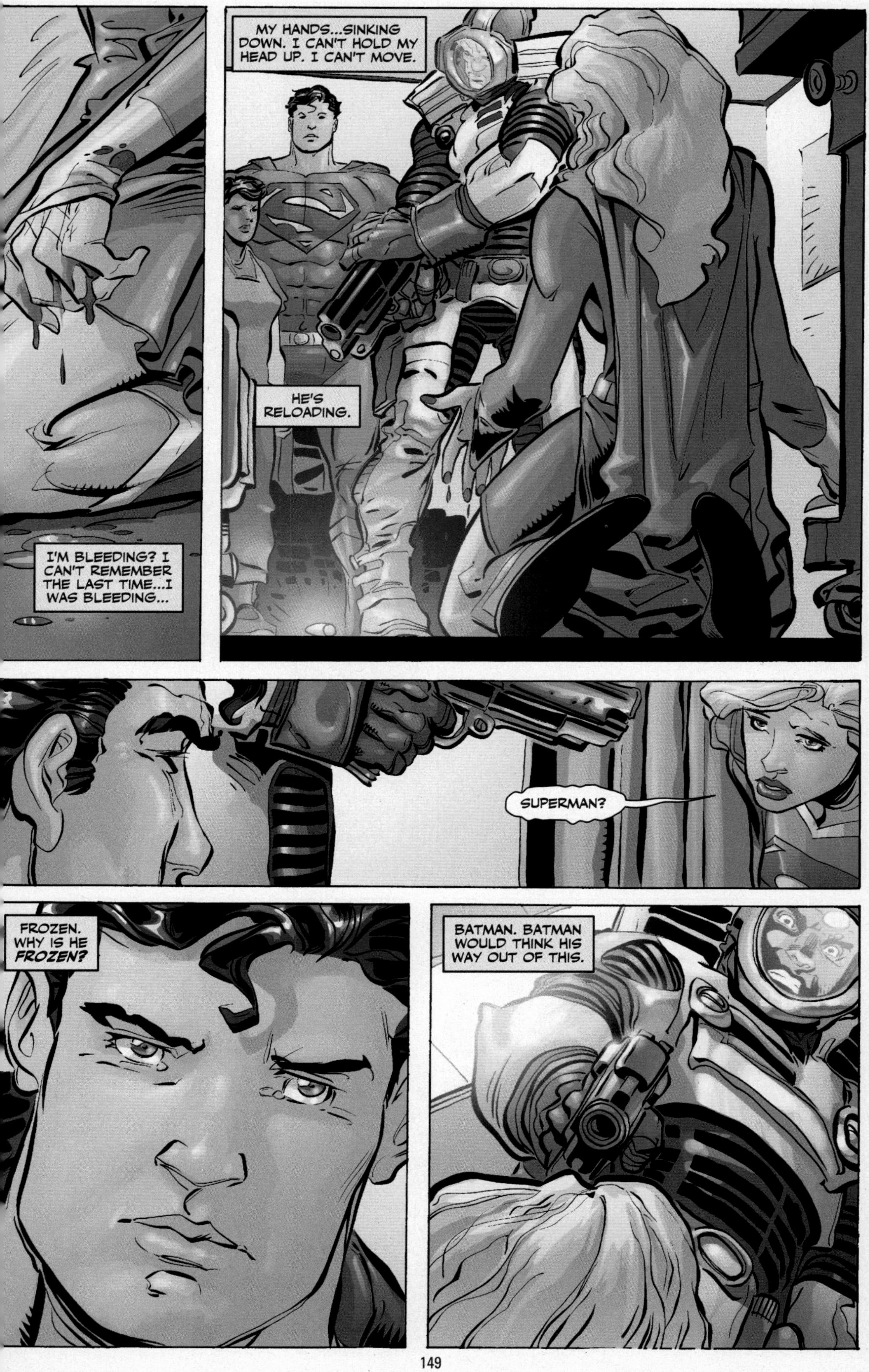
I'M BLEEDING? I CAN'T REMEMBER THE LAST TIME...I WAS BLEEDING...
MY HANDS...SINKING DOWN. I CAN'T HOLD MY HEAD UP. I CAN'T MOVE.
HE'S RELOADING.
SUPERMAN?
FROZEN. WHY IS HE *FROZEN?*
BATMAN. BATMAN WOULD THINK HIS WAY OUT OF THIS.

BATMAN WOULD *SAY* SOMETHING. TRICK HIM. STALL FOR TIME.

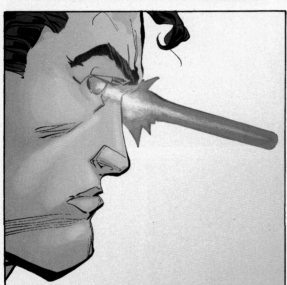

HE WOULDN'T JUST THINK ABOUT DYING.

WHY ARE YOU DOING THIS?

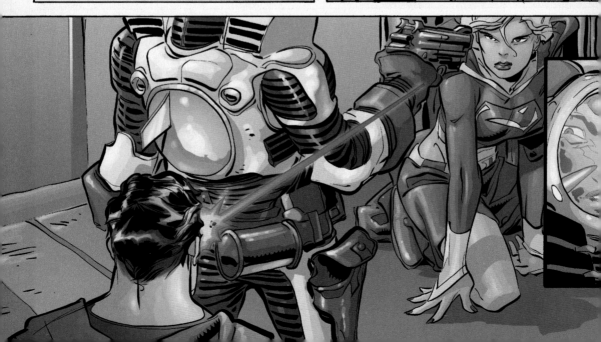

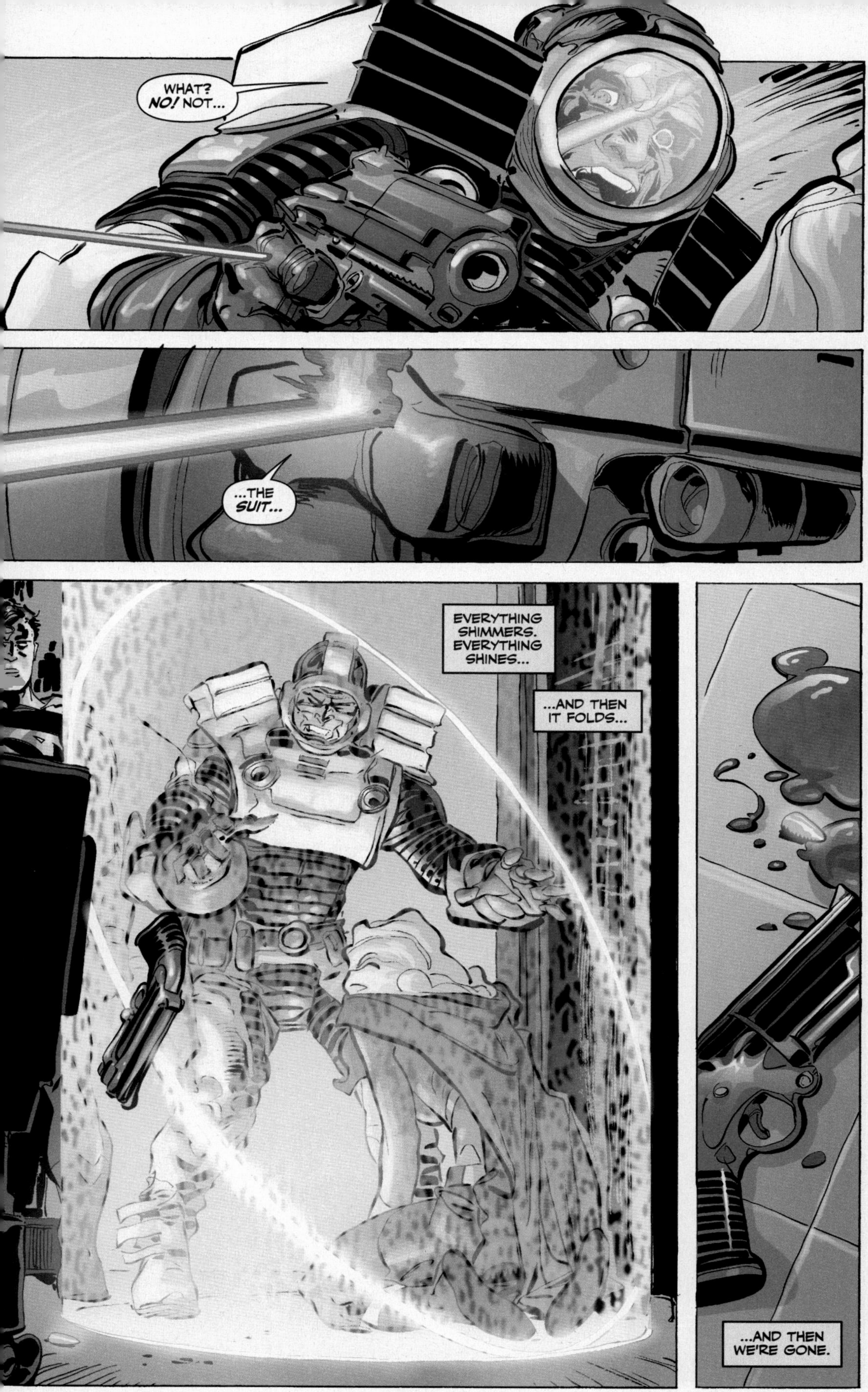
WHAT? NO! NOT...
...THE SUIT...
EVERYTHING SHIMMERS. EVERYTHING SHINES...
...AND THEN IT FOLDS...
...AND THEN WE'RE GONE.

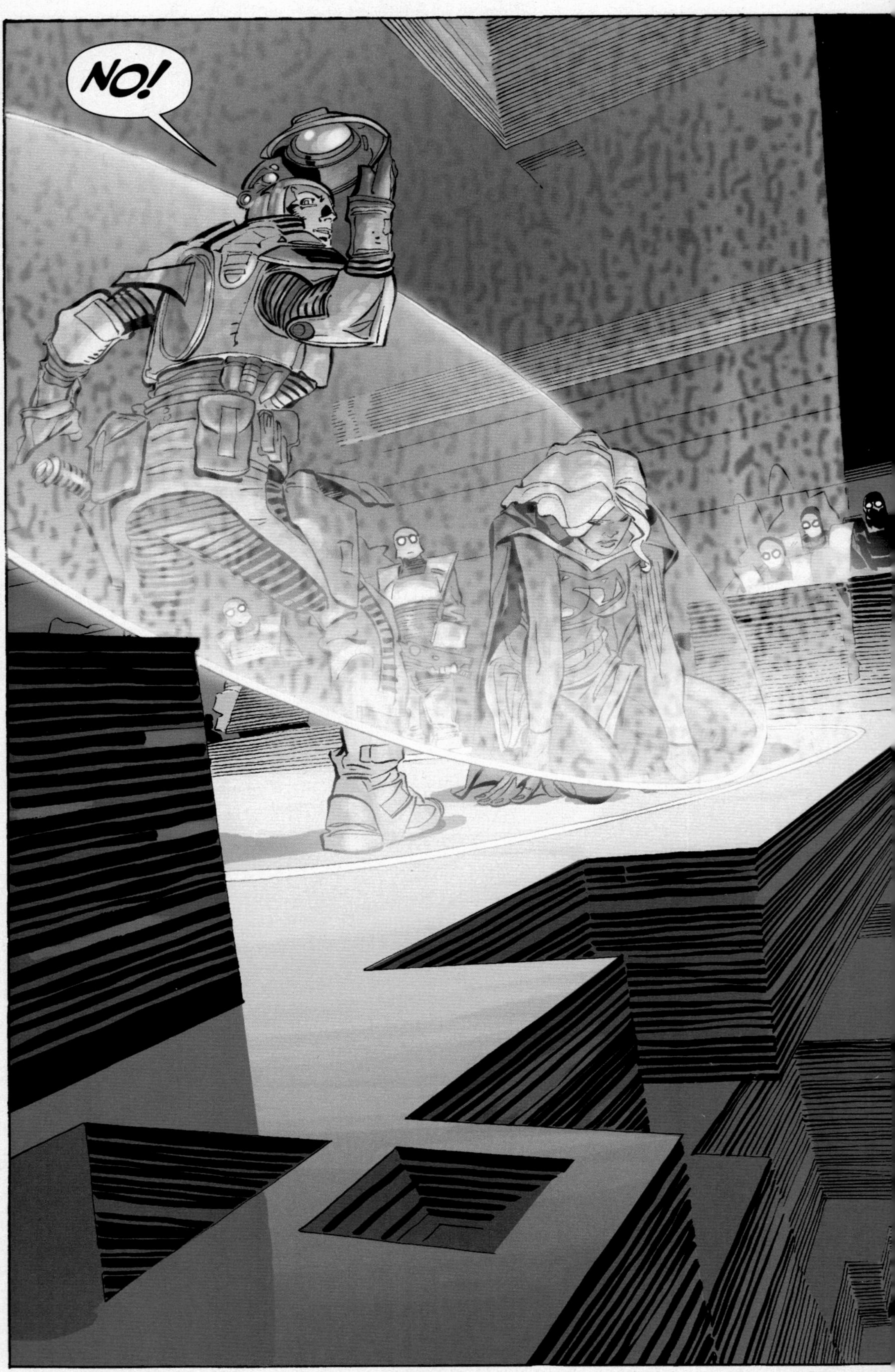
NO!

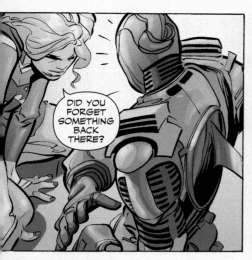

DID YOU FORGET SOMETHING BACK THERE?

LIKE YOUR KRYPTONITE GUN?

AHH!

FIRE.

WH AM

153

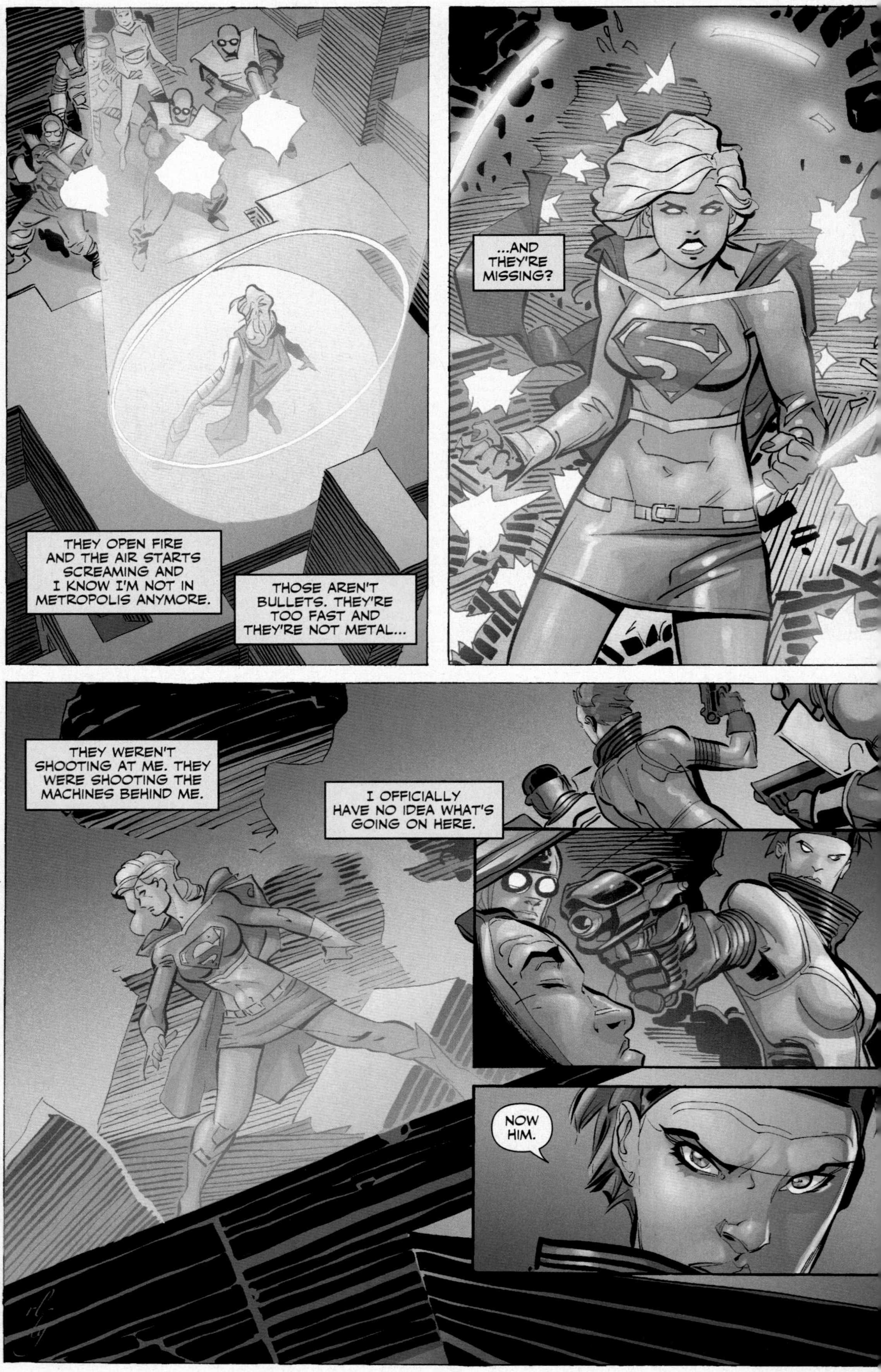
THEY OPEN FIRE AND THE AIR STARTS SCREAMING AND I KNOW I'M NOT IN METROPOLIS ANYMORE.
THOSE AREN'T BULLETS. THEY'RE TOO FAST AND THEY'RE NOT METAL...
...AND THEY'RE MISSING?
THEY WEREN'T SHOOTING AT ME. THEY WERE SHOOTING THE MACHINES BEHIND ME.
I OFFICIALLY HAVE NO IDEA WHAT'S GOING ON HERE.
NOW HIM.

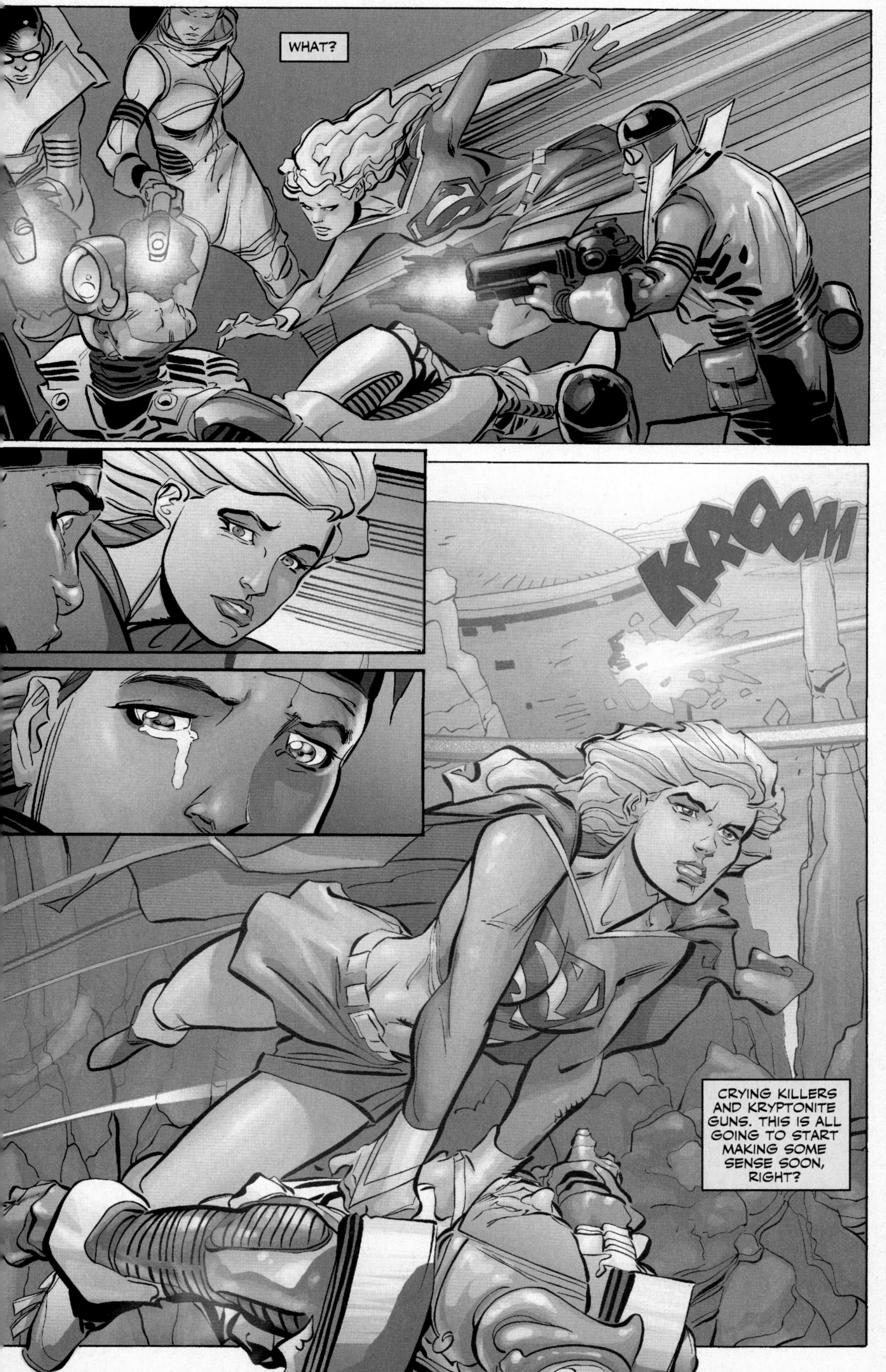
WHAT?
KROOM
CRYING KILLERS AND KRYPTONITE GUNS. THIS IS ALL GOING TO START MAKING SOME SENSE SOON, RIGHT?

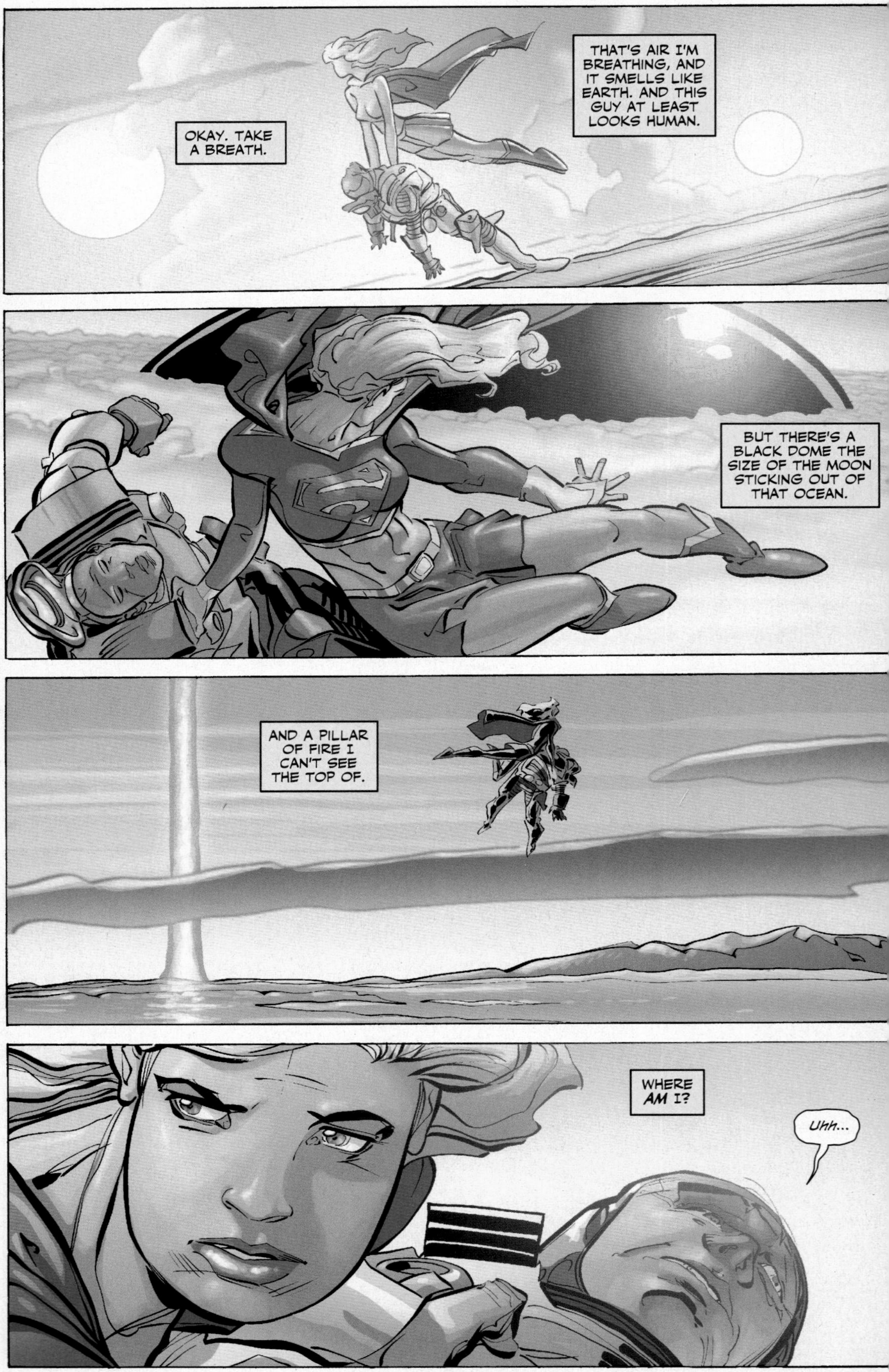
OKAY. TAKE A BREATH.
THAT'S AIR I'M BREATHING, AND IT SMELLS LIKE EARTH. AND THIS GUY AT LEAST LOOKS HUMAN.
BUT THERE'S A BLACK DOME THE SIZE OF THE MOON STICKING OUT OF THAT OCEAN.
AND A PILLAR OF FIRE I CAN'T SEE THE TOP OF.
WHERE *AM* I?
Uhh...

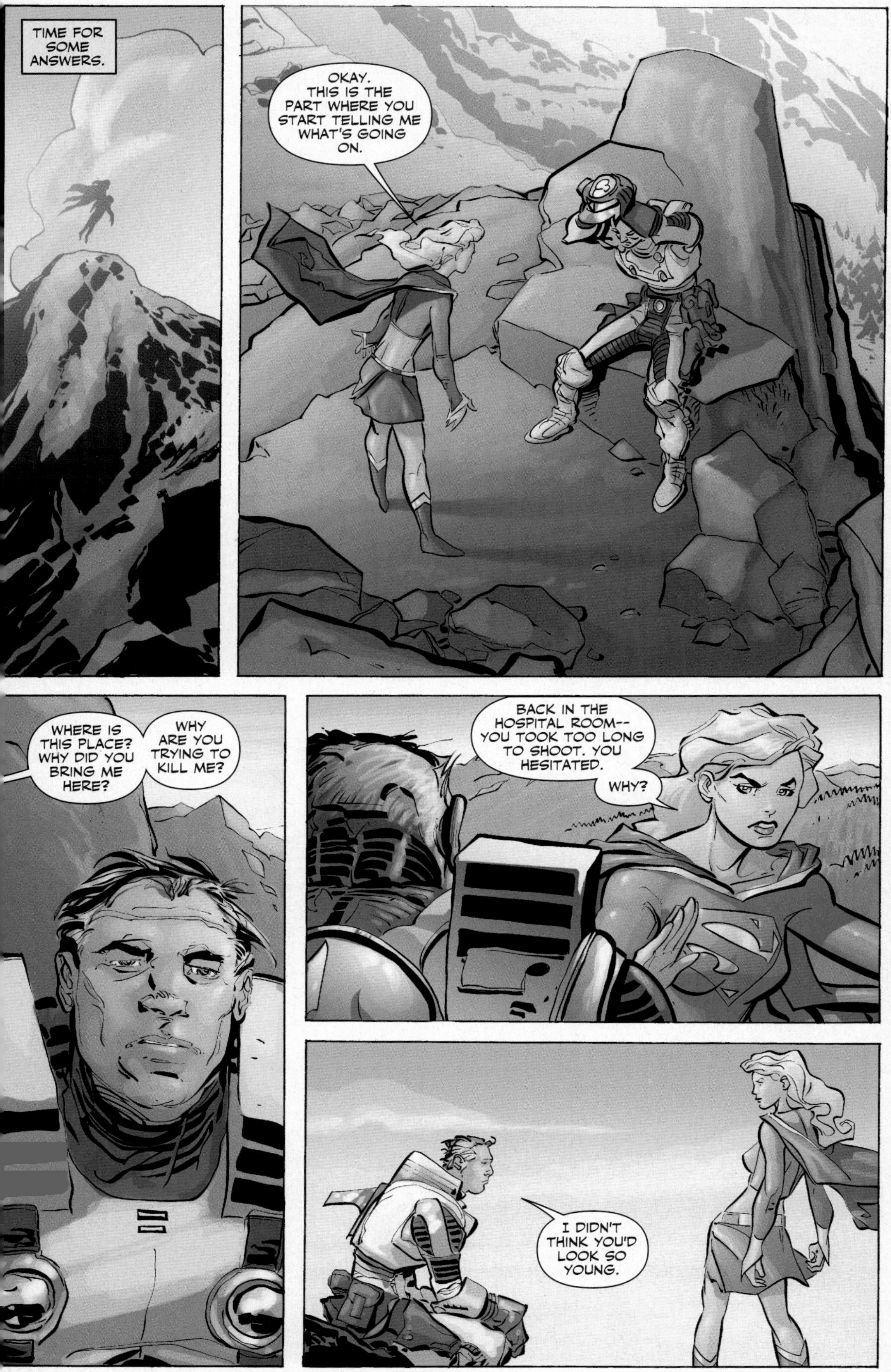

TIME FOR SOME ANSWERS.
OKAY. THIS IS THE PART WHERE YOU START TELLING ME WHAT'S GOING ON.
WHERE IS THIS PLACE? WHY DID YOU BRING ME HERE?
WHY ARE YOU TRYING TO KILL ME?
BACK IN THE HOSPITAL ROOM-- YOU TOOK TOO LONG TO SHOOT. YOU HESITATED.
WHY?
I DIDN'T THINK YOU'D LOOK SO YOUNG.

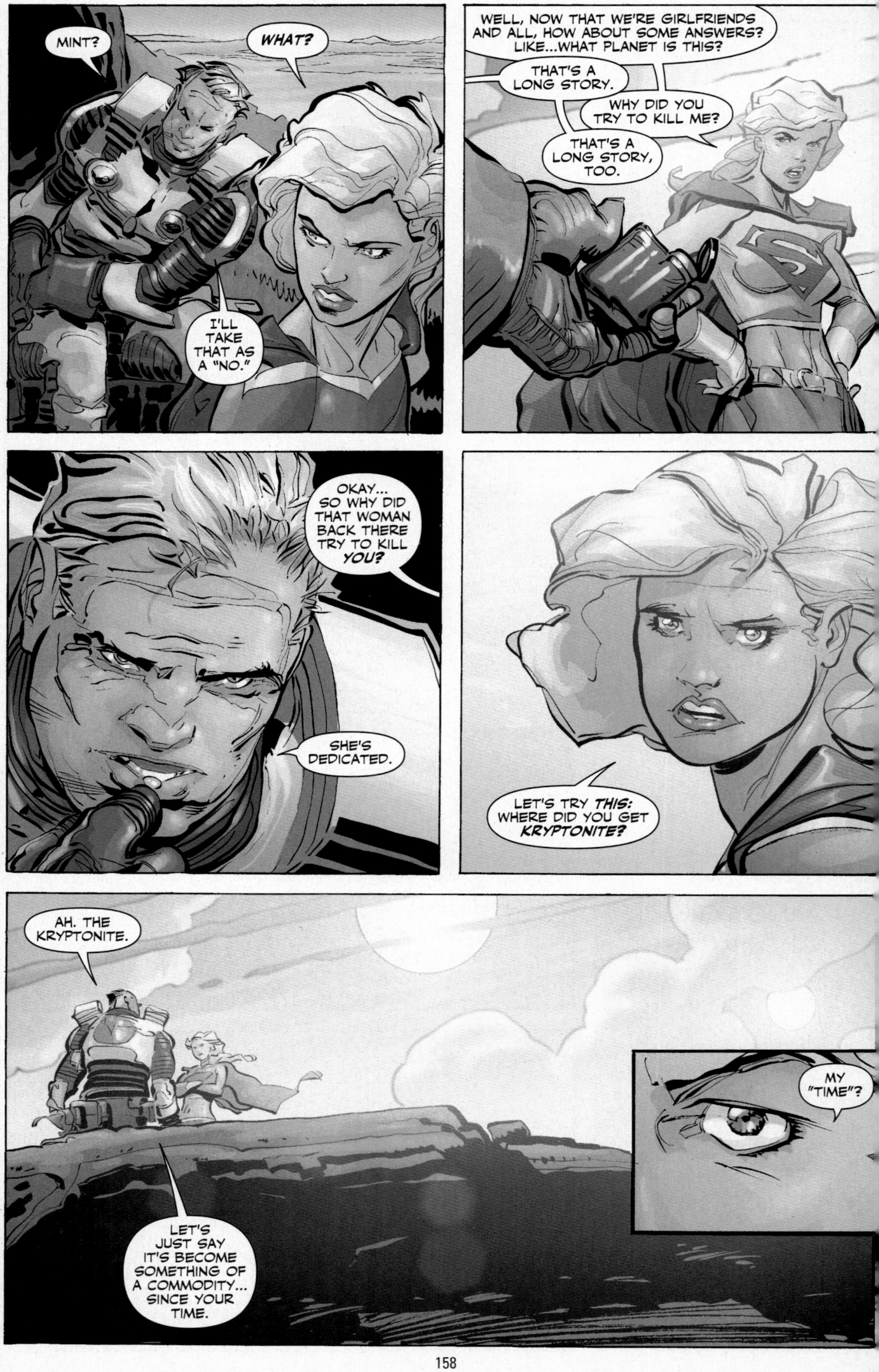
MINT?
WHAT?
I'LL TAKE THAT AS A "NO."
WELL, NOW THAT WE'RE GIRLFRIENDS AND ALL, HOW ABOUT SOME ANSWERS? LIKE...WHAT PLANET IS THIS?
THAT'S A LONG STORY.
WHY DID YOU TRY TO KILL ME?
THAT'S A LONG STORY, TOO.
OKAY... SO WHY DID THAT WOMAN BACK THERE TRY TO KILL YOU?
SHE'S DEDICATED.
LET'S TRY THIS: WHERE DID YOU GET KRYPTONITE?
AH. THE KRYPTONITE.
LET'S JUST SAY IT'S BECOME SOMETHING OF A COMMODITY... SINCE YOUR TIME.
MY "TIME"?

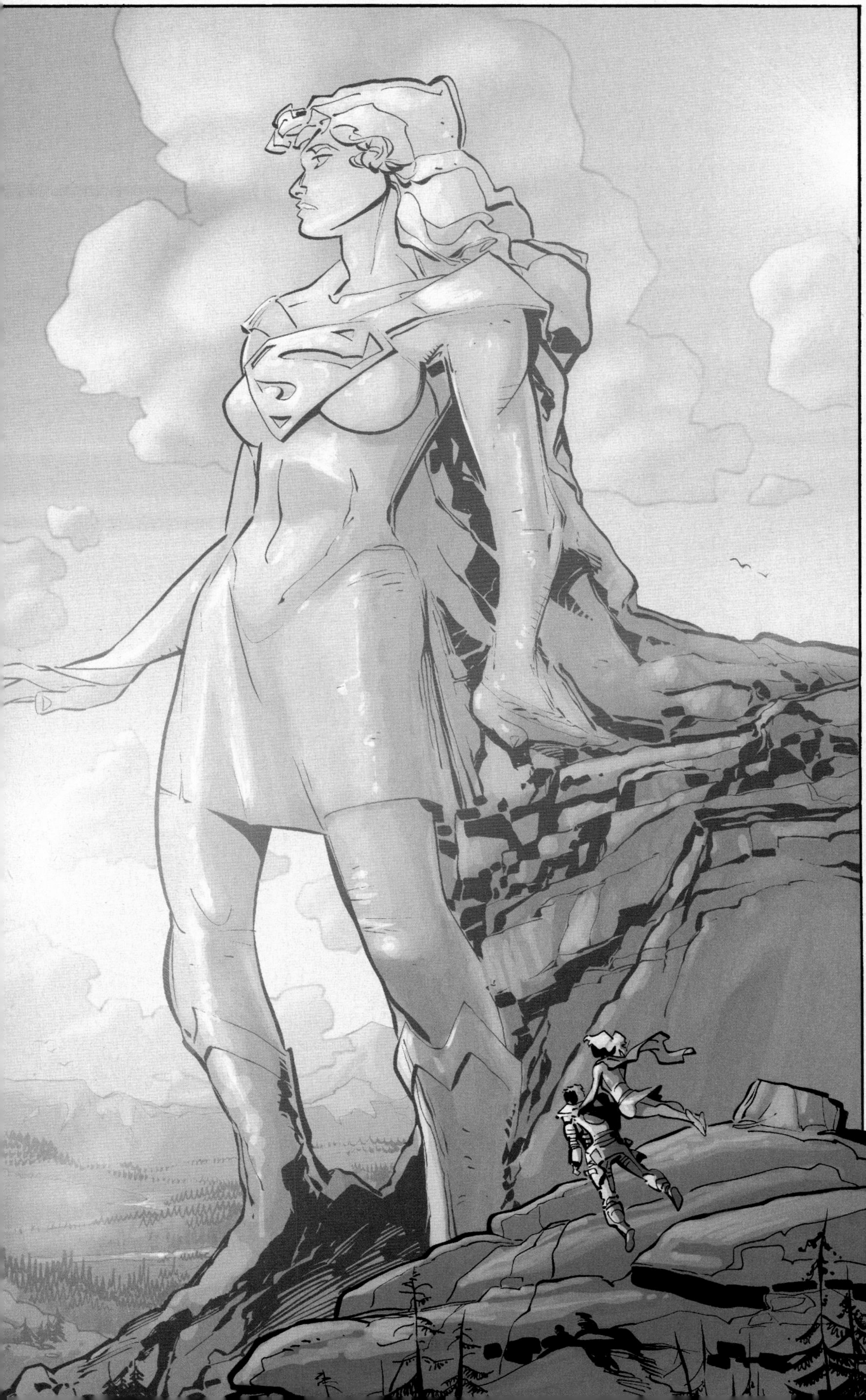

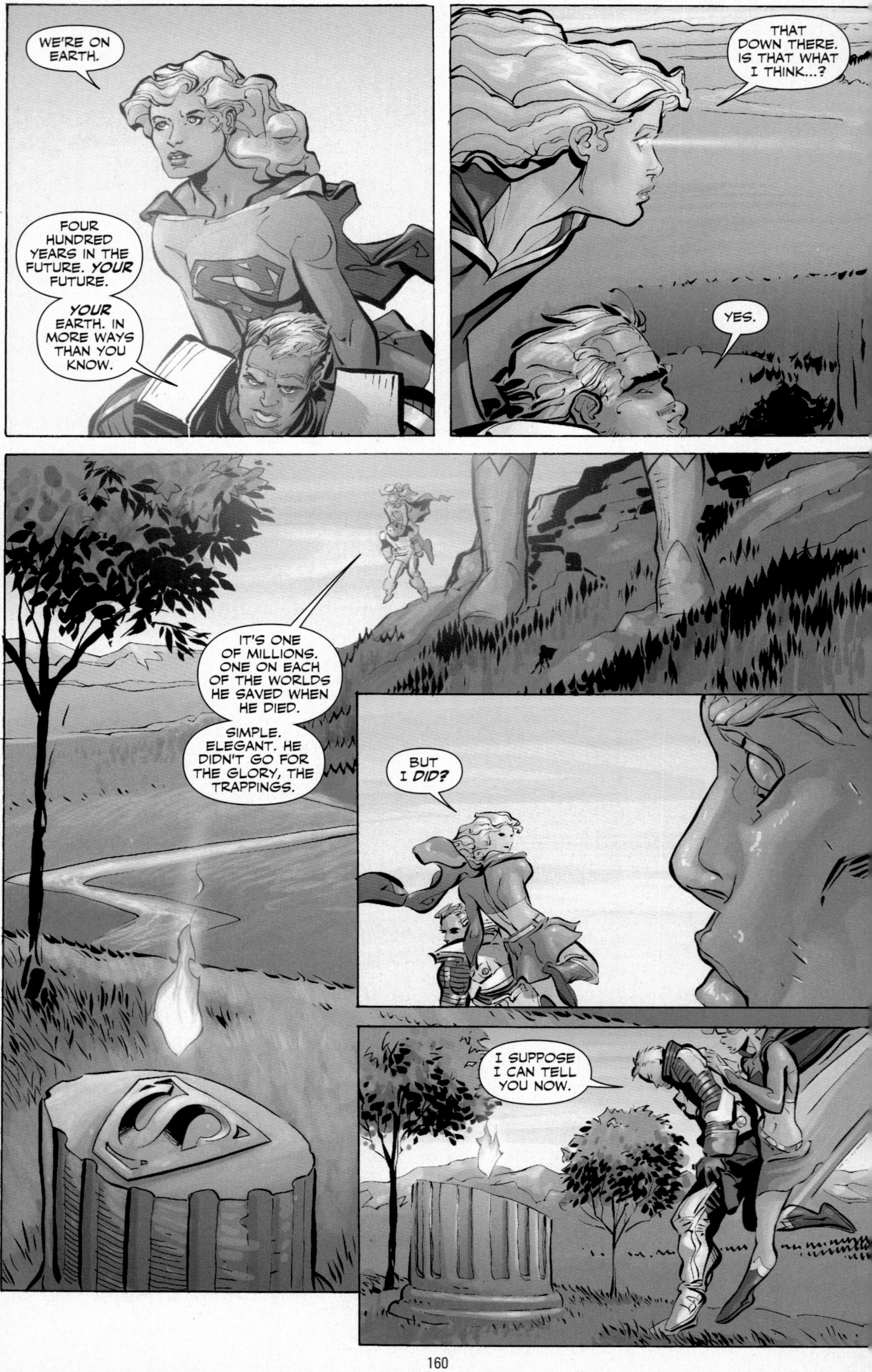
WE'RE ON EARTH.
FOUR HUNDRED YEARS IN THE FUTURE. YOUR FUTURE.
YOUR EARTH. IN MORE WAYS THAN YOU KNOW.
THAT DOWN THERE. IS THAT WHAT I THINK...?
YES.
IT'S ONE OF MILLIONS. ONE ON EACH OF THE WORLDS HE SAVED WHEN HE DIED.
SIMPLE. ELEGANT. HE DIDN'T GO FOR THE GLORY, THE TRAPPINGS.
BUT I DID?
I SUPPOSE I CAN TELL YOU NOW.

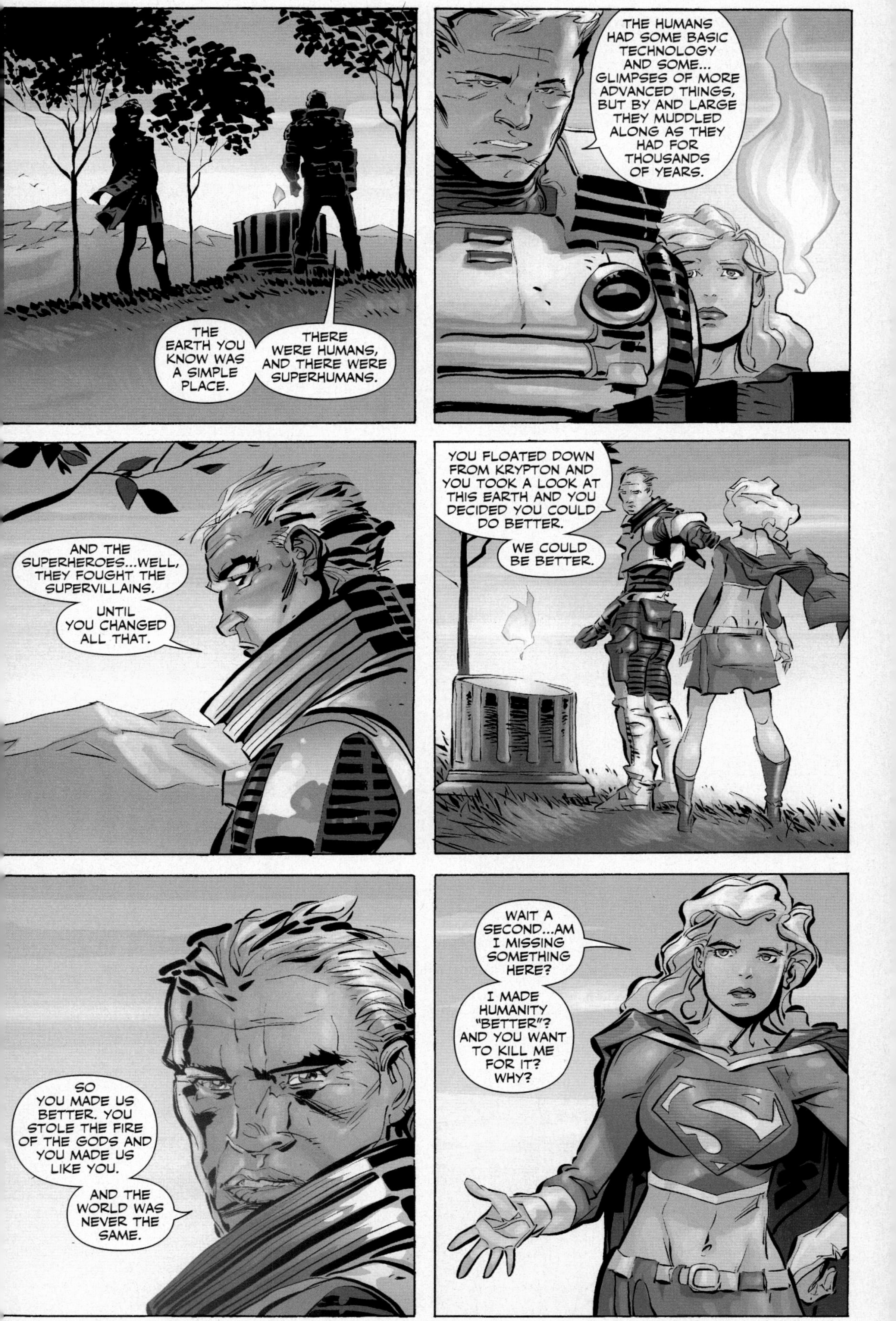
THE EARTH YOU KNOW WAS A SIMPLE PLACE.
THERE WERE HUMANS, AND THERE WERE SUPERHUMANS.
THE HUMANS HAD SOME BASIC TECHNOLOGY AND SOME... GLIMPSES OF MORE ADVANCED THINGS, BUT BY AND LARGE THEY MUDDLED ALONG AS THEY HAD FOR THOUSANDS OF YEARS.
AND THE SUPERHEROES...WELL, THEY FOUGHT THE SUPERVILLAINS.
UNTIL YOU CHANGED ALL THAT.
YOU FLOATED DOWN FROM KRYPTON AND YOU TOOK A LOOK AT THIS EARTH AND YOU DECIDED YOU COULD DO BETTER.
WE COULD BE BETTER.
SO YOU MADE US BETTER. YOU STOLE THE FIRE OF THE GODS AND YOU MADE US LIKE YOU.
AND THE WORLD WAS NEVER THE SAME.
WAIT A SECOND...AM I MISSING SOMETHING HERE?
I MADE HUMANITY "BETTER"? AND YOU WANT TO KILL ME FOR IT? WHY?

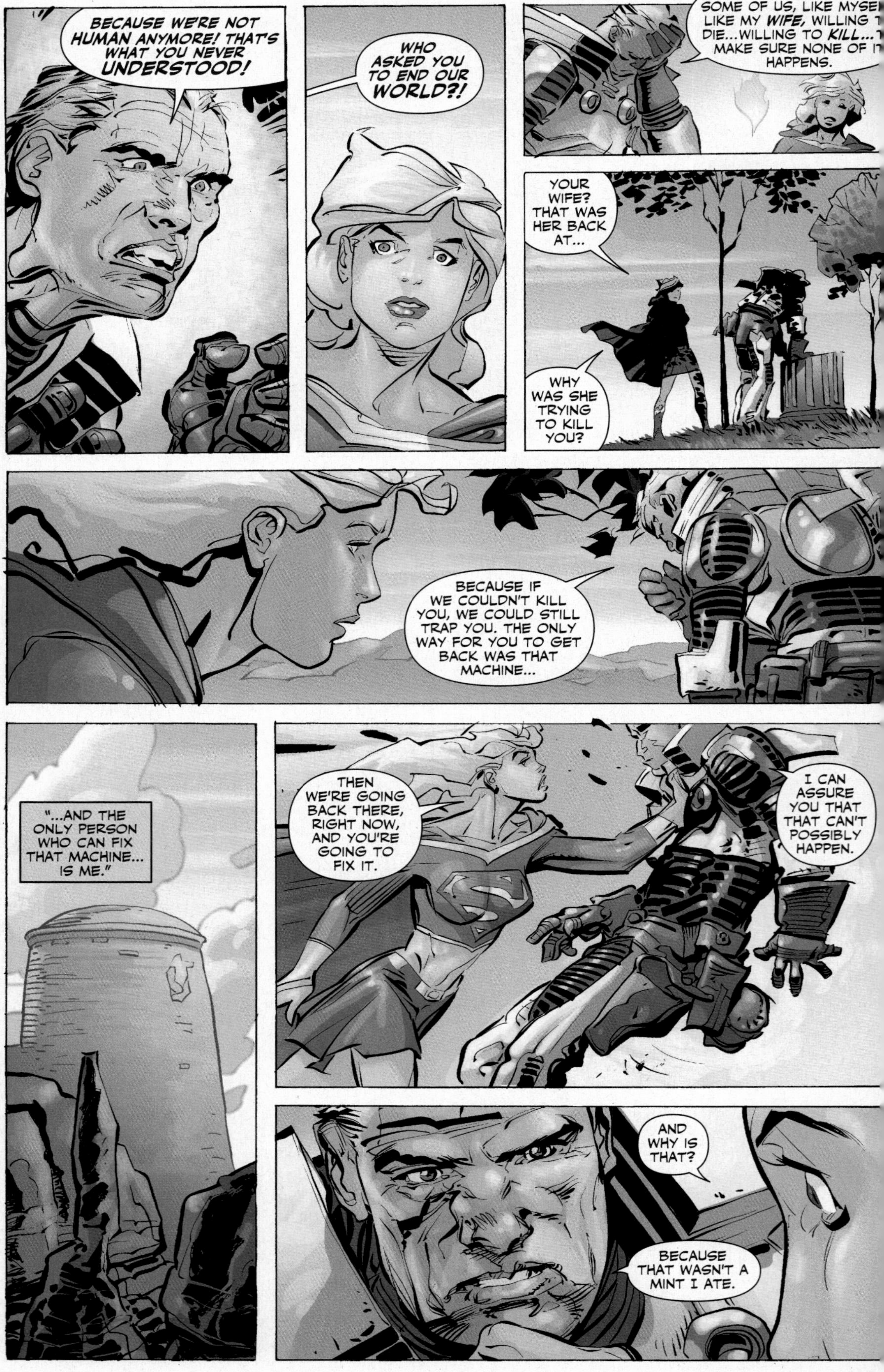
BECAUSE WE'RE NOT HUMAN ANYMORE! THAT'S WHAT YOU NEVER UNDERSTOOD!
WHO ASKED YOU TO END OUR WORLD?!
ANYWAY...THERE ARE SOME OF US, LIKE MYSE LIKE MY WIFE, WILLING T DIE...WILLING TO KILL... MAKE SURE NONE OF IT HAPPENS.
YOUR WIFE? THAT WAS HER BACK AT...
WHY WAS SHE TRYING TO KILL YOU?
BECAUSE IF WE COULDN'T KILL YOU, WE COULD STILL TRAP YOU. THE ONLY WAY FOR YOU TO GET BACK WAS THAT MACHINE...
"...AND THE ONLY PERSON WHO CAN FIX THAT MACHINE... IS ME."
THEN WE'RE GOING BACK THERE, RIGHT NOW, AND YOU'RE GOING TO FIX IT.
I CAN ASSURE YOU THAT THAT CAN'T POSSIBLY HAPPEN.
AND WHY IS THAT?
BECAUSE THAT WASN'T A MINT I ATE.

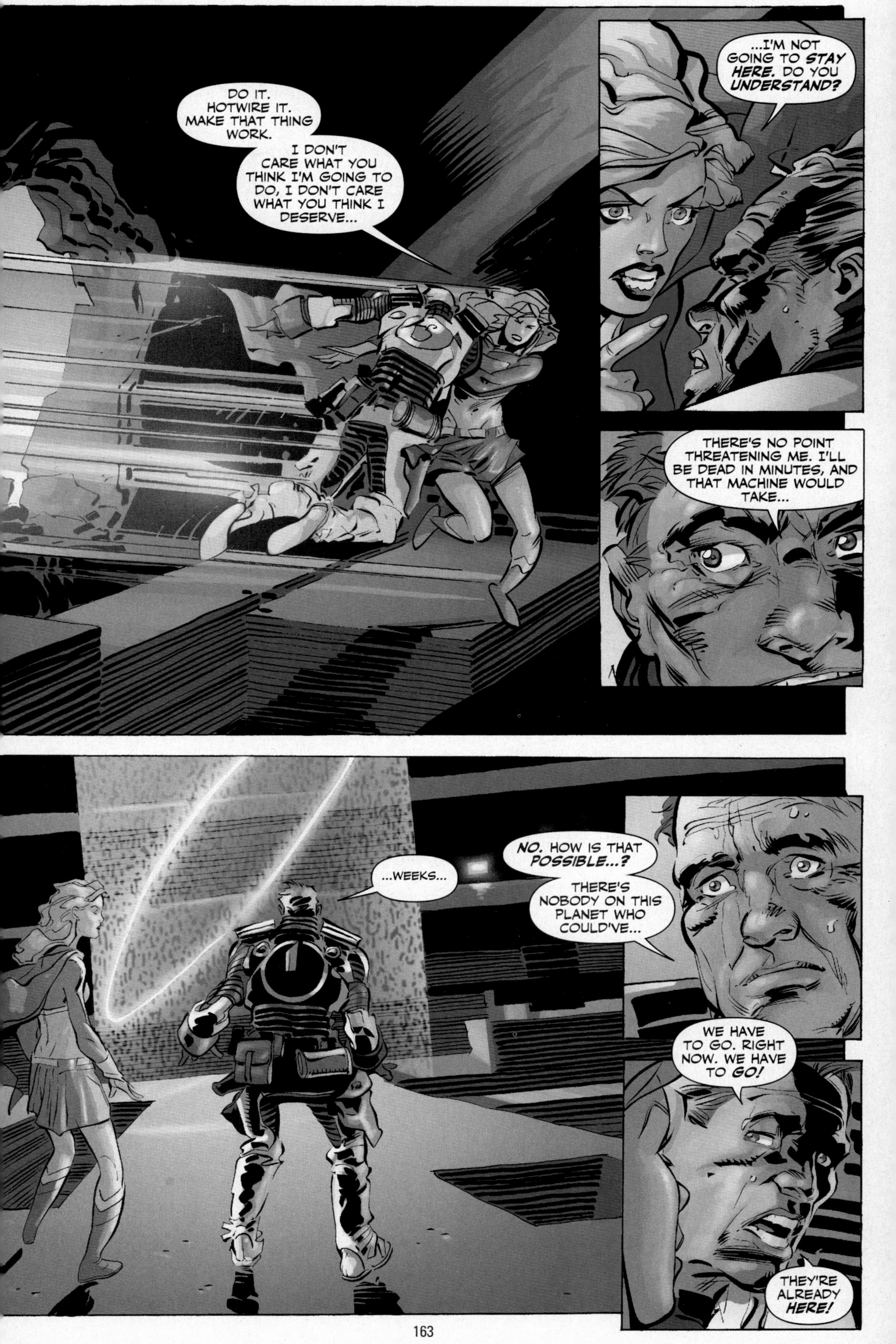
DO IT. HOTWIRE IT. MAKE THAT THING WORK.
I DON'T CARE WHAT YOU THINK I'M GOING TO DO, I DON'T CARE WHAT YOU THINK I DESERVE...
...I'M NOT GOING TO STAY HERE. DO YOU UNDERSTAND?
THERE'S NO POINT THREATENING ME. I'LL BE DEAD IN MINUTES, AND THAT MACHINE WOULD TAKE...
...WEEKS...
NO. HOW IS THAT POSSIBLE...?
THERE'S NOBODY ON THIS PLANET WHO COULD'VE...
WE HAVE TO GO. RIGHT NOW. WE HAVE TO GO!
THEY'RE ALREADY HERE!

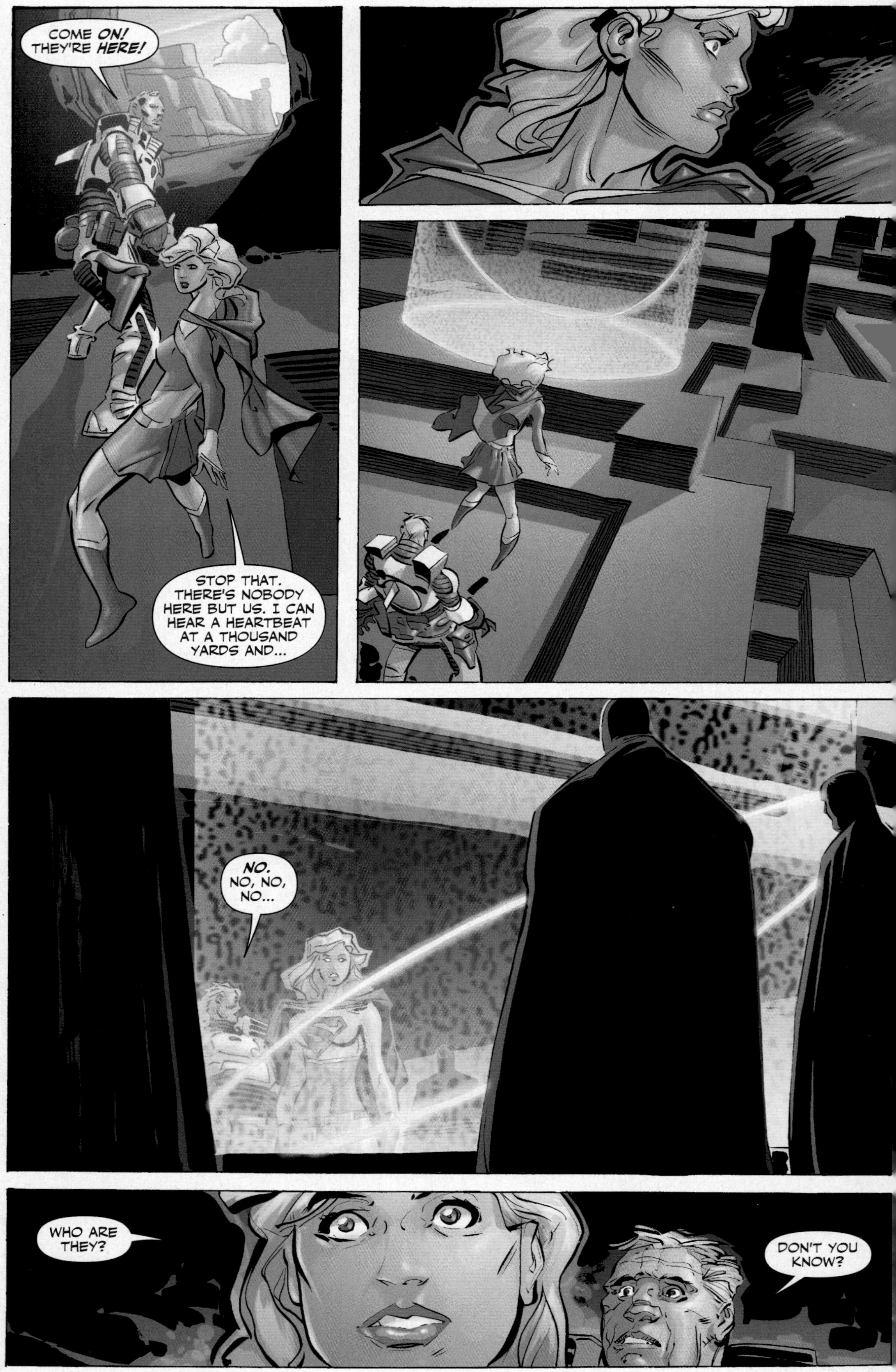
COME ON! THEY'RE HERE!
STOP THAT. THERE'S NOBODY HERE BUT US. I CAN HEAR A HEARTBEAT AT A THOUSAND YARDS AND...
NO. NO, NO, NO...
WHO ARE THEY?
DON'T YOU KNOW?

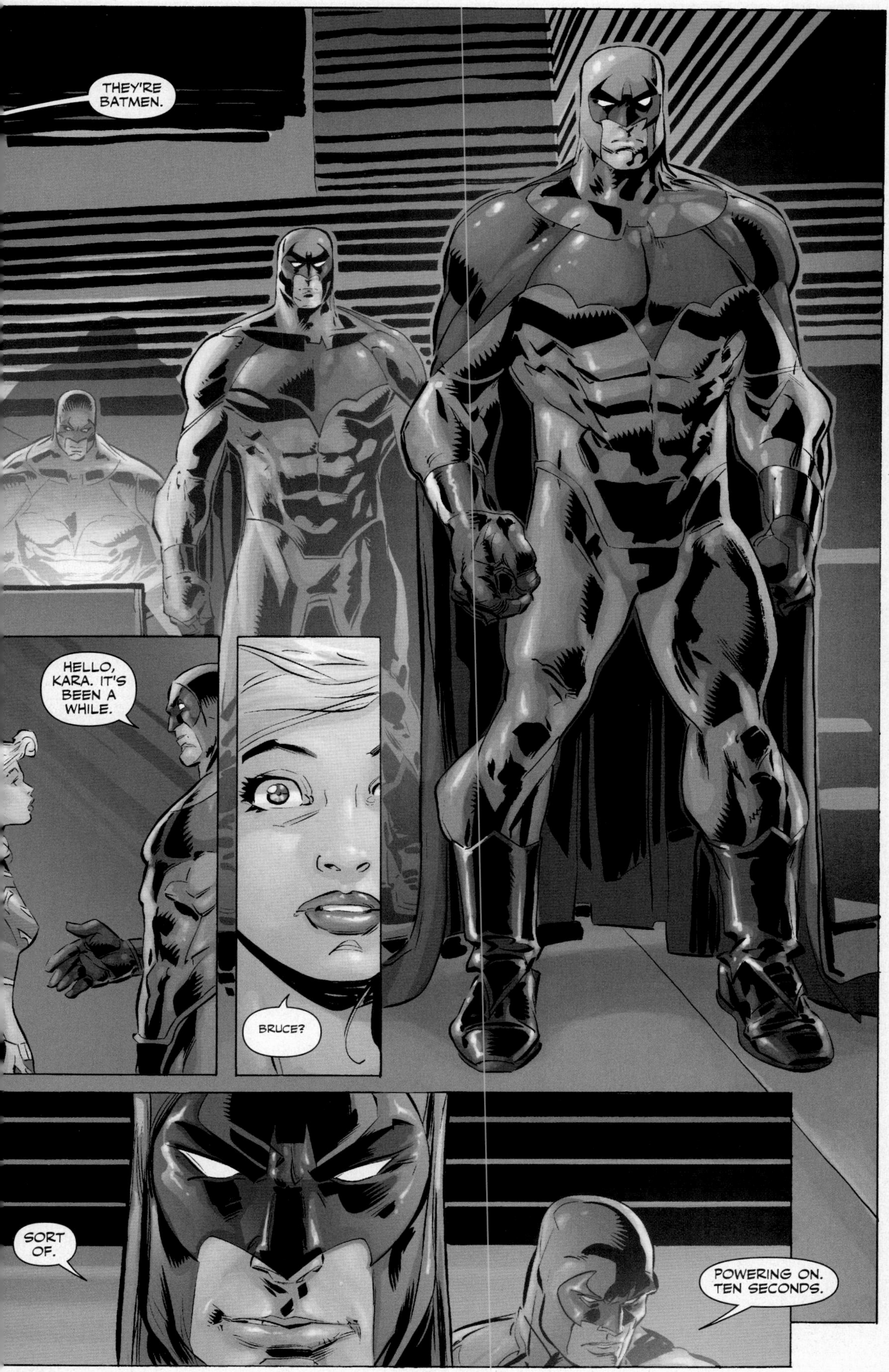
THEY'RE BATMEN.
HELLO, KARA. IT'S BEEN A WHILE.
BRUCE?
SORT OF.
POWERING ON. TEN SECONDS.

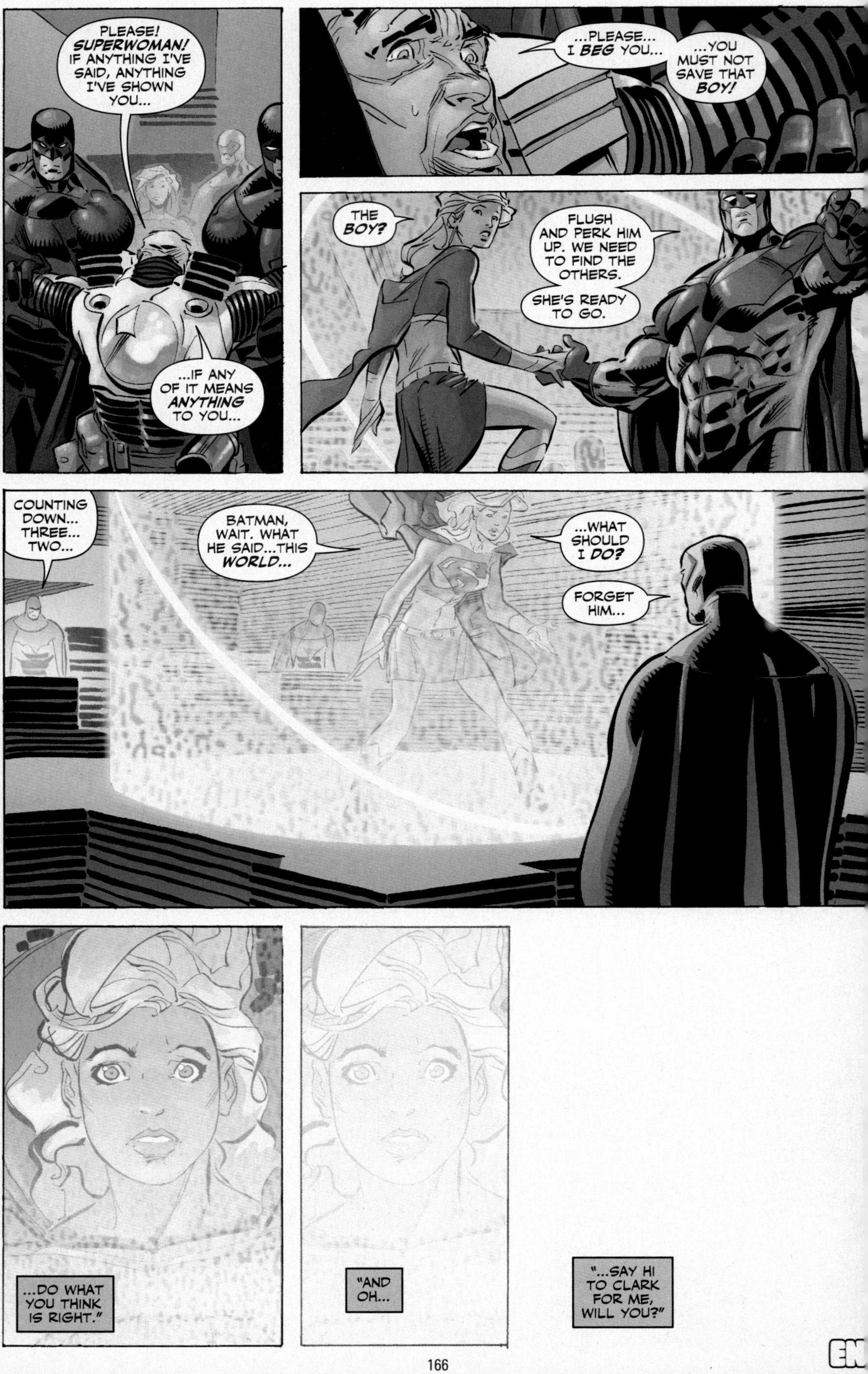
PLEASE! SUPERWOMAN! IF ANYTHING I'VE SAID, ANYTHING I'VE SHOWN YOU...
...IF ANY OF IT MEANS ANYTHING TO YOU...
...PLEASE... I BEG YOU...
...YOU MUST NOT SAVE THAT BOY!
THE BOY?
FLUSH AND PERK HIM UP. WE NEED TO FIND THE OTHERS.
SHE'S READY TO GO.
COUNTING DOWN... THREE... TWO...
BATMAN, WAIT. WHAT HE SAID...THIS WORLD...
...WHAT SHOULD I DO?
FORGET HIM...
...DO WHAT YOU THINK IS RIGHT."
"AND OH...
"...SAY HI TO CLARK FOR ME, WILL YOU?"

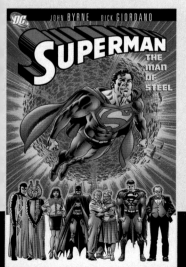

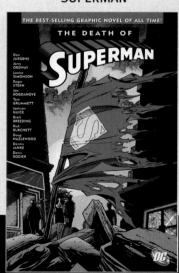